HAMLET

Shakespearean Criticism
(Advisory Editor: Joseph G. Price)
Vol. 4

Richard Burton as Hamlet and Claire Bloom as Ophelia in the "nunnery scene" from the 1953 Old Vic production directed by Michael Benthall. Photograph by Angus McBean. Courtesy of the Harvard Theatre Collection.

HAMLET
Critical Essays

Joseph G. Price

GARLAND PUBLISHING, INC. • NEW YORK & LONDON
1986

Library of Congress Cataloging-in-Publication Data

Hamlet : critical essays.

  (Shakespearean criticism ; vol. 4)
  Bibliography: p.
  1. Shakespeare, William, 1564–1616. Hamlet—
Addresses, essays, lectures. I. Price, Joseph G.
II. Series.
PR2807.H2625 1986   822.3′3   82-48287
ISBN 0-8240-9241-4 (alk. paper)

Printed on acid-free, 250-year-life paper
Manufactured in the United States of America

Contents

General Editor's Preface   ix

Introduction   xi

Part 1: The Play

G. L. Kittredge, *Shakespeare: An Address, 1916, Apr. 23*   3

Samuel Johnson, "Endnote to *Hamlet*"   7

E. E. Stoll, *Hamlet: An Historical and Comparative Study*   9

Maynard Mack, "The World of *Hamlet*"   39

H. D. Kitto, *Form and Meaning in Drama*   59

Francis Fergusson, *The Idea of a Theater*   65

D. G. James, *The Dream of Learning*   77

Harry Levin, *The Question of Hamlet*   99

Sheldon P. Zittner, "Hamlet, Duellist"   123

Susan Snyder, *The Comic Matrix of Shakespeare's Tragedies*   145

Marco Mincoff, "The Structural Pattern of Shakespeare's Tragedies"   191

Part 2: Hamlet the Character

R. A. Foakes (ed.), *Coleridge on Shakespeare*   201

William Hazlitt, *Characters of Shakespeare's Plays*   207

Augustus Schlegel, *Course of Lectures on Dramatic Art
and Literature*   217

A. C. Bradley, *Shakespearean Tragedy*   221

Levin Schücking, *Character Problems in Shakespeare's Plays*   229

Ernest Jones, *Hamlet and Oedipus*   243

A. J. Waldock, *Hamlet: A Study in Critical Method*   259

P. Gottschalk, *The Meanings of Hamlet*   267

Part 3: Scenes and Characters

Samuel Johnson, "Notes to 'to be or not to be'"   285

Francis Gentleman, "To Be or Not to Be"   287

Harley Granville-Barker, *Prefaces to Shakespeare*   289

John Dover Wilson, *What Happens in Hamlet*   297

John C. Bucknill, *The Mad Folk of Shakespeare*   315

A. C. Bradley, *Shakespearean Tragedy*   323

Harold Jenkins, "Introduction," *The Arden Hamlet*   329

Samuel Johnson, "Note to Polonius"   337

G. L. Kittredge, "Introduction," *Hamlet*   339

Nigel Alexander, *Poison, Play, and Duel*   341

Harold Jenkins, "Introduction," *The Arden Hamlet*   379

Part 4: Language

Madeleine Doran, *Shakespeare's Dramatic Language*   387

Inga-Stina Ewbank, "*Hamlet* and the Power of Words"   417

Part 5: The Theatre

Samuel Pepys, *Diary and Correspondence*, August 31, 1668   451

Mr. MacKenzie, *The Mirror*, April 22, 1780   453

Thomas Davies, *Dramatic Miscellanies*   455

Charles Shattuck, *The Hamlet of Edwin Booth*   459

Henry Irving, "An Actor's Notes on Shakespeare"   465

George Bernard Shaw, "Hamlet," 2 October, 1897   475

Muriel St. C. Byrne, "Fifty Years of Shakespearian
     Production"   483

Richard L. Sterne, *John Gielgud Directs Richard Burton
     in Hamlet*   487

Part 6: Hamlet in Fiction

Henry Fielding, *Tom Jones*   499

Goethe, *Wilhelm Meister*   503

Charles Dickens, *Great Expectations*   507

James Joyce, *Ulysses*   511

Bibliography   515

General Editor's Preface

The Garland series is designed to bring together the best that has been written about Shakespeare's plays, both as dramatic literature and theatrical performance. With the exception of some early plays which are treated in related combinations, each volume is devoted to a single play to include the most influential historical criticism, the significant modern interpretations, and reviews of the most illuminating productions. The collections are intended as resource companions to the texts. The scholar, the student, the reader, the director, the actor, the audience, will find here the full range of critical opinion, scholarly debate, and popular taste. Much of the material reproduced has been extremely difficult for the casual reader to locate. Original volumes have long since been out of print; definitive articles have been buried in journals and editions now obscure; theatrical reviews are discarded with each day's newspaper.

"The best that has been written" about each play is the criterion for selection, and the volumes represent the collective wisdom of foremost Shakespearean scholars throughout the world. Each editor has had the freedom and responsibility to make accessible the most insightful criticism to date for his or her play. I express my gratitude to the team of international scholars who have accepted this challenge. One would like to say with Keats "that is all/Ye know on earth, and all ye need to know," but the universality of Shakespeare will stimulate new responses, yield fresh meanings, and lead new generations to richer understandings of human nature.

Generally the essays have been reproduced as they appeared originally. Some concessions in punctuation, spelling, and documentation have been made for the sake of conformity. In the case of excerpts, notes have been renumbered to clarify the references. A principle of the series, however, is to reproduce the full text, rather than excerpts, except for digressive material having no bearing on the subject.

Joseph G. Price

Introduction

At the beginning of the twentieth century, the great American scholar G. L. Kittredge spoke disparagingly of almost three hundred years of *Hamlet* criticism: "Almost everything that has been written about this drama is out of focus."[1] In the New Arden edition of the play published in 1982, Harold Jenkins updated the complaint: "The 'nunnery' scene, as it is called, and indeed Ophelia's whole part in the play, has been generally misunderstood: it is not too much to say that the failure to get Ophelia right has frustrated the interpretation of the tragedy."[2] Two principal reasons for such dissatisfaction emerge from the critical history of *Hamlet*: one lies within the critic, the other within the text—oddly enough within the very quality which accounts for the play's artistic triumph. Kittredge illustrates the first when he says, "Your Hamlet is not my Hamlet, for your ego is not my ego. Yet both your Hamlet and mine are really existent; and mine is as much to my life as yours to yours—and both are justifiable, if your personality and mine have any claim to exist."[3] Jenkins illustrates the second reason when he argues that the neglect of a major element distorts the interpretation of the entire play. The subjective response of the critic and the seemingly infinite variety within the text have led to the dismay voiced by critic after critic with the commentaries of predecessors.

The objectivity of the critic is always suspect, for we all recognize the difficulty of achieving a Keatsian capability to negate the self and render a detached analysis of the text. No literary work, perhaps no work of art, however, has elicited such subjective criticism as *Hamlet*. Uniquely with this play, the critic seems compelled either to express what *Hamlet* evokes in him or to portray an image of its protagonist sketched along the lines of the critic's personality and philosophy. Part II of this volume offers ample evidence, but one need only recall Coleridge's meditative Hamlet, Goethe's fragile Hamlet, Freud's Oedipal Hamlet, Rebecca West's bad Hamlet to indicate the stream of subjectivity. Again uniquely, the critic so often shuns any pretense at objectivity. Hazlitt writes, "It is we who are Hamlet." More pompously, Coleridge acknowledges, "I have a smack of Hamlet in me myself." Victor Hugo begins, "We who are Hamlet. . . ." Frank Walters insists, "We are all Hamlets in our own time." Santayana confides, "In Hamlet our incoherent souls see their own image." As actor and producer, Beerbohm Tree comments, "We are all potential Hamlets." And most stunningly, German critics throughout the nineteenth century wrestled with the concept, "Deutschland ist Hamlet."

I mean no disparagement. No one doubts that the magnetism of the play and the genius of its author are rooted in the inexplicable identification which the reader singly and the audience collectively feel with the character of this seventeenth century revenger. In a sense, it is Aristotelian empathy turned upside down. We do not move out of ourselves to identify with Hamlet; we bring him down from the outsize world of the stage into the pit to become one of us. As the history of the play attests, no dramatic character seems as real to us as Hamlet. Critical explanations of this phenomenon have illuminated the comprehensive soul of Shakespeare's character in which so many find reflection. They have taught us much about ourselves. They have contributed to the psychic expansion of Burbage's Hamlet at the Globe to the archetypal Hamlet of our culture.

Yet Kittredge and Jenkins are justified in protesting against the distortions which such criticism inflicts upon the play. As early as 1710, Shaftesbury had described *Hamlet* as a one-character play, and this thread has been woven ever since into studies which perhaps culminate in Ernest Jones's *Hamlet and Oedipus*. The more objective critic must enlarge his focus, for it is not insignificant that this is Shakespeare's longest play, four hours in modern production, certainly well over three if the full text was acted on the Elizabethan stage. The very length should signal that quality which constitutes the play's artistic triumph, what Dr. Johnson brilliantly perceived:

> If the dramas of Shakespeare were to be characterised, each by the particular excellence which distinguishes it from the rest, we must allow to the tragedy of *Hamlet* the praise of variety.[4]

Sir Philip Sidney encapsulates Renaissance theory when he declares the function of poetry is to teach and to delight, and the delight springs from variety. Did Shakespeare consciously set out to embody this in *Hamlet*? Was this the basis for its great success in its own time?

We cannot know. This great variety, however, has caused a second set of problems for the critic and, in turn, dissatisfaction with *Hamlet* criticism. There seem to be too many pieces to the puzzle. The critic is thwarted; the credibility of his argument reduced through his sins of omission. The rebuttal charges, "But you didn't consider Hamlet's relationship with the pirates!" So Harold Jenkins objects to the neglect of Ophelia and concludes that this neglect has frustrated the interpretation of the entire play. The entire canon of criticism reverberates with accusations that A ignored imagery, that B concentrated only on soliloquies, that C neglected theatrical practices, that Z has failed to consider the question of adultery before the murder. Not even major book-length studies such as John Dover Wilson's *What Happens in Hamlet*, Harry Levin's *The Question of Hamlet*, Nigel Alexander's *Poison, Play, and Duel* confront all the issues raised by the full text; to a much slighter degree do slanted works such as Eleanor Prosser's *Hamlet and Revenge* and L. C. Knight's *An Approach to Hamlet*. The omissions and undue emphases in *Hamlet* criticism imperil interpretation to a greater extent than in other Shakespearean plays. Shakespeare embraces so much here that the critic is challenged to match the creative imagination which visualized the drama unfolding on stage. That imagination too may have faltered, and we may point an accusing finger at Shakespeare if the text is correct: there is a major difference in tone and psychological make-up if Hamlet is a young university student rather than a thirty-year-old scholar.

As general editor of this series, I have asked editors of individual plays to select what they consider to be the best that has been written about the plays. This suggests a narrowing of focus, an intensive examination of the play under the light of its best critics. Alas, *Hamlet* cannot be treated accordingly. What has happened historically in the criticism of this play, and what this volume hopes to do, is to enlarge the focus. The selections have been chosen to expand the reader's construct so that he may experience fully what Maynard Mack terms "the world of Hamlet." The problems of madness and delay are debated amply within the volume; so too is the mental stability of Hamlet. But when he objected to the narrow limits of earlier criticism, Kittredge planted the seed that has borne such fruit in our ripening understanding of the play:

> On the contrary, it is the tragedy not of an individual but of a group; and in its structure it is balanced, in the most delicate and unstable equilibrium, between two great personages—Hamlet and the King. It is a duel to the death between well-matched protagonists; so well-matched indeed, that neither triumphs, but they destroy each other in the end.[5]

Even this seems too narrow a view of the play; the seed, however, has flourished so that this volume begins with what I see as the major contribution of the last fifty years, the critical treatment of *Hamlet* the play, not the character. The approaches range from the theatrical, as in Francis Fergusson's essay, to the philosophical as advanced by D. G. James. There is greater discussion of theme than heretofore: in *Hamlet*, modern critics assert, Shakespeare tests the problematical nature of reality. The play itself is enveloped in mystery, and that cannot be plucked out only from the heart of Hamlet's mystery, for the embracive themes are mortality (Mack), evil (Kitto), doubt (Levin), and human conduct (James). In articles as diverse as Sheldon Zittner's which locates the play in Elizabethan social codes and Susan Snyder's highly original study which forces us to rethink the comic function in tragedy, there flows the turbulent current of alienation and scepticism. Throughout Part I, the computer might key into recurrent words like myth, mystery, ritual, doubt. Our understanding of *Hamlet* is enriched greatly by the perspective and methodology of modern critics. One hopes that the thematic message carries us beyond the tribute paid by previous generations, each holding up its mirror to Shakespeare.

Part II contains the more traditional essays in that they treat of the character of Hamlet, his motives, and his "madness," the question of delay, and finally the post-Freudian psychoanalysis of his personality. Perhaps the reader's favorite passages from Coleridge or Bradley are not included, but my choices have been made to convey the full range of the argument. The Hamlet of Hazlitt is the "prince of philosophical speculators," marked "by refinement of thought and sentiment." The Hamlet of Schlegel "has a natural inclination for crooked ways; he is a hypocrite towards himself." To Bradley, "That Hamlet was not far from insanity is very probable." For Schücking, the character is neurotic, a manic depressive. The last three essays constitute a debate on the legitimacy of psychoanalytic criticism as against textual evidence. Jones lays out the case for the psychoanalytic solution to the mystery of Hamlet's character. Waldock insists upon the primacy of the text and, although he admits to a "psychic hurt" in Hamlet, rejects any exploration of the subconscious. Gottschalk mediates in that he supports the psychoanalytic method if the work evokes the mythic in the audience whether wilfully in the text or not.

If the great variety within the play, its very magnitude, has caused problems even for its most insightful critics, some of the very finest criticism has come in the analysis of its parts. Soliloquies, scenes, and characters are explicated in Part III. Polonius has had his defenders since Dr. Johnson. Ophelia, especially after Eliot had done her in in *The Wasteland*, has been more of a target than her father until recently. Nigel Alexander and Harold Jenkins restore the balance. Certainly, Shakespeare gives her a charm in her first appearance that rivals the appeal of his romantic heroines. Granville-Barker's defense of the dumb-show and his reading of the entire play-within-the-play, I think, has not been superceded. The excerpt from John Charles Bucknill's *The Mad Folk of Shakespeare* might have been placed among the analyses of Hamlet's character, but particularly distinctive is his explication of one scene, Act II, scene ii. In predating Freud, his work is of historical interest and anticipates later commentary on melancholy and the divided personality, a small justification for twentieth century criticism, which has been accused of reading *Hamlet* disproportionately through the eyes of Freud.

Space alone has dictated the limits of Part IV. Much current work in rhetoric, language, style, and poetics is contributing to our understanding of the play and Shakespeare's techniques. The two pieces by Madeleine Doran and Inga-Stina Ewbank are among the best. For the purpose of this volume, each has a coherence and completeness that will suggest other possibilities to the reader.

Marvin Rosenberg's plans for the stage history of *Hamlet* run to two large volumes. Obviously, the choices for Part IV, "The Theatre," are necessarily scant and idiosyncratic. We know that the play, with its extended "run," was exceptionally popular from its first performance. We have the report of two amateur ship productions in 1607 and 1608 to attest to its expanding appeal:

> I have sent the interpreter, according to his desire, aboard the *Hector* where he broke fast, and after came aboard me, where we gave the tragedy of *Hamlet*.
> ....
> I invited Captain Hawkins to a fish dinner, and had *Hamlet* acted aboard me; which I permit to keep my people from idleness and unlawful games, or sleep.

The continuous popularity is attested by the comments which I have included from Pepys, Mackenzie, and Davies, who also remind us that the plays were examined through productions and actors' interpretations until nineteenth century critics closeted Shakespeare in the study. Davies illustrates as well the theatrical effectiveness of the Ghost which, along with the opening scenes, has been praised throughout the stage history—no doubt aided by the legend that Shakespeare played the role. Charles Shattuck's delightful recapitulation of Booth's success as Hamlet reveals as much about American bardolatry as it does about the performance. The interdependence of theatrical and literary criticism is presented superbly in Shaw's review of Forbes-Robertson's portrayal and in Sir John Gielgud's instructions to Richard

Burton and the entire cast in the now famous 1964 production. As an example, Gielgud's critical approach to the enduring problem of Polonius led to Hume Cronyn's memorable interpretation.

I have mentioned Hamlet as archetype, and this mythic figure has arisen out of the countless representations in art and popular culture. Even for the marginally educated, no reference to Shakespeare need be cited when the old Jack Benny film, "To Be Or Not To Be," is publicised in a remake in 1983. No reference to *Hamlet* was cited, fortunately, in a food advertisement captioned by "To thine ownself be good." The reader who turns first to the cartoon page of his daily newspaper finds a caricature asking, "To compute . . . or not to compute . . . that is the question/Whether 'tis nobler in the memory bank . . . to suffer the slings and circuits of outrageous functions" and so on. A fisherman browsing through his issue of *Sports Illustrated* is directed to a new fly called Hamlet's cloud because "most fish are like Polonius. They see what they want to see." A politician is called Hamlet-like, and the conjuration damns him for indecisiveness and delay. The archetype pervades our popular culture.

He pervades our art. Four examples from novels of the eighteenth, nineteenth, and twentieth centuries are represented as a small token of the Hamlet myth in Part VI. No other character stalks the centuries as he does; no other character typifies our brooding over cosmic and interior changes as he does. For the image evokes so much more than doubt and delay. Each of us is embodied in the character who puzzles over the most elemental conflict in human nature, the struggle among intellect, will, emotion, and sensation:

> Thus conscience does make cowards of us all,
> And thus the native hue of resolution
> Is sicklied o'er with the pale cast of thought,
> And enterprises of great pitch and moment
> With this regard their currents turn awry
> And lose the name of action;
> . . . .
>   I do not know
> Why yet I live to say this thing's to do,
> Sith I have cause, and will, and strength, and means
> To do't.

Notes

1. *Shakspere: An address, 1916, Apr. 23*, p. 40.
2. p. 149.
3. *Shakspere: An Address*, p. 12.
4. *The Plays of William Shakespeare*, ed. by Isaac Reed, vol. 10, p. 524.
5. *Shakspere: An Address*, p. 40.

PART I:
The Play

G. L. Kittredge

From *Shakspere: An Address, 1916, Apr. 23*

As with our fellow-creatures in real life, so is it with our fellow-creatures in Shakspere. There neither is nor can be any exclusive or orthodox interpretation. Each of us must read the riddle of motive and personality for himself. There will be as many Hamlets or Macbeths or Othellos as there are readers or spectators. For the impressions are not made, or meant to be made, on one uniformly registering and mechanically accurate instrument, but on an infinite variety of capriciously sensitive and unaccountable individualities—on *us*, in short, who see as we can, and understand as we are. Your Hamlet is not my Hamlet, for your ego is not my ego. Yet both your Hamlet and mine are really existent; and mine is as much to my life as yours to yours—and both are justifiable, if your personality and mine have any claim to exist. You shall convert me if you can, for I am docile and accessible to reason; but, when all is said, and you have taught me whatever is teachable, there must still remain, in the last analysis, a difference that is beyond reconciliation, except in the universal solvent of our common humanity. Otherwise you and I and Hamlet are not individuals, but merely types and symbols, or (worst of worst) stark formulas, masquerading as God's creatures in a world that is too full of formulas already.

These principles, however, give no license to capricious propaganda. For there is one corrective and restraining proviso. Somewhere there exists, and must be discoverable, the solid fact—and that fact is Shakspere's Hamlet or Macbeth or Othello. And this actual being is not to be confused, in your apprehension or in mine, with any of the figures that we have constructed, each for himself, by the instinctive reaction of our several personalities

3

under the poet's art. Each of us has a prescriptive right to his own Hamlet; but none of us has a charter to impose it either upon his neighbor or upon himself as the poet's intent. We should recognize it rather, and cherish it, as our private property—as something that we have ourselves achieved when our minds and hearts have been kindled by a spark from his altar or a tongue of flame from his Promethean fire.

* * * * * * *

In the first place, the subject of Hamlet is not the tragedy of the Prince of Denmark; it is not the tragedy of any individual: it is the tragedy of a group, of the whole royal family; and their fate involves the destruction of the family of Polonius, which is very close to the royal line, so close that the Danish mob sees nothing extraordinary in the idea of seating Laertes upon the throne.

> Caps, hands, and tongues applaud it to the clouds, "Laertes shall be king—Laertes king!"

The tragic complex is almost indescribably entangled, despite the simplicity of the main plot; yet it is brought out with perfect clearness. The moving cause is not the murder: it is the guilty passion of Gertrude and Claudius, to which the murder is incidental. Claudius did not kill his brother, merely, or even chiefly, to acquire the kingdom: he killed him to possess the queen. That was his leading motive, though of course the other is not excluded. Nothing is more striking in the story than the passionate attachment of the guilty pair. And to clinch the matter, we have the words of Claudius himself in that matchless soliloquy when he tries to pray and only succeeds in reasoning himself, with pitiless logic and an intellectual honesty of which only the greatest minds are capable, into assurance of his own damnation.

> But O what form of prayer
> Can serve my turn? Forgive me my foul murther?
> That cannot be, since I am still possess'd
> Of those effects for which I did the murther—
> My crown, mine own ambition, and my queen!

Mark the ascending series—and the queen is at the top of the climax. That is where Claudius puts her when he strips his soul bare, and forces it to appear, naked and shivering, before the all-seeing eye.

Again, consider the situation of the queen. Conscious of adultery, but innocent of all complicity in the murder, she is torn asunder by her love for her husband and her love for her son. She would have peace, peace, when there is no peace. And so would Claudius, for his wife's sake, until he learns that somehow Hamlet has found out the truth, and that it must be war to the knife. Yet he must destroy the son without alienating the mother. And so he becomes his own Nemesis, for the queen drinks to Hamlet from the chalice prepared by Claudius for his enemy. Two lines condense the tragedy of Claudius and Gertrude:

> Gertrude, do not drink!
> It is the poisoned cup—it is too late!

In this web of crisscross tragic entanglements Polonius is meshed—Polonius, benevolent diplomatist and devoted father—and with him the son and daughter whom he loves with the pathetic tenderness of an old and failing man, and who return his affection as it deserves. The details need no rehearsal, but one point calls for emphasis: the deliberate parallelism of situation which makes Laertes the foil to Hamlet.

They have the same cause at heart: vengeance for a father is their common purpose. But their characters are sharply contrasted. For Laertes strikes on headlong impulse, without balancing and without scruple. If those critics are right who censure Hamlet for alleged inaction, for weakness of will, for being unequal to his task, then Laertes should be commended. For he does precisely what they seem to require of Hamlet. But I hear no praise of Laertes, even from the sternest of Hamlet's judges. How can they praise him, indeed? For his rash singleness of purpose makes him false to his own code of honor and degrades him to the basest uses. Yet there is no alternative in logic. Laertes, I repeat, is Hamlet's foil; and if Hamlet is wrong, Laertes must be right.

Veritably, we are at a nonplus if we regard this complex and tangle of tragic situations as a one-part play, or—what is much the same thing—as a mystery of temperament to which the sole character of the hero is the master-key.

No. Hamlet is not the tragedy of a weak-willed procrastinator, of the contemplative nature challenged by fate to fill the rôle of a man of action. On the contrary, it is the tragedy not of an individual but of a group; and in its structure it is balanced, in the most delicate and unstable equilibrium, between two great personages—Hamlet and the King. It is a duel to the death between well-matched antagonists; so well-matched indeed, that neither triumphs, but they destroy each other in the end. Almost everything that has been written about this drama is out of focus. For Claudius is either belittled or disregarded; and—Hamlet's real obstacle being thus cleared from his path by a complete misrepresentation of the facts—a new obstacle is called into being to account for his delay: namely, a complete misrepresentation of his mental and moral character.

Samuel Johnson

From *The Plays of William Shakespeare*

If the dramas of *Shakespeare* were to be characterised, each by the particular excellence which distinguishes it from the rest, we must allow to the tragedy of *Hamlet* the praise of variety. The incidents are so numerous, that the argument of the play would make a long tale. The scenes are interchangeably diversifed with merriment and solemnity; with merriment that includes judicious and instructive observations, and solemnity, not strained by poetical violence above the natural sentiments of man. New characters appear from time to time in continual succession, exhibiting various forms of life and particular modes of conversation. The pretended madness of *Hamlet* causes much mirth, the mournful distraction of *Ophelia* fills the heart with tenderness, and every personage produces the effect intended, from the apparition that in the first act chills the blood with horror, to the fop in the last, that exposes affectation to just contempt.

The conduct is perhaps not wholly secure against objections. The action is indeed for the most part in continual progression, but there are some scenes which neither forward nor retard it. Of the feigned madness of *Hamlet* there appears no adequate cause, for he does nothing which he might not have done with the reputation of sanity. He plays the madman most, when he treats *Ophelia* with so much rudeness, which seems to be useless and wanton cruelty.

Hamlet is, through the whole play, rather an instrument than an agent. After he has, by the stratagem of the play, convicted the King, he makes no attempt to punish him, and his death is at last effected by an incident which *Hamlet* has no part in producing.

The catastrophe is not very happily produced; the exchange of weapons is rather an expedient of necessity, than a stroke of art.

7

A scheme might easily have been formed, to kill *Hamlet* with the dagger, and *Laertes* with the bowl.

The poet is accused of having shewn little regard to poetical justice, and may be charged with equal neglect of poetical probability. The apparition left the regions of the dead to little purpose; the revenge which he demands is not obtained but by the death of him that was required to take it; and the gratification which would arise from the destruction of an usurper and a murderer, is abated by the untimely death of *Ophelia*, the young, the beautiful, the harmless, and the pious.

Elmer Edgar Stoll

From *Hamlet: An Historical and Comparative Study*

Confessions in soliloquy, moreover, are generally confirmed,—are, in Shakespeare's tragedy at least, never contradicted by the comment of other characters in a position to know,
or by the confidences imparted to them by the character himself.
Hamlet eventually tells Horatio of his uncle's guilt and his own
purpose, but not of his difficulties or failures in carrying it out. To
Horatio (or to himself, indeed) he never complains of any specific
dereliction of duty such as sparing the King at prayer. Nor to any
one is he known to have a defect. No one ever ventures to speak
of him slightingly or critically. Why does not the King, Laertes, or
Fortinbras despise him for a scholar and dreamer, at least, instead
of taking him as they all do for the worthy son of his warrior sire?
Why does not the Queen once sigh, or Horatio sadly shake his
head? He is a courtier, soldier, scholar, the expectancy and rose of
the fair state, cries Ophelia and there is no suggestion that she is
saying it as one who does not know. It is the accepted opinion.
The King fears him, and shrinks from bringing him to account for
Polonius' death, he says, because of the great love the general
gender bear him. The sinful Queen quails under his rebuke, and
yet loves him too well to betray his confidence. And, as often in
Shakespeare's tragedies, at the end of the play judgment to the
same effect is pronounced on his character by a disinterested
party, like the chorus of the Greeks. The closing funeral orations,
observes Professor Schick, are always spoken by the dramatist
himself.[1] "Let four captains," cries Fortibras,

> Bear Hamlet, like a soldier, to the stage,
> For he was likely, had he been put on,

> To have proved most royally; and, for his passage,
> The soldiers' music and the rites of war
> Speak loudly for him.
> Take up the bodies. Such a sight as this
> Becomes the field, but here shows much amiss.
> Go, bid the soldiers shoot.

A royal salute is given. For no one else in death has Shakespeare let the trumpets blare and cannon thunder; but this youth, says the man whom Hamlet himself had emulated, would have made a kingly king. It is like the judgment pronounced at the end by Cassio on Othello; like that pronounced by Antony on Brutus; and like that pronounced by Octavius on Antony himself and his queen. But in none of these cases is the praise so unmingled with blame, as if (were the poet to have his way) the villian, fate, and false fortune, not the hero himself, must bear the whole heavy burden. Critics there are who have thought the Fortinbras said it all in irony, but not those who are most in sympathy with Shakespeare's art.[2] So the words could not have been understood; or even if they had been, they would have disturbed that note of calm and reconciliation which Shakespeare in his great tragedies always reaches at the close. No respectable person in his dramas, for that matter, consciously or unconsciously speaks lightly of the dead. The poet's own personal humor, it would seem, did not sally across the confines of the frivolous or profane.

Here, or somewhere, one would have expected comment on Hamlet's shortcomings, his weakness or tragic fault. Instead, there is only praise from his friends, fear and hatred from his enemies. How is it possible, then, that a tragic fault or weakness could have been intended?[3] Not only do Shakespeare's heroes know their faults, like Lear at the beginning, or Othello at the end, as Hamlet says he does not (and would seem to have none to know), but their friends and enemies know them too. The Fool and Kent know Lear's, Lady Macbeth her husband's, Enobarbus Antony's, Cassius Brutus', and Iago Othello's;[4] but Horatio, Ophelia, Gertrude, Laertes, Fortinbras, who at the end avers that as a king he would have proved right royally, even Claudius himself, find in Hamlet no weakness at all! Only Horatio, of course, who alone is in the secret of the murder, could know of the procrastination or suspect it. He does not even hint at it. But Laertes might at least have belittled his swordsmanship, Polonius his statesmanship, and Claudius at times might have questioned his formidableness as a foe. Indeed, who so likely to know his own fault as Hamlet himself? At every other point (and at this as well!) he, like other Shakespearean characters, knows himself even as he is known.[5]

Nor can it be urged that Hamlet's defect is too private and delicate a matter to be touched upon. On the stage the secrets of the heart must rudely be brought to light; on the stage people know and talk about all sorts of things that no one would know or talk about off it. Even of our stage this is true, where there is greater reticence, and how much more is it true of the Elizabethan! Even Schiller and Ibsen must needs, in such cases, have recourse to comment, and they wrote for a more intellectual audience than Shakespeare's. Wallenstein too doubts, hesitates, procrastinates, though not, like Hamlet, episodically, but throughout the play. And he knows his own shortcoming, though at some points his friends know it better. Illo and the Countess know it: Terzky and Wrangel lay their fingers on or near the spot.[6] And Ibsen, who also wrote for audiences, not readers, though for audiences such as one seldom sees, found it necessary to bring Solness' apprehensions and Peer Gynt's indefinable evasions into the plain light of day. All the workmen know that the Masterbuilder cannot climb high towers, and openly his friends and enemies dissuade him from it or urge him on. And as for Peer Gynt, his career of hedging and dodging and "going round about" is made clear to us by words not only from his own lips but from those of the Dovre King, the Lean One, and the Button-Moulder.[7]

The charges, then, which Hamlet brings against himself are not, though they might well be, confirmed or substantiated. Instead, the evidence points the other way. In addition to what we have already considered, there is the fact that the two soliloquies of self-reproach are so contrived as to end each in a definite resolve, and that a resolve which is kept. "The play's the thing," in the one case; "From this time forth my thoughts be bloody or be nothing worth," in the other. Both times Hamlet, upon consideration, mends his ways: he turns from his sin of inaction, and his repentance is unto life. But the action he resolves on, you say, is not to the point—not revenge. You say this, however, because you are a critic, or a psychologist; or because you have read others' criticisms of the play; or because you have read the play more than you have seen it. In both cases it is action, not collapse; in both cases it is action which has to do with the King and with thwarting him; what is more, in both cases it is action which wholly satisfies the speaker himself. After the second soliloquy he complains of himself, questions himself, no more. And that the audience will observe, and are meant to observe, much more readily than the circumstance that the action is not the supreme one of killing the King. So the dramatist is enabled to content his audience, shield his hero, and still prolong his play.

*   *   *   *   *   *   *

Likewise Hamlet's doubt of the Ghost has been taken for no honest doubt. It is remarkable that scholarly critics continue to do this,[8] although it has long been known that the doctrine that ghosts were masquerading devils was then the enlightened Protestant opinion. If this doctrine had not been taken account of by the dramatist he would simply have been behind the times. As Spalding[9] has shown, it was the doctrine of the Reformers and of such theologians as Hooper and King James I. Says the martyred Bishop, in his *Declaration of the Holy Commaundementes of Allmyghtye God* (1550):

> Those abuse the name of God that seek help of damned spirits, or of such souls as be departed out of this world, as Saul did, . . . or those that by necromancy, or such like enchantments, abuse the name of God to resuscitate dead bodies, or call spirits departed unto the body again; which is nothing else but an illusion and craft of the devil to make men believe lies.[10]

This has to do only with the summoning of the spirits, and it is possible that the Bishop would not have denied that at times ghosts are real enough. But James VI of Scotland, presently to be Shakespeare's sovereign, is quite explicit:

> *Epistemon.* When they appeare vpon that occasion, they are called Wraithes in our language: Amongst the *Gentiles* the diuell vsed that much, to make them beleeue that it was some good spirit that appeared to them then, either to forewarne them of the death of their friend, or else to discouer vnto them the will of the defunct, or what was the way of his slaughter, as it is written in the booke of the histories prodigious: and this way he easily deceiued the *Gentiles*, because they knew not God: and to that same effect is it, that he now appeares in that maner to some ignorant Christians: for hee dares not so illude any that knoweth that, neither can the spirit of the defunct returne to his friend, or yet an Angel vse such formes.—*Dæmonologie*, III, i.[11]

This doctrine is of the soundest, for Henry Smith, "Silver-tongued Smith," one of the most eloquent of London preachers in the great Queen's reign, who died in 1591, speaking of ghosts in his *Pilgrim's Wish*, declares:

> Thus the deuill hath many wayes to deceive; and this is one and a dangerous one to draw us from Gods word to visions, and dreames and apparitions, upon which many of the doctrines of the Papists are grounded. They had neuer heard of Purgatory but for those spirits that walked in the night, and told them that they were the soules of such and such, which suffered in fire, till their Masses, and almes, and Pilgrimages did ransome them out: so these night-spirits began Purgatorie, and Purgatorye begat Trentals as one Serpent hatcheth another.[12]

And Andrew Willet, in his *Hexapla in Exodum* (1608), p. 81, to the same effect:

> The divels doe counterfeit the spirits and the soules of the dead; by this means the divell more strongly deceiveth, seeing men are readie to heare their parents and friends departed.[13]

So Robert Burton, in his *Anatomy* (1621):

> These kind of Devils many times appear to men . . . counterfeiting dead men's ghosts, as that of Caligula, which (saith Suetonius) was seen to walk in Lavinia's garden, where his body was buried.[14]

This, which is Hamlet's view, had already passed out of the realm
of controversy into poetry before him; and the Red Cross Knight
cries in answer to the voice of Fradubio when it comes to him out
of the tree:

> What voyce of damned Ghost from Limbo Lake,
> Or guilefull spright wandring in empty aire,
> Both which fraile men do oftentimes mistake,
> Sends to my doubtfull eares these speaches rare?
>
> *Faerie Queene*, I,ii,32. (Cf. II, xi, 39)

And like Hamlet, he too fears that "out of his weakness" the Devil
"abuses" (that is, *deceives*) him. But the skepticism of Sir Thomas
Browne in his *Religio* (1642), I, Sect. 37, goes farther, and declares
the devils no mimics or counterfeits, but the ghosts themselves,
in so far as there are any:

> I believe that these apparitions and ghosts of departed
> persons are not wandering souls of men, but the unquiet
> walks of devils, prompting and suggesting us into mischief,
> blood, and villainy; instilling and stealing into our hearts,
> that the blessed spirits are not at rest in their graves, but
> wander solicitous of the affairs of the world.[15]

In the same spirit Bacon interprets modern miracles as the "illusions of spirits,"[16] and Milton does the same with oracles.

The honest doubt or distrust of the supernatural, moreover, is
the recognized thing in old stories and plays. However real and
indubitable the ghost in Shakespeare may be, he is doubted by
the person who had trembled in his presence. There are the
several and various cases of Richard III, of Brutus, of Macbeth.
And so it is in Tirso's (1571–1648) *Infanzón de Illescas*.[17] Don Pedro,
the King, thinks, after the ghost has disappeared, that it was a
malicious trick of the Queen's or his brother's. The doubt of the
reality of the ghost is the natural psychological reaction of the
beholder, once it has vanished. The fear that is may be an evil
spirit is equally natural, and also, as here, a means of making a
situation, or of retarding the action and prolonging the play. For
purposes of story-making this Protestant—supposedly morbid or
pusillanimous—misgiving that the spirit may be an evil one, is
really ancient and pagan. Stout Odysseus, after Leucothoe had

given him the girdle and bid him plunge into the sea, murmurs to himself: "Perhaps this is some god who wishes to destroy me, by ordering me to quit my vessel. I will not do it." And Hamlet's own scruple is none other than that of the elder Hamlet, Orestes (himself surely not weak of heart or of hand), when in Euripides he confesses to Apollo that "there came a dreadful thought into my heart that it was some fiend I had listened to when I seemed to hear thy voice."[18] The simplicity and sincerity of Odysseus and Orestes, surely, is [sic] above suspicion, beyond cavil.

If Hamlet, then, were to be represented as deceiving himself when he doubts the Ghost, he should have been given a reason less plausible and natural. If he were meant to be skeptical, he should have been given a reason more original and novel in his day. An hallucination he might have called it, and left the devil out. But if either impression were the one Shakespeare had meant to convey, he could hardly have managed worse. Hamlet doubts the Ghost, but his doubts are so simple and sincere that he can share them with Horatio unabashed, and at once proceed to put them to the proof. He gives the play, and upon the blenching of the King his doubts are forever settled. "I'll take the Ghost's word," he cries, "for a thousand pound." But if the play had been a pretext or subterfuge, would he not have forgotten the pretended purpose of it—noted the King's guilt but not remembered the word of the Ghost? Or if he had been the incorrigible skeptic that since Coleridge and Schlegel's day he has been thought to be, would he not have doubted still? Leontes continues to doubt Hermione's innocence after the oracle is delivered which he had sought. But Hamlet's doubt is as simple as old Hieronimo's. Belimperia's letter he thinks a trap; but having learnt the truth through the intercepted letter of Pedringano, he, like Hamlet, seeks no further, doubts no more. In the plot of both plays doubt seems to perform an identical function. In Hamlet's case, moreover, it is prepared for, not dragged in. The pretext, if such it be, occurs long before he has need of it, or can have a "forefeeling"[19] of such need, the Ghost having as yet not unsealed his lips:

> Be thou a spirit of health or *goblin damned* . . .

Nor is that a sign that his wit is diseased if we remember Brutus' question as he faces Cæsar's ghost:

Art thou some god, some angel, or some devil?

Indeed, there are several passages, as Spalding has shown,[20] which imply that the night on the platform both Hamlet and Horatio were fully aware that a ghost was a dubious and dangerous thing.

It is of course to be admitted that Hamlet otherwise does not act as if he doubted—does not in any way change his attitude to the King. In the nunnery scene he tells Ophelia that those who are married—*all but one*—shall live; and in the play scene he is insulting and menacing from the start. But that is Shakespeare's way. Leontes, after all, does not doubt Hermione, Posthumus does not doubt Imogen, Othello does not doubt Desdemona after the temptation scene. Doubt means suspension of belief, or wavering betwixt belief and disbelief. These heroes do not waver—do not simply fail to believe their wives true, but positively believe them false. Shakespeare has no technique, we have noted, for presenting hesitation or irresolution, deliberation or debate; and of doubt may be said the same. His characters are on the one side or the other—they do not tarry in the twilight—amid the debatable lands—in between. Not intellect is the centre of their being but emotion and imagination. If they doubt, it is, as with Hamlet, only to make assurance doubly sure. Hamlet's doubt of the King's guilt, then, is not searching and thorough-going, but it is not therefore to be considered specious or unreal. If he fails to take his doubt to heart we are not therefore to think his doubt a pretext. It is not so much he who fails to take his doubt to heart as it is his maker. Though natural enough in the character, his doubt mainly serves as a *retardierendes Moment* in the story; and it is not by us to be taken psychologically—least of all for such a reason as that it was not taken psychologically by Shakespeare himself.

The greatest hoax, however, that Hamlet is supposed to have played on himself is when he spares the King at prayer. He shrinks from the deed, but he deceives his conscience by the promise of a more complete and horrible vengeance when the King is about an act that has no relish of salvation in it. With the numerous remoter explanations offered we shall not conern ourselves, whether it be a lack of will power, his unwillingness to kill a defenceless man, or an aversion to killing in general. What interests us is whether in this matter he deceives himself at all.

Here again the reason actually given is, for a revenge play, right and proper. It is consistent, in the first place, with the rest of the play. In Shakespeare's final version Hamlet retains not merely this but many other bloody Kydian sentiments and qualities. "Would I had met my dearest foe in Heaven, Horatio," Hamlet exclaims as he thinks of his mother's wedding, "or ever I had seen that day." "Now could I drink hot blood," he cries before he goes to his mother's bedchamber, just before he meets the King. And on his trip to England he does not hesitate to send Rosencrantz and Guildenstern to their death, as he puts it, "not shriving-time allowed." The reason he gives himself for postponing vengeance, moreover, tallies completely with the Ghost's own tale of his bitter lot, and thereby the audience is prepared to accept his reason. Hamlet says:

> He took my father grossly and full of bread,
> With all his crimes broad blown, as flush as May;
> And how his audit stands who knows save Heaven?
> But in our circumstance and course of thought
> 'Tis heavy with him. And am I then reveng'd
> To take him in the purging of his soul,
> When he is fit and season'd for his passage?

And his father had said before that:

> Cut off even in the blossoms of my sin,
> Unhousel'd, disappointed, unanel'd,
> No reckoning made, but sent to my account
> With all my imperfections on my head,
> O, horrible! O, horrible! most horrible!

In the second place, any one who is familiar with revenge tragedy, whether that of the ancients or of the Renaissance, is aware that the principle which prevails in it is an eye for an eye, a tooth for a tooth; and the blow in return may be greater but not less than the injury. Even with the selfsame axe which felled Agamemnon the son must needs smite the murderess and her paramour. "The justice of it pleases." And the answer to Hamlet's question is that neither in classical nor in Renaissance tragedy would he seem to be revenged if he took the King in the purging of his soul.

Indeed, the expression of a longing to kill both body and soul, which in this case Samuel Johnson thought too horrible to be read or uttered, is far from rare in Elizabethan drama and literature. Two perfect parallels are found in early prose. There is that in the *Brief Discourse of the Spanish State, with a Dialogue annexed, entitled Philobasilis* (1590), p. 24:

> One of these monsters meeting his enemie unarmed, threatened to kill him if he denied not God, his power, and essential properties, viz. his mercy, suffrance, etc., the which when the other, desiring life, pronounced with great horror, kneeling upon his knees; the hero cried out, *nowe will I kill thy body and soule*, and at that instant thrust him through with his rapier.[21]

And there is that in Nash's *Jack Wilton* (1594):

> [Cutwolf has led his enemy on, in the hope of saving himself, to utter abominable blasphemies and devote his soul to the devil.] "These fearefull ceremonies brought to an end, I bad him ope his mouth and gape wide. He did so (as what will not slaues do for feare?); therewith made I no more ado, but shot him full into the throat with my pistoll; no more spake he after; so did I shoot him that he might neuer speak after, or repent him."[22]

Quite so, in the anonymous *Alphonsus Emperor of Germany* (published 1654) Alexander induces his victim to renounce the joys of heaven as the price of his life, and in that moment takes his life as well:

> *Alphonsus.* Alphonsus doth renounce the joyes of Heaven,
>   The sight of Angells and his Saviours blood,
>   And gives his soul unto the Devills power.
> *Alexander.* Thus will I make delivery of the Deed,
>   Die and be damn'd, now am I satisfied.
>
> V, i.

Heywood in his *Gynaikeion, or Nine Bookes of Various History Concerninge Women* (1624), tells a similar story of "a gentleman of Mediolanum,"

> "that hauing his enemie at his mercie, held his steeletto to his heart, and swore that unlesse he would instantly abiure his faith, and renounce his Sauiour, had he a thousand liues he would instantly (with as many wounds) despoile him of

all; which the other for feare assenting to, and he, hauing
made him iterate ouer and ouer his unchristianlike blasphe-
mies, in the middle of his horrible abiuration stabd him to
the heart, uttering these words, See, I am reueng'd of thy
soule and bodie at once; for as thy bodie is desperate of life,
so is thy soule of mercie." (P. 400)[23]

So in John Ford's *'Tis Pity She's a Whore* (1627) V, iv, the servant
suggests to the infuriated Soranzo, whose wife has been guilty of
incest with her brother: "Let my hot hare [her brother] have law[24]
ere he be hunted to his death, that, if it be possible, he post to hell
in the very act of his damnation."[25]

Without such ingenious contrivances to make it effective,
moreover, there is still more frequently expressed the simple and
emphatic wish to send your victim's soul to hell. It is thus that
Belimperia admonishes her tardy father-in-law.

> For heere I sweare, in sight of heauen and earth,
> Shouldst thou neglect the loue thou shouldst retaine,
> And giue it ouer, and deuise no more,
> Myselfe should send their hatefull soules to hell,
> That wrought his downfall with extreamest death.
> *Spanish Tragedy*, IV,i,25–30.

In the same spirit Hieronimo invokes further vengeance on these
murderers the moment that he has killed them.

> Upon whose soules may heauens be yet auenged
> With greater far than these afflications.
> IV, iv, 173–74.

And at the very end of the play the Ghost of Andrea in fifteen
specific lines allots to each of them his own particular portion of
damnation and everlasting pain. Indeed, there is every evidence
that to Kyd's account is to be reckoned this sentiment of Hamlet's
which we are now considering.

It is a sentiment frequently met with on the lips of heroes of
that type of Senecan tragedy to which the *Spanish Tragedy* and
Hamlet belong. Frequently it takes the form of embittering the
victim's last moments by taunting him with thoughts of the hell
to which he is hastening. So it is in *Antonio's Revenge* (1599) V, ii,
100–104; the *First Part of Jeronimo* (1602?) I, iii, 79–80; Tourneur's

Revenger's Tragedy (1607) III, iv; and Webster's *White Devil* (1612) V, i, pp. 117–118 (1857, vol. ii). In Italian tragedy of the sixteenth century, it would seem, the Senecan *atrocitas* took a form still nearer to that in *Hamlet*. Merope, at least, in the tragedy of that name by Pomponio Torelli (1589), finding the supposed murderer of her son asleep, will not kill him so. He would die "too happy"; but she would harm, if she could, both body and soul ("insieme il corpo e l'alma").[26] And she rouses him for the same reasons as Beaumont and Fletcher's Evadne when she rouses her King out of his sleep.

> Yet I must not
> Thus tamely do it, as he sleeps; that were
> To rock him to another world, etc.
>
> *Maid's Tragedy* (1609), V, ii.

But some of these may seem to us rather sorry ladies and gentlemen, of whom better were not to be expected, though as a matter of fact they have not so much blood on their heads as the high-souled Prince. To reassure us, there is, in a play in which Shakespeare himself had a hand, the *Second Part of Henry VI* (1591–2), Iden, the philosophizing and moralizing squire of Kent, who says, as he kills the rebel Cade:

> And as I thrust thy body in with my sword,
> So wish I, I might thrust thy soul to hell.
>
> IV, x, 84–85

And in Belleforest's novel, the hero is almost as vindictive as our Senecan Hamlet:

> "Et pour ce va," he cries as he fells him with his hand, "et estant aux enfers ne faux de compter à ton frere, que tu occis meschamment, que c'est son fils qui te fait faire ce message a fin que soulagé par ceste memoire, son ombre s'appaise parmy les esprits bien heureux."—(*Lyon*, 1576) p. 259.

Amleth keeps the body to show to the Danes that they may wreak vengeance on it,—

> affin que ce soit vous qui punissez le tronc, et charoigne morte, puis que vivât il n'est peu tomber en voz mains, pour

en faire entiere la punition et vengeance et rassasier vostre colere, sur les oz de celuy, etc.—*Ib.* p. 271.

So he bids them burn the body and scatter the ashes, putting "the sparks of pity" far from them,

affin que ny la cruche d'argent, ou cristal, ny un sacré tombeau soient le repos des reliques, et ossements d'un homme si detestable.

* * * * * * *

There are several ways in which self-deception can be made apparent on the stage, none of which is here employed. Chief of these is that the reason given should itself be far-fetched, transparently thin and specious. In the novel it may be less so, but on the stage a subterfuge must fairly look like one. There is no mistaking Falstaff's, Bob Acres', or Hjalmar Ekdal's. But, just as in real life, if it be a natural or usual reason we do not wink or look askance. Hamlet's reason is natural, we have seen, and consistent, and people nowadays think it not such simply because they do not enter into the spirit of Elizabethan drama. People began to complain of it only far along into the eighteenth century,—the author of *Some Remarks* in 1736, "A Well-wisher and Admirer" in a letter to Garrick in 1742,[27] Johnson in 1765, Tom Davies in 1785.[28] It was too terrible, said one and all. They had been alienated, by now, from the Senecan tradition—

Verbannet ist der Sitten falsche Strenge—

the humane and sentimental spirit reigned. They complained of his reason, but they did not presume to doubt it. Then, by a trick of the human brain which has, hundreds of times, repeated itself in the history of literature (as indeed in the history of religion too) what they did not like they instinctively put from them and explained away. So, by his words in 1784, Richardson, the Glasgow professor, became the voice of his age: "The sentiments that Hamlet expresses when he finds Claudius at prayer, are not, I will venture to affirm, his real ones."[29]

Another way of securing the effect of self-deception is by means of repetition. As I have remarked elsewhere, if here the man were really meant to flinch, he would be made to do so once

more. In all times, and particularly in early times, in order to make
a point dramatists have found it necessary to drive it home; and
there would be a special necessity for this in the case of so difficult
a matter as self-deception in tragedy. There is such a necessity
even in matters less difficult. If Brutus is an impractical idealist,
he must thwart Cassius's worldly prudence, not only in the matter of the oath but also in the matter of letting Antony speak to
the People and in the strategy at Philippi. If Coriolanus is proud
and contemptuous, he must be made not once but twice to undertake to win the favor of the People and break down in the doing of
it. But Hamlet, flinching, if you will, when the King is delivered
into his hands at prayer, at his next opportunity to kill a man
who, apparently, is the King, *kills* him; and there is only one thing
for an audience to think of that. In the very next scene he has
caught the King, as he thinks, "about an act that has no relish of
salvation in it," and is as good as his word. It is not the King—but
what, then, is the King about when the Prince catches him in the
end? Trafficking in death and treachery, poisoning foils and
bowls. It has paid to wait. "This physic doth but prolong thy sickly
days," Hamlet had confidently said as he left his uncle on his
knees. It was not the speech, as the event proves, of one who fails
in deeds and takes refuge in words.

Nay, but there again he is deceiving himself, the critics protest. He doesn't really believe it is the King, they say despite the
plain intention of the text,[30] or, he is striking out frantically
because of his failure before; or, he can act on the spur of the
moment, as he cannot in resolute fulfilment of a duty; or, he can
stab a man through the arras, but not eye to eye, not face to face.
One wonders whether these writers ever stop to consider how a
stage play is made, or how audiences, or even readers, make shift
to comprehend it. There is a recognized method and medium of
expression, a language of the drama, in short,—"simple and sensuous," and certainly sensible,—which one must speak and the
other understand. And if it be to me a language not wholly
strange and foreign, there is only one possible way (without
explicit comment to guide us) whereby Hamlet can, as here, be
represented as shrinking from the deed and at the same time
deceiving himself,—and that is by acting as he did before. If now
he had hesitated; if now again he had deferred the hour of

reckoning and prolonged the King's sickly days; or if once afterwards he had been given an opportunity and failed to take advantage of it: then it would have been clear that his hesitation before
had been a fault, and the reason he gave a swindle. Since he does
not hesitate, but strikes instantly, on the spur of the moment, it is
clear that the reason for delay he had given was an honest reason,
and that he now stoutly keeps his word.

Still another, a third way, of presenting self-deception, is that
just now suggested—explicit comment. This may be by the character himself, or by the others on the stage. It is strange indeed
that in this, Shakespeare's most subtle and difficult play (though
not so subtle and difficult as criticism has made it) there should
have been, as we have seen, no comment on the tragic fault, if
such there be. Shakespeare's other chief characters, even those
who, like Lear, would in real life have known themselves but
slenderly, know their weaknesses very well; but Hamlet "does not
know" nor does any of his friends. And as for the self-deception,
it is Shakespeare's wont to make that perfectly clear. There may
be the comment of another, as when Othello cries "not a jot, not a
jot!" in rejoinder to Iago's remark, "I see this hath a little dash'd
your spirits." "I' faith I fear it has," he insists, with hypocritical
regret and icy candor. But when there are no witnesses the
character must needs bear witness against himself. There is in
Othello another instance of this, when Iago for the moment dallies
with the notion that he cannot be called a villain; and one in this
very play when Hamlet falls a' cursing like a very drab and catches
himself at it.[31] It is strange that Shakespeare thought good plainly
to label this case of self-deception, and yet let the presumably
momentuous cases like the resolve on the play as the thing, the
sparing of the King at prayer, and the summoning up of his
energies on his departure for England, go unmarked. It is strange
that he should let Hamlet trip himself up when he unpacks his
heart with words, and yet never let him detect himself—suspect
himself—in culpable evasion, or once doubt he should do the deed
when the occasion called. That Shakespeare should do thus, and
yet conceive of Hamlet as deceiving himself thus, is too strange a
thing to be.

Nothing vexes a popular dramatist more than to be misunderstood—for him there is not the consolation in store that there is

for poet or prophet—but according to the critics Shakespeare in
Hamlet must have courted it. He would make, for once, not a play
for the stage but a puzzle and riddle for the ages! And as chance
would have it—for what is art, to be sure, but a matter of
chance?—it turned out to be the first of stage plays in England,
and for two hundred years no one realized that there was a riddle
at all! But we know in our souls that the right element of art is
not chance and the unexpected; not obscurity or confusion. Even
the most esoteric art must find ready access to the minds and
hearts of men, and drama must find it swiftly and surely. Elsewhere, as we have seen, Shakespeare has not thought it beneath
his dignity to furnish comment on the tragic fault, if there be one,
or on the self-deception. Now Shakespeare is far less restricted in
his appeal, less exacting in his demands upon the attention and
understanding—more popular, in short—than Ibsen. But with
what elaborate repetition and variation of situation, with what
cunning contrast of character with character and of character
with circumstance, and with what plenitude of comment, Ibsen
presents to us the self-righteous self-deception of Helmer in the
Doll's House or the sentimental self-deception of Hjalmar in the
Wild Duck! In the *Doll's House* comment is provided through Nora;
in the *Wild Duck* through Relling and the comically—patheti-
cally—mistaken Gina, Gregers, and Hedvig. Thus upon the self-
deception in the two plays many rays of light converge; but in
Hamlet it is otherwise.

One thing at least the dramatist might have done in case he
shrank from having others perceive Hamlet's propensity or from
having him perceive the mental process on the occasion himself. If
really he beguiled himself when he spared the King, why on a
later occasion, particularly in his last soliloquy, before setting out
for England, does he not clearly recognize it? Why is he, the most
reflective and analytic character in Shakespeare, never permitted
to bring against himself any definite charge, whether of self-
deception or of conscious dereliction of duty?

* * * * * * *

The conclusion of a play is one of the surest indexes to your
dramatist's thought. It is so with the Greeks, for with them there

is always the final choral comment; it is so with Ibsen, for in the
end he has stripped the soul of the hero or heroine bare; it is
equally so with the Elizabethans. The chorus here, we have already seen, is Fortinbras. But what is Hamlet himself concerned
for at the last, after his work is done? Mainly for his "wounded
name."

> Report me and my cause aright
> To the unsatisfied!

Nothing in the words or the situation will justify any interpretation except that Hamlet is anxious to have the world know why
he had killed his uncle the King. For his name suffers not at all
because of his procrastination; no one knows of the murder of his
father, still less of his spirit's mandate. Hamlet's interest is in his
name being cleared, his reputation being righted, and after that in
the news from England, and in the succession to the throne. Not
a thought has he for any fault or defect[32] such as Othello reveals
in his last words for his. Not a thought, either, for his triumph
over it. "Done after all," is what he should say to himself if he
were the crippled, aspiring but despairing, spirit the critics have
taken him to be. Dramatic art—human nature itself—would demand no less. If the tragedy be, as the critics maintain, internal,
here, if nowhere else, that fact must come to light. The audience
must see it, if the other characters do not. But Hamlet's only
interests now are in things external—his name, the news, his
father's crown. "The rest is *silence*," the critics pick up his words to
answer; and they put a world of meaning into the phrase that
could never have been intended, because it could never have been
understood. The words simply mean:—I am a dead man, the rest
must go untold.

What goes untold Horatio is to tell. (In Shakespeare what ever
goes untold, and to him is of moment? His words—of all men's—
were neither faint nor few.) Horatio has been commissioned to
give the "complete official report." But this is to come, he says,
after the play is over, and that implies that it would be only what
the audience already know. Meantime he gives a summary of it,
the headlines, so to speak, without, however, hinting at any
failure or shortcoming in the hero. To him, the Prince's friend,
the tragedy is not by any means what we are inclined to take it

for—simply the tragedy of Hamlet's soul. "So shall you hear," he cries to the wondering Danes at the end:

> Of carnal, bloody, and unnatural acts,
> Of accidental judgments, casual slaughters,
> Of deaths put on by cunning and forc'd cause,
> And, in this upshot, purposes mistook
> Fallen on the inventors' heads.

A tragedy, that is to say (though so much else besides that) of intrigue, fate, and blood. And exactly such it was taken to be in the earliest extended criticism, to which we have already alluded, that in James Drake's *Antient and Modern Stages Survey'd* (1699):

> Nothing in Antiquity can rival this plot for the admirable distribution of Poetick Justice. The Criminals are not only brought to execution, but they are taken in their own Toyls, their own Stratagems recoyl upon 'em, and they are involved themselves in that mischief and ruine, which they had projected for *Hamlet*. *Polonius* by playing the Spy meets a Fate, which was neither expected by nor intended for him. *Guildenstern* and *Rosencrans*, the Kings Decoys, are counter-plotted, and sent to meet that fate, to which they were trepanning the Prince. The Tyrant himself falls by his own plot, and by the hand of the Son of that Brother, whom he had Murther'd. *Laertes* suffers by his own Treachery, and dies by a Weapon of his own preparing. Thus every one's crime naturally produces his Punishment, and every one (the Tyrant excepted) commences a Wretch almost as soon as a Villain.[33]

To something of the same effect is the opinion of the author of *Some Remarks* (1736) as he touches on poetic justice in the death of Laertes and the Queen:

> The Death of the Queen is particularly according to the strictest rules of Justice: for she loses her life by the villainy of the very Person who had been the Cause of all her Crimes.—P. 48.

It was the tragedy as a whole in which these critics were interested and Horatio's words lend them ample justification. They knew less about psychology than more recent Hamlet critics, but they were nearer in spirit to Shakespeare's art; and, as they insisted on the importance of the effect of the whole rather than on the importance of the leading character, they were nearer, in their old-fashioned way, to the secret of dramatic art in general.

Such is the text—intrigue, fate, and blood—and what of the score? Others before me have remarked upon the melodramatic quality of the great tragedy, the abundance of sound and fury in it, of all that takes the eye, fills the ear, and shocks both;[34] and no one so shrewdly as the philosophical and literary critic Professor Bradley has noted the quantity of noise required by the old stage-directions and implied in the play itself. Cannon roar whenever the King takes a rouse, kettle-drum and trumpet bray out the triumph of his pledge, and "Danish marches," "hautboys," and "flourishes" celebrate his movements. According to the unabridged text of the last scene the cannon (robuster equivalent, as Mr. Bradley observes, of our melodramatic pistol) should be kept booming continually,—when Hamlet "gives a hit" and the King drinks to him, when Fortinbras draws near on his march back from Poland, and when the body of the irresolute dreamer is borne with a warrior's honors to the grave. "Go bid the soldiers shoot," cries Fortinbras; whereupon, according to the Folio, "a Peale of Ordenance are shot off." So it was at least in 1623;[35] but never was it so when you or I have been at the theatre.

There is no irony intended,—none, as this cutting shows, that we today are inclined to put up with, at any rate. Even in Shakespeare's day it would have been considered barbarous if there were. But it is thought to be a triumph of Shakespeare's art that out of this sensational material—"well-nigh every stimulant of popular excitement he could collect"—he made the most mysterious and inward of his dramas. To my thinking, and, if facts prove anything, to that of our modern producers as well, the triumph would have been greater were the form better suited to the spirit. The world does not move if the earth does, and harmony, not incongruity, is the secret of art in the time of Shakespeare as in the time of Synge. "A strange harmony of discords," says Mr. Bradley; but there is plenty of that sort of thing in Elizabethan art without adding to it this incomprehensible variety.[36] It is easy thus oracularly to dispose of the matter, but one wonders how this harmony arises—or why to secure it the dramatist went so far afield. In the sixteenth century, as in the twentieth, no great poet would have chosen to tell, or succeeded in telling, the subtle tale of a soul that criticism has thought to hear, athwart all this booming and trumpeting, and this mass of violent and bloody action in which man is pitted against man, Hamlet against Claudius, Polonius, Laertes, the pirates, Rosencrantz and Guildenstern, instead of an enemy seated in the depths of his bosom. Shakespeare may have been in error, to be sure, led astray in the last scene in particular by his love of sensation, or his audience's love of it. But the endings of his other plays are not like this, and there is no such noise and tumult at the death of Othello and Macbeth, who were warriors, or of Lear, who was a king. Why should Shakespeare, in error, do here what he has not done elsewhere,—introduce repeated cannon shots at the close of this, presumably the most mysterious and inward of his dramas? The dramatist could not have been thus led astray from habit or by his audience's expectations—still less could he have exerted himself so vigorously to lead his audience astray and defeat his purpose. If there were such inwardness to the tragedy we may be sure that he would have had us suspect it: he would not have battered our ear-drums, instead.

But the dramatist is not thus in error if his drama be one—of character, to be sure, but of intrigue, fate, and blood. If Hamlet was not an irresolute dreamer but an intrepid young prince who had fought off his enemies through the four acts, and now fell at the end of the fifth only after he had slain them all, then "the soldiers' music and the rites of war," which Fortinbras orders "for his passage," are but his due. They are like a wreath or chaplet on his brow, from a soldier to a soldier, from the son of the con-quered to the conqueror's son.[37] Let them speak loudly for him, cries Fortinbras, for loudly a soldier salutes a soldier's grave. Here is no irony, but pathos, rather, for Hamlet had not lived out even a warrior's years;[38] but the main and prevailing note is that of tragic triumph. He was a pretty fighter, and this fight, says Fortinbras, was worthy of the field, and well has earned him a soldier's burial. There is on earth no end so fair, thought the Norseman, and Shakespeare and all England with him—then as now.

Thus there is nothing inappropriate in the artillery. And if a dramatist dealing with an heroic subject would not have put the like into his stage directions today, it is simply because "we have changed all that." We have no cannon just as we have generally no sound and fury, no fighting at funerals, no leaping into graves. But the shots fired when Hamlet gives his hits do not offend us when our hero appears to us sound and stalwart, and the scene— as story, not as psychology—is played for all it is worth. The shots make you hear what your eye may not be quick enough to see; the shots speak the language of the stage. Such portentous emphasis, to be sure, is not in our vein; but it is proper enough in a play in which there has been such violence of speech and demeanor in almost every act. And in this final scene of the revenge, toward which we have been impatiently looking, Shake- speare may well have felt warranted in scoring for full orchestra, and letting his thunders loose. This is the scene of scenes, where the energies of the Prince, checked and pent up throughout the play, are to be let loose. And if it was for such a brave and high occasion, not a weakling's desperate spasm, Shakespeare did not ill to call in the artillery. He may have made the error of over- emphasis, which he often makes—like a true Englishman, said Dryden long ago, "he knows not when to give over"—but he did not make the error, which he elsewhere never makes, of mistak- ing and defeating his own purpose. The great dramatist may overdo, but he does not do one thing thinking he is doing another. He does one thing, even to the point of calling in the artillery to make it clear; and it is the critics, far from the tumult and thunders of his theatre, who think he is doing another.

But what of our hero? In ridding him of his fault have we also robbed him of his charm? If not weak and erring, he is still unfortunate enough, unhappy enough, to be tragic. And all the individuality of his utterance and the poetry of his nature are left us—if not untouched, unspoiled. To what Hazlitt, Bradley, and Raleigh have in general to say of these no one will demur. Only the morbid psychology—the diseased spirit and limping will—is here denied him. His melancholy is not the melancholy of pessi- mism; his irony and cynicism are those of one who mourns his father, and his memory of a mother, not one who has lost his hold on life. At the end his interests are external, we have seen, but his soul is in them. Never before in the history of the world, I suppose, were words used so marvelously to show a man's chang-

ing moods as here—when he pardons Laertes, when he turns to
his people, who loved him, to clear his name, when he wrests the
cup out of Horatio's hand and prays him to live to clear it for him,
and when he peers into the future for the news from England and
to see Fortinbras seated on his father's throne. And I trust that
not one quivering accent or hovering intonation of the verse need
be lost to us if he be thought to speak in a manly strain. The
pathos is simpler, that is all. His body is wounded but his spirit is
whole, and he is not ready and glad to turn his face to the wall.
Like a man he clings to his friends, is concerned for the welfare of
the kingdom, but is concerned above all for his name and honor.[39]
Like a man he struggles against death to tell his story himself, and
wrests away the cup that his friend may live to tell it. "By
heaven," he cries, "I'll have it!" The nineteenth-century Hamlet
would not have had the strength or self-assertion to do that, or
say that; he would not have had even the desire. "This trivial
game of life,"[40] which he is presumed to despise, how much, even
at his last gasp, he seems to care for it all! And by his interpretation, which we have been presenting, Hamlet's most famous
utterance gains more perhaps, than it loses.

> O good Horatio, what a wounded name,
> Things standing thus unknown, shall live behind me!
> If ever thou didst hold me in thy heart,
> Absent thee from felicity awhile
> And in this harsh world draw thy breath in pain
> To tell my story,

There is less point, to be sure, to the words "in this harsh world
draw thy breath in pain." The frail and shrinking spirit of the
accepted Hamlet had found the world harsher than has ours. But
why should *he* have his story told, or have Horatio draw his
breath in pain to tell it? If all of it were to be told, surely he
himself had rather draw the veil—had rather let Horatio drain the
cup. But for our Hamlet the story is only not long enough, and he
yearns to live a bit longer in the telling of it by his friend. He is a
lord of the Renaissance and loves name and fame. He dies young,
dies in the moment of his triumph, dies, as it must seem to others,
with all this blood on his head. This is his triple tragedy, as
Shakespeare, I think, intended it,—a simpler and nobler, possibly

less interesting and piquant, conception than the usual one, though one not less appealing. To some it may even be more interesting because it seems to be more nearly what Shakespeare intended—more like him and his age.

NOTES

1. I.e., so far as authority is concerned. Generally they are much in character, however, though in Octavius's eulogy of Antony it is hard to make this out.
2. Cf. Professor Trench, *Shakespeare's Hamlet* (1913), pp. 238 ff. (The *Times* rightly demurred to such an opinion.)
3. Both Professor Baker and Professor Lewis have recently pointed out the fact that not always in Shakespeare is a tragic fault to be found.
4. And the pride of Coriolanus and the villainy of Richard are known to everybody.
5. A friend calls my attention to the fact that in thus interpreting Hamlet's reproaches, as well as in the general conception of Hamlet as not irresolute, I am following Swinburne, in his *Study of Shakespeare* (1895), pp. 161–69. I had not read this particular passage for some years:

    "That Hamlet should seem at times to accept for himself, and even to enforce by reiteration of argument upon his conscience and his reason, some such conviction or suspicion as to his own character tells much rather in disfavour than in favour of its truth. A man whose natural temptation was to swerve, whose inborn inclination was to shrink and skulk aside from duty and from action, would hardly be the first and last person to suspect his own weakness, the one only unbiassed judge and witness of sufficiently sharp-sighted candour and accuracy to estimate aright his poverty of nature and the malformation of his mind."

    The only point at which I am constrained to dissent from the great poet's judgment is where, having recognized that "the signal characteristic of Hamlet's inmost nature is by no means irresolution or hesitation or any form of weakness," he adds, "but rather the strong conflux of contending forces." But he lets it go at that, and in the discussion as a whole he is as remarkable for his clearness of perception as his readers (*quorum pars!*) have been for their dulness. He wrote in 1879, how many have gone on writing since! But Swinburne foresaw how it would be; and after he shows how Shakespeare has endeavored to exhibit Hamlet's courage and resourcefulness in the expedition to England, he adds, with a smile, the words quoted here on p. iv.

6. *Illo:* Der Einzige, der dir schadet, ist der Zweifel. (*Picc.*, II, vi.)
    Die Wahl ist's was ihm schwer wird; drängt die Noth,
    Dann kommt ihm seine Stärke. (*Picc.*, III, i.)
    Wrangel: Eh man überhaupt dran denkt, Herr Fürst! (*Tod*, I, v.)
    Gräfin: Nur in Entwürfen bist du tapfer, feig
    In Thaten. (*Tod*, I, vii.)

7. Both plays are pieces of symbolism. But the symbolists' methods seem to be about the only ones nowadays whereby these indefinable matters can effectively be brought upon the stage. Warranted by this convention, concreteness and explicitness do not offend.

8. Scholars seem often to keep their antiquarian knowledge and their criticism in separate compartments, as students of the Bible do theirs. Mr. E. K. Chambers, whose learning in matters Elizabethan is of course far in excess of anything I can pretend to, nevertheless speaks of Hamlet as "covering his weakness with unreal reasons" (*Warwick* ed.). He surely knows that *per se* the Prince's doubt of the Ghost and his reason for sparing the King were, for a revenge-play, very real.

9. *Elizabethan Demonology* (1880), pp. 53 ff.

10. Parker Society ed., p. 326. I regret that I have not the unmodernized text at hand, but the original is very rare.

11. I quote from *Workes* (1616), p. 125, but this particular treatise first appeared in 1579.

12. Hunter's *Illustrations* (1845), ii. p. 211. But I use the text of *The Sermons*, etc. (1631) pp. 262–63.

13. Quoted by Halliwell-Phillips, *Memoranda on Hamlet*, p. 9.

14. Shilleto ed., i, pp. 220–21.

15. Cited by Coleridge. Cf. to the same effect the last chapter of Bk. I of the *Pseudodoxia*, where he interprets most superstitions as the result of the Devil's contriving.

16. *Advancement of Learning*, I, iv, 9.

17. I, iv.—On this subject see my article on Ghosts in Shakespeare, *M. L. P.*, xxii., 217–18.

18. *Orestes*, ll. 1668–69; and also Orestes in the *Electra*, l. 979: "Surely it was a fiend in the likeness of the god that commanded this." The word in both cases is *alastor*. Again, in the *Iphigeneia in Tauris*, Orestes complains that "Phoebus deceived us by his prophecies." In the first two instances the parallel is clear—it is the revenger of his father's death, doubting, momentarily, the genuineness of the mandate of revenge which he has received from the other world. For evidence of the influence of Euripides on the old *Hamlet*, see the *Appendix*.

19. I allude to Professor Bradley's subtle and much-praised device for explaining something quite different,—why Hamlet should decide upon madness (his "safety-valve," and his first evasion) at once, and not—for the first time—after he had found his courage ebbing. Hamlet had a "forefeeling" of his need. (*Op. cit.*, pp. 120–21). Of this Shakespeare gives no hint, and surely nothing could be further removed from the spirit of his or any dramatic art. A play is not a puzzle. Besides, this notion interferes with Mr. Bradley's own conception of Hamlet as a strong man. See my article, *Kittredge Anniversary Papers*, p. 269.

20. Pp. 55–59. Cf. in particular the echo of James VI's words. Horatio cries:

> What if it tempt you toward the flood, my lord,
> Or to the dreadful summit of the cliff,
> Etc.

> *Dæmonologie* (III, ii):
> It is to obtaine one of two things thereby, if he [the Devil] may: The one is the tinsell of their life, by inducing them to such perillous places, at such time as he either followes or possesses them, which may procure the same, and such like, so farre as God will permit him, by tormenting them to weaken their bodie, and cast them into incurable diseases.

21. Cited by Reed, Furness, i, p. 283.

22. McKerrow, ii, p. 326. In his notes Mr. McKerrow refers also to Browne's *Religio Medici*, the anonymous notes, ed. Sayle, i, p. 1, where the same story is told. The passages from Nash and the *Alphonsus* are cited by Creizenach.

23. Referred to by McKerrow, *ut supra*.

24. A hunting term, meaning a head start.

25. This is parallel to Hamlet at another point, III, iii, 90:

> When he is drunk asleep, or in his rage,
> Or in the incestuous pleasure of his bed.

26. Ed. Verona (1723), pp. 381–82.

27. From Dublin, *Private Correspondence of David Garrick* (1831), i, p. 14.

28. III, p. 104: "The first actor who rejected this horrid soliloquy was Mr. Garrick." From the letter cited above it appears that in 1742 Garrick had not rejected it. "Well-wisher" beseeches him to omit it, as "a terrible blot and stain to a character, that, were it not for that, would be complete." But as yet no one went behind the returns. Voltaire (*v. ante*) in 1761 took the reality of the motive for granted. (*Œuvres*, xxiv, p. 198). And the author of *Miscellaneous Observations on Hamlet*, 1752, in commenting on Hamlet's words "I his sole son, do

this same Villain send To Heaven," makes this observation and no more: "Hamlet means by it that he was his *only* son, and conse-quently ought to be his chief avenger, instead of doing an Act of Kindness to his Assassin" (p. 39).

29. *Essays on Shakespeare's Characters* (1798), p. 131. See above, p. 8, note 22.

30. "Is it the King?"—"I took thee for thy better." And the intention being so plain, even the cleverest critics, before the days of Romanti-cism, refrained from tampering with it; as Voltaire (Œuvres, 24, p. 198), and the author of *Some Remarks* (1736): "Our Hero had not put him to Death, had he not thought it to have been the Usurper hid behind the Arras (pp. 43–44). Even Davies, in 1784 (*Miscellanies*, Ed. 1785, iii, pp. 104–5) in criticising Voltaire's carelessness, whom he seems to misunderstand, makes the same observation as he: "Had he read the play . . . he would have known that Hamlet imagined that the person he had killed was the King himself." Throughout his long commentary Davies nowhere suggests the likelihood of self-deception or unconscious fiction.

31. In the soliloquy "O What a Rogue," Act II, ii, 610 ff.—This sort of self-deception is not complete, for in the end the deceiver knows that he deceives himself. But no other sort is possible in soliloquy, at least in Elizabethan tragedy. The obvious irony of double-tongued soliloquies, such as Falstaff's, is only an apparent exception. (See my "Falstaff," *Mod. Phil.*, xii, pp. 233–34). If I may be permitted to quote from my article *"Anachronism in Shakespeare Criticism,"* (*ib.*, April, 1910, pp. 561–62): "Whatever a character says in soliloquy concerning his motives is for the information of the audience and is necessarily true. Iago is a liar no doubt, but it is to confound fact with fiction and knock the props from under Shakespeare's dramatic framework to hold that Iago's soliloquies are lies—that he lies to the audience, lies to himself. His word concerning his motives, like the theological reason Hamlet renders himself for sparing the King at prayer, must be taken at its face value. There is no chance of the audience discounting it, for they have no other clue." And that applies to the suggestion which Professor Bradley entertains as to Prince Hal's deceiving himself in his first soliloquy (*Oxford Lectures*, 1914, p. 254). I refer to the words: "I know you all and will awhile uphold the unyok'd humour of your idleness," etc. If a case of self-deception, how was the audience to discover that it is? Instead of being un-pleasant and unnatural to them, as it is to us, this soliloquy pre-served in their eyes the reputation of a famous English King.

32. Mr. Stopford Brooke, for instance (*Ten More Plays of Shakespeare*, N.Y., 1913, p. 137), declares that he has. What I am insisting on, however,

is not that the best critics generally lend their authority to such an interpretation, but that here, if anywhere, such sentiments would, if the critics otherwise are right, necessarily appear. And they do not appear.

33. *Allusion-Book*, ii, pp. 424–25.

34. In recognizing this melodramatic element in *Hamlet* (as in all of Shakespeare's tragedies, indeed) we do it no injustice. That in Shakespeare, as in the tragedy of the ancients, there is more of this than there is in *Ghosts* or *Rosmersholm* no one can candidly deny. By the very distinction of the *genres* they observed, ancient and Renaissance tragedy was allotted the realm of terror and horror—"the manacles of kings," as the familiar phrase of Scaliger has it, "slaughters, despairs, executions, exiles, loss of parents, parricides, incests, conflagrations, battles, loss of sight, tears, shrieks, lamentations, burials, epitaphs, and funeral songs." That was the precept for Renaissance tragedy, founded on the practice of that time and earlier times, and Elizabethan tragedy was, in so far, classical.

35. Generally the entry of Fortinbras and his last words are omitted, the last cannon-shot, of course, along with these. In the later prompt-books, such as Booth's and Irving's, cannon-shots are indicated only twice—at the words the "King drinks" (or "Give me to drink") and at Osrick's "A hit!." Irving omits the first, but requires a "shot within" to signalize the approach of the ambassadors.

36. I cannot but think that Bulthaupt, an excellent critic too, and much after Mr. Bradley's own heart, is franker: "Die tragische Färbung fehlt dem Schlusse ganz und gar, und es ist widerlich, ihn auf der Bühne zu sehen, wenn uns die drei ersten Acte mit dem magischen Zwang ihrer Entwickelung gebannt, wenn uns," etc. *Dramaturgie* (1894) ii, pp. 270–71. But before one condemns the close as inharmonious had one not better consider whether it may not harmonize with a play a bit different from that which one had conceived? It is in the same spirit that Bulthaupt (p. 325) complains of the inappropriateness of Hamlet's being ready and fit to fight, and of his having "been in continual practice." This makes him too businesslike and to the point; it shows that he is no weakling and intends revenge! It would have been logical for Bulthaupt—but I am glad he refrained—to have recourse to Loening's interpretation—that the practice is part of Hamlet's prescribed daily regimen. Like many other Germans, Loening thinks the Prince sick in body as well as in soul. How foreign is either supposition to Shakespeare's art!

37. Hamlet was born, says the Gravedigger, the day that his father overcame the elder Fortinbras. This may, as Professor Schick says,

be a circumstance not without significance. It is only a casual remark, but Hamlet is frequently mentioned in connection with his
father, and never with a slight upon the Prince.

38. There can be no question about this, though exactly how young he
is it is difficult to say. Repeatedly he is called "young," or his "youth"
is touched upon,—by Polonius, the Ghost, Ophelia, and the King.
(See the Concordance for these words and "young man.") He is not
so young to be sure, as in Quarto 1; he does not call the King
"father" as he does there (twice in III, ii) and in the *Fratricide Punished*,
and no doubt did in the lost play. Shakespeare's finished Hamlet is
too reserved and dignified, too subtle and mature, for that. And in
Quarto 2 Shakespeare has added some touches, which by inference,
at any rate, convey the impression of a somewhat greater age. The
Gravedigger says he went at his trade the day that our last King
Hamlet overcame Fortinbras. That, he says a bit later, was the day
young Hamlet was born. And finally he answers up, and tells the
Prince that he has been sexton here, man and boy, thirty years.
Hence Hamlet must be thirty. And that prepares us for another
added touch in Quarto 2—when near the end the Queen says that
Hamlet is "fat and scant of breath." Both additions, together with
the suppression of such details as I have mentioned in Quarto 1,
may have been deliberately designed, as has been thought, either to
make Hamlet mature enough for the reflections Shakespeare puts in
his mouth or to fit the part for an older actor like Burbage. But with
the additions it is dubious. As for the Gravedigger's remarks one
wonders whether Shakespeare expected the audience to put two and
two together in that fashion. What Shakespeare is interested in, and
the audience too, is the humors of the Gravedigger and his concrete
and circumstantial way of dating.

And as for "fat and scant of breath," those few words so precious
to the pathologists, it is to me incredible that Shakespeare ever put
the first of these into the text. That is not sound textual criticism, I
know; but if ever an emendation seemed imperative it is here. "Hot"
might easily have been so mistaken, (or to suit the actor it might
deliberately have been replaced); and the advantage of such a word is
not only that it does not clash with Hamlet's youthful elegance—
"the glass of fashion and the mould of form"—"that unmatcht form
and feature of blown youth"—and with his being in "continual
practice" as a fencer; but also that it is in keeping with the King's
words to Laertes as he arranges for the poisoned bowl—"when in
your motion you are hot and dry" (IV, vii, 158. Cf. Quarto 1: "In all
his heate," etc.; and F. P. IV, v; "wenn er erhitzt"). Besides, it fits
better the occasion. One doesn't need his brows wiped if one be fat

or scant of breath either, but one does if overheated. Or if one be really fat, why should it be noticed only here at the end? It is natural enough at this exciting moment for the Queen to remark upon a condition newly arisen, but not upon a permanent one. Her son is no fatter now than when he returned from his voyage, or (when we remember the actual shortness of the time involved) than he was at the beginning of the play. But the chief point is that the word "hot" keeps intact the dramatic situation as "fat" does not. At the word "hot" we are reminded of the King's words as he arranged for the bowl, and when the Queen invites Hamlet to drink we fear, for the space of four speeches, that he may. He had declined to drink with the King; now that he is hot he may, we fear, drink with the Queen. But his being overheated, it turns out, is the very cause of his refraining. "I dare not drink yet, madam; by and by"—"Come let me wipe thy face." If we have "hot," then, it is, fortunately, clearer that here again at the very end Hamlet is cleverer than the King—to the very end is more than a match for him.

39. These things men nowadays would not hold dearest of all, but an Elizabethan would.

40. See Mr. Yeats's *Ideas of Good and Evil* (London, 1907), p. 162. For a century and more *Hamlet* criticism has been the vehicle of men's melancholy and pessimism.

Maynard Mack

"The World of *Hamlet*"

My subject is the world of *Hamlet*. I do not of course mean
Denmark, except as Denmark is given a body by the play; and I do
not mean Elizabethan England, though this is necessarily close
behind the scenes. I mean simply the imaginative enviroment that
the play asks us to enter when we read it or go to see it.

Great plays, as we know, do present us with something that
can be called a world, a microcosm—a world like our own in being
made of people, actions, situations, thoughts, feelings and much
more, but unlike our own in being perfectly, or almost perfectly,
significant and coherent. In a play's world, each part implies the
other parts, and each lives, each means, with the life and meaning
of the rest.

This is the reason, as we also know, that the worlds of great
plays greatly differ. Othello in Hamlet's position, we sometimes
say, would have no problem; but what we are really saying is that
Othello in Hamlet's position would not exist. The conception we
have of Othello is a function of the characters who help define
him, Desdemona, honest Iago, Cassio, and the rest; of his history
of travel and war; of a great storm that divides his ship from
Cassio's, and a handkerchief; of a quiet night in Venice broken by
cries about an old black ram; of a quiet night in Cyprus broken by
sword-play; of a quiet bedroom where a woman goes to bed in her
wedding sheets and a man comes in with a light to put out the
light; and above all, of a language, a language with many voices in

Reprinted from *The Yale Review*, Vol. 41 (1952), pp. 502–23, by permission of the author.

it, gentle, rasping, querulous, or foul, but all counterpointing the one great voice:

> Put up your bright swords, for the dew will rust them.

> O thou weed
> Who art so lovely fair and smell'st so sweet
> That the sense aches at thee. . . .

> Yet I'll not shed her blood
> Nor scar that whiter skin of hers than snow,
> And smooth as monumental alabaster.

> I pray you in your letters,
> When you shall these unlucky deeds relate,
> Speak of me as I am; nothing extenuate,
> Nor set down aught in malice; then must you speak
> Of one that loved not wisely but too well;
> Of one not easily jealous, but being wrought,
> Perplex'd in th' extreme; of one whose hand,
> Like the base Indian, threw a pearl away
> Richer than all his tribe. . . .

Without his particular world of voices, persons, events, the world that both expresses and contains him, Othello is unimaginable. And so, I think, are Antony, King Lear, Macbeth—and Hamlet. We come back then to Hamlet's world, of all the tragic worlds that Shakespeare made, easily the most various and brilliant, the most elusive. It is with no thought of doing justice to it that I have singled out three of its attributes for comment. I know too well, if I may echo a sentiment of Mr. E. M. W. Tillyard's, that no one is likely to accept another man's reading of *Hamlet*, that anyone who tries to throw light on one part of the play usually throws the rest into deeper shadow, and that what I have to say leaves our many problems—to mention only one, the knotty problem of the text. All I would say in defense of the materials I have chosen is that they seem to me interesting, close to the root of the matter even if we continue to differ about what the root of the matter is, and explanatory, in a modest way, of this play's peculiar hold on everyone's imagination, its almost mythic status, one might say, as a paradigm of the life of man.

The first attribute that impresses us, I think, is mysteriousness. We often hear it said, perhaps with truth, that every great
work of art has a mystery at the heart; but mystery of *Hamlet* is
something else. We feel its presence in the numberless explanations that have been brought forward for Hamlet's delay, his
madness, his ghost, his treatment of Polonius, or Ophelia, or his
mother; and in the controversies that still go on about whether
the play is "undoubtedly a failure" (Eliot's phrase) or one of the
greatest artistic triumphs; whether, if it is a triumph, it belongs to
the highest order of tragedy; whether, if it is such a tragedy, its
hero is to be taken as a man of exquisite moral sensibility (Bradley's view) or an egomaniac (Madariaga's view).

Doubtless there have been more of these controversies and
explanations than the play requires; for in Hamlet, to paraphrase
a remark of Falstaff's, we have a character who is not only mad in
himself but a cause that madness is in the rest of us. Still, the very
existence of so many theories and counter-theories, many of
them formulated by sober heads, gives food for thought. *Hamlet*
seems to lie closer to the illogical logic of life than Shakespeare's
other tragedies. And while the causes of this situation may be
sought by saying that Shakespeare revised the play so often that
eventually the motivations were smudged over, or that the original old play has been here or there imperfectly digested, or that the
problems of Hamlet lay so close to Shakespeare's heart that he
could not quite distance them in the formal terms of art, we have
still as critics to deal with effects, not causes. If I may quote again
from Mr. Tillyard, the play's very lack of a rigorous type of causal
logic seems to be part of its point.

Moreover, the matter goes deeper than this. Hamlet's world is
preëminently in the interrogative mood. It reverberates with questions, anguished, meditative, alarmed. There are questions that in
this play, to an extent I think unparalleled in any other, mark the
phases and even the nuances of the action, helping to establish its
peculiar baffled tone. There are other questions whose interrogations, innocent at first glance, are subsequently seen to have
reached beyond their contexts and to point towards some pervasive inscrutability in Hamlet's world as a whole. Such is that tense
series of challenges with which the tragedy begins: Bernardo's of
Francisco, "Who's there?" Francisco's of Horatio and Marcellus,

"Who's there?" Horatio's of the ghost, "What art thou . . . ?" And then there are the famous questions. In them the interrogations seem to point not only beyond the context but beyond the play, out of Hamlet's predicaments into everyone's: "What a piece of work is a man! . . . And yet to me what is this quintessence of dust?" "To be, or not to be, that is the question." "Get thee to a nunnery. Why wouldst thou be a breeder of sinners?" "I am very proud, revengeful, ambitious, with more offences at my beck than I have thoughts to put them in, imagination to give them shape, or time to act them in. What should such fellows as I do crawling between earth and heaven?" "Dost thou think Alexander look'd o' this fashion i' th' earth?. . . and smelt so?"

Further, Hamlet's world is a world of riddles. The hero's own language is often riddling, as the critics have pointed out. When he puns, his puns have receding depths in them, like the one which constitutes his first speech: "A little more than kin, and less than kind." His utterances in madness, even if wild and whirling, are simultaneously, as Polonius discovers, pregnant: "Do you know me, my lord?" "Excellent well. You are a fishmonger." Even the madness itself is riddling: How much is real? How much is feigned? What does it mean? Sane or mad, Hamlet's mind plays restlessly about his world, turning up one riddle upon another. The riddle of character, for example, and how it is that in a man whose virtues else are "pure as grace," some vicious mole of nature, some "dram of eale," can "all the noble substance oft adulter." Or the riddle of the player's art, and how a man can so project himself into a fiction, a dream of passion, that he can weep for Hecuba. Or the riddle of action: how we may think too little— "What to ourselves in passion we propose," says the player-king, "The passion ending, doth the purpose lose"; and again, how we may think too much: "Thus conscience does make cowards of us all, And thus the native hue of resolution Is sicklied o'er with the pale cast of thought."

There are also more immediate riddles. His mother—how could she "on this fair mountain leave to feed, And batten on this moor?" The ghost—which may be a devil, for "the de'il hath power T'assume a pleasing shape." Ophelia—what does her behavior to him mean? Surprising her in her closet, he falls to such perusal of her face as he would draw it. Even the king at his prayers is a riddle. Will a revenge that takes him in the purging of his soul be vengeance, or hire and salary? As for himself, Hamlet realizes, he is the greatest riddle of all—a mystery, he warns Rosencrantz and Guildenstern, from which he will not have the heart plucked out. He cannot tell why he has of late lost all his mirth, forgone all custom of exercises. Still less can be tell why he delays: "I do not know Why yet I live to say, 'This thing's to do,' Sith I have cause and will and strength and means To do't."

Thus the mysteriousness of Hamlet's world is of a piece. It is not simply a matter of missing motivations, to be expunged if only we could find the perfect clue. It is built in. It is evidently an important part of what the play wishes to say to us. And it is certainly an element that the play thrusts upon us from the opening word. Everyone, I think, recalls the mysteriousness of that first scene. The cold middle of the night on the castle plat-form, the muffled sentries, the uneasy atmosphere of apprehen-sion, the challenges leaping out of the dark, the questions that follow the challenges, feeling out the darkness, searching for identities, for relations, for assurance. "Bernardo?" "Have you had quiet guard?" "Who hath reliev'd you?" "What, is Horatio there?" "What, has this thing appear'd again tonight?" "Looks 'a not like the king?" "How now, Horatio! . . . Is not this something more than fantasy? What think you on 't?" "Is it not like the king?" "Why this same strict and most observant watch . . . ?" "Shall I strike at it with my partisan?" "Do you consent we shall acquaint [young Hamlet] with it?"

We need not be surprised that critics and playgoers alike have been tempted to see in this an evocation not simply of Hamlet's world but of their own. Man in his aspect of bafflement, moving in darkness on a rampart between two worlds, unable to reject, or quite accept, the one that, when he faces it, "to-shakes" his disposition with thoughts beyond the reaches of his soul—com-forting himself with hints and guesses. We hear these hints and guesses whispering through the darkness as the several watchers speak. "At least, the whisper goes so," says one. "I think it be no other but e'en so," says another. "I have heard" that on the crowing of the cock "Th' extravagant and erring spirit hies To his confine," says a third. "Some say" at Christmas time "this bird of dawning" sings all night, "And then, they say, no spirit dare stir

abroad," "So have I heard," says the first, "and do in part believe
it." However we choose to take the scene, it is clear that it creates
a world where uncertainties are of the essence.

Meantime, such is Shakespeare's economy, a second attribute
of Hamlet's world has been put before us. This is the problematic
nature of reality and the relation of reality to appearance. The
play begins with an appearance, an "apparition," to use Marcellus's term—the ghost. And the ghost is somehow real, indeed the
vehicle of realities. Through its revelation, the glittering surface
of Claudius's court is pierced, and Hamlet comes to know, and we
do, that the king is not only hateful to him but the murderer of
his father, that his mother is guilty of adultery as well as incest.
Yet there is a dilemma in the revelation. For possibly the apparition *is* an apparition, a devil who has assumed his father's shape.

This dilemma, once established, recurs on every hand. From
the court's point of view, there is Hamlet's madness. Polonius
investigates and gets some strange advice about his daughter:
"Conception is a blessing, but as your daughter may conceive,
friend, look to 't." Rosencrantz and Guildenstern investigate and
get the strange confidence that "Man delights not me; no, nor
woman neither." Ophelia is "loosed" to Hamlet (Polonius's vulgar
word), while Polonius and the king hide behind the arras; and
what they hear is a strange indictment of human nature, and a
riddling threat: "Those that are married already, all but one, shall
live."

On the other hand, from Hamlet's point of view, there is
Ophelia. Kneeling here at her prayers, she seems the image of
innocence and devotion. Yet she is of the sex for whom he has
already found the name Frailty, and she is also, as he seems either
madly or sanely to divine, a decoy in a trick. The famous cry—
"Get thee to a nunnery"—shows the anguish of his uncertainty.
If Ophelia is what she seems, this dirty-minded world of murder,
incest, lust, adultery, is no place for her. Were she "as chaste as
ice, as pure as snow," she could not escape its calumny. And if she
is not what she seems, then a nunnery in its other sense of
brothel is relevant to her. In the scene that follows he treats her
as if she were indeed an inmate of a brothel.

Likewise, from Hamlet's point of view, there is the enigma of
the king. If the ghost is *only* an appearance, then possibly the

king's appearance is reality. He must try it further. By means of a second and different kind of "apparition," the play within the play, he does so. But then, immediately after, he stumbles on the king at prayer. This appearance has a relish of salvation in it. If the king dies now, his soul may yet be saved. Yet actually, as we know, the king's efforts to come to terms with heaven have been unavailing; his words fly up, his thoughts remain below. If Hamlet means the conventional revenger's reasons that he gives for sparing Claudius, it was the perfect moment not to spare him— when the sinner was acknowledging his guilt, yet unrepentant. The perfect moment, but it was hidden, like so much else in the play, behind an arras.

There are two arrases in his mother's room. Hamlet thrusts his sword through one of them. Now at last he has got to the heart of the evil, or so he thinks. But now it is the wrong man; now he himself is a murderer. The other arras he stabs through with his words—like daggers, says the queen. He makes her shrink under the contrast he points between her present husband and his father. But as the play now stands (matters are somewhat clearer in the bad Quarto), it is hard to be sure how far the queen grasps the fact that her second husband is the murderer of her first. And it is hard to say what may be signified by her inability to see the ghost, who now for the last time appears. In one sense at least, the ghost is the supreme reality, representative of the hidden ultimate power, in Bradley's terms—witnessing from beyond the grave against this hollow world. Yet the man who is capable of seeing through to this reality, the queen thinks is mad. "To whom do you speak this?" she cries to her son. "Do you see nothing there?" he asks, incredulous. And she replies: "Nothing at all; yet all that is I see." Here certainly we have the imperturbable self-confidence of the worldly world, its layers on layers of habituation, so that when the reality is before its very eyes it cannot detect its presence.

Like mystery, this problem of reality is central to the play and written deep into its idiom. Shakespeare's favorite terms in *Hamlet* are words of ordinary usage that pose the question of appearances in a fundamental form. "Apparition" I have already mentioned. Another term is "seems." When we say, as Ophelia says of Hamlet leaving her closet, "He seem'd to find his way without his eyes," we mean one thing. When we say, as Hamlet says to his mother in the first court-scene, "Seems, Madam! . . . I know not 'seems,'" we mean another. And when we say, as Hamlet says to Horatio before the play within the play, "And after, we will both our judgments join In censure of his seeming," we mean both at once. The ambiguities of "seem" coil and uncoil throughout this play, and over against them is set the idea of "seeing." So Hamlet challenges the king in his triumphant letter announcing his return to Denmark: "Tomorrow shall I beg leave to see your kingly eyes." Yet "seeing" itself can be ambiguous, as we recognize from Hamlet's uncertainty about the ghost; or from that statement of his mother's already quoted: "Nothing at all; yet all that is I see."

Another term of like importance is "assume." What we assume may be what we are not: "The de'il hath power T' assume a pleasing shape." But it may be what we are: "If it assume my noble father's person, I'll speak to it." And it may be what we are not yet, but would become; thus Hamlet advises his mother, "Assume a virtue, if you have it not." The perplexity in the word points to a real perplexity in Hamlet's and our own experience. We assume our habits—and habits are like costumes, as the word implies: "My father in his habit as he liv'd!" Yet these habits become ourselves in time: "That monster, custom, who all sense doth eat Of habits evil, is angel yet in this, That to the use of actions fair and good He likewise gives a frock or livery That aptly is put on."

Two other terms I wish to instance are "put on" and "shape." The shape of something is the form under which we are accustomed to apprehend it: "Do you see yonder cloud that's almost in shape of a camel?" But a shape may also be a disguise—even, in Shakespeare's time, an actor's costume or an actor's role. This is the meaning when the king says to Laertes as they lay the plot against Hamlet's life: "Weigh what convenience both of time and means May fit us to our shape." "Put on" supplies an analogous ambiguity. Shakespeare's mind seems to worry this phrase in the play much as Hamlet's mind worries the problem of acting in a world of surfaces, or the king's mind worries the meaning of Hamlet's transformation. Hamlet has put an antic disposition on, that the king knows. But what does "put on" mean? A mask, or a frock or livery—our "habit"? The king is left guessing, and so are we.

What is found in the play's key terms is also found in its imagery. Miss Spurgeon has called attention to a pattern of disease images in *Hamlet*, to which I shall return. But the play has other patterns equally striking. One of these, as my earlier quotations hint, is based on clothes. In the world of surfaces to which Shakespeare exposes us in Hamlet, clothes are naturally a factor of importance. "The apparel oft proclaims the man," Polonius assures Laertes, cataloguing maxims in the young man's ear as he is about to leave for Paris. Oft, but not always. And so he sends his man Reynaldo to look into Laertes' life there—even, if need be, to put a false dress of accusation upon his son ("What forgeries you please"), the better by indirections to find directions out. On the same grounds, he takes Hamlet's vows to Ophelia as false apparel. They are bawds, he tells her—or if we do not like Theobald's emendation, they are bonds-in masquerade, "Not of that dye which their investments show, But mere implorators of unholy suits."

This breach between the outer and the inner stirs no special emotion in Polonius, because he is always either behind an arras or prying into one, but it shakes Hamlet to the core. Here so recently was his mother in her widow's weeds, the tears still flushing in her galled eyes; yet now within a month, a little month, before even her funeral shoes are old, she has married with his uncle. Her mourning was all clothes. Not so his own, he bitterly replies, when she asks him to cast his"nighted color off." "Tis not alone my inky cloak, good mother"—and not alone, he adds, the sighs, the tears, the dejected havior of the visage—"that can denote me truly."

> These indeed seem,
> For they are actions that a man might play;
> But I have that within which passes show;
> These but the trappings and the suits of woe.

What we must not overlook here is Hamlet's visible attire, giving the verbal imagery a theatrical extension. Hamlet's apparel now is his inky cloak, mark of his grief for his father, mark also of his character as a man of melancholy, mark possible too of his being one in whom appearance and reality are attuned. Later, in his madness, with his mind disordered, he will wear his costume in a corresponding disarray, the disarray that Ophelia describes so vividly to Polonius and that producers of the play rarely give sufficient heed to: "Lord Hamlet with his doublet all unbrac'd, No hat upon his head; his stockings foul'd, Ungarter'd, and down-gyved to his ankle." Here the only quesion will be, as with the madness itself, how much is studied, how much is real. Still later, by a third costume, the simple traveler's grab in which we find him new come from shipboard, Shakespeare will show us that we have a third aspect of the man.

A second pattern of imagery springs from terms of painting: the paints, the colorings, the varnishes that may either conceal, or, as in the painter's art, reveal. Art in Claudius conceals. "The harlot's cheek," he tells us in his one aside, "beautied with plaster-ing art, Is not more ugly to the thing that helps it Than is my deed to my most painted word." Art in Ophelia, loosed to Hamlet in the episode already noticed to which this speech of the king's is prelude, is more complex. She looks so beautiful—"the celestial, and my soul's idol, the most beautified Ophelia," Hamlet has called her in his love letter. But now, what does beautified mean? Perfected with all the innocent beauties of a lovely woman? Or "beautied" like the harlot's cheek? "I have heard of your paintings too, well enough. God hath given you one face, and you make yourselves another."

Yet art, differently used, may serve the truth. By using an "image" (his own word) of a murder done in Vienna, Hamlet cuts through to the king's guilt; holds "as 'twere, the mirror up to nature," shows "virtue her own feature, scorn her own image, and the very age and body of the time"—which is out of joint— "his form and pressure." Something similar he does again in his mother's bedroom, painting for her in words "the rank sweat of an enseamed bed," making her recoil in horror from his "counter-feit presentment of two brothers," and holding, if we may trust a stage tradition, his father's picture beside his uncle's. Here again the verbal imagery is realized visually on the stage.

The most pervasive of Shakespeare's image patterns in this play, however, is the pattern evolved around the three words, show, act, play. "Show" seems to be Shakespeare's unifying image in *Hamlet*. Through it he pulls together and exhibits in a single focus much of the diverse material in his play. The ideas of seeming, assuming, and putting on; the images of clothing, painting, mirroring; the episode of the dumb show and the play within the play; the characters of Polonius, Laertes, Ophelia, Claudius, Gertrude, Rosencrantz and Guildenstern, Hamlet himself—all these at one time or another, and usually more than once, are drawn into the range of implications flung round the play by "show."

"Act," on the other hand, I take to be the play's radical metaphor. It distills the various perplexities about the character of reality into a residual perplexity about the character of an act. What, this play asks again and again, is an act? What is its relation to the inner act, the intent? "If I drown myself wittingly," says the clown in the graveyard, "it argues an act, and an act hath three branches; it is to act, to do, to perform." Or again, the play asks, how does action relate to passion, that "laps'd in time and passion" I can let "go by Th' important acting of your dread command"; and to thought, which can so sickly o'er the native hue of resolution that "enterprises of great pitch and moment With this regard their currents turn awry, And lose the name of action"; and to words, which are not acts, and so we dare not be content to unpack our hearts with them, and yet are acts of a sort, for we may speak daggers though we use none. Or still again, how does an act (a deed) relate to an act (a pretense)? For an action may be nothing but pretense. So Polonius readying Ophelia for the interview with Hamlet, with "pious action," as he phrases it, "sugar [s] o'er The devil himself." Or it may not be a pretense, yet not what it appears. So Hamlet spares the king, finding him in an act that has some "relish of salvation in 't." Or it may be a pretense that is also the first foothold of a new reality, as when we assume a virtue though we have it not. Or it may be a pretense that is actually a mirroring of reality, like the play within the play, or the tragedy of *Hamlet*.

To this network of implications, the third term, play, adds an additional dimension. "Play" is a more precise word, in Elizabethan parlance at least, for all the elements in *Hamlet* that pertain to the art of the theatre; and it extends their field of reference till we see that, every major personage in the tragedy is a player in some sense, and every major episode a play. The court plays, Hamlet plays, the players play, Rosencrantz and Guildenstern try to play on Hamlet, though they cannot play on his recorders—

here we have an extension to a musical sense. And the final duel, by a further extension, becomes itself a play, in which everyone but Claudius and Laertes plays his role in ignorance: "The queen desires you to show some gentle entertainment to Laertes before you fall to play." "I . . . will this brother's wager frankly play." "Give him the cup."—"I'll play this bout first."

The full extension of this theme is best evidenced in the play within the play itself. Here, in the bodily presence of these traveling players, bringing with them the latest playhouse gossip out of London, we have suddenly a situation that tends to dissolve the normal barriers between the fictive and the real. For here on the stage before us is a play of false appearances in which an actor called the player-king is playing. But there is also on the stage, Claudius, another player-king, who is a spectator of this player. And there is on the stage, besides, a prince who is a spectator of both these player-kings and who plays with great intensity a player's role himself. And around these kings and that prince is a group of courtly spectators—Gertrude, Rosencrantz, Guildenstern, Polonius, and the rest—and they, as we have come to know, are players too. And lastly there are ourselves, an audience watching all these audiences who are also players. Where, it may suddenly occur to us to ask, does the playing end? Which *are* the guilty creatures sitting at a play? When is an act not an "act"?

The mysteriousness of Hamlet's world, while it pervades the tragedy, finds its point of greatest dramatic concentration in the first act, and its symbol in the first scene. The problems of appearance and reality also pervade the play as a whole, but come to a climax in Acts II and III, and possibly their best symbol is the play within the play. Our third attribute, though again it is one that crops out everywhere, reaches its full development in Acts IV and V. It is not easy to find an appropriate name for this attribute, but perhaps "mortality" will serve, if we remember to mean by mortality the heartache and the thousand natural shocks that flesh is heir to, not simply death.

The powerful sense of mortality in *Hamlet* is conveyed to us, I think, in three ways . First, there is the play's emphasis on human weakness, the instability of human purpose, the subjection of humanity to fortune—all that we might call the aspect of failure in man. Hamlet opens this theme in Act I, when he describes how from that single blemish, perhaps not even the victim's fault, a man's whole character may take corruption. Claudius dwells on it again, to an extent that goes far beyond the needs of the occasion, while engaged in seducing Laertes to step behind the arras of a seemer's world and dispose of Hamlet by a trick. Time qualifies everything, Claudius says, including love, including purpose. As for love—it has a "plurisy" in it and dies of its own too much. As for purpose—"That we would do, We should do when we would, for this 'would' changes, And hath abatements and delays as many As there are tongues, are hands, are accidents; And then this 'should' is like a spendthrift's sigh, That hurts by easing." The player-king, in his long speeches to his queen in the play within the play, sets the matter in a still darker light. She means these protestations of undying love, he knows, but our purposes depend on our memory, and our memory fades fast. Or else, he suggests, we propose something to ourselves in a condition of strong feeling, but then the feeling goes, and with it the resolve. Or else our fortunes change, he adds, and with these our loves: "The great man down, you mark his favorite flies." The subjection of human aims to fortune is a reiterated theme in *Hamlet*, as subsequently in *Lear*. Fortune is the harlot goddess in whose secret parts men like Rosencrantz and Guildenstern live and thrive; the strumpet who threw down Troy and Hecuba and Priam; the outrageous foe whose slings and arrows a man of principle must suffer or seek release in suicide. Horatio suffers them with composure: he is one of the blessed few "Whose blood and judgment are so well co-mingled That they are not a pipe for fortune's finger To sound what stop she please." For Hamlet the task is of a greater difficulty.

Next, and intimately related to this matter of infirmity, is the emphasis on infection—the ulcer, the hidden abscess, "th' imposthume of much wealth and peace That inward breaks and shows no cause without Why the man dies." Miss Spurgeon, who was the first to call attention to this aspect of the play, has well remarked that so far as Shakespeare's pictorial imagination is concerned, the problem in *Hamlet* is not a problem of the will and reason, "of a mind too philosophical or a nature temperamentally unfitted to act quickly," nor even a problem of an individual at all. Rather, it is a condition—"a condition for which the individual himself is apparently not responsible, any more than the sick man is to blame for the infection which strikes and devours him, but which nevertheless, in its course and development, impartially and relentlessly, annihilates him and others, innocent and gulity alike." "That," she adds, "is the tragedy of *Hamlet*, as it is perhaps the chief tragic mystery of life." This is a perceptive comment, for it reminds us that Hamlet's situation is mainly not of his own manufacture, as are the situations of Shakespeare's other tragic heroes. He has inherited it; he is "born to set it right."

We must not, however, neglect to add to this what another student of Shakespeare's imagery has noticed—that the infection in Denmark is presented alternatively as poison. Here, of course, responsibility is implied, for the poisoner of the play is Claudius. The juice he pours into the ear of the elder Hamlet is a combined poison and disease, a "leperous distilment" that curds "the thin and wholesome blood." From this fatal center, unwholesomeness spreads out till there is something rotten in all Denmark. Hamlet tells us that his "wit's diseased," the queen speaks of her "sick soul," the king is troubled by "the hectic" in his blood, Laertes meditates revenge to warm "the sickness in my heart," the people of the kingdom grow "muddied, Thick and unwholesome in their thoughts"; and even Ophelia's madness is said to be "the poison of deep grief." In the end, all save Ophelia die of that poison in a literal as well as figurative sense.

But the chief form in which the theme of mortality reaches us, it seems to me, is as a profound consciousness of loss. Hamlet's father expresses something of the kind when he tells Hamlet how his "[most] seeming-virtuous queen," betraying a love which "was of that dignity That it went hand in hand even with the vow I made to her in marriage," had chosen to "decline Upon a wretch whose natural gifts were poor To those of mine." "O Hamlet, what a falling off was there!" Ophelia expresses it again, on hearing Hamlet's denunciation of love and woman in the nunnery scene which she takes to be the product of a disordered brain:

> O what a noble mind is here o'erthrown!
> The courtier's, soldier's, scholar's, eye, tongue, sword;
> Th' expectancy and rose of the fair state,
> The glass of fashion and the mould of form,
> Th' observ'd of all observers, quite, quite down!

The passage invites us to remember that we have never actually seen such a Hamlet—that his mother's marriage has brought a falling off in him before we meet him. And then there is that further falling off, if I may call it so, when Ophelia too goes mad— "Divided from herself and her fair judgment, Without the which we are pictures, or mere beasts."

Time was, the play keeps reminding us, when Denmark was a different place. That was before Hamlet's mother took off "the rose From the fair forehead of an innocent love" and set a blister there. Hamlet then was still "Th' expectancy and rose of the fair state"; Ophelia, the "rose of May." For Denmark was a garden then, when his father ruled. There had been something heroic about his father—a king who met the threats to Denmark in open battle, fought with Norway, smote the sledded Polacks on the ice, slew the elder Fortinbras in an honorable trial of strength. There had been something godlike about his father too: "Hyperion's curls, the front of Jove himself, An eye like Mars . . . , A station like the herald Mercury." But, the ghost reveals, a serpent was in the garden, and "the serpent that did sting thy father's life Now wears his crown." The martial virtues are put by now. The threats to Denmark are attended to by policy, by agents working deviously for and through an uncle. The moral virtues are put by too. Hyperion's throne is occupied by "a vice of kings," "a king of shreds and patches"; Hyperion's bed, by a satyr, a paddock, a bat, a gib, a bloat king with reechy kisses. The garden is unweeded now, and "grows to seed; things rank and gross in nature Possess it merely." Even in himself he feels the taint, the taint of being his mother's son; and that other taint, from an earlier garden, of which he admonishes Ophelia: "Our virtue cannot so inoculate our old stock but we shall relish of it." "Why wouldst thou be a breeder of sinners?" "What should such fellows as I do crawling between earth and heaven?"

"Hamlet is painfully aware," says Professor Tillyard, "of the baffling human predicament between the angels and the beasts, between the glory of having been made in God's image and the incrimination of being descended from fallen Adam." To this we may add, I think, that Hamlet is more than aware of it; he exemplifies it; and it is for this reason that his problem appeals to us so powerfully as an image of our own.

Hamlet's problem, in its crudest form, is simply the problem of the avenger: he must carry out the injunction of the ghost and kill the king. But his problem, as I ventured to suggest at the outset, is presented in terms of a certain kind of world. The ghost's injunction to act becomes so inextricably bound up for Hamlet with the character of the world in which the action must be taken—its mysteriousness, its baffling appearances, its deep consciousness of infection, frailty, and loss—that he cannot come to terms with either without coming to terms with both.

When we first see him in the play, he is clearly a very young man, sensitive and idealistic, suffering the first shock of growing up. He has taken the garden at face value, we might say, supposing mankind to be only a little lower than the angels. Now in his mother's hasty and incestuous marriage, he discovers evidence of something else, something bestial—though even a beast, he thinks, would have mourned longer. Then comes the revelation of the ghost, bringing a second shock. Not so much because he now knows that his serpent-uncle killed his father; his prophetic soul had almost suspected this. Not entirely, even, because he knows now how far below the angels humanity has fallen in his mother, and how lust—these were the ghost's words—"though to a radiant angel link'd Will sate itself in a celestial bed, And prey on garbage," Rather, because he now sees everywhere, but especially in his own nature, the general taint, taking from life its meaning, from woman her integrity, from the will its strength, turning reason into madness. "Why wouldst thou be a breeder of sinners?" What should such fellows as I do crawling between earth and heaven?" Hamlet is not the first young man to have felt the heavy and the weary weight of all this unintelligible world; and, like the others, he must come to terms with it.

The ghost's injunction to revenge unfolds a different facet of his problem. The young man growing up is not to be allowed simply to endure a rotten world, he must also act in it. Yet how to begin, among so many enigmatic surfaces? Even Claudius, whom he now knows to be the core of the ulcer, has a plausible exterior. And around Claudius, swathing the evil out of sight, he encounters all those other exteriors, as we have seen. Some of them already deeply infected beneath, like his mother. Some noble, but marked for infection, like Laertes. Some not particularly corrupt but infinitely corruptible, like Rosencrantz and Guildenstern; some mostly weak and foolish like Polonius and Osric. Some, like Ophelia, innocent, yet in their innocence still serving to "skin and film the ulcerous place."

And this is not all. The act required of him, though retributive justice, is one that necessarily involves the doer in the general guilt. Not only because it involves a killing; but because to get at the world of seeming one sometimes has to use its weapons. He himself, before he finishes, has become a player, has put an antic disposition on, has killed a man—the wrong man—has helped drive Ophelia mad, and has sent two friends of his youth to death, mining below their mines, and hoisting the engineer with his own petard. He had never meant to dirty himself with these things, but from the moment of the ghost's challenge to act, this dirtying was inevitable. It is the condition of living at all in such a world. To quote Polonius, who knew that world so well, men become "a little soil'd i' th' working." Here is another matter with which Hamlet has to come to terms.

Human infirmity—all that I have discussed with reference to instability, infection, loss—supplies the problem with its third phase. Hamlet has not only to accept the mystery of man's condition between the angels and the brutes, and not only to act in a perplexing and soiling world. He has also to act within the human limits—"with shabby equipment always deteriorating," if I may adapt some phrases from Eliot's *East Coker*, "In the general mess of imprecision of feeling, Undisciplined squads of emotion." Hamlet is aware of that fine poise of body and mind, feeling and thought, that suits the action to the word, the word to the action; that acquires and begets a temperance in the very torrent, tempest, and whirlwind of passion; but he cannot at first achieve it in himself. He vacillates between undisciplined squads of emotion and thinking too precisely on the event. He learns to his cost how easily action can be lost in "acting," and loses it there for a time himself. But these again are only the terms of every man's life. As Anatole France reminds us in a now famous apostrophe to Hamlet: "What one of us thinks without contradiction and acts without incoherence? What one of us is not mad? What one of us does not say with a mixture of pity, comradeship, admiration, and horror, Goodnight, sweet Prince!"

In the last act of the play (or so it seems to me, for I know there can be differences on this point), Hamlet accepts his world and we discover a different man. Shakespeare does not outline for us the process of acceptance any more than he had done with Romeo or was to do with Othello. But he leads us strongly to expect an altered Hamlet, and then, in my opinion, provides him. We must recall that at this point Hamlet has been absent from the stage during several scenes, and that such absences in Shakespearean tragedy usually warn us to be on the watch for a new phase in the development of the character. It is so when we leave King Lear in Gloucester's farmhouse and find him again in Dover fields. It is so when we leave Macbeth at the witches' cave and rejoin him at Dunsinane, hearing of the armies that beset it. Furthermore, and this is an important matter in the theatre— especially important in a play in which the symbolism of clothing has figured largely—Hamlet now looks different. He is wearing a different dress—probably, as Granville-Barker thinks, his "sea-gown scarf'd" about him, but in any case no longer the disordered costume of his antic disposition. The effect is not entirely dissimilar to that in *Lear*, when the old king wakes out of his madness to find fresh garments on him.

Still more important, Hamlet displays a considerable change of mood. This is not a matter of the way we take the passage about defying augury, as Mr. Tillyard among others seems to think. It is a matter of Hamlet's whole deportment, in which I feel we may legitimately see the deportment of a man who has been "illuminated" in the tragic sense. Bradley's term for it is fatalism, but if this is what we wish to call it, we must at least acknowledge that it is fatalism of a very distinctive kind—a kind that Shakespeare has been willing to touch with the associations of the saying in St. Matthew about the fall of a sparrow, and with Hamlet's recognition that a divinity shapes our ends. The point is not that Hamlet has suddenly become religious; he has been religious all through the play. The point is that he has now learned, and accepted, the boundaries in which human action, human judgment, are enclosed.

Till his return from the voyage he had been trying to act beyond these, had been encroaching on the role of providence, if I may exaggerate to make a vital point. He had been too quick to take the burden of the whole world and its condition upon his

limited and finite self. Faced with a task of sufficient difficulty in
its own right, he had dilated it into a cosmic problem—as indeed
every task is, but if we think about this too precisely we cannot
act at all. The whole time is out of joint, he feels, and in his young
man's egocentricity, he will set it right. Hence he misjudges
Ophelia, seeing in her only a breeder of sinners. Hence he misjudges himself, seeing himself a vermin crawling between earth
and heaven. Hence he takes it upon himself to be his mother's
conscience, though the ghost has warned that this is no fit task
for him, and returns to repeat the warning: "Leave her to heaven,
And to those thorns that in her bosom lodge." Even with the king,
Hamlet has sought to play at God. *He* it must be who decides the
issue of Claudius's salvation, saving him for a more damnable
occasion. Now, he has learned that there are limits to the before
and after that human reason can comprehend. Rashness, even, is
sometimes good. Through rashness he has saved his life from the
commission for his death, "and prais'd be rashness for it." This
happy circumstance and the unexpected arrival of the pirate ship
make it plain that the roles of life are not entirely self-assigned.
"There is a divinity that shapes our ends, Roughhew them how
we will." Hamlet is ready now for what may happen, seeking
neither to foreknow it nor avoid it. "If it be now, 'tis not to come;
if it be not to come, it will be now; if it be not now, yet it will
come: the readiness is all."

The crucial evidence of Hamlet's new frame of mind, as I
understand it, is the graveyard scene. Here, in its ultimate symbol, he confronts, recognizes, and accepts the condition of being
man. It is not simply that he now accepts death, though Shakespeare shows him accepting it in ever more poignant forms: first,
in the imagined persons of the politician, the courtier, and the
lawyer, who laid their little schemes "to circumvent God," as
Hamlet puts it, but now lie here; then in Yorick, whom he knew
and played with as a child; and then in Ophelia. This last death
tears from him a final cry of passion, but the striking contrast
between his behavior and Laertes's reveals how deeply he has
changed.

Still, it is not the fact of death that invests this scene with its
peculiar power. It is instead the haunting mystery of life itself
that Hamlet's speeches point to, holding in its inscrutable folds
those other mysteries that he has wrestled with so long. These he

now knows for what they are, and lays them by. The mystery of evil is present here—for this is after all the universal graveyard, where, as the clown says humorously, he holds up Adam's profession; where the scheming politician, the hollow courtier, the tricky lawyer, the emperor and the clown and the beautiful young maiden, all come together in an emblem of the world; where even, Hamlet murmurs, one might expect to stumble on "Cain's jawbone, that did the first murther." The mystery of reality is here too—for death puts the question, "What is real?" in its irreducible form, and in the end uncovers all appearances: "Is this the fine of his fines and the recovery of his recoveries, to have his fine pate full of fine dirt?" "Now get you to my lady's chamber, and tell her, let her paint an inch thick, to this favor she must come." Or if we need more evidence of this mystery, there is the anger of Laertes at the lack of ceremonial trappings, and the ambiguous character of Ophelia's own death. "Is she to be buried in Christian burial when she wilfully seeks her own salvation?" asks the gravedigger. And last of all, but most pervasive of all, there is the mystery of human limitation. The grotesque nature of man's little joys, his big ambitions. The fact that the man who used to bear us on his back is now a skull that smells; that the noble dust of Alexander somewhere plugs a bunghole; that "Imperious Caesar, dead and turn'd to clay, Might stop a hole to keep the wind away." Above all, the fact that a pit of clay is "meet" for such a guest as man, as the gravedigger tells us in his song, and yet that, despite all frailties and limitations, "That skull had a tongue in it and could sing once."

After the graveyard and what it indicates has come to pass in him, we know that Hamlet is ready for the final contest of mighty opposites. He accepts the world as it is, the world as a duel, in which, whether we know it or not, evil holds the poisoned rapier and the poisoned chalice waits; and in which, if we win at all, it costs not less than everything. I think we understand by the close of Shakespeare's *Hamlet* why it is that unlike the other tragic heroes he is given a soldier's rites upon the stage. For as William Butler Yeats once said, "Why should we honor those who die on the field of battle? A man may show as reckless a courage in entering into the abyss of himself."

H. D. Kitto

From *Form and Meaning in Drama*

As we said at the outset, the first thing that strikes us, or should strike us, when we contemplate the play is that it ends in the complete destruction of the two houses that are concerned. The character of Hamlet and the inner experience that he undergoes are indeed drawn at length and with great subtlety, and we must not overlook the fact; nevertheless, the architectonic pattern just indicated is so vast as to suggest at once that what we are dealing with is no individual tragedy of character, however profound, but something more like religious drama; and this means that unless we are ready, at every step, to relate the dramatic situation to its religious or philosophical background—in other words, to look at the play from a point of view to which more recent drama has not accustomed us—then we may not see either the structure or the meaning of the play as Shakespeare thought them.

Why do Rosencrantz and Guildenstern die, and Ophelia, and Laertes? Are these disasters casual by-products of "the tragedy of a man who could not make up his mind"? Or are they necessary parts of a firm structure? Each of these disasters we can refer to something that Hamlet has done or failed to do, and we can say that each reveals something more of Hamlet's character; but if we see no more than this we are short-sighted, and are neglecting Shakespeare's plain directions in favour of our own. We are told much more than this when we hear Horatio, and then Laertes, cry "Why, what a King is this!," "The King, the King's to blame";

Reprinted from *Form and Meaning in Drama*, pp. 329–334, by H. D. Kitto (1959), by permission of Methuen and Company.

also when Guildenstern says, with a deep and unconscious irony "We here give up ourselves . . . ," and when Laertes talks of "contagious blastments." Shakespeare puts before us a group of young people, friends or lovers, none of them wicked, one of them at least entirely virtuous, all surrounded by the poisonous air of Denmark (which also Shakespeare brings frequently and vividly before our minds), all of them brought to death because of its evil influences. Time after time, either in some significant patterning or with some phrase pregnant with irony, he makes us see that these people are partners in disaster, all of them borne down on the "massy wheel" to "boisterous ruin."

In this, the natural working-out of sin, there is nothing mechanical. That is the philosophic reason why character and situation must be drawn vividly. Neither here nor in Greek drama have we anything to do with characters who are puppets in the hands of Fate. In both, we see something of the power of the gods, or the designs of Providence; but these no more override or reduce to unimportance the natural working of individual character than the existence, in the physical world, of universal laws overrides the natural behaviour of natural bodies. It is indeed precisely in the natural behaviour of men, and its natural results, in given circumstances, that the operation of the divine laws can be discerned. In *Hamlet*, Shakespeare draws a complete character, not for the comparatively barren purpose of "creating" a Hamlet for our admiration, but in order to show how he, like the others, is inevitably engulfed by the evil that has been set in motion, and how he himself becomes the cause of further ruin. The conception which unites these eight persons in one coherent catastrophe may be said to be this: evil, once started on its course, will so work as to attack and overthrow impartially the good and the bad; and if the dramatist makes us feel, as he does, that a Providence is ordinant in all this, that, as with the Greeks, is his way of universalising the particular event.

Claudius, the arch-villain, driven by crime into further crime, meets at last what is manifestly divine justice. "If his fitness speaks . . ." says Hamlet; the "fitness" of Claudius has been speaking for a long time. At the opposite pole stands Ophelia, exposed to corruption though uncorrupted, but pitifully destroyed as the chain of evil uncoils itself. Then Gertrude, one of Shakespeare's

most tragic characters: she is the first, as Laertes is the last, to be
tainted by Claudius; but while he dies in forgiveness and reconciliation, no such gentle influence alleviates her end. In the bedchamber scene Hamlet had pointed out to her the hard road to
amendment; has she tried to follow it? On this, Shakespeare is
silent; but her last grim experience of life is to find that "O my
dear Hamlet, the drink, the drink! I am poisoned"—poisoned, as
she must realise, by the cup that her new husband had prepared
for the son whom she loved so tenderly. After her own sin, and as
a direct consequence of it, everything that she holds dear is
blasted. Her part in this tragedy is indeed a frightening one. She is
no Claudius, recklessly given to crime, devoid of any pure or
disinterested motive. Her love for her son shines through every
line she speaks; this, and her affection for Ophelia, show us the
Gertrude that might have been, if a mad passion had not swept
her into the arms of Claudius. By this one sin she condemned
herself to endure, and, still worse, to understand, all its devastating consequences: her son driven "mad," killing Polonius, denouncing herself and her crime in cruel terms that she cannot
rebut, Ophelia driven out of her senses and into her grave—
nearly a criminal's grave; all her hopes irretrievably ruined. One
tragic little detail, just before the end, shows how deeply Shakespeare must have pondered on his Gertrude. We know that she
has seen the wild struggle in the graveyard between Laertes and
Hamlet. When the Lord enters, to invite Hamlet to the fencing-
match, he says: "The Queen desires you to use some gentle
entertainment to Laertes before you fall to play." "She well in-
structs me," says Hamlet. What can this mean, except that she
has vague fears of Laertes' anger, and a pathetic hope that Hamlet
might appease it, by talk more courteous than he had used in the
graveyard? It recalls her equally pathetic wish that Ophelia's
beauty and virtue might "bring him to his wonted ways again."
The mischief is always much greater than her worst fears. We
soon see how Hamlet's gentle entertainment is received by
Laertes; and she, in the blinding flash in which she dies, learns
how great a treachery had been prepared against her Hamlet.

We cannot think of Gertrude's death, and the manner of it,
without recalling what the Ghost had said: Leave her to Heaven.
But if we are to see the hand of Providence—whatever that may

signify—in her death, can we do other with the death of Polonius? A "casual slaughter"? A "rash and bloody deed"? Certainly;
and let us by all means blame Hamlet for it, as also for the
callousness with which he sends Rosencrantz and Guildenstern
to their doom; but if we suppose that Shakespeare contrived these
things only to show us what Hamlet was like, we shall be treating
as secular drama what Shakespeare designed as something
bigger. In fact, Hamlet was *not* like this, any more than he was, by
nature, hesitant or dilatory; any more than Ophelia was habitually mad. This is what he has become. The dramatist does indeed
direct us to regard the killing of Polonius in two aspects at once: it
is a sudden, unpremeditated attack made by Hamlet, "mad," on
one who he hopes will prove to be Claudius; and at the same time
it is the will of Heaven:

> For this same lord
> I do repent; but Heaven hath pleased it so
> To punish me with this and this with me,
> That I must be their scourge and minister.

Surely this is exactly the same dramaturgy that we meet in
Sophocles' *Electra.* When Orestes comes out from killing his
mother, Electra asks him how things are. "In the *palace,*"* he says,
"all is well—if Apollo's oracle was well." Perhaps it was a "rash and
bloody deed"; it seems to bring Orestes little joy. We may think of
it what we like; Sophocles does not invite us to approve, and if we
suppose that he does, we have not understood his play, or his
gods. Apollo approves, and Orestes, though he acts for his own
reasons, is the gods' "scourge and minister." Polonius, no unworthy Counsellor of this King, a mean and crafty man whose
soul is mirrored in his language no less than in his acts, meets a
violent death while spying; and that such a man should so be
killed is, in a large sense, right. Hamlet may "repent"; Orestes
may feel remorse at a dreadful act, but in each case Heaven was
ordinant.

The death of Laertes too is a coherent part of this same
pattern. To this friend of Hamlet's we can attribute one fault; nor
are we taken by surprise when we meet it, for Shakespeare has
made his preparations. Laertes is a noble and generous youth, but
his sense of honour has no very secure foundations—and Polo-

nius' farewell speech to him makes the fact easy to understand. His natural and unguarded virtue, assailed at once by his anger, his incomplete understanding of the facts, and the evil suggestions of Claudius, gives way; he falls into treachery, and through it, as he comes to see, he is "most justly killed."

Of Rosencrantz and Guildenstern, two agreeable though undistinguished young men, flattered and suborned and cruelly destroyed, there is no more to be said; but there remains Hamlet, last and greatest of the eight. Why must he be destroyed? It would be true to say that he is destroyed simply because he has failed to destroy Claudius first; but this is "truth" as it is understood between police-inspectors, on duty. The dramatic truth must be something which, taking this in its stride, goes much deeper; and we are justified in saying "must be" since this catastrophe too is presented as being directed by Providence, and therefore inevitable and "right." If "there is a special providence in the fall of a sparrow," there surely is in the fall of a Hamlet.

Of the eight victims, we have placed Claudius at one pole and Ophelia at the other; Hamlet, plainly, stands near Ophelia. In both Hamlet and Ophelia we can no doubt detect faults: she ought to have been able to see through Polonius, and he should not have hesitated. But to think like this is to behave like a judge, one who must stand outside the drama and sum up from a neutral point of view; the critic who tries to do this would be better employed in a police-court than in criticism. We must remain within the play, not try to peer at the characters through a window of our own constructing. If we do remain within the play, we observe that what Shakespeare puts before us, all the time, is not faults that we can attribute to Ophelia and Hamlet, but their virtues; and when he does make Hamlet do things deserving of blame, he also makes it evident on whom the blame should be laid. The impression with which he leaves us is not the tragedy that one so fine as Hamlet should be ruined by one fault; it is the tragedy that one so fine should be drawn down into the gulf; and, beyond this, that the poison let loose in Denmark should destroy indiscriminately the good, the bad and the indifferent. Good and bad, Hamlet and Claudius, are coupled in the one sentence "If his fitness speaks, mine is ready." That Claudius is "fit and seasoned for his passage" is plain enough. Is it not just as plain that Hamlet is equally "ready?" What has he been telling us, throughout the play, but that life can henceforth have no meaning or value to him? Confronted by what he sees in Denmark, he, the man of action, has been reduced to impotence; the man of reason has gone "mad"; the man of religion has been dragged down to "knavery," and has felt the contagions of Hell. There is room, though not very much, for subtle and judicious appraisal of his character and conduct; the core of his tragedy is not here, but in the fact that such surpassing excellence is, like the beauty and virtue of Ophelia, brought to nothing by evil. Through all the members of these two doomed houses the evil goes on working, in a concatenation

> *Of carnal, bloody and unnatural acts,*
> *Of accidental judgments, casual slaughters,*
> *Of deaths put on by cunning and forced cause,*

until none are left, and the slate is wiped clean.

The structure of *Hamlet*, then, suggests that we should treat it as religious drama, and when we do, it certainly does not lose either in significance or in artistic integrity. As we have seen more than once, it has fundamental things in common with Greek religious drama—yet in other respects it is very different, being so complex in form and texture.

NOTES

*I italicise this word in order to represent Sophocles' untranslateable μέν, which suggests a coming antithesis that in fact is not expressed.

Francis Fergusson

From *The Idea of a Theater*

If one could see a performance of *Hamlet*, uncut, unbroken by intermissions, and employing the kind of simple make-believe which Shakespeare, with his bare stage, must have intended, we should find much to enthrall us besides the stories themselves. The stories, of course, start at once, and are felt continuously as working themselves out: fate, behind the scenes, makes, from time to time, its sudden pronouncements. But on-stage, the music and the drums and the marching of royal and military pageantry, are directly absorbing, and they assure us that something of great and general significance is going on. From time to time the stage is emptied; the pageantry is gone; the stories seem to be marking time—and Hamlet emerges, alone, or with one or two interlocutors. Sometimes he suffers his visions before us; sometimes he makes jokes and topical allusions; sometimes he spars with his interlocutors like the gag-man in a minstrel show, or the master of ceremonies in a modern musical.

The scenes of pageantry are all civic or military or religious rituals; the changing of the guard, the formal assembling of the court of Denmark, the funeral of Ophelia. Though they all have their relevance to the interwoven stories of the play and to the discordant purposes of the various characters, their chief function is to show forth the main action or underlying theme, at various stages in its development. At these ritual moments the plot-lines are, as it were, gathered together; the issues are held in suspension, and we are reminded of the traditional social values in which all have some sort of stake.

Reprinted from *The Idea of a Theater*, pp. 112–27, by Francis Fergusson (1949), by permission of Princeton University Press.

Hamlet's monologues, and his nimble exchanges with Polonius or Rosencrantz and Guildenstern, his "topical allusions" to drunkenness or to the state of the theater, make a very different kind of theatrical appeal. He steps out of the narrative course of the play, out of the "world of Denmark" which is the basic postulate of the make-believe, refers directly to the parallels between "Denmark" and the England of his audience. From one point of view Shakespeare seems to be counting on the inherent dramatic and theatrical interest which this character has apart from the story—permitting him, like the first violin in a concerto, a cadenza on his own, after which we are returned to the matter in hand. From another point of view, Hamlet's "improvized" moments are carried by our confidence in him as "chief reflector": we look to him, as to the ritual scenes, to show us the underlying theme of the whole.

Both the ritual and the improvisational elements in *Hamlet* are essential—as essential as the stories—in the structure of the whole. The Elizabethan theater, at once as frankly "theatrical" as vaudeville, and as central to the life of its time as an ancient rite, offered Shakespeare two resources, two theatrical "dimensions" which the modern naturalistic tradition of serious drama must try, or pretend, to do without. In the table on the following pages I have shown the chief ritual and the chief improvisational scenes in relation to the main parts of the plot.

If one thinks over the succession of ritual scenes as they appear in the play, it is clear that they serve to focus attention on the Danish body politic and its hidden malady: they are ceremonious invocations of the well-being of society, and secular or religious devices for securing it. As the play progresses, the rituals change in character, from the dim but honest changing of the guard, through Ophelia's mock rites, to the black mass of Claudius' last court. And it appears that the improvisational scenes bear a significant and developing relationship to the rituals. In general, they throw doubt upon the efficacy of the official magic, as when Hamlet refuses to take Claudius' first court at its face value; yet even the most cutting ironies of Hamlet do not disavow the mystery which the rituals celebrate, or reject the purposes that inform them.

The rituals, the stories, and the improvisations together make the peculiar rhythm of *Hamlet* as a performance. Denmark is shown as waiting, as it were, in the darkness of its ineffective ceremonies and hollow communal prayers while the infection, "mining all within," divides every man in secret from every other and bursts forth, from time to time, in savage but brief and ineffective fights.

But before examining the sequence of rituals, with its center in the players scene, it is necessary to endeavor to support the view that the Elizabethan theater had, in fact, this ritual aspect: that Shakespeare's audience, like that of Sophocles, was prepared to accept his play not only as an exciting story but as the "celebration of the mystery" of human life.

* * * * * * *

Shakespeare's theater, because of its ancient roots and its central place in society, permitted the development of ritual drama—or at least a drama which had this dimension as well as others. In the structure of *Hamlet* the rituals, as distinguished from the plots, serve to present the main action at various points in its development. Shakespeare uses them in much the same way in which Henry James used his "social occasions" to present the main theme of *The Awkward Age*. The structure of *Hamlet* could be described in Henry James's words: "A circle consisting of a number of small rounds disposed at equal distance about a central object. The central object was my situation, my subject in itself, to which the thing would owe its title, and the small rounds represented so many distinct lamps, as I liked to call them, the function of each of which would be to light up with all due intensity one of its aspects. . . . I revelled in this notion of the Occasion as a thing by itself." That is the important point: the social rite or occasion is taken as a thing by itself; it enables the author to assemble his dramatis personae in a wider light than any of their individual intelligences could provide. If my analysis of *Hamlet* is correct, the rituals (though they have deeper meanings than James's social gatherings) are also "occasions" of this kind: lamps lighting the rottenness of Denmark (the basic situation of the play) and the many-sided action which results, at various points in its course, and in various aspects.

In the table showing the relation of the plot to the ritual scenes and the improvisations, the players' scene is at the center. It has a ritual aspect, it is Hamlet's most ambitious improvisation,

THE PARTS OF THE PLOT	RITUAL SCENES	IMPROVISATIONAL ENTERTAINMENT
The Prologue	Act I, sc. 1 The changing of the Guard	
	Act I, sc. 2 Claudius' First Court	
The Agons—development of conflicting purposes of various characters; contrasts of their stories; "purposes mistook"; indecision and fighting in the dark		Act I, sc. 4. Hamlet's sermon on drunkenness (in Denmark and/or England)
		Act II, sc. 2 Hamlet exchanges wisecracks with Polonius, Rosencrantz, Guildenstern, and the players.
		Act III, sc. 2 Hamlet's charge to the players—his opinions on the art of acting.
		RITUAL AND ENTERTAINMENT
The Climax, Peripety, and Recognitions; all narrative strands brought together		Act III, sc. 2 The performance of Hamlet's play is both rite and entertainment, and shows the Prince as at once clown and ritual head of the state.

The Pathos or "sparagmos," both of the state and the individuals, leading to the epiphany or "collective revelation" of the general disease. (Cf. Toynbee's "schism in the state and schism in the soul")	Act IV, sc. 5 Ophelia's Madness is a mock ritual, a mixture of false and lewd marriage, and false and savage funeral; refers also to the funeral of Hamlet's father and Gertrude's false marriage. Alternates with rebellion in the state.	Act V Hamlet jokes and moralizes with the Gravedigger and Horatio. He feels like the gag-man and the royal victim in one. Gravedigger corresponds to Polonius.
The Epiphany, or Final Vision of the underlying truth of the action	Act V, sc. 1 Ophelia's funeral. A "maimed rite" but a real death. Act V, sc. 2 The duel between Hamlet and Laertes. This duel is surrounded with all the ceremonies of Claudius' Court, like the players' scene, and Claudius' other loud and drunken celebrations; but every element in it is false or mistaken: a mockery of invocation; and it eventuates in death, and "resurrection" in the shape of Fortinbras, who, now that Claudius' regime is gone, can appear with his new faith and hope.	

and it is the climax and peripety of the whole complex plot-scheme. If one can understand this scene, one will be close to grasping Shakespeare's sense of the theater, and his direct, profoundly histrionic dramaturgy.

The prologue contains two rituals, the changing of the guard and Claudius' first court. The changing of the guard is conducted by the honest and simple-minded soldiers, in perfect good faith: the welfare of the state is conceived in the most obvious and acceptable terms, and with the solemnity and authority of the military function. The motives of the soldiers are not impugned; and the only ironic angle we get on this scene is due to the arrival of the Ghost, which clearly suggests that the military rite is not an appropriate means for dealing with the actual danger. Claudius' court, on the other hand, is conducted by the new King; and here we feel (both in the light of Hamlet's disabused view of Claudius, and in the light of the visit of the Ghost) that there is something false about Claudius' discharge of the royal function. Together the two scenes establish the fact of danger and the common concern with the threatened welfare of the state. But they throw ironic lights upon each other. The point of view of the regime is in conflict with that of the simple soldiers. Neither the soldiers nor the regime have the magic for dealing with the Ghost; and it appears that the rituals of the state in general are false or mistaken.

The many conflicts, which the prologue presents as it were in suspension, are further developed (though without coming to direct issue) during the rest of the first act, the second act, and the first scene of Act III. Then (bringing the climax, peripety, and recognition) comes Hamlet's improvised ritual, the players' scene. Hamlet, as the "chief reflector," the widest consciousness in literature, as Henry James called him, is aware of what the soldiers see, of what Claudius sees, and of what the Ghost sees, and he is torn by all the conflicts implicit in these partial values and myopic vested interests. His "ritual occasion" is thus an answer to both rituals in the prologue; and at the same time (because he has also seen what the Ghost sees) it is an answer to, and a substitute for, the inadequate or false ritual order of Denmark. It is itself a "ritual" in that it assembles the whole tribe for an act symbolic of their deepest welfare; it is false and ineffective, like the other public occasions, in that the Danes do not really understand or intend the enactment which they witness. It is, on the other hand, not a true ritual, but an improvisation—for here the role of Hamlet, as showman, as master of ceremonies, as clown, as night-club entertainer who lewdly jokes with the embarrassed patrons—Hamlet the ironist, in sharpest contact with the audience on-stage and the audience off-stage, yet a bit outside the literal belief in the story: it is here that this aspect of Hamlet's role is clearest. But notice that, if Hamlet is the joking clown, he is also like those improvising Old Testament prophets who, gathering a handful of dust or of little bones, or a damaged pot from the potter's wheel, present to a blind generation a sudden image of their state. It is in the players' scene that the peculiar theatricality of *Hamlet*—ritual as theater and theater as ritual; at once the lightest improvisation and the solemnest occasion—is most clearly visible.

What then is the image, the parable, the "fear in a handful of dust," which Hamlet thus places—with all the pomp of court and all the impudence of the night-club entertainer—in the very center of the public consciousness of Denmark?

The most detailed analysis I know of the players' scene is Mr. Dover Wilson's, in his excellent book, *What Happens in Hamlet*. The reader is referred to that study, and to its companion-piece, Granville-Barker's book on *Hamlet*, for a discussion of the theatrical problems which the scene presents and for an understanding of the complexity of the scene as a whole, wherein the focus of the audience's attention is shifted from Hamlet (the "central reflector") to Horatio, to the Queen, to Ophelia, to the King—as though the play-within-a-play were being lighted from many angles by reflection from many mirrors. My purpose here is only to describe Hamlet's play itself, in order to show how it reveals the malady of the regime in all its ambiguity, mystery, and spreading ramifications. For this little play is indeed an all-purpose mousetrap—and it catches more than the conscience of the King.

First of all the play presents the hidden crime (the murder of a king and the more or less incestuous theft of his queen and his throne) upon which, as in *Oedipus*, all the threads of the interwoven plots depend. It is the presentation of this literal fact which has the immediate effect upon the innocent bystanders of the

court and upon the innocent groundlings in the audience, though
in Hamlet's violent view none are innocent. Because the security
of the regime and the purposes of its supporters depend either
upon ignorance or concealment, the public representation of the
crime is itself an act of aggression, Hamlet's attack, the turning
point in the story. This attack reaches the guilty Claudius first,
Gertrude second, Polonius third; then Laertes and Ophelia. And
at length it clears the way for Fortinbras, the new faith and the
new regime.

But though the fact of murder, incest, and usurpation is
clearly presented, the time of the murder—is it still to come?—is
vague; and the dramatis personae in the playlet are shifted about
in such a way as to leave the identity of the criminal in question,
and so to spread the guilt. The actual crime was that of Claudius;
but in the play the guilty one is nephew to the King. This could
mean (as Polonius and Gertrude seem to think) a direct threat by
Hamlet to Claudius; it also means that Hamlet (who had admitted
to himself a "weakness and melancholy" which makes him subject
to devilish solicitations, and who had assured Ophelia, that "I am
myself indifferent honest, yet I could accuse me of such things it
were better my mother had not borne me") had granted Claudius,
in advance, that he too is at least potentially guilty. Neither
Hamlet nor Shakespeare seem to rule out a Freudian interpretation of the tangle; Hamlet comes close to representing himself as
the diagrammatic son of the Oedipus complex, killing the father
and possessing the mother. Yet his awareness of such motivations
lifts the problems from the level of pathology to that of drama; he
sees himself, Claudius, Denmark, the race itself, as subject to
greeds and lusts which the hypocritical façade of the regime
guiltily conceals.

Thus the literal meaning of the playlet is the fact of the crime;
but the trope and the anagoge convey a picture of the human in
general as weak, guilty, and foolish: the deepest and most sinister
version of the malady of Claudius' regime in Denmark. This
picture should emerge directly from the staging of the playlet
before the corrupt and hypocritical court, under the inspired and
triumphant irony of the regisseur-prince. The whining of pipes,
the parade of mummers, the wooden gestures of the dumb-show,
the tinkle of the rhymes, should have the magical solemnity of a

play-party or children's singing-game ("London bridge is falling down"). Yet because of the crimes represented, this atmosphere is felt as unbearably weak and frivolous, a parody of all solemn rites. If this playlet invokes the magic potency of the theater ("the play's the thing") it does so with as much despairing irony as love. The staging is crude and childish: Hamlet's actors vainly take things into their own hands, and the court audience is as condescendingly unperceptive (until the scandal dawns on them) as any cynical crowd at a Broadway opening.

Hamlet's audience on-stage (and perhaps off-stage as well) misses the deeper meanings of his play. Yet he and his author have put it as simply as possible in the weary couplets of the Player-King. The Player-King seems to stand for Hamlet's father, and thus for the Ghost; and he speaks in fact with the clarity but helplessness (in this world) of the dead—addressing the frivolous Player-Queen without much hope of understanding. Since he is Hamlet's puppet, he speaks also for Hamlet, and since he is the King, he stands also for Claudius. Claudius, in the course of the play, will gradually acquire a helplessness like that of the Ghost; a faithlessness and an indecision like that of Hamlet. It is the function of the Player-King to state as directly as possible that gloomy and fatalistic sense of human action which is the subject of the play, and which all the various characters have by analogy.

The way to show this in detail would be to study the action of each character and to show what frivolity and gloomy faithlessness they have in common, but this would take too long. The point may be briefly illustrated by juxtaposing a few utterances of Hamlet and Claudius with analogous couplets of the Player-King:

Hamlet: There's a divinity that shapes our ends,
Act V Rough-hew them how we will.

Scene 2 Was't Hamlet wronged Laertes? Never Hamlet:
. . . . .
. . . . Hamlet denies it.
Who does it then? His madness.

Claudius: My stronger guilt defeats my strong intent:
Act III And, like a man to double business bound,

Scene 3 I stand in pause where I shall first begin,
And both neglect.

Act IV Not that I think you did not love your father,
Scene 7 But that I know love is begun by time,
And that I see, in passages of proof,
Time qualifies the spark and fire of it.
There lives within the very flame of love
A kind of wick or snuff that will abate it,
And nothing is at a like goodness still,
For goodness, growing to a plurisy,
Dies in his own too much. That we would do,
We should do when we would, for this "would" changes
And hath abatements and delays as many
As there are tongues, are hands, are accidents;
And then this "should" is like a spendthrift sigh,
That hurts by easing.

Player Our wills and fates do so contrary run
King: That our devices still are overthrown,
Our thoughts are ours, their ends none of our own.

What to ourselves in passion we propose,
The passion ending, doth the purpose lose.

Purpose is but the slave to memory
Of violent birth, but poor validity.

The speeches of Hamlet and Claudius which I have quoted
come late in the play, when both of them gain a deathly insight
into their destinies—the hidden and uncontrolled springs of their
own and others' actions. Even Claudius sees so deeply at this
moment that he gets the sense of human action which all the
characters have by analogy. His speech to Laertes (Act IV,
scene 7) is, moreover, both made more ironic and more general by
being addressed to Laertes in order to deceive him into a course
which is contrary to his deepest purposes and best interests. As
for Hamlet, his sense of pathos, of the suffering of motivations
beyond our understanding or control, does not save him from
violent outbursts any more than that of Claudius does. Shakespeare usually grants his victims a moment of great clarity when it

is too late—and then shows them returning, like automatons, to "ravin down their proper bane" and die.

But the chief point I wish to make here is that the Player-King presents very pithily the basic vision of human action in the play, at a level so deep that it applies to all the characters: the guilty, the free, the principals, the bystanders, those in power and the dispossessed. This vision of course comes directly from the crime of Claudius and the other "accidental judgements, casual slaughters, purposes mistook" (as Horatio describes them when summing up for Fortinbras) upon which the complicated plot depends; yet this generalized vision is more terrible than any of the particular crimes, and much more important for understanding Hamlet's motivation. To this point I shall return later.

The immediate effect of Hamlet's play comes by way of the concrete scandal which brings the climax and peripety of the narratives. The presentation of the play is Hamlet's attack; it succeeds; it convicts Claudius' regime, and "the lives of many" that depend upon it, of impotence and corruption. After that revelation all is lost (just as Macbeth is lost after the banquet scene)—and the desperate devices of the King and Laertes, the brief folly of Polonius, and the unimpeded progress of Fortinbras, in the healthy rhythm of the march, are seen as clearly fated or doomed.

For this reason also the "rituals" which follow the players' scene have a different quality from those which precede it. Since the regime has lost its manna—been "shown up"—the rituals in Acts IV and V, marking the stages of the collective pathos and epiphany, are clearly presented as mad or evil. Ophelia's mad ritual presents the "sparagmos" or tearing asunder of the individual and society at once ("schism in the state and schism in the soul"); mingling marriage and funeral, lewdness and prettiness, love and destruction to the accompaniment of plotting and rebellion. Ophelia's funeral is a real death but a "maimèd rite"; the duel between Hamlet and Laertes is ostensibly a ritual and actually a murder. With the assembling of the court and the royal family for the duel, the picture of Claudius' regime (the collective revelation of his black masses) is complete.

In the succession of "ritual scenes" with its center and climax in Hamlet's little play, it is obvious that Hamlet himself plays a central role. In the two rituals of the prologue he is, like the audience, a mere puzzled and troubled bystander. After the hidden struggles of Act I, II, and III, he presents, with his play, his own black mass, his own parody of a rite. He does not appear for the "tearing asunder" of Ophelia's madness, for this marks the pathos of the regime, and of the lives that depend directly on it; and his life (wherever it may be) has already withdrawn from all loyalty to Claudius' Denmark. But he returns to record Ophelia's truncated funeral in his cold, spent, but clear awareness; and to take his fated role in the duel at the end. I have endeavored to study the rituals as marking the progress of the "play as a whole"; but it is evident that in the play, and in the order of the rituals, Hamlet himself is both chief "agonist" and central "reflector." With this in mind it is possible to offer an interpretation of the role of Hamlet in relation to Shakespeare's idea of the theater, and the traditional social values which the play assumes.

D. G. James

From *The Dream of Learning*

In trying to speak of *Hamlet*, I give myself some comfort by saying at once that I shall be content to play the role of a Teucer to the Ajax of Mr. Granville-Barker. Mr. Granville-Barker concluded his essay on *Hamlet* with these words:

> In England, for the best part of a century before *Hamlet* was written, and for sixty years after, the finer issues of the spiritual revolution which the Renaissance had begun were obscured by secular discord, persecution, and civil war; and the ensuing peace left them hardened into formula. To the popular mind thus distressed and coarsened, the finer issues implicit either in play or character might well make small appeal. Nor would they be likelier to touch the conscience of the positive eighteenth century. Not till it was waning, and many men had come to find their set creeds unsatisfying, till they began to ask the old essential questions once again, to have a better answer if they might, did the Hamlet of spiritual tragedy come by his own; then to become, indeed, the typical hero of a new "age of doubt." It was as if Shakespeare, so alive to the spirit of his own time, had been in this mysteriously attuned besides to some
>
> > prophetic soul
> > Of the wide world dreaming on things to come.
>
> While our age of doubt endures and men still cry despairingly "I do not know. . . ." and must go on uncomforted, the

Reprinted from *The Dream of Learning*, pp. 33–62, by D. G. James (1951), by permission of Oxford University Press.

> play will keep, I should suppose, its hold on us. If a new age
> of faith or reason should succeeed, or one for a while too
> crushed by brute reality to value either, Hamlet may then be
> seen again simply as the good Polonius saw him.[1]

In these, as I believe, profound words, is the essence of what I
have to say. I am not, I trust, unmindful of all the work which has
gone to exhibiting to us the Elizabethan Hamlet; but those who
have illuminated the play by historical research have not themselves been unmindful that Hamlet was not merely contemporary
with his age; and the mind of Shakespeare is not, I take it,
expressible as a function of a number of features of the age in
which Shakespeare lived. The historian must accept the creative-
ness of the rare and great mind as itself a brute fact, and as a
major brute fact; there is no resolving it away; it is peculiar,
unique, and inexplicable; it is creative both of itself and of its
civilization. The apparently simple category of cause and effect
does not apply here; in such a mind, the facts and features of its
age are material worked upon and transfigured into expressive
symbols. Indeed, the symbol is not a statement or even a translation of the fact; instead, the fact emerges into clear light in the
form of the symbol which alone is the full because significant fact.
Thus, *Hamlet* better helps us to understand the Elizabethan uncertainty about ghosts than books written by lesser contemporaries
of Shakespeare whose study of these things is far more partial
and abstract than Shakespeare's treatment of them in his play.

I am not here chiefly concerned with these matters. I wish
only to suggest that we may go too far in seeing Shakespeare as
one *behind* whom we must look in order to understand him; we
may rightly look to what came after. There is much, indeed, in
Bacon which was of the Middle Ages and of the Renaissance; but
the core of him was what we can only call modern; he was one of
the first of the moderns; his vision of things was creative of, and
is better understood in the light of, what came after him; and
what makes Bacon important and gives to him his splendid literary powers is, I venture to say, his modernity. What was of the
Middle Ages in him and of the Renaissance, is, of course, of deep
interest to us; but it is not this which makes him loom so large,
which indeed gives him his peculiar greatness, and secures for
him the attention and admiration of all succeeding generations.

And so it is, I think, with Shakespeare. He was, in all truth, as
Mr. Granville-Barker says, greatly alive to the spirit of his own
time; but he, like Bacon, was prophetic, though of different
things. The "finer issues of the spiritual revolution" of his time
are still our issues; it is Hamlet as a figure expressive of modernity which holds our rapt contemplation; he, too, is one of the
first, and is perhaps the greatest, of the moderns. The spirit of
Bacon is still potently alive; so is Hamlet's. We read, in a nineteenth-century poet, that we are

> Light half-believers of our casual creeds,
>   Who never deeply felt, nor clearly will'd,
> Whose insight never has borne fruit in deeds,
>   Whose vague resolves never have been fulfill'd;
>   For whom each year we see
> Breeds new beginnings, disappointments new;
>   Who hesitate and falter life away,
>   And lose tomorrow the ground won today;

and it is natural to acknowledge that Arnold's description of us is
true enough. But Arnold's lines, fine as they are, are a poetry of
brief statement; Shakespeare's play is the detailed image, the
elaborately wrought symbol, of this unresolved distress of modernity. Our modern world, at its outset, beheld itself here, here
defined, and in that measure created; here it has continued to
behold itself; this play, far more than any other work of art or
philosophy, has held our fascinated study. Bacon, I have said, was
prophetic; and yet he looked to a conclusive event, an absolute
achievement through knowledge which was also power. But
Shakespeare, in *Hamlet*, was also, I have said, prophetic; but he
saw uncertainty, ignorance, failure, and defeat. I do not say he
saw, even in *Hamlet*, only these things; but that he saw at least
these things, we cannot deny. Bacon looked to unquestioning
religious faith and to natural philosophy; but Hamlet certainly
had no unquestioning faith; he had no philosophy, natural or
other; and his problems were hardly to be resolved by the use of
scientific method, or knowledge, or experiment.

I cannot, within my limits, proceed to a systematic study of the
play of *Hamlet*: I must move discursively, but not, I trust, evasively.

I have suggested where, as it seems to me, the centre of the play lies. Some have seen Hamlet as congenitally indisposed to action: Goethe and Coleridge saw him largely in this way. But in fact, the play forbids this; and Ophelia's description of Hamlet is no doubt intended to suggest to us a difference between the Hamlet we see now and the Hamlet of earlier days. He had been the courtier, the soldier, and the scholar,

> The expectancy and rose of the fair state,
> The glass of fashion, and the mould of form,
> The observed of all observers . . .[2]

But now he is quite, quite down. New circumstances have arisen, and in them he is distracted, uncertain of his way, unable to resolve an intolerable state of things; and the play presents this man in this condition, what he does and what happens to him. This indeed is not all it does; but this it does chiefly.

To see Hamlet as merely a perplexed mind, an uncertain intellect, would be grossly to simplify; no play could be enacted out of such abstracted matter. Hamlet is a man of strong passion, if he is also one of weak will; but the weakness of his will and the strength of his feelings, whether of contempt and disgust for Claudius or of admiration for Horatio, are of a piece with his intellectual condition; and if I appear to speak of Hamlet as of some ghostly and bloodless intellectual, it will not be in entire forgetfulness of the rest of him. Nor, if I appear to lift Hamlet out of the play and seem to offend against a canon of contemporary criticism, shall I forget the risks I am running. I must indeed ask forbearance for what cannot, within the scope at my disposal, be a full-length study of the play; I shall proceed with what I acknowledge to be a limited purpose in view; I only think that nothing that I say is in the last resort at odds with any full consideration of the play as a work of dramatic art.

Now we have, in the first place, to see Hamlet as a man uncertain of his duty in the circumstances in which he finds himself. Ought he to murder the murderer of his father and the seducer of his mother? That is the question:

> To be, or not to be: that is the question:
> Whether 'tis nobler in the mind to suffer
> The slings and arrows of outrageous fortune,

> Or to take arms against a sea of troubles,
> And by opposing end them? To die,—to sleep . . .

I am not unaware that I am plunging into, to say the least, debated territory. But it is better, I think, for me to declare myself at once and make clear where, on this battlefield, I stand and fight; and Mr. Granville-Barker would, I am sure, forgive me if for the moment I make Dr. Johnson my Ajax; he stands four-square, if shot at, in this as in his other battles. His interpretation of this soliloquy seems to me incomparably the best yet offered. The thought of the soliloquy is not, at the outset, of suicide at all, but of personal immortality: whether we are to be or not to be, to live or in truth to die; and in the context of this thought, which recurs at the conclusion of the lines I quoted (. . . and by opposing end them? To die,—to sleep . . .), Hamlet asks whether it be nobler to suffer the slings of fortune or to take arms against troubles and end them. Hamlet's mind is moving fast: we may read the "that is the question" as referring both backwards and forwards; and the two questions, Whether we shall live or die? and, Whether it is nobler to suffer or to take arms against our troubles? are tied up with each other and are in Hamlet's mind quite inseparable. Certainly, the thought of suicide occurs later with the talk of a bare bodkin making a quietus for us; this is one way of taking arms against a sea of troubles; and then Hamlet's thought turns at once, again, to death and a life to come. He had spoken first of taking arms against others with the chance that he be killed; and his mind had passed at once to the thought of what might come in another world than this. Now he speaks of killing himself; and now, again, his mind turns to what would come in another world.

> For who would bear the whips and scorns of time . . .
> When he himself might his quietus make
> With a bare bodkin? who would fardels bear . . .
> But that the dread of something after death,
> The undiscover'd country from whose bourn
> No traveller returns, puzzles the will . . .?

We do offence to the speech, or so it seems to me, unless we see Hamlet contemplating first, the killing of others with perhaps, then, his own death, and second, a suicide; both are ways of

taking arms against a sea of troubles; and the taking arms in
either form is seen against the fearful background of a world to
come in which condign punishment may be inflicted by a righ-
teous God. What kind of an eternity will the taking up of arms,
whether against others or oneself, bring one? Therefore the
overriding question is, Whether 'tis nobler . . .? This we must
know; for God, if there be a God, may punish us through eternity
for a wrong choice. There is the intrinsic ethical question,—
Which is in itself nobler? But Hamlet ties up this question along
with the thought of eternal sanctions imposed by God. If there
were no after-life it would not matter, or matter less, which line
he took; but he cannot here, upon this bank and shoal of time,
jump the thought of a life to come. There is, then, an ethical
question; there is also a metaphysical and religious question; and
to neither does he know the answer.

I only emphasize here, in passing, Hamlet's fearful imagination of a life after death. I venture to think we often underrate
this. Here, indeed, we need to remember how close these Elizabethan days were to the Middle Ages; here we must hold our
modernity in restraint. If we need to illustrate further that in this
matter Hamlet was not fetching excuses for delay, we may look at
lines Shakespeare wrote in another play a few years later. In
Measure for Measure the Duke has urged Claudio to be absolute for
death: the afflictions of life make death sweet. Later in the same
scene, Isabella has told Claudio that "the sense of death is most in
apprehension." But the reply of Claudio, given indeed to Isabella
but coming in effect as a reply both to her and to the Duke, is
dreadful in its imagination:

> Ay, but to die, and go we know not where;
> To lie in cold obstruction and to rot . . .
> . . . and the delighted spirit
> To bathe in fiery floods, or to reside
> In thrilling region of thick-ribbed ice;
> To be imprison'd in the viewless winds,
> And blown with restless violence round about
> The pendent world; or to be worse than worst
> Of those that lawless and incertain thought
> Imagine howling: 'tis too horrible!
> The weariest and most loathed worldly life

That age, ache, penury and imprisonment
Can lay on nature is a paradise
To what we fear of death.

Hamlet too had "lawless and incertain thought"; and it will not do
to say that here, in the face of this, Hamlet is finding extravagant
or recondite reasons for his hesitation. Since the days when these
lines were written the eschatological imagination has fallen steadily back before the onset of naturalism. A. C. Bradley merits our
gratitude, and I should be the last man to speak of him without
deep respect; but an English Hegelian would be intelligibly disposed to underrate Hamlet's fear of other worlds and to say that
his thought, if it moved on these lines, was a symptom merely of a
morbid and diseased state. My own wish is frankly to elevate
Hamlet's intellectual distresses to an equality in importance with
his emotional state; the strength of the emotional shock he has
suffered is equalled by the weakness of his mind in the face of
difficult moral and metaphysical issues. Hamlet was, after all, an
intellectual. We must bear in mind that Shakespeare was the first
to make him a member of a university; and *Hamlet* was acted
before the universities of Oxford and Cambridge. (We may also
recall, with alarm, that Polonius had been a member of a university; some will further note, and with still greater alarm, that he
had clearly, when at the university, been a member of the Dramatic Society.) But my point is that *Hamlet* is not a tragedy of
excessive thought; so far as we are to see the cause of Hamlet's
destiny in intellectual terms, it is a tragedy not of excessive
thought but of defeated thought. Hamlet does not know; and he
knows of no way of knowing. And then comes the line,

Thus conscience does make cowards of us all;

resolution is sicklied o'er, and enterprise loses the name of action.
It is hard to know what it is right to do; and we do not know
whether in fact we live after we die, and in a universe in which a
moral order asserts itself. No doubt Shakespeare had to be careful
how he expressed the issues which confronted Hamlet. But the
plain issue was, Does God exist or not? What was at stake in
Hamlet's mind was nothing less than the greatest which confronts our mortal minds.

"Conscience does make cowards of us." There has been, I am aware, much dispute as to what the word means here. For my part, I find not the least difficulty in believing that the word carries both its usual meaning and that of "reflection and anxious thought." It is a platitude of Shakespeare study that Shakespeare could, with wonderful ease, charge a word with two or three meanings at once; there is hardly a page of Shakespeare which does not illustrate this; and, in any case, the word "conscience" means for us all both a command to do what is right and anxious reflection as to what is, in fact, the right thing to do. If I had to choose (what I feel under no compulsion whatever to do) between the two meanings proposed, I should unhesitatingly choose the former and usual meaning. A. C. Bradley was cross (in a footnote) with the *Oxford Dictionary* for giving its authority to construing "conscience" in this passage as meaning "moral sense or scrupulousness"; and he declares that "in this soliloquy Hamlet is not thinking of the duty laid upon him at all." But how then can he begin to explain the lines,

> Whether 'tis nobler in the mind to suffer . . .
> Or to take arms . . .?

It is precisely his duty Hamlet thinks of, and of his duty, which he finds it hard to decide, in relation to a possible world to come; and the difficulty of knowing what is right, and the uncertainty of our last destiny, together puzzle and arrest the will. Conscience requires that we do what is right; but then, what *is* right or wrong in these circumstances? Anxious reflection discloses no clear conviction; nor does it provide knowledge of a world to come. This is the moral and metaphysical uncertainty in which Hamlet finds himself. He does not know and cannot find out. Conscience makes demands; but it also provides no clear moral or metaphysical sense. Until he finds himself in this climacteric condition, life has gone on smoothly enough; but now, and suddenly, he knows that he lacks the insight, or the knowledge, or the faith, which will steady him, and carry him forward in a single and continuous course of action. In this, Hamlet knows he is different from Horatio, whose calm and steadily appointed way of life we are expected to admire. Horatio is precisely one who in suffering all, suffers nothing; he has accepted the first alternative Hamlet had proposed to himself: "whether 'tis nobler in the mind to suffer the slings and arrows. . . ." Horatio has, we are expected to understand, decided that it is nobler so to suffer, and he has taken the buffets and the rewards of fortune with equal thanks; he knows his line and he is steady in it. Hamlet has not decided; and hence his peculiar distress.

It is very important to observe the play here on the word "suffer." Horatio is one who suffers everything and suffers nothing. What does this mean? I take it to mean, in the first sense, that Horatio accepts equally the fortunes and misfortunes of life; he embraces his good fortune with restraint and he endures his misfortunes. Therefore, in the second sense, he suffers nothing; he is not put out or mastered by circumstance; he is master of himself and of circumstance; he sustains a steady and imperturbable calm. In the one sense of the word, he takes what comes, without rebellion against it; he does not oppose it to end it; he is thus passive. But in the other sense, he is precisely not passive, but pre-eminently active and creative in his life. Such a steadiness and even tenour, in a philosophy of "suffering," Hamlet does not possess. Horatio is one who, in suffering all, suffers nothing; Hamlet is one who, in suffering nothing, suffers everything. He is active where Horatio is passive, and passive where Horatio is active. His passivity is of the wrong sort; he is blown about by every gust of passion. But it is the same when he is active: his activity, like his passivity, is an affair of passion merely. Judgement is not in it. He is passion's slave, played on like a pipe, lapsed in time and circumstance, unaccountable, now listless, now violent.

But we must remark how Hamlet speaks of Horatio; he does so in words of passionate admiration. His election had sealed Horatio for himself because in suffering all, Horatio suffered nothing; and it is the man who is not passion's slave whom he would wear in his heart's core. How clearly he would be like Horatio! And yet, in the face of what has happened, ought he to be like Horatio? or ought he not to take up arms against his troubles, and violently end them and perhaps thereby himself? He did not know. The ghost had given Hamlet specific instructions to contrive nothing against his mother:

> . . . leave her to heaven,
> And to those thorns that in her bosom lodge,
> To prick and sting her.

But ought he perhaps to leave Claudius to heaven also? When his guilt was proved beyond any doubt, Hamlet still did not kill him; he left him alone, giving a reason, plausible enough in Hamlet's eyes, in the eyes of his audience, and in our eyes, and yet inhabiting a middle region between sincerity and insincerity. We are told that in explaining why he does not there kill the King, Hamlet was sincere; it was a belief of the time. But it was certainly not universal. Claudius at least could have told him it was nonsense; Claudius has made just clear to us what was necessary if he, Claudius, was to win heaven. And could a Hamlet who half his time believed neither in heaven nor hell, sincerely and with a whole mind say these things? He leaves Claudius, and goes off to rage at his mother.

Conscience, says Hamlet, makes cowards of us; we are made afraid by it; and who of us does not know that this is true? In the soliloquy in Act IV (How all occasions do inform against me) the same thought is uppermost. God has given us capability and godlike reason; we may, Hamlet certainly does not, live in a bestial oblivion of it. What he charges himself with is excess of scruple in employing it in his moral difficulties, thinking too precisely on the event; his scruples, he says, are craven; or at least they are one part wisdom and three-quarters cowardice:

> A thought which, quarter'd, hath but one part wisdom
> And ever three parts coward.

He is disposed to upbraid himself for letting all things sleep; but he also acknowledges, even in his bitter reproachment of himself, that he is at least one-quarter wise in thinking precisely on the event: he could not do other than think precisely on such momentous issues. But then, if his precise thinking issues in no results, no assured decision, no clear path of duty, how can he be other than afraid of doing one thing rather than the other? He has cause and will and strength and means to do it; yes, all these he has; but has he the conscience to do it? That is the question; and conscience makes cowards of us. But where is a resolution of this distress to come from? From thinking precisely on the event?

Apparently not; Hamlet is a thinker and has thought enough. Then let him plunge, and do what no doubt most people would expect of him; he talks fustian at himself about greatly finding quarrel in a straw when honour's at the stake; and this in future will be his line. But will it? Of course not. It is better to have three-quarters cowardice and one quarter wisdom than four quarters of bravado and tomfoolery; and Hamlet knows this well enough. But where and how will he find escape from this proper and rightminded cowardice? This is his problem; and it is, I suppose, everybody's problem.

I am aware that I may well be manifesting a deplorable cocksureness in all this. But at least I shall make clear what I intend; and I confess to some impatience with what seems to me the present-day willingness to give up Hamlet for a mystery. Now it is true, no doubt, that we must not see the play as merely an affair of the character of its hero. But few of us will deny that Hamlet's procrastination is the major fact in the play and that it was intended by Shakespeare to be so. But are we really to find his procrastination a mystery and to leave it a mystery? Is there really anything mysterious about a man who has come to no clear and practised sense of life, and who in the face of a shocking situation which quite peculiarly involves him, shuffles, deceives himself, procrastinates, and in his exasperation cruelly persecutes the person he loves best in the world? Is this beyond our understanding? If we fail to understand it, is it not only because it is all so near to us and not because it is far off in Elizabethan times? Conscience, Hamlet said, makes cowards *of us all*. He was thinking of himself not as the exception, but as the rule.

Even if what I have said is true, it may still be replied that I am building up too much from the great soliloquies of Acts III and IV. There is much before, between, and after these speeches; there is indeed, round about them, the play as a whole. But I trust I may be allowed to make a few observations in further defence of what I have been saying. A. C. Bradley declared that it was only late in the play that Shakespeare gives any ground for thinking that Hamlet doubted what his duty was. In Act V, Scene ii, he has been speaking of his uncle, and he asks:

> . . . is't not perfect conscience
> To quit him with this arm? and is't not to be damn'd
> To let this canker of our nature come
> In further evil?

Certainly, the question is asked; and here at least (as Bradley tacitly acknowledges) "conscience" means conscience and no mistake; and with the thought of conscience comes again the thought of a world after this one—"is't not to be damned . . .?" But certainly, if this were all we had to go on, it would not be a great deal; it comes too late in the play. I have spoken of two of the soliloquies, those of Acts III and IV. Of the soliloquy in Act IV (How all occasions) and of that in Act II (Oh, what a rogue and peasant slave am I), Bradley remarks that in them Hamlet bitterly reproaches himself "for the neglect of his duty. When he reflects on the possible causes for this neglect he never mentions among them a moral scruple."[3] In fact I think, as I have suggested, that this, so far as it refers to the soliloquy in Act IV, is not true: it is thinking too precisely on the event which is there put down for the cause of the delay. But leaving that aside, we have to take account of the circumstances in which these two speeches are made. The first is made immediately after the players have shown him their paces; the second after Fortinbras has marched through against Poland. The player and the soldier come upon him—how could they else?—as deep and bitter reproaches. Nothing could be more natural than this: the player and the soldier move easily and naturally into their appointed actions; they suffer no arrest or inhibition; and Hamlet is filled with shame when he thinks of himself. What then could be truer, in any delineation of human nature, than that his mind should then, in face of those whose inner lives get so little in the way of their duties, turn to the second of his great alternatives, to taking arms against a sea of troubles and, as Mr. Granville-Barker says, to "brute capacity for deeds of blood"? These are not occasions of mere reflection; the shame of his helplessness goads him towards the more violent of the two choices. But in between these two soliloquies comes, in Act III, the soliloquy which every schoolboy knows by heart and which the world has always put down for the essence of Hamlet. Here he is under the stress of no immediate instigation which would merely rouse his blood and allay his judgement. Here he comes quietly on and speaks; and that very night the play is to be performed at Court. We are in a part of the play where the time-sequence of the action is given with unmistakable clarity. Hamlet had agreed with the player, when arranging to have *The Murder of Gonzago* performed, that it should be the following night; and early in the scene in which Hamlet speaks the great soliloquy it has been made clear that the play is to be performed that night. There has been previously, as Mr. Granville-Barker remarked, "a spell of timelessness"; and now the carefully defined temporal sequence is "used," said Mr. Granville-Barker, "to validate the dramatic speed, even as was timelessness to help slow the action down" and give a vague impression of inaction and delay. The tension tightens; Hamlet may have no doubt in his heart of the King's guilt; but soon there will be proof; and then, if ever, Hamlet must make his decision. At this point, Hamlet comes on and speaks his speech; and the purpose of this speech must be above all to define the issues. If, after the play-scene, he is not to act, we must be given fair reason: we must understand it; and the reason is as I have tried to expound it. This soliloquy is therefore central; on this, if on anything, the play turns. In the anguish of uncertainty which he here expresses he sees Ophelia and speaks his cruellest words to her. Then the play-scene; then a lifting of the tension in a measure, as he talks to Rosencrantz and Guildenstern. Then he is summoned to his mother and it is of his mother he thinks. It is midnight and he could drink hot blood; but still it is of his mother he thinks, not of his uncle. He goes to his mother but alights upon the King as he goes. But he does not kill him; he shuffles out of it and talks off his exasperation to his mother. But all is over. Very soon he will be in effect a prisoner, on his way to England. It is indeed, as he goes, that he hears of Fortinbras; and he ends his long soliloquy with,

> Oh, from this time forth,
> My thoughts be bloody, or be nothing worth.

But he had said something like this after hearing the Player; he had afterwards had his proof and his chance; and nothing had come of it. He may say what he likes about his thoughts being bloody; but this they will never be. "My thoughts be bloody, or be nothing worth"; but was his thinking precisely on the event "worth nothing"? It was at least one-quarter wisdom; and Hamlet, storm as he will at himself, will not throw up that wisdom for mere thoughts and deeds of blood. As Mr. Granville-Barker said, here is the end of a movement—the second movement—of the play. A new movement will begin; but Hamlet will not design and accomplish its ending. Someone else will do that.

I suggest, therefore, that it is not only what a careful inspection of the speech discloses that we have to take into account; there is also the crucial position of the speech in the action of the play as a whole. And to this I add that we must see this speech as close to, indeed as of a piece with, the conversation with Horatio in which Hamlet declares the quintessence of Horatio's mind and character which he so admires. This conversation occurs later in the third act and immediately before the play-scene; the moral and intellectual confusion of Hamlet, and then the calm and impregnable bearing of Horatio, are driven hard home as the inner spiritual setting of the ensuing climax of the play.

But it is not only this. Everywhere in this play there is uncertainty and doubt; everywhere also there is incalculable and almost incredible conduct. In belief as in conduct nothing is firm and clear. If we look to belief: the ghost may be an honest ghost; he may be the devil; he may be an illusion. Man has an immortal soul; he is also the quintessence of dust. Death may be a nothing, or a sleep, or its world may contain a heaven and a hell. It may be right to leave criminals to the action of heaven; it may also be right to find quarrel in a straw when honour (whatever that may be) is at the stake. There may be a God to point his canon at self-slaughter; but also there may not be, and only, in his place, a congregation of vapours. And if we look to the conduct of others: a brother can murder his brother whose wife he has seduced, and he can smile and be a villain. A loving wife will betray her husband and promptly marry again with no obvious compunction; and before these two a Court will cringe and crawl. Ophelia will apparently play in with the others. Of clarity of belief and clarity of conduct there is nothing. The world has crumbled to shifting sand; there is nothing which is firm and no one on whom to rely. Except indeed Horatio, who in suffering all suffers nothing; who has made a choice; and him Hamlet wears in his heart's core, ay, in his heart of heart.

But can we, before we go further, say anything which is at all clear about the fundamental ethical issue which confronted Hamlet? I think it is possible to do so; and to do so in the first place in terms of an opposition, with which Hamlet plays a good deal, between "blood" and "judgment." Hamlet has said to Horatio that he suffers nothing in suffering all; and he goes on to say that they are blessed

> Whose blood and judgment are so well commingled
> That they are not a pipe for fortune's finger
> To sound what stop she please. Give me that man
> That is not passion's slave . . .

"Blood," here, is the same as "passion," and together are opposed to "judgment," a word which is frequent in Shakespeare's plays of this time. In the first Act, Laertes tells Ophelia to regard Hamlet's favours as "a fashion, and a toy in blood"; Hamlet tells his mother that at her age

> The hey-day in the blood is tame, it's humble,
> And waits upon the judgment; and what judgment
> Would step from this to this?

And then again, he says of himself, in the soliloquy in the fourth Act,

> How stand I then,
> That have . . .
> Excitements of my reason and my blood . . .

The opposition of these two is frequent and clear. Besides, the King speaks of Ophelia in her madness as

> Divided from herself and her fair judgment,
> Without the which we are pictures, or mere beasts;

and this chimes in with Hamlet's

> What is a man,
> If the chief good and market of his time
> Be but to sleep and feed? a beast, no more.
> Sure he that made us with such large discourse,
> Looking before and after, gave us not
> That capability and god-like reason
> To fust in us unused.

It is clear that what is of the blood is animal and is opposed to judgement, which is reason; and Hamlet in one place declares that reason is from God and god-like.

Now we observe that Hamlet, in the soliloquy in the fourth Act, speaks of "excitements of my reason and my blood": both his reason and his blood are roused, he says; and in the mood in which he finds himself after hearing of Fortinbras, he implies that both his reason and his blood require that he takes arms. But in the speech to Horatio he speaks of blood and judgement, which are also passion and reason, being so well commingled in Horatio that he is neither a pipe for fortune to play upon nor a slave of passion; this is part and parcel, apparently, of Horatio's power to suffer all and to suffer nothing; and Horatio is also

> as just a man
> As e'er his conversation coped withal.

In order to try further to illumine this pair of terms, I turn for a moment from *Hamlet* to *Troilus and Cressida*. A little later I shall try to offer something in the way of justifying my turning to this play. But I look now, without apology, to the scene in *Troilus* where Hector, Troilus, Helenus, and Paris discuss the whole matter of the cause and rightness of the Trojan War. Shall they return Helen to the Greeks? And Hector begins the debate by saying that

> modest doubt is call'd
> The beacon of the wise, the tent that searches
> To the bottom of the worst.

Modest doubt is the beacon of the wise and tents into the depths, and Hector denies that it can be reasonable to decline to give up Helen. It is Troilus who replies: he passionately denies that the "worth and honour" of a King can be weighed against "fears and reasons." What he calls "honour" and "greatness" are infinite; "reasons" are but so many miserable counters. Helenus comes out on the side of Hector; and Troilus turns on him to say,

> Nay, if we talk of reason,
> Let's shut our gates and sleep: manhood and honour
> Should have harehearts, would they but fat their thoughts
> With this cramm'd reason: reason and respect

Make livers pale and lustihood deject,

where "respect" means "anxious consideration."
Then, when Hector declares that Helen is not worth holding, and
Troilus replies by asking

What is aught but as 'tis valued?

Hector in turn replies that

. . . value dwells not in particular will;
It holds his estimate and dignity
As well wherein 'tis precious of itself
As in the prizer.

Value, that is to say, is not something arbitrarily placed by the
individual or "particular will" upon an object or act; it is something
there to be discovered, and presumably by reason.

I cannot now follow in close sequence this remarkable debate;
I quote again only Hector's words to Troilus which occur later in
the scene:

. . . is your blood
So madly hot that no discourse of reason,
No fear of bad success in a bad cause,
Can qualify the same?

and Troilus replies that the reasons of Hector and the ravings of
Cassandra

Cannot distaste the goodness of a quarrel
Which hath our several honours all engag'd
To make it gracious.

But the purpose and issue of this debate is clear: reasons, discourse of reason, modest doubt, "respect" are set over against
honour, blood, dignity, glory; the one side proclaims reason and
modest doubt, the other declares that these "make livers pale and
lustihood deject." I see here the fundamental issue which also
agitates Hamlet. Fortinbras and Troilus hold, in these matters, the
same role: when honour's at the stake they act against all considerations of reason and modest doubt. Hamlet does not do so; he
cannot do so; and at the lowest estimate, his not doing so has one-
quarter part of wisdom. He cannot forbear to place the check of

reason and judgement upon passion, blood, and honour. He
wants a just commingling of the two; the sheer mastery of himself by unreflecting blood will not serve. But no doubt

> reason and respect
> Makes livers pale and lustihood deject.

It is this which, I think, lies at the centre of the play; and with this
great ethical issue is joined the questioning of last things of which
I have spoken earlier.

I have looked to *Troilus and Cressida* for light on *Hamlet*. I look
now briefly, beyond Shakespeare's own work, for further light.
Bacon had certainly read Montaigne, and there is much that
might be said on that subject. But it seems certain to me that
Shakespeare also had read Montaigne before writing *Hamlet* and
Troilus. I cannot now attempt to give chapter and verse; but the
evidence that can be compiled is, it seems to me, decisive. It is not,
however, necessary for my purpose to prove that this is so: I wish
only to mention briefly those things in which Shakespeare in
these plays manifests a mind deeply concerned with matters
discursively treated by Montaigne.

There is of course Montaigne's scepticism. But it is not of this
only that, recalling what I have just been saying, I think now.
Everybody knows that it has frequently been thought, and rea-
sonably enough, that some lines in the soliloquy in Act III derive
from an essay in the Third Book; in that essay Montaigne gives a
loose version of some passages which occur in the Apology of
Socrates; and, if we are at all right in thinking that Shakespeare
read these pages, it is striking to reflect that here at least he
encountered a version of a part of the *Apology*. I shall quote soon a
few sentences from the *Apology*, not as in Montaigne's version,
but in a close translation; I do so in order further to emphasize,
what is my main thesis, that the play of *Hamlet* has for its soul and
centre a passionate and deeply reflective concern with the problem of conduct; and if this is so, it is natural to bring together in
our minds Shakespeare and Socrates. Socrates, we know, declared that he turned away from natural philosophy to concern
himself with conduct; we have seen that Bacon wished to turn the
energies of human inquiry back into natural philosophy; in *Hamlet*

we see Shakespeare writing one of his greatest plays, after reading an essay by Montaigne in which Socrates is exhibited as the model and pattern of human wisdom.

> You do not speak wisely . . . if you think a man of any worth should weigh the risks of life against the risks of death. What he should consider is only whether what he does is right or wrong, and is the action of a good or a bad man. . . . For, my friends, to fear Death is only to think yourself wise when you are not; it is to think you know when in fact you do not know. For no one can be sure that Death is not the greatest of all benefits; but men fear it in the firm belief that it is the greatest of all evils. But is it not the most contemptible kind of ignorance to think you know when you do not? . . . For to be dead is one of two things: either it is as good as being nothing, so that a dead man has no consciousness of anything; or it is, as people say, a transition and a moving of the soul's abode from here to another place.
>
> Now if to be dead is to be unconscious and, as it were, a sleep in which dreams do not appear, how wonderful a benefit Death becomes! Let a man compare a night in which he sleeps without dreaming with other nights and days of his life. Then let him reflect carefully and declare how many of those days and nights he has passed to more advantage and more pleasantly than his night of dreamless sleep. I think that, whether he is a private citizen or the great Persian King himself, he would find that he could count them on one hand. Now if Death were a dreamless sleep, I certainly would count it a great gain: the whole of time would then be no longer than a night. But if, instead, Death is a change of abode from here to another place, and if it is true, as we are told, that all the dead are there, what greater boon can there be . . . ? For if a man on coming to the other world escapes from so-called judges and finds real judges . . . is his change of abode of no account? . . . But you, my judges, must be of good hope when you think of Death. Have in mind this one truth: that nothing evil can befall a good man in life or in death; and the Gods are never unmindful of him.

I have quoted these passages from the *Apology*, not as they are given in Montaigne, but in a close translation, because I venture to think we shall better understand Shakespeare's play by a read-

ing of Plato than by indulging the naturalistic temper of our time
and seeking therefore to see Shakespeare only as a professional
playwright, who dealt cleverly with intractable material or contrived merely to stretch out a play for the appointed time. Socrates spoke these words near to his death; Hamlet spoke his
words with death, as he might well think, not far off. Socrates
knew his line; he knew where he stood; and he was ready.
Shakespeare exhibits Hamlet as a man seeing indeed the issues,
and with his imagination complicated by centuries of Christian
eschatology, but not knowing his line or where he stood; he was
not ready. He could not keep his mind in a pious and cheerful
agnosticism of what came after; and he could not do so because he
swayed between the clamour of a traditional moral code which
might be only the clamour of blood, passion, and revenge, and the
calm demands of what might be true judgement and reason.
What he should do was not clear to him, in the face of his dreadful
situation; and not knowing this, he could not calmly face the
prospect of a world to come. By Socratic standards he fell short
and was lost; he was not enough of a philosopher after all.

He falls short by the standards of Socrates; and he falls short
by the standards of Montaigne, who holds up Socrates for a
paragon of virtue and wisdom. The burden of much of Montaigne's writing is the folly of passion which masters conduct.

> I know how to deal in publike charges without departing
> from my selfe. This sharpnesse and violence of desires hin-
> dreth more then steade the conduct of what we undertake,
> filling us with impatience to the events, either contrary or
> slow, and with bitternesse and jealousie towards those with
> whom we negotiate. Wee never governe that thing well
> wherewith we are possessed and directed. . . . He that is
> besotted with this violent and tyrannicall intention doth
> necessarily declare much indiscretion and injustice. The vio-
> lence of his desire transports him. . . . Philosophie wills us to
> banish choller in the punishment of offences; not to the end
> revenge should be more moderate, but contrary, more
> weighty and surely set on. . . . When my wil gives me to any
> party, it is not with so violent a bond that my understanding
> is thereby infected. . . . See why that man doth hazzard both
> his honour and life on the fortune of his rapier and dagger;
> let him tell you whence the cause of that contention ariseth:

he cannot do so without blushing, so vaine and frivolous is
the occasion.[4]

And later, in the essay in which passages from the *Apology* are
rendered, Montaigne illustrates from his own experience what he
means when he says: "I am a man that willingly commit my selfe
unto fortune, and carelessly cast my selfe into her armes"; and
then he concludes his essay by saying that "ordinary judgements
are exasperated into punishment by the horror of the crime; And
that enmildens mee. The horror of the first murther makes me
feare a second; And the uglinesse of one cruelty induceth me to
detest all maner of imitation of it. To me, that am but a plaine
fellow . . . may that concerne which was reported of Charillus
. . . : 'He must needs be good, since he is so to the wicked.'"[5]
Montaigne says elsewhere that the two extremes of men are the
philosophers who have attained to "noble Stoical impassibility,"
and the simple and, as he calls them, "rurall men"; the middle
region, he says, "harboureth stormes";[6] and these storms are
storms of intellectual doubt and speculation which are mingled
with strong and violent emotions. Hamlet is a man having a sense
of the high stoical impassibility; he beholds it lived by Horatio; and
Horatio he wears in his heart's core. But he is also moved, and
naturally, by the passions of disgust and revenge; what they say
may be right; "is't not perfect conscience to kill him with this
arm?" He does not rise to the demands of philosophy; he cannot
sink into passion; he inhabits a middle region where philosophy
and passion, judgement and honour, reason and blood, annul each
other and leave him, for all essential purposes, helpless and angry,
passive and violent.

NOTES

1. *Prefaces to Shakespeare*, Third Series, London, 1937, third impression,
   1944, pp. 328–29.
2. Quotations from Shakespeare are made from the *Arden* editions.
3. *Shakespearean Tragedy*, London, second edition, 1920, p. 97.
4. World's Classics edition of Florio's translation, 1904–06, iii. pp. 293–
   306.
5. Ibid., pp. 365–66.
6. Ibid., p. 308.

Harry Levin

From *The Question of Hamlet*

Drama in outline, as we run no danger of forgetting, can be little more than a student's paradigm of drama in the round. Lambs' *Tales from Shakespeare* show a closer kinship to Grimms' *Fairy Tales* than to the plays that they so blandly recount. Voltaire utilized a synopsis of *Hamlet* as a *reductio ad absurdum* in his notorious attack on Shakespeare. Yet when we have a chance to walk through the script, pausing here and there on our pedestrian tour for brief citations, we may notice elements of design which frequently get lost in actual performance. The most exciting part of the story, Hamlet's journey by sea and fight with pirates, must be narrated at a second and a third remove. What is more unfortunate, these narrations are usually cut on the stage, with a weakening effect upon our impression of Hamlet's character. Not that Hamlet's character is slighted by the actors who star in our theaters; his lines, constituting almost forty per cent of the text, are subject to abridgement less than the rest of it. On the other hand, the seven soliloquies, massive as they may seem when detached from their context, do not constitute much more than five per cent of the whole. Theatrical bowdlerization tends to reduce the dialogue, thereby concentrating the monologue, and underlining the romantic notion of a statuesque figure who broods apart, who thinks too much, who shies away from the others. But Hamlet questions the others as well as himself. He is the chief participant in a dynamic series of oral encounters, though they end by isolating him all the more. All too often we

Reprinted from *The Question of Hamlet*, pp. 47–75, by Harry Levin (1959), by permission of Oxford University Press.

view the play as an opera, awaiting the famous set-pieces as if they were arias, and overlooking the dramatic tensions in the give-and-take of the recitative.

In reconsidering *Hamlet*, we cannot pretend that we are unaware of what happens next or how it all comes out. Knowing what will finally be decided, critics have grown impatient over its agonies of decision, and have blamed Hamlet for undue procrastination. But what may be a foregone conclusion to them must be an open question to him, as we have reminded ourselves by watching the process unfold, and observing how the tone is set through the interaction of questions, answers, and unanswered speculations. Having rehearsed the play once with an emphasis on the interrogative mood, let us push the interrogation further by returning to certain indicative passages, tracing now an inner train of thought, and later placing it in a broader perspective. *Interrogatio* is classified—by the rhetorician, Henry Peacham—as a form of *pathopoeia*, which in turn is neither more nor less than a device for arousing emotions: "Examples hereof are common in Tragedies." *Dubitatio*, our next figure of speech and thought, is less emotional and more deliberative. As it is defined by Abraham Fraunce, in *The Arcadian Rhetorike*, "Addubitation or doubting is a kinde of deliberation with our selues." The orator deliberates between rival options: either to revenge or not to revenge, whether a visitant comes from heaven or hell. For doubt is that state of mind where the questioner faces no single answer nor the lack of one, but rather a choice between a pair of alternatives. Etymologically, the word stems from *dubitare*, which means precisely to hesitate in the face of two possibilities. The structure of *Hamlet* seems, at every level, to have been determined by this duality. "A double blessing is a double grace (I.iii.53)."

Similarly, the texture is characterized by a tendency to double and redouble words and phrases. From the very first scene, the speeches abound in hendiadys: "gross and scope," "law and heraldry." Sometimes the paired nouns are redundant synonyms: "food and diet," "pith and moment"—Saxon balancing Latin as in the doublets of Sir Thomas Browne. Adjectives or verbs are coupled at other times: "impotent and bedrid," "countenance and excuse." This reduplication seems to be a habit of courtly diction into which Hamlet himself falls now and then: "the purpose of playing . . . is . . . to show . . . the very age and body of the time his form and pressure (III.ii.21–5)." By the count of R. A. Foakes, no less than 247 such pairings are scattered through the play. They are doubtless more ornamental than functional; yet they charge the air with overtones of wavering and indecision. The Clown goes farther with his equivocations, putting his finger on serious ambiguities. And Hamlet goes too far with his *double-entendres*, besmirching the maidenly innocence of Ophelia. Claudius, in his opening address to the Council, establishes himself as a practiced exponent of stately double-talk. With unctuous skill, he manages a transition from the old King's death to himself and his inherited queen. Antithesis is condensed into oxymoron: "delight and dole," "defeated joy." Some of these mannerisms will have their echo in the stilted language of the Play-King: "Grief joys, joy grieves, on slender accident (III.ii, 209)." The formal style is a mask, which accords with the dress and etiquette of the court; Claudius is virtually winking, when he speaks of "an auspicious and a dropping eye (I.ii.11)." Hamlet, speaking informally and ironically to Horatio, sums up the paradoxical situation:

> The funeral bak'd meats
> Did coldly furnish forth the marriage tables. (180–81)

The incrimination of Claudius by the Ghost, duly recorded in the book of Hamlet's brain, is an object-lesson in duplicity. Claudius himself is unremittingly conscious of the distinction between the "exterior" and "the inward man." Both in communing with himself and in dealing with others, he seldom fails to distinguish between words and deeds, or face and heart. He introduces Gertrude by publicly casting her in a dual role, "our sometime sister, now our queen," as he does his nephew shortly afterward, "my cousin Hamlet, and my son." Hamlet resentfully picks up the implications, and caustically refers to his "uncle-father and aunt-mother." On the premise that "man and wife is one flesh," he preversely carries the logic of incest to its conclusion by bidding farewell to Claudius as his "dear mother." He prefaces his interview with Gertrude by resolving to act a part: "My tongue and soul in this be hypocrites." He will "speak daggers" to her, and she will admit that his words are "like daggers." Addressing her as "your husband's brother's wife," he implores her to keep aloof from Claudius, though she may feel otherwise inclined: "Assume a virtue, if you have it not." It is the recommendation of worldly wisdom that La Rochefoucauld would moralize: "Hypocrisy is the tribute that vice pays to virtue." Molière's *Misanthrope* would reject such sophistications; Alceste stands squarely for virtue disdaining vice; like the ingenuous Hamlet, he knows not "seems." But Hamlet, unlike Alceste, learns to live at court, in an arena where men and women must be actors and actresses. He must learn an etymology which may not have struck him during his humanistic studies at Wittenberg—that the word "hypocrite," in the original Greek, designated an actor.

Claudius, invoking the "twofold force" of prayer, acknowledges his own hypocrisy, caught as he is between guilt and repentance:

> . . . like a man to double business bound,
> I stand in pause where I should first begin. (III.iii.41–2)

A moment later, Hamlet will stand in pause before the double business of whether Claudius should be saved or damned, and will give him the benefit of an unforeseen doubt. The smiling villain is a double-dealer; but so is Hamlet, in another sense. At the beginning he is single-minded, all of a piece, all melancholia; then he puts on his mask and plays the antic, carrying his buffoonery to the verge of hysteria; his disposition is manic in the presence of others and depressive when he is by himself. Where the vicious Claudius assumes an air of respectability, the virtuous Hamlet must assimilate the atmosphere of licentiousness. He must set aside the high-minded idealism of Castiglione's *Courtier*, "The courtier's, scholar's, soldier's eye, tongue, sword," and take up the time-serving realism of Machiavelli's *Prince*. It is the role of Polonius, as chamberlain, to profess the one and practice the other. While he privately expounds a philosophy of keeping up appearances, he prides himself on his capacity for seeing through them. Master of ceremonies, he bustles about, arranging formalities according to protocol; but he is also a master of palace intrigue, who sneaks behind curtains to spy; and, with him, the play oscillates between ceremonious public hearings and furtive whisperings behind the scenes, so to speak. With the twin figures of Rosencrantz and Guildenstern, the double-dealing is symmetrically personified. Since they invariably hunt in couples, their roles are interchangeable. Each of them has an introductory speech of exactly the same length and rhythm, and in each case the keyword is "both."

Thanks, Rosencrantz and gentle Guildenstern,

the King responds, and the Queen preserves the symmetry by adding:

Thanks, Guildenstern and gentle Rosencrantz.

Hamlet's singleness and singularity set him off from this duplication and conformity on the part of his schoolfellows. His tragic solitude is emphasized by the comic aspect of their behavior, as they vie with each other in flattering the King and the Queen or in evading the Prince. "I am most dreadfully attended," he complains, meaning that he is badly served—and, more intimately, that he is haunted by a ghost. Well may he jest with Rosencrantz and Guildenstern about the harlotry of the goddess Fortune, since they are turning out to be fortune-seekers, royal spies, and unfaithful friends. Yet he retains one true friend, who is a Damon to his Pythias, equally impervious to "Fortune's buffets and rewards"; and in that short, rare, half-embarrassed interim of sincerity between his advice to the Players and their play, Hamlet praises Horatio because he is not "a pipe for Fortune's finger / To sound what stop she please." After "The Mousetrap" has been sprung, with Horatio counterspying upon Claudius, Hamlet calls for recorders and enacts his metaphor with Rosencrantz and Guildenstern. Fortune's finger may sound their stops, but they cannot pluck out the heart of his mystery. "S'blood, do you think I am easier to be play'd on than a pipe?" And, having told them off, having demonstrated his own virtuosity by plucking out the mystery of Claudius, he continues the music-lesson by teasing Polonius, who can be played on like any courtly instrument. Within a confused and crowded hour, the elderly politician is dead, and Hamlet is being hustled off to England, dreadfully attended by Rosencrantz and Guildenstern. When he turns back to challenge Claudius, Hamlet will be unarmed—as he writes in his letter, "naked"—and, as he adds in a postscript, "alone."

It is this isolation from all the others, this alienation from his environment, that has made Hamlet the spiritual patron of many a disinherited modern hero. He has a confidant, to be sure, in Horatio; but Horatio, in spite of his devotion, can hardly do more than echo Hamlet's dubieties. Involved in a complex and subtle network of human relations, all of them strained, Hamlet sees himself "benetted round with villanies." His father is dead through suspected foul play; his mother has remarried under dubious and technically immoral circumstances; his uncle, to whom he is naturally antipathetic, would seem to be culpable on both of those counts. Love, between Hamlet and Ophelia, is an excluded possibility from the very first time it is mentioned; we hear of it mainly from the other side, through a series of warnings and farewells; and it is from Ophelia's grave that Hamlet dares at last to avow what might have been. Laertes imprecates him with "treble woe"; for Ophelia, too, has been triply isolated; cut off and crazed by her lover's defection, her brother's absence and her father's accident, she could do nothing but wander to muddy death. Thus family ties are broken while, on the plane of the state, the social order is jeopardized internally and externally. "The people muddied," Laertes makes his appearance as the leader of their revolt. The invasion of Denmark by Norway under Fortinbras, long threatened and averted earlier, becomes a virtual conquest by default. These mishaps, domestic and dynastic, have their counterparts in that cosmic disorder of which the Ghost is the portent. It heralds the anarchy that we behold. It presupposes a chaos which is left, with darkling hints, to our imagination.

This world, in Hamlet's opening description, is "an unweeded garden." Well-tended gardens always stand for the norms of nature in Shakespeare's imagery; here the blight is traceable not merely to neglect, but to a kind of perverse cultivation; and Gertrude will be cautioned by Hamlet against spreading compost on the weeds. The Ghost is manifestly a sign that something is rotten; more problematically, it points a course of action for setting things right. By obeying its supernatural behest, Hamlet might solve the political and personal problems at one fell swoop, removing his uncle from his father's throne and from his mother's bed. But, having been led to question all that seems most familiar, how can he be expected to trust the unknown? Hence, according to James Russell Lowell, "Hamlet doubts everything." Doubt is "The beacon of the wise," says Hector in *Troilus and Cressida*; moreover, it is a probe for the wounded, "the tent that searches To th' bottom of the worst." It is the rhetorical pattern that formulates the philosophical outlook of skepticism. By Sir Walter Ralegh's definition, "The Skeptick doth neither affirm, nor denie any Position; but doubteth of it." And since a skeptic is by derivation an onlooker, his doubts are hesitations. As a doubter, Hamlet cannot be considered idiosyncratic; his consciousness that the time is out of joint was widely shared by late Elizabethans. Experimental science, "New Philosophy," as John Donne was lamenting, "calls all in doubt." The well-ordered cosmos of Ptolemaic astronomy was being displaced by the planetary system of Copernicus, wherein the sun no longer revolved around the earth and man was no longer the center of creation. So Hamlet could write to Ophelia:

> Doubt thou the stars are fire;
>   Doubt that the sun doth move;
> Doubt truth to be a liar;
>   But never doubt I love.

As a poet who mixes cosmology with intimacy, Hamlet obviously belongs to the Metaphysical School. The purport of his stanza does not differ much from the conclusion of Arnold's "Dover Beach," the affirmation that, in a universe of illusion and pain, the only true relationship is love. But Hamlet recants his love soon afterward, while Ophelia herself is enveloped from first to last in an astral nimbus of uncertainty. Her first speech, in response to her brother's parting request, is the question, "Do you doubt that?" Her last rites are curtailed by the Priest because "Her death was doubtful." The tenderness of lovers can be no more than a trivial fond record which Hamlet must erase from his tablets of memory. Only the filial relationship can retain its meaning for him; and it is, to put it mildly, a peculiar one; for he is not the son and heir of his father so much as the son and revenger of a ghost; he is, we might deduce, the incarnate member of an unhallowed trinity. It may be significant that, although the late King was called Horwendill in the chronicle, he too is named Hamlet in the play. The name is introduced with reference to him, "our valiant Hamlet," whereas no one refers to "young Hamlet" until the closing lines of the introductory scene. "Young Fortinbras" has already come under discussion as the son of old King Fortinbras, who was slain and whose Norwegian army was defeated by the elder Hamlet. The invidious parallel will be clinched by the fact that the younger Hamlet was born on the day of his father's victory; and that was the day, as we shall likewise discover, when the Gravedigger started to ply his callous trade.

Though the part of the Ghost is dignified by our awareness that Shakespeare appeared in it, though it has its portentous harangue, it is confined to four scenes and is mute in two of them. Yet it is omnipresent, *hic et ubique*. Like the defunct Captain Alving in Ibsen's *Ghosts*, Hamlet the Elder dominates the lives of those who have survived him. The opening scene evokes the recollection of his military exploits against Poland and Norway; the attempt to identify him particularizes, one by one in the mind's eye, his physical characteristics; the harangue includes a first-hand account of his bodily dissolution after his poisoning. The disembodied presence that emerges is fully armed, wearing a beaver and bearing a truncheon, with grizzled beard and sorrowful countenance: an awesome figure of heroic proportions. "Remember me" is his hollow farewell from the battlement. And, in the Queen's closet, he objurgates, "Do not forget." Claudius and Gertrude, of course, would urge the consolations of forgetfulness, that decaying weed of Lethe wharf. In their funereal commonplaces, they point out that the death of parents is not a unique but a universal bereavement, and that every father has lost a father before him back to the origins of the race. This line of reasoning proves to be a better warrant for Hamlet's cult of remembrance, for the qualms of succession he feels as a son, the child's reluctance to grow up, the youth's assumption that an intervening generation protects him from death. Looking backward toward those bygone fathers who have been sons in their time, Hamlet can envision the Ghost as an archetypal forbear, as our composite ancestry, the dead hand of the past, the constraining weight of tradition.

The roots of Hamlet's story, like those of Beowulf's, go deep into the bleak and marshy soil of Norse folklore. It comes down to us from the sagas of the Vikings, out of darker ages into the Renaissance, through a process of literary recension elaborate and sensitive enough to have been finally influenced by Montaigne. Shakespeare's immediate source, the French collection of *Histoires tragiques* by Belleforest, comments upon the barbarity of Scandinavian customs as exemplified in the tale. In that tragical history there was no need to conceal the slaying, and consequently no secret to impart by supernatural means. The Ghost, with its lugubrious refrain "Hamlet, revenge!," seems to have been the most popular adjunct of an earlier and cruder dramatic version than Shakespeare's. Shakespeare refined upon this material by surrounding it with mystery. Skillful adapter that he was, he exploited its very resistance to adaptation. He showed revenge as a harsh and brutal convention, more honored in the breach than in the observance. He seems to have understood how a legend can owe its strength to survival, how its encrustations and stratifications can recapitulate the traditional stages of cultural development, and how its inherent discrepancies can dramatize a conflict between primitive instinct and civilized restraint. This conflict, as between the two Hamlets, may be respectively symbolized by the soldier's truncheon and the scholar's book. The lapse of a generation separates them, dating from the defeat of Fortinbras, as well as from the Play-King's marriage, just thirty years ago. How exactly that same round number marks Hamlet's age would seem to vary with our confidence in the Gravedigger's roundabout testimony. Most readers prefer to visualize a younger Hamlet; most actors are bound to present a somewhat older one.

"Must I remember?" Hamlet has asked himself, before the Ghost has answered for him in the imperative. Could he ever forget? Back in his study at Wittenberg, could the young intellectual have escaped from the shade of the dead hero, and have ceased to measure himself—man and boy—by the father-image? His uncle-father is no more like Hamlet the Elder "Than I to Hercules," Hamlet the Younger declares. Thereby he disparages his own prowess, along with that of his father's successor, who has rebuked him for "unmanly grief." Whatever his inclination, he is not allowed to lead the contemplative life; he must be active, willy-nilly; and to avenge his father would, in effect, be to step into his father's shoes. "Let Hercules himself do what he may," nevertheless every dog will have his proverbial day, and the Younger will somehow come into his own. But his Herculean standards will still be set by the past glories of the warrior King. With all his imperfections, all the Elder's faults, the defects of his soldierly virtues, he remains the embodiment of mankind in the fullness of manhood.

> He was a man, take him for all in all.
> I shall not look upon his like again.

Soon after pronouncing this kingly epitaph, as irony will have it, Hamlet will look upon the paternal likeness again. Whether that phantom is animated by an immortal soul or by an evil genius will be the doubt that continues to trouble Hamlet, as he threads his way between shadows and substances, trying to discriminate spirit from matter. "The body is with the King, but the King is not with the body." Hamlet's ambiguous relation to his father is mirrored by the ambiguous identity of the Ghost in the background. Both are related to the ambiguity in the foreground, the strategic role of the two-faced Claudius and the running contrast between his person and that of his predecessor, more than kin, less than kind.

The link between man and man, ideally, is brotherhood. Here it has been subverted into fratricide, the underlying offence, as the offending brother keenly discerns in his self-examination: "It hath the primal eldest curse upon't." It came into the world, bringing death along with it, in direct consequence to the original sin of our ultimate parents. Hence, when the Gravedigger turns up the first of his skulls, Hamlet regards it "as if 'twere Cain's jawbone." Although the sinful Claudius is branded by that Biblical prototype, his more humane brother attracts comparisons of a more classical sort, such as the implied resemblance to Hercules. The fraternal antipathy is stated, in Hamlet's First Soliloquy, by the equation: "Hyperion to a satyr." True royalty is, appropriately, a sun-god; the sensual interloper is a goatish caricature of a human being; and that polarity stretches, across the whole scale of creation, from the superhuman to the subhuman. Hamlet's allusion to the sun breeding maggots in a dead dog, "being a god kissing carrion," is a prose variation upon the same theme. But, in this instance, fleshly weakness takes the shape of mortality rather than sensuality. Both themes are interconnected through, for example, the monologue of the Ghost, which proceeds from the carnal to the charnel, from the falling-off of the Queen to the after-effects of the poison. Gertrude, for her failure to observe the proprieties of mourning, has been invidiously compared to "a beast that wants—" and the phrase describing what it is that differentiates men from beasts was originally Montaigne's—"discourse of reason." The allegation becomes a generalization in Hamlet's Seventh Soliloquy, which examines the uses and the abuses of reason:

> What is a man,
> If his chief good and market of his time
> Be but to sleep and feed? A beast, no more. (IV. iv.33–5)

Gods are invoked to canonize men at their best, animals to stigmatize men at their worst. Improvising doggerel after the play, Hamlet likens his father to the ruler of the gods, "Jove himself." The epithet for his uncle, preordained by the rhyme, is "ass"; but Hamlet, in high spirits, substitutes "pajock" or peacock. Later epithets are less flattering—paddock, bat, gib, ape. Claudius is envisaged calling Gertrude his "mouse," and wallowing in "an enseamed bed" with her like two pigs in a sty. A nobleman, an Osric, may be "a beast"; but if he is also a "lord of beasts," if he possesses land and livestock, others will be as obsequious to him as he is to the royal family. Such is the way of the world, though it mystifies Hamlet. During the reign of the elder Hamlet, people made faces at Claudius; now that he is enthroned, they pay large sums for his "picture in little." This comment is elicited by the popularity of the child-actors, which has driven the Players away from their city, where they performed under the sign of Hercules. Having been dispossessed, they are entertained at Elsinore with some warmth of fellow-feeling by Hamlet. His association of ideas, linking their theatrical competition to his obsession with his stepfather, foreshadows the Closet Scene—or, more specifically, the Portrait Scene, where Gertrude is violently confronted by Hamlet with a pair of miniatures, pictures in little of both her husbands.

> Look here upon this picture, and on this,
> The counterfeit presentment of two brothers. (III.iv.53–4)

Using the rhetorical figure known as *icon* or verbal portraiture, a favorite Shakespearean embellishment, Hamlet portrays his father at full length and in Olympian majesty. It is an idealized portrait, a classicized image in the Renaissance manner, combining "Hyperion's curls" with Jove's forehead, the eye of Mars, and the posture of Mercury:

> A combination and a form indeed
> Where every god did seem to set his seal
> To give the world assurance of a man.

Hamlet's depiction is almost a conjuration, inasmuch as it seems to raise the Ghost, "My father, in his habit as he liv'd"—not in armor now, but in the very gown he must have worn on his previous visits to this chamber. But Gertrude is blind to him; while Hamlet goes on to sketch a companion portrait, denouncing the bloated Claudius as "A king of shreds and patches," a sexual and a political usurper. The brothers are as dissimilar in stature as in merit; indeed, they are like mountain and moor; the one is not worth the twentieth part of the tithe of the other. "What judgment," Hamlet passionately demands of his mother, "Would step from this to this?"

Even the exuberant Host in *The Merry Wives of Windsor* wavers, for a moment, "in perplexity and doubtful dilemma." So the thoughtless Gertrude, all too briefly transfixed by Hamlet's pictorial exhibit, achieves a reluctant glimpse of self-discovery and moral discrimination. However, the interrupted recognition-scene has a much broader significance. Turning in the other direction, Hamlet holds—as it were—the portraits up to his audience. By that express gesture, he brings the intrinsic dualism of the play to its climactic statement, while Shakespeare confronts the age and body of the time with the form and pressure of its greatest doubt. What is a man . . . ? The sustained inquiry still re-echoes after the final soliloquy, to be intermittently resumed in *King Lear* and *Macbeth*. Such was the anxious question of Old Testament ethics, voiced by the Psalmist: "What is man, that thou art mindful of him?" Sophocles propounded the confident answer of humanism, when the chorus in *Antigone* praised mankind as the wonder of wonders, controlling the world through his works, led by his ingenuity toward both good and evil, capable of meeting all

situations save death. Those may well have been the preconditions of tragedy for Hamlet the Elder; he was a man, to say the
very least. It is his long-drawn-out eulogy and his difficult testament that lay down the preconditions of tragedy for Hamlet the
Younger. The latter reveals his training as a humanist when he
exclaims: "What a piece of work is a man!" But the exclamation,
we have noted, has an undertone of interrogation. Hamlet utters
the sentiment in order to qualify it, shifting his focus from the
potentialities to the limitations of the species. If man is a matchless creature, he is "the paragon of animals." To complete the
paradox, he is the last refinement, the "quintessence of dust."

Man, according to medieval Christian tradition, occupies a
middle status within the great chain of being. Created in the
divine image out of dust, lower than the angels and higher than
the brutes, equally endowed with godlike capabilities and bestial
appetites, he may elevate or debase himself through the exercise
of his will. But the Renaissance held a challenge to this scheme of
things, as it did to hierarchies and settled beliefs in other spheres
of culture and society. The unifying but limiting synthesis tended
to break down into two conflicting positions, which Theodore
Spencer has suggestively outlined in his study of Shakespeare's
ideas. Changing attitudes toward human nature, as expressed by
thinkers of the period, oscillate between theological and naturalistic extremes. At one extreme is the "Oration on the Dignity of
Man" by Pico della Mirandola, with its lofty plea for man's self-
liberation through his intellectual and spiritual faculties. At the
opposite pole is Montaigne's "Apology for Ramón Sabunde," with
its devastating critique of the senses and of man's consequent
frailties and confusions. Man's quandary, in choosing between
these polar conceptions of himself, has been aptly set forth by the
laureate of antithesis, Alexander Pope:

> . . . in doubt to act or rest;
> In doubt to deem himself a god, or beast;
> In doubt his mind or body to prefer;
> Born but to die, and reas'ning but to err.

This, in the largest sense, is the alternative that Shakespeare
places before us through the contrasting pictures of two kings,
the slain protector and the menacing slayer. For the Queen, more

immediately, the issue is between two ways of living, which she
has adopted in promiscuous succession. For Hamlet, the decision
is suspended between what was and what is, what should be and
what has become intolerable, between an archetype of the good
life which is the merest shadow of its former self and an embodiment of malefaction which is substantial, successful, and authoritative. Friar Lawrence, in *Romeo and Juliet*, extracts the same lesson
from plants:

> Two such opposed kings encamp them still
> In man as well as herbs—grace and rude will.

Hamlet's discontent with man is generic, though the incredulous smiles of Rosencrantz and Guildenstern seemed to imply
that woman might please him better. To be specific, in his First
Soliloquy, he has identified frailty with womanhood; and he keeps
up a misogynistic barrage which hits its target in the Closet
Scene. By holding up his dramatic mirror to Claudius, he has just
exposed man's depravity. Now, by setting up "a glass" wherein
Gertrude may behold "the inmost part" of herself, he is exposing
woman's culpability. The locale is appropriate to the exposure, if
the Queen's closet serves as her dressing-room, where presumably she applies cosmetics. Therefore the looking-glass may have
its literal place in the scene, while it symbolically links acting with
painting as metaphors of hypocrisy. Artifice, as an aid to beauty,
is a standard topic of anti-feminine satire. "God hath given you
one face, and you make yourselves another." Hamlet sneers in-
congruously during his one scene with Ophelia, having satirized
the follies of dotage during his earlier scene with Polonius. A
vignette of my lady in her chamber, painting an inch thick, is the
culminating example of earthly vanity to which Hamlet juxta-
poses the skull of Yorick. Claudius draws another explicit moral,
in his most revealing aside; his misdeed, glossed over by his
"painted word," is like a "harlot's cheek, beautied with plast'ring
art." Polonius, we might recall, objected to the world "beautified"
in the letter that Hamlet addressed to Ophelia—and we might
further recall that the participle once had carried a special sting
for Shakespeare, when Robert Greene had castigated him as an
upstart crow, beautified with the feathers of elder and better
playwrights.

For Polonius, the objectionable implication is the nuance between "beautified" and "beautiful," the suspicion that his daughter may owe her loveliness to plastering art, that her beauty is as delusive as her honesty, that she is a painted woman. Obviously, she is nothing of the kind; *honi soit qui mal y pense*; and Rebecca West's recent attempt to blacken her character does not speak very charitably for Miss West. While the other characters play their double games, the simple Ophelia is halved by loss of reason; she is divided from her judgment, "Without the which"--as who but Claudius sententiously remarks?—"we are pictures or mere beasts." In some respects, the Closet Scene has its rehearsal in the Nunnery Scene, wherein Hamlet's scathing denunciation of femininity might have been more pertinently directed at Gertrude than at Ophelia. This prurient conversation on sex is, again, the immediate sequel to his meditation on death. It is a characteristic transition from the paternal to the maternal area of concern. If man is a sinner, woman can only be "a breeder of sinners." Birth can be no blessing; not to be born is best; "it were better my mother had not borne me." There has been one marriage too many; hereafter there shall be "no moe marriages." Gertrude, by her hasty and incestuous remarriage, has profaned a sacrament. Hamlet, in his revulsion, will annul that marriage by killing Claudius; but he will give up the notion of wedlock for himself; and, dog in the manger, he will condemn Ophelia to die a virgin. "Those that are married already—all but one—shall live; the rest shall keep as they are. To a nunnery, go." Take the veil, and let the loveless breed of men and women doom themselves to extinction.

The connection between Gertrude and Claudius, regarded by Hamlet as so unnatural, has the effect of inhibiting normal courtship between himself and Ophelia. Instead, it occasions a sort of emotional displacement, which has easily lent itself to Freudian interpretation. Insofar as it may account for the ambivalent zeal with which he harps upon the connubial embraces of his mother and uncle, this is a relevant consideration. Insofar as the Oedipus complex may be a valid conception of the child's unconscious relationship with its parents, it is applicable to everyone, and not peculiarly to Hamlet. To be sure, Hamlet does not leave Gertrude to heaven; his painful dialogue with her so far exceeds the instructions of the Ghost that it invites psychological theorizing;

and the study of the late Ernest Jones is outstanding, among the efforts of psychoanalytic criticism, for the resilience of its argument and for its acquaintance with the subject-matter. It motivates Hamlet's delay by identifying him with Claudius, through whom he has vicariously accomplished the Oedipal feat of murdering his father and marrying his mother. If this be the case, it must be said that Hamlet conceals his sympathy for his uncle from the audience more effectively than he conceals his hostility to, and from, Claudius. In his expressed admiration for his father and in the disgust he displays toward his mother, he seems to have more in common with Orestes than with Oedipus. Certainly, we come closer to Shakespeare's plot with the hero of the *Oresteia*, who is hounded by the Furies if not by a ghost, and who avenges his father's death upon his mother's lover, and upon her as well. The power of such a myth, as Gilbert Murray suggests, may lie in the collective imagination rather than in the individual ego. Yet, the plight of Orestes was not entirely within the family, and his father's murderer was revenging a father of his own.

If brotherhood—the bond between man and man—is degraded in *Hamlet* to fratricide, then love—the bond between man and woman—is perverted to incest. Gertrude may not have been an adulteress during her first husband's lifetime; but she has grossly overstepped a strict barrier by remarrying within the forbidden degrees of kinship. Just as the Portrait Scene presents man at his best and worst, so the two heroines are depicted in opposition to one another, adultery and virginity, the faithless mother and wife versus the faithful daughter and sister. The matron, all too suddenly, has pivoted from a funeral to a nuptial; the maiden, who might well be expecting a nuptial, obtains a sudden funeral. Ophelia's prototype is Jephthah's daughter, the sacrificial victim of ironic mischance. Gertrude's model should be Niobe or Hecuba, the mourning mother or wife; but it is conspicuously not, until the scene where she scatters flowers on Ophelia's grave. Then the bond between woman and woman comes out, her motherly feeling for the motherless girl. Like the momentary flicker of brotherly feeling between Laertes and Hamlet, it is a reminder of the unconsummated romance. The natural freshness of flowers suffuses Ophelia, whereas Gertrude is associated with the artifical enticement of cosmetics. Laertes has begun by warning his sister that Hamlet's love for her will be nipped in the bud, that it is no more than

> A violet in the youth of primy nature,
> Forward, not permanent—sweet, not lasting. (I.iii.7–8)

When she makes her final entrance, mad, she distributes imaginary posies, fitting each presentation to the recipient according to a neatly ordered symbolism. The violets have withered, she laments, on the very day her father died. Both she and Gertrude will wear the flower of pity, "herb of grace," but the Queen must wear her "rue with a difference." Two scenes later, it is Gertrude who announces Ophelia's death; and the wording of Gertrude's choric speech draws, with touching and delicate sympathy, upon the language of the flowers. The orchid to which she alludes as "dead men's fingers" has "a grosser name" which she pointedly avoids: it is "the rampant widow."

The innocent and corrupted ladies, the good and evil kings: these polarities influence Hamlet's course as clearly as if he were Everyman. But existence is really too complicated a problem to be comprehended within the limits of allegory; and Hamlet is by no means an average hero or *l'homme moyen intellectuel.* He is not only— cursed spite!—a prince, with a deferred heritage and a pressing obligation; he is also—or would rather be—a scholar who has studied philosophy, and whose brain is studiously conceived as a "book and volume" whereon experience may be registered and analyzed. His preliminary analysis, as we have seen, takes the inevitable form of a sequence of questions. One question leads to another, and all of them bear either upon the supernatural message or upon the cruel mandate. These two crucial issues are doubts, in the technical sense of our term; each is a kind of deliberation with ourselves, as rhetoric would have it, a hesitation before alternatives. Questioning gives the dialogue its pitch of intensity and its rhythm of agitation. Doubting gives pause, brings intervals of suspense, prompts Hamlet to resume his intermittent monologue. The solitary protagonist seems to wander through a labyrinth, wherein every turning-point marks a new predicament before which he must stop to deliberate. The seven soliloquies are, of course, his deliberations. The First of them, relating to his parents, strikes the note of dejection; the Second, reacting to the Ghost, seals a vow; the Third, inspired by the Player, plans a test. The Fifth, coming after the play, is a resolve to chide the Queen; the Sixth, spoken behind the kneeling King, is a postponement of the revenge; the Seventh, spurred by the army of Fortinbras, is a final call to action.

The Fourth and central soliloquy occupies an exceptional position, both in its context and among the bywords that have winged their way out of literature into life. The generality of its purport has been confirmed by the universality of its appeal. Unlike the other six soliloquies, it does not mention particular events or individuals; nor does it advance the action of the play. Unlike the first three, it does not begin with the interjection, "O!" Its tone is quietly meditative, and so detached that the whole episode has been misplaced in the First Quarto, where the Nunnery Scene precedes the Fishmonger Scene. But its obvious place is at the still midpoint of the play. This comes early in Act III and soon after the soliloquy that terminates Act II; Hamlet's part has no lines between these two soliloquies. In the Third, he has expressed his pent-up emotion and arrived at his projected scheme. In the Fourth, while he awaits his opportunity, he is free to consider the most basic of all predicaments. Though he soliloquizes, he is not altogether *solus*, as it happens. Claudius and Polonius, those "lawful espials," are watching every move from behind their arras; and there is an ironic disparity between the loftiness of Hamlet's thoughts and the baseness of their suspicions. Furthermore, their decoy, Ophelia, is on stage, reading a book of devotion to "colour" her "loneliness"—to serve as a pretext for apparently being unaccompanied. Her sanctimonious father, who could dismiss Hamlet's vows as "sanctified and pious bawds," has pushed her into this provocative role. But Hamlet is too abstracted to be provoked, at least for a while; and her devotional posture, when he does take notice, provokes him to recommend the nunnery.

His loneliness needs no coloring. The convention of the soliloquy, treating his speech as if it were unheard by the other actors, isolates him further from them and brings him closer to us. We are permitted to share the stream of his consciousness. It is a far cry from the oratory of Polonius; hence, to a neo-classicist like Goldsmith, it seemed a "strange rhapsody of broken images." But, though the syntax is quite informal, the movement of ideas is logical. If clauses dangle, it is because the speaker interrupts and argues with himself. The process of dubitation, with its disjunctive *eithers* and *whethers*, usually involves more choices than one; and readers or hearers oversimplify when they equate "to be" with "to suffer" and "to take arms" with "not to be." The method preferred by Renaissance logicians—which does not differ greatly from the selective procedures used today by so-called mechanical brains—was the dichotomy, which chopped its subjects down by dividing them in half and subdividing the resultant divisions into halves again. The result may be bracketed into a diagram of the sort that we find in Robert Burton or Petrus Ramus. Thus, if we leave aside the unpromising consequences of "not to be," the proposition "to be" entails two possibilities: "to suffer," and—if we flinch from that for the moment—"to take arms. . . ." What follows is, once more, a bifurcation. How we may end our troubles by opposing them is equivocal; our opposition may do away with them or with ourselves. This deflects us toward the alternative, "to die"; and if that is truly the end, if death is no more than a sleep, we are back in the dreamless realm of "not to be." But if, instead of oblivion, there are dreams; and if those dreams are nightmares, comparable to the worst sufferings of this life; then we are impaled upon the other horn of the dilemma—"to suffer . . ." "to be. . . ."

Such is the doubter's mode of dialectic, which leads him back—through complementary semi-circles—to his binary point of departure. That is the question, *esse aut non esse*, which metaphysicians from Plato to Sartre have pondered. Hamlet seeks the essence of things in a world of phenomena, where being must be disentangled from seeming; and since the entanglement is a personal one, perhaps a sword is the only means of escape. The ontological question becomes an existential question, and the argument shifts from metaphysics to ethics. "Only one philosophical problem is really serious, and that is suicide," Albert Camus has written. "To decide whether or not life is worth living is to answer the most fundamental question of philosophy." Shakespeare explored that problem repeatedly; in his Roman tragedies he condoned, and even ennobled, the Stoic solution. In *Hamlet* a powerful death-wish is suppressed by the Christian canon against self-slaughter. Yet Horatio professes to be more

Roman than Danish, in this respect; Ophelia dies by self-offence, in the Gravediggers' verdict; and Hamlet's latent impulse becomes the premise for sweeping generalizations. He has joked about Fortune with Rosencrantz and Guildenstern, and has heard the bitch-goddess cursed by the Player. Must one endure her on-slaughts with a Stoic's resignation, Hamlet now asks himself; should one passively submit or actively resist? He envisions him-self taking arms not against her weapons, "slings and arrows," but in an ill-matched combat with a formless and overwhelming enemy, "a sea of troubles." Trouble will come to Claudius like "the ocean" rushing across "the flats." The Gravedigger will act out the conundrum of whether a man drowns himself or is drowned by the water.

Hamlet's image has been severely criticized, cleverly emended, and evasively translated. It is certainly vulnerable from the stand-point of military tactics. But it need not be taken as a mixed metaphor; it is rather a hyperbole. A warrior marching armed into the sea would be improbable yet impressive, ready to stand beside such indomitable British worthies as King Canute apostro-phizing the waves and Mrs. Partington battling the Atlantic. We may take it as a Shakespearean symbol of beleaguered humanity in its strife against the overpowering elements, an ineffectual fight in a noble cause. Its outcome is death—what else?—but what, then, is death? Hamlet's clearest answer will be his enigmatic parenthesis:

> The undiscover'd country, from whose bourn
> No traveller returns.

This passage may have been suggested by Marlowe's *Edward II*, when the free-thinking Mortimer dies like a traveler, who "Goes to discover countries yet unknown." He is approaching the mys-tery from which Hamlet draws back. The phrasing of the latter is significantly garbled in the First Quarto, where we are offered an unauthorized and ungrammatical glance at the vista that Shake-speare has carefully veiled from us:

> The undiscover'd country, at whose sight
> The happy smile, and the accursed damn'd.

It is essential to the soliloquy, as it is to the play, that we remain in the dark about the prospective blessings and banes of the afterlife. "To die—to sleep—." Hamlet stops twice at this precarious equipoise. The first time, his abrupt and elliptical "No more" seems to write off everything else as nothingness; yet it evokes its opposite, Macbeth's "Sleep no more." The second time, Hamlet encounters "the rub," the obstacle in a metaphorical game of bowls. This is the orthodox hypothesis that death may not be an annihilation but another stage of consciousness. "To sleep—perchance to dream." If the discontents of this life are bad dreams, as he has averred to Rosencrantz and Guildenstern, those of the next may be worse; and who shall say which are more real? Having arrived at the impasse, Hamlet buttresses it with two searching rhetorical questions, in which the inflection falls upon the verb, "bear." An unsheathed dagger might settle our account in short order; but we prefer the heartache and calamity of staying alive to "the dread of something after death." The soliloquy, according to Wilson Knight, "concentrates on the terrors of an afterlife." Yet these are far less concretely in evidence than "those ills we have," the evils that flesh is heir to. Like the Duke, sermonizing on death in *Measure for Measure*, Hamlet reasons with life. Shakespeare was always aware of what even Tourneur, in *The Atheist's Tragedy*, fitfully perceived: "It is not death but life that tries us."

Life tries Hamlet with the uttermost severity, and that is why he is comtemplating death. Yet his decision is in favor of life, even though he sustains it through inaction, while enumerating some of the daily burdens that make it so tragic: oppression, pride, love scorned, merit unrecognized. Erasmus, in *The Praise of Folly*, includes a comparable list of human miseries; a wise man, looking down on that abject panorama from a high place, might well be tempted to self-destruction; wherefore Erasmus concludes with his usual inference, that it is folly to be wise. Hamlet is not unmindful of the fool's wisdom when he puts on his antic disposition. But, in introspection, his mentor is Montaigne; the soliloquies are like the *Essays* in balancing arguments with counterarguments, in pursuing wayward ideas and unmasking stubborn illusions, in scholarly illustrations and homely afterthoughts which range from the soul of Nero to John-a-dreams. More than with any other theme, Montaigne confides, he has entertained himself with "imagination of death." If that is "a consummation/ Devoutly to be wished" for Shakespeare, for him it is "a consummation of ones being . . . a quiet rest and gentle sleepe, and without dreames." For him, and often for Shakespeare too, "We wake sleeping, and sleep waking." Montaigne's phraseology—or rather, that of his Elizabethan translator, John Florio—reverberates throughout the play. So does Montaigne's philosophy, insofar as it may be said to ramify from his two postulates: *"philosopher c'est apprendre à mourir"* and *"philosopher c'est douter."* And here it is Montaigne who puts on the antic disposition: "If, as some say, to philosophate be to doubt; with much more reason, to rave and fantastiquize, as I doe, must necessarily be to doubt."

But the Prince of Denmark cannot, like the country gentleman of Bordeaux, sleep soundly on a pillow of incuriosity, dismissing his doubts as bad dreams. Hamlet's pause, at the dead center of the play, is a prelude to "action," the last word in his soliloquy. That is the way in which conscience works in us all, he generalizes, albeit some of his critics have assumed that he is particularizing his own delay. Our spontaneous resolves are weakened by our intellectual compunctions; our will is puzzled before the unknowable. Having taken this long look, he will leap into a quick succession of adventures; he will make choices, right or wrong, thick and fast. The decisive event will be planned by others, and will play unexpectedly into his hands. Horatio will counsel last-minute hesitation, but Hamlet will be ready for anything. His final disjunction is a conditional syllogism: "If it be now, 'tis not to come; if it be not to come, it will be now; if it be not now, yet it will come (V.ii.231-4)." Time will decide, and fate will thereafter seem to have been inevitable. Hamlet consoles himself with a reflection paraphrased from Montaigne: "Since no man knows aught of what he leaves, what is't to leave betimes?" Another question which might be referred to the Ghost, since Hamlet's father seems to have known a good deal about what he left behind. By now that perturbed spirit must be at rest—which may or may not mean nonexistence. Nothing has been revealed about the undiscovered country, although the rottenness of Denmark has been laid bare. Like the nocturnal watches on the platform before the castle, we are relieved when the cock crows, the apparition fades, and russet tinges the sky. In the half-light between knowledge and superstition, science and nescience, we can only be skeptical, neither affirming nor denying but doubting.

One of the most celebrated Hamlets of theatrical history, Tommaso Salvini, summed up the part in a single trait: *il dubbio*. Hamlet is not so much a perplexing personality as he is a state of perplexity into which we enter, the very personification of doubtfulness. His sense of certainty has been fatally ravaged, and with it his trust in others. They are even less sure of things than he is; Polonius obliges him by discerning three different animals in the same cloud; and Osric agrees that the weather is hot or cold, depending upon Hamlet's variable taste. In the absence of some external criterion, he searches within. Whether this earth is a goodly frame or a sterile promontory, whether this air is fretted with golden fire or befouled with pestilent vapors, may depend on which of his two mental portraits we are able to keep in mind. Erasmus, borrowing an example from Plato, recalls those double images of Silenus, one of whose faces was antithetical to the other in every regard: ". . . what outwardly seemed death, yet loking within ye shulde fynde it lyfe: and on the other side, what semed life, to be death: what fayre, to be foule: what riche, beggerly: what cunnyng, rude: what stronge, feable: what noble, vile: what gladsome, sadde: what happie, unlucky: what friendly, unfriendly: what healthsome, noysome." So Erasmus, in the English translation of the *Encomium Moriae* by Sir Thomas Chaloner, adds his testimonial to the conception of man as a two-faced biped. "Briefely the Silene ones beyng undone and disclosed, ye shall fynde all thyngs tourned into a new semblance." Whether that semblance is angelic or demonic, whether the mask indeed is tragic or comic, depends upon the attitude of the beholder.

"There is nothing either good or bad but thinking makes it so," Hamlet explains to Rosencrantz and Guildenstern. The identical situation, the state of Denmark, may seem good to them and bad to him. Similarly, an intellectual might have disagreed with a pair of courtiers about the state of England in 1601, though he could hardly have publicized his plaint. In the year of *Hamlet*, John Donne poured his disillusionment into an elaborate poetic fragment, "The Progress of the Soul," which breaks off with this triplet:

> Ther's nothing simply good, nor ill alone,
> Of every quality comparison,
>   The only measure is, and judge, opinion.

Montaigne, under more tranquil circumstances two decades before, had reached an analogous position in an essay demonstrating "That the taste of goods or evils doth greatly depend on the
opinion we have of them." Of these three formulations, Hamlet's
is the boldest, though his boldness must be qualified by the
realization that he is a fictitious character, speaking not for Shakespeare but for himself, and for himself in a particularly saturnine
humor. Yet he is willing, at all events, to declare that there are no
ethical absolutes, that good and evil are value-judgements determined by relative standards. Troilus, starting from the same
relativism, strives to imbue it with all the enthusiasm that Hamlet
so consciously lacks. "What is aught save as 'tis valu'd?" asks
Troilus. The upshot, for him, is a relentless devaluation of both
the heroic and the romantic ideals. *Troilus and Cressida* has close
affinities with *Hamlet* in composition and in temper; but it terminates with its difficulties unresolved. As for *Hamlet*, it never re-
gains its lost certitudes; nor does it ever relax its movement of
vacillation; but it derives new meaning out of its clash of values;
and its overclouded patterns merge into a grander design. "What
doubt is to knowledge, irony is to the personal life," wrote
another melancholy Dane, Sören Kierkegaard, who was to strike
his balance under the heading of *Either/Or*. That pronouncement
asks for application, when Kierkegaard singles out Shakespeare
as "the grand master of irony."

Sheldon P. Zittner

"Hamlet, Duellist"

Whatever else it is, and it is notoriously *everything* else, *Hamlet* is a play of weapons. Ordnance peals, swords are flourished, there is a "daily cast of brazen cannon," rapiers and daggers are only two of Laertes' weapons; the pike and the great axe are invoked, slings and arrows, partisan and truncheon, foil and target; poison is poured into the porches of the ear or drunk off in goblets; enginers are hoist by their own petard, and there is a memorable bare bodkin. The motif of the duel dominates the play: thus Old Hamlet vanquishes Old Fortinbras in single combat; thus young Hamlet and Laertes destroy each other. The whole struggle between Hamlet and Claudius is conceived of by Hamlet as a duel:

> the pass and fell incensed points
> Of mighty opposites.

The perfection of the duellist's art leads Laertes to France and prepares Hamlet for his return. The exercise of weapons is the measure of men: the fencing that, coupled with "drinking, swearing, quarreling, drabbing," Raynaldo feels may dishonour Laertes; the valour in primitive single combat that gained the elder Hamlet his glory and "all those lands." The use of poison damns Laertes as it doubly damns Claudius. The sword becomes the Christian symbol that (in the traditional stage business) stays a Ghost; on it friendships and secrecies are sworn, kingdoms altered, princes and old fools dispatched. By the swordsman's code of honour

Reprinted from *University of Toronto Quarterly*, Volume XXXIX, Number 1, October 1969, by permission of the author and University of Toronto Press.

Hamlet finds himself wanting. Within the code, he both resigns himself and triumphs. Weapons and their use shift back and forth between the action of the play and its metaphors and symbols. Weapons thus share in the play's central technique by which act and metaphor enrich one another: a player-king shedding significance on a villain playing king, a sick prince on a prince feigning illness, and indeed, the artifice of theatre on the stage that the whole world is.

For such a use of weaponry in literature I know of no "source" and can think of only one precedent. The five-fold shield Hephaestus forges for another doomed and petulant and delaying hero is surrounded by the river Ocean which runs at the limits of the world. In the *Iliad*, too, weapons tragically become the whole of the possible, and the man who takes them up wields, too, what coarsens and destroys him. But in *Hamlet* weaponry has an even more remarkable role. It divides human history into distinct epochs; defining—in the single, almost judicial combat of Old Hamlet and Old Fortinbras—an unrecoverable heroic past; and—in the purchasable ordnance of Fortinbras—what was for Elizabethans the already foreseeable future, the sequestration of violence to the bureaucratic state. Because of what is *in* the play then—not only because of a desire to discover what is in it—I should like to consider the circumstances of personal violence at the time *Hamlet* was written.

Hamlet was composed at the very end of the 1590s during the revival of the "tragedy of blood." The great early success in that genre, Kyd's *Spanish Tragedy*, was revived by Henslowe in 1597. Both adult and children's companies apparently commissioned revenge plays about this time, and *Hamlet* was prompted by the vogue. The vogue itself had two phases. From 1597 to about 1607, revenge tragedy was dominated by a protagonist who undertook blood revenge as a heroic dedication. After the *Revenger's Tragedy*, he was replaced by a revenger-villain, who held the stage until about 1620, when the genre sank.[1] Its jetsam surfaced as Restoration heroics or, better, Restoration farce. In Vanbrugh's *Provok'd Wife*, that archetypal domestic souse, Sir John Brute, propelled by wine, lurches round his wife's gallants, blubbering, "Sir, I wear a sword." "The progression of Kydian hero to villain-revenger was inevitable," Bowers tells us, "owing to the standards

of English morality,"[2] and, one might add, as does Bowers, owing
to the influence of Seneca and of the Italian *novelle*. Yet Seneca and
the Italians had been available long before the revival or the
alteration. The first volume of Painter's *Palace of Pleasure* appeared
in 1566, and the percolation of *novelle* motifs and atmosphere into
the drama increased almost at once. Moreover, despite the differences between the horrendous inflations of Seneca and the deli-
cious trivia of the *novellieri*, on the nature of revenge they were in
odd agreement. In the first act of Seneca's *Thyestes* we are told that

> Nothing avenges crimes
> But what outdoes them. (ll.195–6)

In the seventh tale of the eighth day of the *Decameron*, the disap-
pointed scholar who contrives exquisite tortures for the flirta-
tious Elena (one of which, by the way, Shakespeare seems to have
remembered for *The Winter's Tale*) tells her,

> what I do to you cannot properly be called vengeance but is
> rather punishment, because vengeance should exceed the
> offence. . . .

In short, Seneca and the *novellieri* reinforced the theatricality of
the genre, the absoluteness of its protagonist, but they did not
dictate the time of its revival. Nor are "the standards of English
morality" sufficient explanation of the change in the avenger.
More to the point, research by Lawrence Stone and other histori-
ans allows us to invoke with more security than did Bowers the
circumstances of the decade. The revival roughly coincides with
the vogue for rapier fencing, and the appearance of the avenger-
villain with a speeding up in the process by which the prerogatives
of violence were taken from the English aristocracy and seques-
tered to the State.

   In the art of duelling, as in other arts of civilization, England
was several decades behind the continent. Hamlet practises at
home, but Laertes goes abroad to perfect his swordsmanship, and
when Claudius cites authority for Laertes' skill he cites a French-
man. As late as 1599 George Silver, in his *Paradoxes of Defence*, could
argue for the sword and buckler on patriotic grounds. Yet several
years before, in *I Henry IV* (1.3.230), Hal is denigrated as "that
same sword-and-buckler Prince of Wales." Hotspur's insult is

directed against Hal's lubberly indifference to modern improvements. But, even more than that, Hotspur's insult is the jibe of the aristocrat, for as the intrroduction to Grassi's *True Art of Defence* (1594) informs us, the sword and buckler were already *infra dig*.[3] In 1602 William Bas issued a book actually entitled *Sword and Buckler, or Serving Mans Defence.* Hotspur's contemptuous reference to these weapons is of a piece with his hope that Hal will be "poison'd with a pot of ale." In the 1590s rapier and dagger—first introduced into England perhaps thirty years before—had decisively supplanted the aristocrat's older weapons, in spite of Silver's annoyance at "frog-picking Poiniards" and "bird-spit" rapiers. Italian masters had set up fashionable fencing "colleges" in London, and during the decade at least five English manuals on the rapier and the duelling code, most of them Italian in origin or doctrine, were published.[4]

The shift in weaponry was not only a matter of aristocratic fashion. It was, in our current cant, a "break-through" in technology, apparently a disastrous one. Silver warned that "a full blow upon the head or face with the short sharpe Sword is commonly death."[5] And so it might be. Yet there had been relatively few deaths despite the substantial numbers involved in aristocratic feuds in the earlier sixteenth century. The older weapons, Lawrence Stone assures us, "allowed . . . the most spectacular show of violence with the minimum threat to life and limb." He concludes that fighting with them was little more dangerous than all-in wrestling.[6] This perhaps goes too far. At the end of his *Paradoxes*, Silver boasts of the death of a teacher of Rapier, Ieronimo Saviolo, in an encounter with "a verie tall man, in his fight naturall English." The victor, graced with the also naturall English name of Cheese, had used a sword against Ieronimo's rapier. However, even Silver concluded that in "true fight"—that is, an encounter between skilled antagonists using the short sword—"there is no hurt done."[7] The deadliness of rapiers, he asserts, lies not in "their dangerous thrusts, nor cunningnesse of that Italinated fight, but in the length and unwieldiness thereof." Whatever the efficacy of the short sword, the rapier was certainly more dangerous, especially in the hands of the inexpert. The revival of the "tragedy of blood" occurs about the same time as dramatically increased possibilities for serious personal violence among the court aristocracy.

The possibilities were realized. Stone makes an appalling collection of anecdotes descriptive of an aristocracy "characterized by the ferocity, childishness, and lack of self-control of the Homeric age." The record of duels and challenges in newsletters and correspondence is an imperfect reflection of the actualities. Yet the number recorded rises from only five in the 1580s to nearly twenty in the next decade, and remains somewhat above this until the beginning of the second decade of the seventeenth century.[8] It would seem at first glance that the dangers of the rapier, and the Italianate codes of honour which were popularized with it, ran counter to the government's main effort to "tame" the aristocracy. However, the new importance of the rapier and personal challenge were also checks on aristocratic insolence.[9] Silver grudgingly agreed that the new dangers of rapier fight "hath bred great civilitie amongst our Enlgish nation, that they will not now give the lye" so readily.[10] Even though punctilio might indeed lead to discovering "quarrel in a straw/When honor's at the stake," it prompted the need for self-justifications that inhibited casual violence. And though a Laertes could in his "terms of honor . . . stand aloof" till "elder masters" allowed him precedents for acknowledging his name "ungored," there seems to have been also a bluff English reaction to the extravagance of the Italianate duellist's code. Hence the comedy which ensues in *As You Like It* (5.4) upon Touchstone's discovery that his quarrel "was upon the seventh cause," that is, "upon a lie seven times removed." Shakespeare, probably recalling here Vincentio Saviolo's elaborate exposition of the nature of lies, was not the only dramatist to laugh at a pedantry of violence. But if the dangers of the rapier provoked increasing moral outcry and the increasing intervention of government,[11] they provoked something more important for the theatre, the duellist's introspection.

If the revival of the revenge play coincides roughly with the triumph of the rapier, the alteration of its hero to revenger-villain coincides roughly with the peak in recorded duels and the most strenuous governmental interventions. Yet neither the revival nor the alteration of revenge plays is simply a reflection of existing conditions. They are means by which aristocratic sensibility was altered. The rapier and its code and the reactions to them forced on their exponents a psychological and ethical self-consciousness, and the plays that gathered up such matters had a

similar effect. This is especially the case with *Hamlet*, whose inno-
vation as revenge-play lies precisely in its exploration of the self-
consciousness of the avenger.

When the unexamined life is no longer worth leading, we
begin to examine it. Most of us are not attracted, but driven, to
introspection. These sad commonplaces underlie the vogue for
the rapier and its code. Silver had been quite correct in pointing
out that the rapier was all but useless in the confused opportunities of war, "in serving of the Prince, when men do meet together
in publique fight."[12] The rapier was deadly only in the ceremony
of single combat. But wasn't this the very attraction of the
weapon and its attendant mystique, a chivalry depending on a
weapon irrelevant to the central chivalric obligation of military
service? Miss Kelso's observation is correct; by the 1590s the
distinguishing marks of aristocratic life-style—the exclusiveness
of dress, and armorial bearings, and occupation, and political
autonomy—all the externals—were fading.[13] The rapier and the
code achieved a new popularity at a time when the court aristocrat required new means of setting himself apart, means that
affected both behaviour and self-conception.

Yet finally the vogue is an ironic episode in the taming of the
court aristocracy. It further restricted the use of the bravo and
the household army, further isolated the aristocracy from power
and esteem, and, if we are to believe Silver, further diminished
their exercise of courage and ability. The dangers of the "imperfect fight" of the rapier, Silver writes, "hath transformed our
boyes into men, and our men into boyes, our strong men into
weaknesse, our valiant men doubtfull, and manie worthie men
resolving themselves upon their false resolutions, have most wilfully in the field, with their Rapiers ended their lives."[14]

Silver does all but state the historical paradox. At a time when
they could no longer employ para-military violence through re-
tainers, the English court aristocracy adopted a new style of
violence. But the new style promoted introspection that could
lead to enervation or self-doubt. Further, the inappropriateness of
the weapons (and the code) to a State claiming a monopoly of
violence and justice was inescapable. In short, the court aristocracy became more clearly anomalous by its very attempt to pre-
serve and idealize its prerogatives. The old revenge play was fit

for the stage again because of the quality of the historical moment, a moment which forced the living protagonists of violence into the self-consciousness and deracination which are the stuff of tragedy. This is not to make Hamlets of two gentlemen who in 1609 murdered each other after a spat at cards. It is only to suggest the tragic significance that was there for the sensitive dramatist to grasp. That Hamlet is socially deracinated, though indeed "the expectancy and rose of the fair state"; that he is not of the primitive, heroic past of old Hamlet, nor yet of the vulgar manipulative present of Claudius and the similar future of Fortinbras, suggests that at least one dramatist grasped this significance.

But there are less general relations between the character of Hamlet and the theory and practice of personal violence in the 1590s. The evidence is that Shakespeare knew in detail the most popular of English duelling books, Vincentio Saviolo's *Practise*, which appeared in 1595. Saviolo's fencing school was popular, too, and the man himself a fashionable figure, if we are to judge from the account of him in Florio's *Second Frutes* (1591), and from the rather envious treatment Silver accords him.

Saviolo's *Practise*, dedicated to his patron, the "English Achilles," Robert, Earl of Essex, is in two books, the first an illustrated art of fencing, the second a discussion of the proprieties of "quarrels." It is little more than a translation of Girolamo Muzio's *Il Duello* (1550).[15] The belief that Shakespeare had read Saviolo's *Practise* goes back at least as far as Theobald and Warburton, who first connected it with Touchstone's comic effussion on lies and quarrels.[16]

One chapter of Saviolo's *Practise* is titled "How Gentlemen ought to accept of any Quarrell, in such manner that they may combat lawfully." And this is precisely the problem that confronted both the Prince of Denmark and his creator. At the outset, Saviolo distinguishes the justice of a cause from the justice of an actual combat. Most commonly, Saviolo declares, the combatant who has justice on his side does not act out of a concern for justice,

> but either for hatred or the desire of revenge, or some other particular affection: whence it cometh to passe, that many howbeit they haue the right on their sides, yet come to be overthrowen.[17]

There is a contradiction between Saviolo's exposition of swordsmanship, whose implicit assumption is that skill assures victory, and his assertion that victory depends not on skill or even on the justice of the duellist's cause, but on the spirit in which he takes up his weapons. Saviolo tries to moralize the duel by ascribing victory neither to skill nor to *virtù* in general, but to the specific state of mind of the duellist and the consequent divine disposition of his case:

> For that God whose eyes are fixed euen on the most secret and inner thoughts of our harts, and even punisheth the euil intent of men, both in iust and vniust causes, reserueth his iust chasticements against all offenders, vntil such times as his incomprehensible iudgement findeth to be most fit and seruing to his purpose.[18]

This commonplace has several points of interest. The first is its context. That we discover it in Saviolo ought to disabuse us of the notion that on the one hand there was a code of honour and on the other a body of Christian doctrine, and that the two were completely at war. The second point is the psychological sophistication of the idea of "euil intent" in "iust and vniust causes."

The gist of Saviolo's argument is that

> no man ought to presume to punish another, by the confidence and trust which hee reposeth in his owne valor; but in iudgement and triall of armes, euery one ought to present himselfe before the sight of God, as an instrument which his eternall maiestie hath to woorke with, in the execution of iustice, and demonstration of his iudgement.[19]

Later on, Saviolo uses precisely the word made crucial to discussions of *Hamlet* by Bowers and others: the lawful duellist is "the minister to execute Gods deuine pleasure."[20] The idea of revenge as ministry had entered secular as well as theological discussion.

But Saviolo's most important difference from theologizing writers on the duel lies in giving the avenger's ministry a psychological concreteness. His chapter on lawful combat deals with the most inflammatory occasions for revenge: rape and seduction, adultery, treason, and murder, but his emphasis throughout is on the mind and the motives of the avenger. One ought not, Saviolo writes, to undertake combat for revenge, or "in respect of hatred," or "for some other particular affection," or "to obtain fauour at the Princes handes," or even to "purchase honour" itself. Rather, the avenger "ought as a publique plague, and not as a particular enemie, to persecute him that committeth any of these odious excesses."[21] Even more relevant for us is Saviolo's description of the avenger's self-preparation. The preparation advocated for one outraged by a murder is particularly important. Almost too pat, the passage throws off *Hamlet* materials like a Roman candle: eulogies and deprecations of man, repressions and resignations, the image of Claudius kneeling at God's altar, and therefore to be left unslain.

> And for the same reason, if some man haue committed murder, hee that will combat with him, must not doe it to this ende, onely to wreake the death of him that is murdered, in respect that he was his freend or kinseman, but he ought to call to minde what a noble and excellent creature man is, who being taken away and brought to naught by murder or slaughter, the fairest and noblest woorke which almightie God hath framed, is marred, and spoiled. Insomuch that whosoever committeth murder, dooth dissolue and breake the most perfect peece of woorke that the creator of heauen and earth hath made, and defaceth the image and likeness of God. And for that God in his sacred law hath ordeined, the man-slayers should be carryed from his alter and put to death, the partie that will combate, . . . ought not to vndertake the combate, because he would kill him, but because hee might be as it were, the minister to execute Gods . . . most holy commaundement.[22]

The avenger then, must assume a state of mind that proceeds from ethical contemplation, social awareness, a quenching of passion, and ends in a nerveless resignation to the will of God. The operative phrases in Saviolo's advice are "fall into consideration," "in regarde of all, considering," "each gentleman ought to thinke," "each gentleman having considered and weighted all this," "he ought to call to minde." Saviolo insists continually on the self-consciousness of the avenger, on the disinterestedness that abandons private will to the will of God. Of such avengers Hamlet is the first in the English theatre.

The antipodes of human performance and human profession are always clearer on ancient maps than on our own. One would hesitate to guess what proportion of those gentlemen who met privately to murder one another in suburban woods, or travelled discreetly to Ostend actually went through a purging of passion, an ethical contemplation, an abandonment to providence. Francis Bacon, as ever in the *Essayes* grasping the apparent, called the entire code "a kind of satanicall illusion and apparition of honour; against religion, against lawe, against morall vertue."[23]

But the patterns of literature arise as much from the heroic illusions of belief as from the dwindled actualities of behaviour. In Hamlet's self-conception, in his efforts to free himself from passion, in his speculations on man and men, in his final accord with providence, one discerns, I think, Saviolo's ideal figure, the gentleman duellist who may combat lawfully. I do not suggest that no other contemporary circumstances or traditions of literature or thought were transformed to fashion *Hamlet*. I want only to insist on the situation of the court aristocracy, on the vogue of rapier fight and the new emphasis on its code as partial explanations of why revenge-tragedy and its masterpiece occur when they do, and why Hamlet is what he is.

The importance of understanding the techniques of rapier fencing for the fencing scene itself has been amply recognized at least since Dover Wilson's attempt to reconstruct it.[24] Details of the code are also useful in interpreting moments in the play: the casual suddenness with which we are informed of Hamlet's "continual practice" since Laertes went to France, Laertes' reservations about his honour, Hamlet's *remissione*. Yet more important than such details are the larger relations between *Hamlet* and the ideas we have examined in Saviolo, and the crisis of court aristocratic power.

The play itself is shaped to the world implied by the rapier and the code of honour. In Denmark the noblest spirit is the wholly private prince who will not and cannot suffer in sloth or shark up resolutes or rush to blind revenge. The play reifies and idealises the contemporary situation of the court aristocrat, a man of action denied his former power to maintain his "rights" through private armies, often disdaining the bureaucratic and technical business war had become, and inwardly denying the jurisdiction, validity, or even the possibility of formal judicial process. The play validates the "particularity" of honour not only by the special nature of the outrages done to its hero, but by making wholly appropriate his alienation from a state which is a web of corrupt alliance, and from a formal religion whose own punctilio leads to the affront of "maimed rites" for the innocent Ophelia.

The political isolation of the court aristocracy, expressed in the rapier vogue, has analogues in the treatment of politics in *Hamlet*. The elaborate arrangements of central authority buy off the young and stultify the old; save through the mistake of Polonius' death or the providential impulse of Hamlet's shipboard rashness, these arrangements are invulnerable to the scruple and effort of the single, noble man. In *Lear* the corrupt state and the corrupt individual are metaphoric extensions of one another, and the resolution of Lear's private woes is the resolution of the woes of Britain, just as for Scotland "the time is free" with the death of Macbeth. Yet, though Denmark is Claudius writ large, its style is also like "some vicious mole of nature," ineradicably in the blood after the end of an heroic age. Hamlet never sets the time aright as do Macduff and Edgar. An Osric replaces a Polonius, a Fortinbras a Claudius. This is not to say that the later plays are Utopian or even comforting. Yet they do not insist as does *Hamlet* that the gored state is unhealed and that the only mission of the noblest survivor is the clearing of a single name.

This difference between the thoroughgoing analogy of public and private woe in *Lear* and *Macbeth* and their rather more distant relation in *Hamlet*[25] is not only a result of Shakespeare's formal development toward an art that seamlessly unites its materials. The difference lies in the closeness of *Hamlet* to Shakespeare's concern with anomalies he had already noticed in those sonnets which distinguished the "old age" from the "new." Unlike Lear or Macbeth, Prince Hamlet does not originate, represent, or wholly share a national corruption, for all his self-pitying sadness at it. His life is played out against the giant backdrop of political power, yet it is finally private. The corrupt monolith remains standing. What I am urging here is the historically suggestive portrait Shakespeare gives us of a man who is the flower of his age, yet one whose most passionate thought and most crucial actions cannot greatly affect its course. In this sense Hamlet is far more alienated from power than an Albany or a Macduff.

That Denmark should fall from the hands of a Claudius into

those of a Fortinbras is an irony often enough observed. But the
irony extends through the verbal fabric of the ending of the play.
In Ophelia's rapturous brachylogia: "The courtier's, soldier's, scholar's, eye, tongue, sword," Hamlet is indeed the soldier. Yet Hamlet's behaviour, the

> accidental judgements, casual slaughters,
> Of deaths put on by cunning and forced cause

that mark his progress, are wholly in the personal style of the
duellist, the isolated protagonist. Hence the irony of Hamlet's
burial: a ceremony so appropriate to Fortinbras' limitations, yet so
foreign to what we know of Hamlet. Hamlet must be borne
offstage like a soldier.

> For he was likely, had he been put on,
> To have proved most royal; and, for his passage,
> The soldier's music and the rites of war
> Speak loudly for him.

There is a clear narrowness of spirit in this strongarm Fortinbras.
That Hamlet had been "put on" indeed, had indeed "proved most
royal" in an older sense, escapes him, and (as the eulogy itself
indicates) not only because of his ignorance of Hamlet's story.
The Hamlet we know could neither shark up resolutes like his
eulogist nor, like his pallbearers, swell the ranks to gain a "little
patch of ground." Whatever the image of the soldier elsewhere in
Shakespeare, here Fortinbras' evocation of it is wry praise, for in
the context of the play the strictly private heroism of Hamlet is
contrasted with the opportunist emptiness of

> Two thousand souls and twenty thousand ducats
> [That] will not debate the question

of a straw. The world of the play and its management of the
relations between the political and private suggest the political
alienation of the English court aristocracy and the futile idealisms
it evoked.

If the central situation of the play and its disjoining of the
private from the public fate suggest the situation of the court
aristocracy in the 1590s, the character of Hamlet recalls the
duelling code which these aristocrats turned to for sustenance

and apology. It would be naive to explain Hamlet's interior "development" from his nearly hysterical first response to the ghost to his dreadful calm in the final act by appealing to any single controlling idea. Yet a case can be made for viewing many of Hamlet's changes in the light of Saviolo's psychological prescription for the gentleman avenger. For to call to mind what a noble and excellent creature man is, to consider what it means to bring to naught the noblest work almighty God hath framed; to purge one's mind of passion and particular affection; to submerge the private in the public weal; to undertake combat not because one would kill, but because one would minister; and, finally, having considered and having cleansed and having undertaken, to hazard all and absolutely upon the least tremor of providence—to do it all, is this not to be like Hamlet? And to pay the price of doing it, is this not to become indeed the only tragic prince we now believe in?

I can tease out here only a few of the connections between Saviolo's prescriptions for lawful combat and the character of Hamlet, only a few instances of what I have called its human cost, that is, the suffering men undergo in adhering to a code of conduct that makes excessive or unnatural demands on them. The presence of this human cost I take to be Shakespeare's critique of the code itself—the same critique he accorded any "prescription" for human behaviour. What follows is, I trust, suggestive—first, a glance at Shakespeare's use of the code in satisfying the genetic demands of tragedy, and, second, a longer look at his use of the code in characterizing Hamlet.

The problem of the writer of tragedy is, after all, how to make us love a criminal. The chief modes of deflecting condemnation for the criminal act are, foremost among the Greeks, to insist on human limitation, especially on that perspectival ignorance which cancels our sharpest understanding, revealing it—as in Oedipus— a merely human genius at problem-solving. There is much of this perspectival ignorance in *Hamlet*: antagonists grope through a natural and a metaphysical darkness in Elsinore, by indirections finding out directions only to death. Their deepest plots *do* pall. Among the living, the one who truly knows, Claudius, knows only his guilt. But in Shakespeare, characteristically, our forebearance is also prompted by the exploration of alternative codes of value. We see Macbeth as less dishonorable for the mouth-honour of the rest. Even as we decry the ghastly virility to which Lady Macbeth successfully appeals, we acknowledge its hold on us in acknowledging Macbeth's heroic endurance, his final valour. We are repelled at first by Cleopatra's petty strategies of passion, and then open our heart to her and to Antony after Ventidius' revelations of the still more petty strategies of power. In *Hamlet* the duellist's code serves its turn in humanizing the criminal by discovering for the best and the worst a single name. The "satani-call illusion" is not without attendant idealisms that declare it a perverse anagram of the good.

Much of the middle of the play is dominated by Hamlet's pursuit of the "illusion," by his efforts to achieve Saviolo's pre-scriptions: a mastery of passion, a disinterested security in the justice of his cause, a resignation to providence. These efforts are intermingled; none goes forward programatically. Sometimes, as in his praise of Horatio as Stoic, or in his reaction to the death of Polonius, or in his testing of the King, Hamlet seems to accept and progress along the path prescribed for the lawful avenger. At other times, as in the scenes with his mother or with Ophelia, or in his response to Fortinbras' Polish expedition, Hamlet seems to stray from it. Yet in the main, he moves forward along the lines Saviolo prescribes; and when he does not or cannot, Hamlet acts out the painful costs of the prescriptions. One of Shakespeare's prime concerns, in *Hamlet* as elsewhere, seems to have been the inadequacies of formulas and commonplaces that pretend to pre-scribe or even describe human conduct. Hence, even when it seems most didactic, his theatre is rarely reducible to statement. In *Othello*, for example, representation both elaborates and undoes love-sonnet ideology. Similarly, the conventional saws on lust, all of which could have been gathered from Textor's school-crib, the *Epitheta*, are overturned by their elaboration in Sonnet 129. But perhaps this strategy is clearest in the relation between Shake-speare's Prince Hal and, say, Erasmus' version of the demands of kingship.[26] Hal's confession to Poins that his human appetites are "belike not princely begot," the grim image in which he compares his passions to "wretches fetter'd in our prisons," and his dis-heartening speech on ceremony work out the fearful price of the commonplace that the monarch should be godlike in act and motive, beyond self-interest and desire.

In the character of Hamlet the costs of quenching the passions, of ethical survey and disinterestedness, are put before us in various agonizing forms; and finally, the cost of resignation—death. This exposure of the Procrustean, the unnatural in moral formula and commonplace, is inevitably part of a complete poetic "making," an exhaustion of dramatic materials. But it is not only the means by which the play is other than statement; it is also the means by which statement is subjected to its most vigorous critique. If one were to seek in Shakespeare the clearest representation of the inadequacies of honour, of the emptiness of violence, of the consequences of inhibited passion, of the impossibility of a deracinated disinterestedness—indeed, of all the pernicious aspects of "manliness" that underlies them—one would turn to *Hamlet* rather than to *Romeo and Juliet* or *Othello* or even *Macbeth*. Here heroic privatism at its noblest is taken up on its own terms and most devastatingly and thoroughly represented. The human toll of the "satanicall illusion" is completely reckoned, and there is neither a feud resolved, nor a free time gained, nor even, as in *Othello*, imperfect sensibilities demonically abused, to point to in mitigation. There is only the bleak triumph of retribution. The best and the worst go down together, and the completion of the task enjoined is, after all the anguish, finally as perfunctory and empty as the ritual blare of Fortinbras' success.

Much of Hamlet's delay and mercurial wavering can be viewed as something other than filler, or the paralysis of sensitivity, or psychological realism, or a plumbing of oedipal depths. It is the working out of an assessment of Saviolo's formulas for lawful vengeance. Some scenes put before us the painfulness of Hamlet's attempts to master self-interest and passion: the gross promptings to immediate action, the frustration of recognizing their grossness, the moral taint of arguments for reasonableness, the unnaturalness of proprieties when love and rage shake the very being. Other scenes put before us the guilt and error that attend reason: the irony of the prayer scene, of Polonius' death. And yet other scenes exhibit the costs even of resignation to providence—for murder and preservation at sea prove resignation as guilty as reason and passion, and they lead to depersonalization, the terrible illness about the heart.

In the characterization of Hamlet perhaps the most striking instances of this cost accounting cluster around the essential aristocratic idea—decorum—essential because it not only makes for aristocratic identity in the first place, but also clearly implies the class attitudes toward both passion and reason. I want to look for a moment at the contradictory effects of the idea of decorum: contradictory in that it prompts Hamlet to opposite kinds of behavior, thus revealing its inadequacy as prescription. Propriety, protocol, appearance—all decorum's forms are central to honour and princeliness, central and undermining.

> O, what a rogue and peasant slave am I

Hamlet cries in the famous soliloquy, berating his ignoble passiveness. Yet Hamlet's open-hearted welcome to the players has just been emphatically contrasted with the self-congratulatory smile of that chilly arriviste, Rosencrantz, who evidently was looking forward to the players' discomfiture. So Hamlet's self-denigrating epithets are not merely the classbound callousness of a Coriolanus. They are a way of drawing our attention to a peculiarly aristocratic sensibility whose limitations here will lie not in outward relations, but in itself. Hamlet compares his situation with that of the player, but only with the player's "quality" as mime, and then to his own disadvantage. However, consciousness of class decorums does echo through the soliloquy, and as Hamlet defines his situation, he slips naturally into the language of the duellist.

> Who calls me villain? breaks my pate across?
> Plucks off my beard, and blows it in my face?
> Tweaks me by the nose? give me the lie i' the throat,
> As deep as to the lungs? who does me this?
> Ha!
> 'Swounds, I should take it.

Yet, though he cries vengeance, Hamlet masters his passion. As did his outrage and self-hatred, this mastery comes from an aristocratic sense of decorum, for Hamlet masters his passion by comparing himself to a whore unpacking her heart with words, and to "a very drab, a scullion." In the conclusion of the soliloquy, he determines, with a cool and princely rationality, to test the justice of his cause. This soliloquy has been subjected to subtle linguistic and psychological analysis. But whatever else may be said, Hamlet's conception of his situation as preliminary to a duel, his crucial exhibition of aristocratic self-consciousness, and his movement from self-indulgent passion to an almost disinterested concern with truth, suggest the social rationale and idealisms of the rapier code. In the soliloquy, one observes that decorum is a cue both for passion (outrage at proprieties and rights violated), and for the suppression of passion (as improper to the noble style). Hamlet's disgust at the funeral-wedding baked meats is violent; his observation "ere those shoes were old," terrible. Yet, though he "most powerfully and potently" believes the slanders of Juvenal,[27] the "satirical rogue," against old age, Hamlet also holds it "not honesty to have it thus set down," and warns others not to mock Polonius, for all his own indecorous mockery of the old man—again for Polonius' violation of the decorums of man and father. Similarly, Hamlet's other passionate violations of decorum for decorum's sake, as when he wrestles Laertes in the grave for an ostentation of grief which demeans its occasion, define not only Hamlet's difficulty in maintaining the equanimity that should follow resignation, but define the unnaturalness of decorum as well. Hamlet leaps at once to match Laertes in the very excess he deplores. And we would have him do no less. The scene exhibits, as does the soliloquy, both the nobility and the unnaturalness of decorum, and hence its cost. At last, in Osric, decorum is reduced to an absurdity.

The antecedents of this treatment of aristocratic *amour-propre* suggest that it is more than a demand of the story or shrewd general observation. In Hamlet's upholding and violation of decorum, Shakespeare at last made coherent drama of the turbulent social themes of the sonnets. Hamlet's behavior unites and alters into a universal woe both the self-hatred of "Sonnet 110," in which his wretched fortune leads the player to gore his own thoughts in the vulnerability of motley, and the controlled outrage of "Sonnet 94," in which aristocratic self-containment, the mere mastery of a face, is damned as a loftier and a worse corruption. The character of Hamlet, I would guess, is the product of an intimate, as well as a formally intellectual, encounter with social history.

As with decorum, so with reason and with passion: their proper exercise is difficult, even godlike; their abandonment perhaps even more difficult. Yet they ought not, cannot if we are wholly men, fust in us unused, these great gifts of providence. But the avenger who would combat lawfully must, like Hamlet, suffer their disuse when social forms and plots and passions pall. To trace the transformation of Hamlet to avenger is therefore not to discover simple affirmations, or ideological nullity, or even fashionable contrarieties. It is to arrive at the only necessary ideology of drama: the irreducible complexity of experience; the impoverishing simplism of codes.

Reading Saviolo four centuries later is an encounter with one such code, suspiciously empty now of recognizable human content, apparently the crude rationalization of a viciousness which (at least in this form) society is well rid of. We can justify crimes of passion more easily than we can the bloody triumphs of this cold contrivance which seems to debase reason, faith, and passion alike. Indeed, James I, who both half-encouraged personal violence and vigorously decried it, speaks for the modern outlook in his "Treatise against Duelling" when he states that

> Actes done sodainly and without aduisement differ as much in kynde and qualitie from others that are done aduisedly and with prepensed malice in colde bloud, as reason doth from rage, change from choice and necessitie from temeritie . . .[28]

Yet in *Hamlet* the duellist's code is made accessible to us, made human and shown to be inhumane by the representation of its idealisms and their price. Whatever else one finds in the play, it is not inappropriate to take from it also the image of a young, self-tortured swordsman moved by ambiguous injunctions to uphold a vanished glory. More than one nobleman in the 1590s, with such a sense of patrimony lost to encroaching civil powers, must have dreamed himself in arms at Elsinore. That the actualities were tennis-court brawls, the anachronisms of the tiltyard, or the silly rebellion of Essex are not wholly to the point, perhaps only a measure of how much actuality requires the celebrations of art.

I have so far provided only an historical *Hamlet*, a *Hamlet* for an age. Yet of this play, Blake's aphorism promises to be endlessly right. If "Eternity is in love with the productions of Time," it is surely in love with this of the late 1590s. But what makes *Hamlet* of its age makes it also, I think, of our age and—till biochemistry transform us—of any other. Under Shakespeare's hand, the crisis of aristocratic power and the code which expressed it became hieroglyphs of a universal crisis and its forms: the crisis of young manhood and the course of maturation. Hamlet is no more his father's child, not yet his own man—he is at home among neither kin nor kind; his are the deracinations of all young men. His naive idealizations of childhood dependency in which the familial was the idyllic; his shock on learning that the idyll was only that; his trial of the bitter, even sick uncharitableness that is necessary to end dependency—these, the common course of maturation, domestic and writ little, echo also the alienation, the chivalric nostalgias, the contentiousness that lesser Elizabethans saw as they looked upward and afar at glittering Essexes and Southhamptons. Saviolo's norms for lawful combat are paradigms of the curbing of passion and even of reason which leads to the habits and acceptance of maturity and to their possibilities for fruitful action. All young men have a father in some sense lost, a mother (dare one say it without arousing sensitivities to Freud?) to whom they cannot return in innocence. And all are plagued by history, by contradictory injunctions from the noble dead, impossible to realize or to ignore. The past pops in between their election and their hopes, offering only obligations where they would grasp the heroic freedom that as children they grew to believe was patrimony. The special intensity of *Hamlet* lies in part in its compression of genres and themes: its bringing together of comedy, the play of maturation, with tragedy, the play of death. To this intensity of genre and theme, I suggest, Shakespeare's sympathetic vision of the nature and fate of the English aristocracy in the late 1590s contributed in some measure, as it also contributed to making for all time a play intended for an age.

NOTES

1. Fredson Bowers, *Elizabethan Revenge Tragedy, 1587–1642* (Princeton, 1940), p. 279.
2. Bowers, p. 275.
3. *Giacomo di Grassi, his true Arte of Defence* . . . (London, 1594). The translation is from the Italian edition of 1570, but the introduction dates from the early 1590s.

4. Among these manuals are W. Segar, *The Booke of Honor and Armes* (1589); *Giacomo di Grassi, his true Arte of Defence* (1594); *Vincentio Saviolo, his Practise* (1594); J. Kepers, *The Courtiers Academie* (1598), a translation of Romei's *Discorsi;* George Silver, *Paradoxes of Defence* (1599).

5. George Silver, *Paradoxes of Defence,* in *The Works of George Silver,* ed. C. G. R. Matthey (London, 1898), pp. 21–22.

6. Lawrence Stone, *The Crisis of the Aristocracy 1558–1641* (Oxford, 1965), p. 242. Throughout the early pages of this essay, I depend heavily on Stone's interpretation of the period.

7. Silver, p. 72.

8. Stone, p. 223 ff. The record of duels is to be found in Stone, p. 245. The decisive leap in numbers of recorded duels occurs in the decade of the nineties; cf. Eleanore Prosser, *Hamlet and Revenge* (Stanford, 1967), p. 14, n40, for a different view of the evidence.

9. Stone, p. 245, who cites here Selden's *Duello or Single Combat* (1610), p. 42.

10. Silver, p. 56.

11. Stone, p. 226 ff.

12. See Silver, pp. 9, 32–37, 51–56.

13. Ruth Kelso, "The Doctrine of the English Gentleman," in *University of Illinois Studies in Language and Literature,* 14 (1929), pp. 96–97.

14. Silver, p. 57.

15. Ruth Kelso, "Saviolo and his *Practise,*" *MLN,* 29 (1924), pp. 33–35.

16. See Variorum *As You Like It,* ed. H. H. Furness (Philadelphia 1890), p. 274 n92; also V. K. Whitaker, *Shakespeare's Use of Learning* (San Marino, Cal., 1953), p. 90, who presents strong reasons for believing that Shakespeare had read Saviolo rather than Segar or some other imitator of Muzio. Yet Shakespeare might also have known the man himself, either through the Southhampton circle, with Florio the common link; or might have met him at the Elephant, a tavern mentioned with pleasure in *Twelfth Night,* and a favorite resort of Italians living in London. On this point see G. S. Gargàno, *Scapigliatura Italiana à Londra sotto Elisabetta e Giacomo I* (Firenze, 1923), p. 42.

17. Saviolo, Y5^r.

18. *Ibid.* In the Italian duelling literature, the distinction between *virtù* and virtue is often confusingly stated; see F. R. Bryson, *The Point of Honor in Sixteenth-Century Italy* (New York, 1935), p. 108 ff, and the New Arden *Tempest,* ed. F. Kermode (Cambridge, Mass. 1958), pp. liii–liv.

19. Saviolo, Y5^r.

20. Saviolo, Z1^v.

21. *Ibid.* There are some resemblances here to Aquinas's comments on "virtuous vengeance" in *Summa Theologica,* II–III, Q. 108, Art. 1. The

passage has been noted by J. A. Bryant, Jr., *Hippolyta's View* (Lexington, Ky., 1961), p. 125, following Msgr. I. J. Semper, *Hamlet Without Tears* (Dubuque, Iowa, 1946), p. 19 ff, and—with its Aristotelian antecedents—may have affected the tradition in which Muzio wrote. Bryant does not attempt to demonstrate that Shakespeare had any knowledge of the passage.

22. Saviolo, Z1ᵛ.
23. Stone, pp. 247–49, refers to similar reactions against the code.
24. J. Dover Wilson, *What Happens in Hamlet* (Cambridge, 1959), p. 276 ff. Wilson cites both Silver and Saviolo.
25. The disagreement on this matter is clarified briefly in Whitaker, p. 272.
26. Erasmus, *The Education of a Christian Prince*, trans., L. K. Born (New York, 1936), p. 159. "God is swayed by no emotions, yet He rules the universe with supreme judgment. The prince should follow His example in all his actions, cast aside all personal motives, and use only reason and judgment. God is sublime. The prince should be removed as far as possible from the low concerns of the common people and their sordid desires."
27. See T. W. Baldwin, *W. S. Small Latine*, 2 (Urbana, Ill. 1944), p. 497.
28. "A Treatise Against Duelling," Cotton MS, Titus CIV, fol. 414ᵛ, quoted by Bowers, p. 17.

Susan Snyder

From *The Comic Matrix of Shakespeare's Tragedies*

What has *Hamlet* to do with the comic world? A good deal, when one considers the gravediggers' grisly jokes, the intrusion of comic-garrulous Polonius and Osric into a sphere they do not understand, the Tweedledum-and-Tweedledee pair Rosencrantz and Guildenstern, Hamlet himself as role-player, manipulator, crafty madman, wit, and eiron. Nothing at all, when one sees that Hamlet's superior awareness brings not the liberation promised by comedy but frustration, and that the play transmutes the comic celebration of multiplicity into an existential nightmare of competing perceptions of reality. Yet even this complete inversion of comic values suggests that some patterns in the complex drama become more coherent when viewed from the vantage point of comedy.

The Prince himself shows us how the multiple perspective can create agony rather than assurance. Generations of critics have sought a consistent Hamlet, one whose conviction that he must take revenge is not really at odds with his reluctance to take that revenge. But Hamlet himself sees that they are at odds and tells us so, most clearly in the "O what a rogue and peasant slave" soliloquy that ends Act II. This speech demands close attention if we are to understand Hamlet's superawareness and the dilemma it creates for him as an avenger. Roused by the passioning of the Pyrrhus speech, Hamlet rages at himself for not having already acted against Claudius. The player who wept over Hecuba was moved by a mere fiction, but Hamlet feels himself impotent in the

Reprinted from *The Comic Matrix of Shakespeare's Tragedies*, pp. 91–136, by Susan Snyder (1979), by permission of Princeton University Press.

face of a real event, "a king / Upon whose property and most dear
life / A damn'd defeat was made." From the first self-disgusted
outburst, the speech builds to frenzy:

> Bloody, bawdy villain!
> Remorseless, treacherous, lecherous, kindless villain!
> O, vengeance!

In all this swell of emotion there is self-questioning (am I a
coward?) but no doubt whatsoever of Claudius's guilt and the
rightness of revenge. Claudius is the worst of villains; he made
the "damn'd defeat"; it can only be cowardice that has held back
Hamlet's avenging hand. But a few lines later Hamlet is saying
something quite different:

> The spirit that I have seen
> May be a devil; and the devil hath power
> T'assume a pleasing shape; yea, and perhaps
> Out of my weakness and my melancholy,
> As he is very potent with such spirits,
> Abuses me to damn me. I'll have grounds
> More relative than this.

In this new version of the situation, the Ghost's origins are not
certain at all and so Claudius's guilt is not certain. The action
indicated is not to denounce and kill the King out of hand but to
force a public, confirming confession.

Bradley thought that Hamlet's doubt, opposing as it does his
certainty in the first part of the soliloquy, was an "unconscious
fiction." Other critics have followed him, or have believed in the
doubt rather than the certainty.[1] But the conventions of Elizabethan soliloquy are against fictions in such circumstances,
whether conscious or not.[2] The inconsistency is real. No ingenious analysis should be allowed to smooth away a contradiction
that Shakespeare has made so prominent—especially since this is
not an isolated instance but merely the most sharply focused of
many such inconsistencies in Hamlet as he is shown to us in the
early part of the play. It is better to look where Shakespeare
himself is directing our attention, to the contradiction itself. What
makes a man feel and say one thing in all sincerity, and then in
equal sincerity feel and say its very opposite?

The dynamic of the speech is instructive. It does not move directly from statement to contradiction but changes tone radically at two points. The first howl for vengeance is followed abruptly by "Why, what an ass am I!" Fully inside his passion one moment, Hamlet steps outside the next to view himself objectively: a man raging all by himself, unpacking his heart with words, is a ridiculous object. Rhythm and phrasing here become less broken and exclamatory than in the preceding denunciations of Claudius and himself, but the section ends with another short outburst—"Fie upon 't! foh!" Then there is another shift, into more formal, meditative verse. Emotional thought gives way to a more speculative sort. Significantly, the new mood is signaled by the words "About, my brains."

The dynamic, then, is a move from emotion to reason and from subjective commitment to objective detachment. It is this shift, with the two kinds of awareness it implies, that should command our attention. By this point in the play the audience badly needs some explanation of Hamlet's conduct. The conduct has been puzzling, both as we see it and as others describe it, ever since his wild and whirling words after encountering the Ghost; and the explanations Hamlet offers onstage are not to be trusted. Given its position and its portentous preface ("Now I am alone"), this soliloquy ought to provide the long-awaited insight into Hamlet's situation. And so it does. This is a man caught between subjective surety and his own awareness that it *is* subjective. He is both inside his emotional conviction and outside it looking on.

This is a position of power for a figure like Rosalind-Ganymede in *As You Like It*, where two views are better than one, more whole, and where the need to choose and act can be suspended in the free play of the mind. But Hamlet's situation calls for action, and coherent action is impossible while his two apprehensions remain separate and opposed. In its own way *Hamlet*, like its successor in the chronology of Shakespearean tragedy *Othello*, finds its tragic core in the comic assumptions. But the ways of these plays are as different as their heroes. To be sure, Othello sees the world subjectively, but he does not know he is seeing it subjectively—not until after the tragic decision is made and its consequences are before him. Like most tragic heroes he is very much the alazon, self-deceived and totally committed. As Bradley

long ago pointed out, Othello could have handled Hamlet's prob-
lem.³ It is Hamlet's peculiar tragedy to be flexible where flexibility
is a drawback, to see beyond his own convictions, to be eiron as
well as alazon in a situation that demands the single-minded
alazon response.⁴

As Hamlet's awareness of subjective distortion is such a departure from the usual tragic pattern, it is not surprising that
Shakespeare has called attention to it in smaller ways throughout
the first two acts. Hamlet's comments to Rosencrantz and
Guildenstern earlier in this same scene, for example, show his
special way of perceiving things. "Denmark's a prison," the subjective view, is not allowed to stand unqualified. "*To me* it is a
prison," he adds. The prison is real for Hamlet, but he knows it is
not real for those who "think not so." The same double vision of
the eiron informs his speech "I have of late—but wherefore I
know not—lost all my mirth." The earth is goodly but seems "*to
me*" a sterile promontory; the skies are excellent and majestic but
"*to me*" foul vapors; man is creation's masterpiece, akin to gods and
angels, yet "*to me*" the quintessence of dust. And lest we miss the
general point, he supplies it directly: "There is nothing either
good or bad, but thinking makes it so."⁵

Only an intellectual could be so conscious of the mind's tricks
and deceptions. D. G. James reminds us that so far as we know
Shakespeare was the first to give Hamlet a university back-
ground.⁶ But if his condition is part of his intellectuality, it is
nevertheless abnormal. Intellectuals are not inevitably caught in
impotence between knowing and not-knowing. How has it happened to Hamlet? Certainly unresolved grief has made him melancholy; and Rosalie Colie has observed with insight that in
Hamlet Shakespeare has used the melancholic syndrome as "a
medium for the character's own confusions" and as "an idiom
which to some extent takes for granted the imbalance, the relativism, the insecurities implicit in any judgment."⁷ Montaigne in the
"Apology of Raymond Sebond" offers another perspective when
he describes how the overthrow of one accepted belief calls all
others into question, leaving the doubter nothing to rely on but
his own lonely judgment.⁸ Hamlet's basic belief was in the goodness of his parents and their relationship. Recent events have not
only brought an emotional shock in the loss of his father but have
overthrown established belief by the sudden revelation of his

mother's fleshly weakness. This is the burden of his first soliloquy in Act I, scene ii, an important speech that is clearly meant to define Hamlet's condition of mind *before* he hears the Ghost, the condition out of which he will react to the Ghost's message.

Hamlet begins with his weary distaste for life—"O, that this too too solid flesh would melt"—and goes on to the cause of that distaste, which is not so much grief for his father as disillusion with his mother. Seemingly loving and good, she has betrayed her real nature by posting with wicked speed to incestuous sheets. Hamlet's disjointed words and memories keep coming back to that suddenly opened abyss between how he saw her and what she was. "Why, she would hang on him / *As if* increase of appetite had grown / By what it fed on. . . . / *Like* Niobe, all tears . . . / . . . most unrighteous tears" (my italics). Neither love nor grief was real in Gertrude. Her son is left with powerful emotions to stifle and no sureties to cling to.

The whole scene has been building toward this effect. Hamlet has come on mute and even when addressed by the King has only tossed him contemptuous one-liners without caring if Claudius hears them or not. What rouses him to passionate speech is Gertrude's "Why seems it so particular with thee?" For reply he fires at her a hysterical diatribe against "seems," which we understand only later as a rebuke for those unrighteous tears she shed for her first husband. At the time, the outburst is puzzling to the audience, like everything else about this sullen young prince. It raises the question that he will answer when he is alone; and it is the first sign of the multiple awareness that lies underneath his obsession with seeming, delusion, and subjectivity.[9]

That obsession is apparent in some of Hamlet's other responses in Act I. In the meditation on the "dram of eale," for example, his mind is not on how things are but on how they *look*, how the image of the whole may be altered and distorted by a part. The dram and the humour growing beyond bounds relate loosely to the play's persistent imagery of spreading poison. Hamlet does not say, however, that heavy drinking corrupts Danish lives and morals. He says that the Dane's drinking habits have given them a generally bad name.

> This heavy-headed revel east and west
> Makes us *traduc'd and tax'd of other nations;*

> They *clepe* us drunkards, and with swinish *phrase*
> Soil our *addition*.
>
>   (my italics)

It is an odd turn for his thought to take, all the more so because
he has passed up an opportunity for a direct slur on Claudius—
who is, after all, doing the drinking. Instead of the sneer we
expect, what comes through is Hamlet's preoccupation with seem-
ings and distorted pictures. Even in his rage that soon follows,
when the Ghost tells him what Claudius did, what does Hamlet
single out for his tables of remembrance? That one may smile and
smile, and yet be a villain. He is shaken, not so much by evil *per se*
as by evil hidden under a masquerade of order, affection, good.

The Ghost's accusation of Claudius gets Hamlet's immediate
intuitive assent: "O my prophetic soul!" Yet he has become suspicious of all certainties, superconscious as he is of the distortions
of the mind's eye. Believing the Ghost with his emotions and his
prophetic soul, he is aware that his belief could be false. The
Ghost has spoken to no one but himself. Hamlet knows he is
melancholy, out of balance. And ghosts themselves are problematic beings, not always what they seem. So he knows and does not
know.[10] A man in such a state cannot be a consistent character in
the ordinary sense, because he can demonstrate the grip of subjectivity only by expressing beliefs with passionate conviction and
the need for objectivity only by doubting or contradicting those
beliefs.

Hamlet's later soliloquy, "How all occasions do inform against
me" (IV.iv), shows a similar jar between subjective sureness and
objective wariness. Even as he berates himself for thinking too
precisely on the event and resolves for blood, Hamlet knows
simultaneously that his temporary model, Fortinbras, has no
more grounds for *his* bloody course than a straw or an eggshell.
This monologue, present only in the Second Quarto,[11] reflects
more on the past situation than on the present one, for at the
moment the well-guarded Hamlet hardly has "means" to kill
Claudius, as he says he does. It is interesting that both the
occasions that inform against Hamlet in this way, the player's
speech in Act II and Fortinbras' expedition in Act IV, represent
forms of delusion. The player raves and weeps for a mythical

queen; Fortinbras risks death for a fantasy and trick of fame. In both cases Hamlet feels his own motive to be more real, but the association—I should be like this actor, I should be like this seeker after fantasies—is nevertheless troubling. Even a third spur to action, the Ghost's reappearance in III.iv, is made ambiguous by Gertrude's failure to see and hear it. Hamlet's subjective mazes are not easy to escape.

The Ghost and Fortinbras can lead us further, to two ways in which Shakespeare manipulates the multiple possibilities dear to comedy for tragic tension in *Hamlet*. One, a series of open questions, involves us as spectators in the difficulty of choosing among possibilities; the other, a set of reflector characters, suggests the limitations of freedom and power inherent in any such choice. In this latter regard, it is clear that Fortinbras and the other young men who serve as foils for Hamlet do not suffer his conflict between the heart's convictions and the mind's doubts. Rather, each in his single awareness embodies one or the other term of that conflict. Fortinbras, Laertes, and Horatio are whole in a way that Hamlet is not; yet we see in them as well the limitations that inhere in the single view. Critics have long noted that Hamlet's situation as a son impelled to avenge a dead father is mirrored in the situations of Laertes and Fortinbras. Laertes leaps to his task with no hesitation. When he consigns "conscience" to the profoundest pit (IV.v.129), it is in both senses of the word: he rejects not only moral scruple but also full awareness and consideration. As for Fortinbras, while he might draw the line at poisoned foils, he is similarly bent on honor at the expense of justice. We have it not only from Claudius, whose word might be suspect, but also from the disinterested Horatio that Old Fortinbras' lands were fairly lost.[12] His son's expedition is diverted away from revenge against Denmark, but Fortinbras in his Polish exploit is no more thoughtful than Laertes. The large discourse that looks before and after is foreign to both of them. And Fortinbras' unthinking action, however Hamlet may envy it, is as fruitless in its way as Laertes'. His conquest in Poland means nothing, and he gains the lands he really wants by *not* fighting for them.

While Laertes and Fortinbras act out Hamlet's subjective side and show its insufficiency as a guide for action, we have for the objective side Horatio, the man that is not passion's slave. Horatio gets high praise from Hamlet (as indeed do Fortinbras and Laertes), but he is finally as insufficient as they. In Horatio, Hamlet says admiringly, blood and judgment are well commingled. Actually, from what we see of him, Horatio's "blood" is so well subdued to judgment as to be almost nonexistent. Significantly, Hamlet sees as the happy result of this commingling not decisive action but a kind of stoicism.[13] Horatio's capacity for detached endurance, however admirable in the abstract, answers Hamlet's own case no better than the emotional rashness of Fortinbras and Laertes. Horatio is an adviser, a go-between, an explainer, but not a doer. We should not forget that the one action in the play that he initiates on his own, although he is not allowed to carry it out, is suicide.

In short, to consider any of these partial reflectors by the side of Hamlet is to become aware of the diminution involved in narrowing down from multiple possibilities to one actuality. In tragedy the eiron retains his superiority to others even while his greater capacities are the cause of his torment.

Horatio illuminates Hamlet's conflict of perceptions in another way. He is the validator, called on first to test the apparition seen by the sentries and then, more centrally, to give objective confirmation of Claudius's guilt. The context of Hamlet's praise of his detachment is the Prince's desperate need of that calm vision to confirm his own apprehension, or to correct its distortion. Directly after his tribute to Horatio he explains:

> There is a play to-night before the King;
> One scene of it comes near the circumstance
> Which I have told thee of my father's death.
> I prithee, when thou seest that act afoot,
> Even with the very comment of thy soul
> Observe my uncle. If his occulted guilt
> Do not itself unkennel in one speech,
> It is a damned ghost that we have seen,
> And my imaginations are as foul
> As Vulcan's stithy. Give him heedful note;
> For I mine eyes will rivet to his face;
> And, after, we will both our judgments join
> In censure of his seeming.
>
>   (III.ii.73–85)

It is usually assumed that Hamlet gets the reassurance he wants when he and Horatio talk after the play has broken off and the King and court have left the stage. But what does Horatio really say?

> *Ham.* O good Horatio, I'll take the ghost's word for a thou-
> sand pound. Didst perceive?
> *Hor.* Very well, my lord.
> *Ham.* Upon the talk of the poisoning.
> *Hor.* I did very well note him.
> *Ham.* Ah, ha!
>
> (III.ii.280-285)

What did Horatio perceive and note? Claudius has not unken-neled his guilt in words; he has only gone off in some agitation. Hamlet has told us himself that powerful dramatic speech would "appal the free" as well as "make mad the guilty."[14] None of the courtiers seems to suspect anything (except, perhaps, that Ham-let himself is madder and more dangerous than ever). Possibly Horatio is trying to temper Hamlet's excitement with his own moderation, but why withhold a simple yes? He is strangely noncommital, even ambiguous.[15] Yet Horatio is not habitually indefinite: at various points in the action he wants Hamlet not to follow the Ghost, advises Gertrude to see Ophelia, counsels Ham-let to forgo the duel with Laertes, all with admirable clarity. It would seem that what Shakespeare wanted in this exchange, onstage at least, was something short of decisive confirmation. (The theater audience does not doubt any longer, I think; but they have already heard Claudius's guilty aside in III.i.) Horatio is still not sure, and Hamlet must go off to his fateful encounters with the King and Queen, once again subjectively certain but with no clearly validated course of action. Not until Act V, when he is faced with the undisputable evidence of Claudius's murderous move against his nephew, does Horatio condemn the King. By that time, as we shall see, the dilemma has been resolved another way, and his confirmation has no importance.

As validator, then, Horatio functions by not functioning. He calls attention to Hamlet's problem of knowledge by refusing to confirm or deny. The same could be said of Shakespeare himself, who in this tragedy of competing realities introduces an unusual number of open questions and resolves as few of them as possible.

The most obvious of these, as I suggested above, is the Ghost. What is he and where does he come from? Dover Wilson has shown that there was no single accepted contemporary view about ghosts. For some they were actual spirits of the dead whose commands had to be obeyed, while others saw them as devils assuming familiar shapes to work evil on men, and still another opinion refused them any existence at all except as delusions of the mind.[16] All three possibilities are raised in *Hamlet*. Horatio speaks to the apparition as the dead king's spirit which must be pacified ("If there be any good thing to be done, / That may to thee do ease . . .") but also as a hallucination ("Stay, illusion") and as an imposter:

> What art thou that usurp'st this time of night
> Together with that fair and warlike form
> In which the majesty of buried Denmark
> Did sometimes march?[17]

The sentries show similar confusion about "this thing." Hamlet himself does not know how to react when the Ghost appears to him. Is it a spirit of health or a goblin damned? Even after he has heard the Ghost's story, his response is not unambiguous: "O all you host of heaven! O earth! What else? / And shall I couple hell?"[18] It seems clear that Shakespeare is trying to leave the question of the Ghost's provenance wide open, unsettling any individual spectator's convictions by introducing the other possibilities. The audience is not allowed to part company with Hamlet, to rest secure in certainty while he hesitates and doubts. The technique indeed, as Wilson says, justifies Hamlet's unsureness, but it does more: it involves the audience experientially in that unsureness.[19]

The Ghost is far from the only open question in the play: Is the marriage of Claudius and Gertrude incestuous? Is Hamlet the rightful heir to the Danish throne, cheated out of his inheritance by a usurper? Practitioners of historical criticism have sought to establish definitively how the average Elizabethan would have answered these questions. Wilson, for example, offers a well-researched, unequivocal yes to both.[20] But on these points, which should be very clear if their proper interpretation is as important as Wilson says it is, Shakespeare is noticeably equivocal. The council of state has approved the royal marriage (I.ii.14–16), and no one except Hamlet seems to feel uneasy about it. Perhaps, as critics often assume, the Danish court is corrupt from the beginning. But where is the evidence? Polonius is commonplace but not vicious. Hamlet, indeed, calls the marriage incestuous, and so does the Ghost. Once again we are made not just to see Hamlet's dilemma but to share it, feeling on the one side his sureness of wrongdoing and on the other the disturbing absence of external confirmation. And once again Shakespeare is exploiting an already existing ambiguity of attitude in his society. To marry one's brother's widow was normally forbidden, but the marriage of a widowed queen ("imperial jointress") to the new king could nevertheless be approved as wise policy. Advantages in terms of resolving dynastic rivalries could overrule the usual sanctions against incest.[21]

The question of Hamlet's succession raises the same possibility of more "truths" than one. Wilson may be right in asserting that Shakespeare's audience would think of the Danish constitution in terms of what they were used to, the English system of inherited rule. Not until Act V is it made clear that the Danish monarchy is elective rather than hereditary. On the other hand, the audience has heard very early in the play about a nearby kingdom, Norway, in which the crown has passed to the dead king's brother rather than to his son, apparently in the normal course of things.[22] In any case, we must be less than certain about Hamlet's rights to the throne simply because so little is made of them in the play. Council and court say nothing. Do we assume Claudius has bribed them all? Gertrude says nothing. Yet her other reactions assure us that her love for Claudius has not canceled out her love and concern for Hamlet. If a major injustice has been done to him, would she not be aware of it? Horatio says nothing. Even that politically minded pair Rosencrantz and Guildenstern, while they hint that Hamlet is ambitious, never suggest that he has a real claim to the throne. Hamlet himself flirts with the ambition motive in various contexts of deception, but in soliloquy he says not a word of being cheated out of a crown. When he denounces Claudius to Gertrude as "cutpurse of the empire" (III.iv.99), he may mean that his uncle stole the throne from the legitimate heir—or he may mean simply that Claudius won the kingdom by treacherous murder rather than by merit or open conquest. His only direct reference to the choice of king, which comes very late in the play (V.ii.65), implies that he himself was a likely candidate for the throne, though by no means the undoubted successor. Claudius popped in between the election and his *hopes*, not his rights. With so little support for its instinctive reaction based on familiar rules of primogeniture, the audience is left in a state of uncertainty that must color response to many scenes. In I.ii, for example, Claudius's careful deference to Polonius and the council and his naming of Hamlet as his chosen successor to the throne may be seen as signs of a shaky title, but they may just as well be seen as a new king's attempts at magnanimity and good government. We simply do not know, and by not knowing we re-create in ourselves another version of Hamlet's dilemma of conflicting perceptions.

Shakespeare raises the questions in *Hamlet* in such a way as to forestall any easy resolution, going to some pains to nurture rather than dispel ambiguity. The germs of ambiguity are already there, in that more than one defensible view existed on each issue. The point, again and again, is not one or the other "right" answer but the doubt. Other questions reinforce these. How guilty is Gertrude? Is Hamlet's grief natural or excessive? Even the central question—did Claudius in fact murder his brother?—is left in doubt until the third act. This last uncertainty is the most difficult for us to re-create in our experience of *Hamlet*. Everyone knows the end of the story. It is rare to find a student who is unfamiliar with the outlines of the plot, even if he has never read or seen the play. When, some years ago, I did come across one who had somehow escaped foreknowledge, I was intrigued when he reported that up to the moment in the prayer scene when Claudius's own words condemned him, he had thought the King might be innocent. My student was a little ashamed, thinking that his late enlightenment showed him unperceptive. But in fact his experience probably came closer to Shakespeare's intention than that of his knowing classmates.[23] *Hamlet* should be, but too rarely is, in Stephen Booth's phrase, "the tragedy of an audience that cannot make up its mind."[24]

For both Hamlet and the audience the eiron state of awareness is uncomfortable. To perceive more truths than one is to be
sure of no truth. Nevertheless, it is still a position of superiority.
The other characters take up a good part of the play's action
demonstrating that to be sure, alazon-fashion, is generally to be
wrong.

In this connection the nature of the initiating event, the
murder, is very important, as is the kind of imagery it generates.
The Ghost tells Hamlet that after the poison entered his ear "a
most instant tetter bark'd about, / Most lazar-like, with vile and
loathsome crust, / All my smooth body" (I.V.71–73). The symptoms were everywhere, but the source and working of the poison
were concealed. So it is with Denmark, where Claudius has not
only polluted the springs of public and private health (lawful
monarchy, ties of blood) but has set himself up as a counterfeit
spring of health: false father, false king. His crime has bred not
only corruption but confusion about that corruption. As Maurice
Charney says, refining on the general disease motif stressed by
Wolfgang Clemen, "If there is indeed a leitmotif of disease
imagery stemming from the Ghost's narration, it does not refer
merely to disease in general, but to the hidden disease, the disease
that is deliberately concealed."25 Thus, its ramifications take in
not only the painted harlot's cheek, the ulcer filmed over while
rank corruption infects unseen, and the secret disease feeding on
the pith of life, but also the hidden corpse of Polonius that will
announce its presence eventually by the stench of decay. This last
implies directly what the others imply indirectly, that the concealed evil will at some time come to light. "Foul deeds will rise, /
Though all the earth o'erwhelm them, to men's eyes." And so it
happens in the last scene, when the ulcer breaks open and its
poison is finally exposed by Laertes' shout "The King, the King's
to blame."26

But through the early acts we see the symptoms rather than
the cause. Something is rotten, and the whole early movement is
toward finding out what that thing is. Diverse ways of seeing the
action *become* the action. The question What is wrong with Denmark? is defined by most of the characters as What is wrong with
Hamlet? The answers they give prove that Hamlet the eiron has
good reason to suspect the single, subjective truth, for they are all

inadvertent self-definitions. The impulse to interpret Hamlet according to the interpreter's own concerns and fears, so noticeable
in Coleridge and Freud, Stephen Dedalus and J. Alfred Prufrock,
begins inside the play itself.[27]

Each of the interpreting characters could well say with Hamlet, "By the image of my cause I see / The portraiture of his"
(V.ii.77–78). Gertrude, uneasy about her own conduct, sees
at the root of Hamlet's trouble her husband's death and her
"o'erhasty" marriage (II.ii.56–57). Claudius, conscious of his own
hidden guilt, thinks Hamlet must harbor a corresponding dangerous secret:

> There's something in his soul
> O'er which his melancholy sits on brood;
> And I do doubt the hatch and the disclose
> Will be some danger.
>
> (III.i.164–167)

Others offer different but equally self-revealing interpretations.
And here another, more direct use of comedy in *Hamlet* for tragic
effect becomes apparent. Comedy's tendency is expansive and
inclusive, but like any genre or convention it is ultimately defined
by the limits within which it treats the human condition. In the
case of the opposed modes of comedy and tragedy, these limits
operate not so much on subject matter as on point of view: love
and jealousy are perceived tragically in *Othello*, while death itself
becomes comic in *The Old Wives' Tale*. Thus, if the tragic focus is to
be on attitudes and limited perceptions, as in *Hamlet*, the perspectives evoked by comic convention can be especially useful as
misinterpreters. This is a particular application of the "irrelevance" function already observed in the Friar and the Nurse in
Romeo and Juliet. Here, it is clearest in Polonius and Osric.

Polonius naturally sees Hamlet's derangement as "the very
ecstasy of love" (II.i.102) because his spiritual home is comedy.
Like the clown, he is in love with words. He has all the inconse-
quential garrulity of Juliet's Nurse and is forever attempting,
though not achieving, the verbal brilliance of Mercutio. Insofar as
Polonius can be envisioned apart from the grim events of Claudius's Denmark, he would not be out of place in *Love's Labour's Lost*,
chewing on the scraps of language with Armado and Holofernes.

Busy as he is, he always has time to crack the wind of a phrase, to make up a fine metaphor and then kindly translate it into plain language lest he go over the heads of his audience. He cannot express an opinion without his own brand of wit, however urgently his hearers may wish for more matter, with less art. As a connoisseur of words, Polonius is, inevitably, a literary critic. "Beautified Ophelia," he thinks, is a vile phrase, but "mobled queen" is good. In spite of this blessing on adjectival obscurity, however, he is impatient at the length of the player's Pyrrhus speech; and Hamlet dismisses him, significantly enough, as one who cares only for comedy: "Prithee say on. He's for a jig, or a tale of bawdry, or he sleeps" (II.ii.493–494). Poor Polonius, who fancies himself the complete critic and can parade before us all the dramatic kinds! His pastoral-comicals and tragical-historicals proliferate irrelevantly for their own sake and of their own accord, words outrunning meaning in the manner of the comic monologue.

The same is true of his aphorisms and *sententiae*, although what Polonius trots out as verbal decoration sometimes has ironic applications quite concealed from the complacent speaker. He counsels prudence, caution, and high-minded integrity to Laertes, more as a pleasing form of words than as an order he expects Laertes to follow (or why send Reynaldo to spy?). But Laertes' failure in just these qualities will lead to his downfall. Arranging Ophelia in a holy pose for less than holy purposes, Polonius cannot resist the facile moral: "We are oft to blame in this: / 'Tis too much prov'd, that with devotion's visage / And pious action we do sugar o'er / The devil himself" (III.i.46–49). What is just another cliché for him pierces to the core of Claudius's sick conscience. Here as elsewhere Polonius's words reverberate suddenly through the play's deep waters while he, all unaware, bobs on the surface like a cork.

From the beginning right up to his death, Polonius behaves as if he were in a comedy. Suspicious of his children, spying on Laertes and interfering in Ophelia's love affair, he casts himself first as the traditional obstructive father. But like Bottom in "Pyramus and Thisbe," Polonius would like to play all the parts. Having brought about the comic impasse, Hamlet's supposed love madness, he switches to a manipulator role, the better to contrive a happy ending.[28] What he has in mind we are not told, but we can be sure that Polonius would not mind being father-in-law to the next king of Denmark. And so he would be, if *Hamlet* were in fact a romantic comedy.

Even after hearing Hamlet revile Ophelia, Polonius holds stubbornly to his belief that the Prince is mad for love and advises that the Queen question Hamlet in private before he is sent to England. Presumably the distraught lover would be more likely to confess his romantic problems to a sympathetic mother than to his stepfather or to the father of the lady in question. Such a suggestion, if we are meant to infer it, enhances the terrible irony in that last attempt to soften Hamlet, for we know that he thinks of his mother with tormented disgust, as an adulteress driven by lust to connive at murder. Instead of pouring out love confidences the son will beat his mother to her knees with rebukes of her own gross appetites. And by that time Polonius will be dead.

Polonius has always been right before, as he makes Claudius admit, and he has verbally staked his life on being right this time (II.ii.152–155). He loses. It is not a comedy after all, and the bustling intriguer finds at last that in this tense, shadowy world, to be busy is some danger. He dies because he is where he should not be, in the place of a greater figure. Thrust in among the affairs of the mighty, he is like the clown Hamlet earlier described to the players, irrelevant to the "necessary question."[29]

Polonius's complete consistency as a comic character creates a cumulative irony. Beyond such immediate effects as that inadvertent catching of the King's conscience, there is the larger irony of a subjective vision, coherent but quite distorted, seeing what we see but getting it all wrong. His total unawareness exacerbates our awareness. Most ironic of all, it is the death of this irrelevant intruder that sets the play unalterably on course to the final catastrophe. Out of the murder of Polonius come Ophelia's madness and suicide; Laertes' rage for revenge and the King's poison plot; and the deaths of Laertes, Gertrude, Claudius, and Hamlet himself. Hamlet's grim joke—"This man shall set me packing"—is all too prophetic. In some ways, Polonius's death is the structural equivalent of Mercutio's in *Romeo and Juliet*, but the differences are important. Mercutio embodies the comic possibilities available to the characters until the middle of the play. When he dies, these possibilities disappear before our eyes, and a potential comedy becomes a tragedy. Polonius never offered Hamlet any valid escape from his dictated course of revenge, although in his pretensions to wit and literary taste he is a parodic reminder of the wide world of intellectual interests that was open to Hamlet before Denmark closed in around him like a prison. For all that, Polonius's longing for a central role in the action is finally fulfilled: not in the comedy he imagined but in the tragedy that is, not as the lively manipulator but as the last of the play's fathers to be killed and the first to be avenged.

For the family affairs of Polonius, Laertes, and Ophelia are similarly drawn into the tragic orbit from outside. At first, as Francis Fergusson observes, they function as a kind of domestic comedy, related to the main action through contrasts of tone and depth. We see one world in which Hamlet is trying to evade a stepfather he despises and to bear a terrible burden of revenge imposed on him by his own father from beyond the grave. Juxtaposed is a smaller, safer world in which Laertes evades *his* omnipresent father by retreating to Paris and Polonius tries to reach him, not across the abyss of eternity but over the measurable distance between Denmark and France, not with dread commands but with "assays of bias" and "slight sullies."[30] But when Polonius becomes relevant by dying, so to speak, his children follow him into tragic roles, roles which have already been adumbrated by Hamlet himself: distracted mourner and suicide, rebel and avenger.

After Polonius becomes part of the tragedy in death, his comic function is carried on by Osric. Even more remote from the true springs of the action than Polonius, Osric has all his elder's chattering inconsequence and delight in fashionable jargon. Like Polonius he is a born go-between—busy, anxious to please—and like him he knows nothing of the people he goes between. In the middle of Hamlet's solemn discourse of death and providence, soon after he has described his struggle with Claudius as "the pass and fell incensed points / Of mighty opposites," comes young Osric to invite Hamlet to a friendly duel arranged by Claudius. The "young" is itself significant. Usually Shakespeare puts it before a name to avoid confusion with the senior bearer of that name, as in the case of Young Siward in *Macbeth* and occasionally

"young Hamlet" and "young Fortinbras" in this play. There is,
however, no Old Osric in *Hamlet*. Osric is labeled "young," by
Shakespeare in the Folio stage direction and then by the King and
the attendant lord, to emphasize for us his ignorance of what is
going on around him. Here again he recalls Polonius, "that great
baby" (II.ii.377). They are both children among adults, playing
with toys while the world collapses above their heads.

Like Laertes, Fortinbras, and Horatio, Polonius and Osric in
their limitations serve as partial reflectors for the multifaceted
Hamlet. In their case the limitations are so drastic as to effect not
just conventional measurement of greatness but comic parody.
Osric is obviously setting up as the next glass of fashion and mold
of form at the Danish court. His painfully elegant manners and
strained vocabulary are a comic distortion of the Prince's easy
grace and wit. The whole Osric encounter affords one last display
of Hamlet's mastery, as he shifts with disconcerting suddenness
from the blunt to the exaggeratedly foppish: "Put your bonnet to
his right use; 'tis for the head. . . . The concernancy, sir? Why do
we wrap the gentleman in our more rawer breath?" (V.ii.93, 121–
122). Osric has taken over a corollary function of Polonius, as
butt.

Polonius presents a comic version of Hamlet's intellectual side.
A university man himself, he has studied logic and recognizes it
when he sees it.

> *Pol.* Will you walk out of the air, my lord?
> *Ham.* Into my grave?
> *Pol.* Indeed, that's out of the air. [*Aside*] How pregnant some-
>   times his replies are!
>
> (II.ii.205–207)

What he sees, though, is only the superficial connection. The
tragic logic of Hamlet's obsession with death escapes him. Polonius and Hamlet are both amateurs of the theater, but Polonius's
parade of dramatic jargon only sets off Hamlet's true sense of the
play and its power. Hamlet gives detailed instructions to the
players on their art, stages and interprets a play himself, acts a
variety of roles throughout the action as he penetrates the disguises of others. When Polonius played a role it was, inevitably,
that of a victim—Julius Caesar.

The parallel between Polonius and Osric is clearest in the following passages, where Shakespeare uses the same device to make the same comic point:

> *Ham.* Do you see yonder cloud that's almost in the shape of a camel?
> *Pol.* By th' mass, and 'tis like a camel indeed.
> *Ham.* Methinks it is like a weasel.
> *Pol.* It is back'd like a weasel.
> *Ham.* Or like a whale?
> *Pol.* Very like a whale.
>
> (III.ii.366–372)

> *Osr.* I thank your lordship; it is very hot.
> *Ham.* No, believe me, 'tis very cold; the wind is northerly.
> *Osr.* It is indifferent cold, my lord, indeed.
> *Ham.* But yet methinks it is very sultry and hot for my complexion.
> *Osr.* Exceedingly, my lord; it is very sultry, as 'twere—I cannot tell how.
>
> (V.ii.94–100)

It is not just that Polonius and Osric lack firm convictions and defer to the Prince. They have the herd instinct. Their shifts from weasels to whales and cold to hot are exaggerated forms of comic accommodation, the opposite of tragic integrity.

Two of Hamlet's other butts, Rosencrantz and Guildenstern, carry out the herd motif in a different way. It would be pleasingly tidy if these two represented a parody of the soldier Hamlet to parallel Osric's of the courtier and Polonius's of the scholar. Unfortunately, there is no evidence of anything of the kind, except insofar as soldiers may be more politically minded than courtiers (which is doubtful) or scholars. The main comic function of Rosencrantz and Guildenstern is to operate visually and aurally as a pair.

Anyone who teaches *Hamlet* finds that students tend to mix up the two names and talk of Rosenstern and Guildencrantz. There is, in fact, no good reason to keep them straight, for these two answer perfectly the demand of Giraudoux's Président for an assembly-line humanity with interchangeable parts.[31] Their

names are a perfect metrical match, which Shakespeare takes care
to emphasize:

> *King.* Thanks, Rosencrantz and gentle Guildenstern
> *Queen.* Thanks, Guildenstern and gentle Rosencrantz.
>
> (II.ii.33–34)

Also exactly matched, as Harry Levin has noted, are their opening
speeches in this scene: a half line, two full lines, and another half
line for each, in the same rhythm.[32] Often they speak turnabout,
dividing a continued account between them. One never appears
without the other. No one ever speaks of Rosencrantz without
Guildenstern—or, of course, vice versa. The two may differ externally in feature or dress, but inside they are indistinguishable,
perversions of those identical twins in which comedy delights.
Bergson's notion of comedy as human beings submerging their
individuality in mechanical repetition helps us see the comic foil
effect of their perpetual twoness as they flank Hamlet, revealing
his loneliness as well as his greatness. In Rosencrantz and Guildenstern it becomes apparent that there is a sinister side to the
submergence of the individual which comedy ratifies by its drive
toward pairing and social harmony, as there is a sinister side to
many of the other comic assumptions. Nonpersons, they reject
personal responsibility.[33] If they were accused of betraying their
friend, their answer might be that of another notable pair in
Shakespearean tragedy, the tribunes in *Coriolanus:* "We do it not
alone."[34] Behind one there is always the other, and behind both
there is society at large, the state.

For these good citizens Rosencrantz and Guildenstern, a dilemma like Hamlet's is impossible. The state must be served. And
to serve the state is to serve the King, "that spirit upon whose
weal depends and rests / The lives of many" (III.iii.14–15). Not for
them the torments of plural consciousness, the fear of subjective
distortion. If the King's weal is the ultimate good, then to do right
they have only to carry out the King's wishes.

Unaware of any questions that cannot be dealt with in political
terms, Rosencrantz and Guildenstern naturally misinterpret
Hamlet's problem as frustrated ambition. Denmark feels too narrow to him, hints Rosencrantz, because Claudius and not Hamlet
is its king.[35] Later, when they ask him directly what is wrong and

Hamlet replies, "Sir, I lack advancement," there is no question in Rosencrantz's mind how he should interpret this general remark. "How can that be, when you have the voice of the King himself for your succession in Denmark?" (III.ii.331–333). But the political interpretation defines only the narrow perceptions of Rosencrantz and Guildenstern, not the heart of Hamlet's mystery. Like Polonius they guess wrong, and like Polonius they suffer for it. The death (one singular noun will do for both) of these two does not incorporate them into the tragedy in the way that Polonius's did, but it has its own irony. Their respect for the royal seal, the emblem of majesty, causes them to deliver their own death warrant to England. Obedient ciphers to the end, they "go to 't," casualties in a war they did not understand.

Unconscious of the issues at stake, relentlessly ordinary in the face of the extraordinary, these four (three?) characters—Polonius, Osric, Rosencrantz and Guildenstern—function somewhat as the porter does in *Macbeth* or the clown in *Antony* and *Cleopatra*, to throw into relief the tragic shape of events and to measure the protagonist's stature. But they are also a part of the action, interwoven in it as the one-appearance porter and clown are not, because the generic anomalies they call into play comment directly on the nature of Hamlet's tragedy. As misinterpreters they make us aware, as Hamlet himself is painfully aware, that men see only what they can and want to see, not necessarily what is there. Yet it is also true that, for all their limitations and ultimate futility, the viewpoints these characters introduce into the play remind us that there are "worlds elsewhere," alternative ways of life governed by premises other than the confining one of revenge. That is, they illuminate both sides of this unusual tragic hero, who is both eiron and alazon. Where the usual movement of tragedy is constriction, narrowing into a no-alternative course, it is exactly Hamlet's tragic situation that he must resist such constriction and the resistance renders him impotent. By having Polonius and the others act out their comic-social preoccupations, Shakespeare creates a certain sense of various possibility—especially when Hamlet takes up the diversions these people offer him and plays with them on their own terms. At the same time, the element of parody and the gulf between any of these perspectives and what we would wish for Hamlet denies validity to them as real possibilities. Shakespeare thus presents a play world that is at once claustrophobic and expansive, to keep us attuned to Hamlet's own division between the subjective thrust toward violent action (alazon) and the objective awareness of more than one reality (eiron).

The physical play world reinforces this effect of variety without real alternatives. The stage action never leaves Denmark, almost never leaves Elsinore, so that the audience can share Hamlet's sense of being closed in. Yet we are also made conscious of the wide arena that is available to other young men, if not to Hamlet. The disparate, unfocused journeys in the play's background—Fortinbras threatening from Norway, then traveling to Poland and finally to Elsinore; Horatio coming from Wittenberg; Laertes going off to Paris—all these may be untidy, as Goethe's Wilhelm Meister complained,[36] but it is a functional untidiness. Those trips here and there keep us aware that mobility and adventure are the norm for young men in *Hamlet*. Only Hamlet himself, the most receptive to new possibilities, must stay cooped up in his private prison. Getting away is the first action he attempts in the play. But Claudius will not let him escape to Wittenberg, and the journey planned for him later is to his death in England.

That never-completed trip turns out to be fated, for it does eventually lead to his death. But it is also freeing, for when he returns, he has got beyond the old dilemma of the eiron. New experience—the pirate adventure and the discovery and reversal of the death warrant—brings new knowledge, and this time the knowledge is not crippling but enabling. The offstage voyage is the setting for this change, allows it through the chances of the sea, in a way even *means* it, as the unsettling forests of Shakespeare's romantic comedies came to signify new directions for their protagonists.

But in the first part of the play Hamlet's multiple awareness brings him only anguish at his constriction and unsureness about his cause. His torment illuminates that element in the tragic described by Karl Jaspers: "Man's mind fails and breaks down in the very wealth of its potentialities."[37] Yet somewhere behind Hamlet's inaction is the sense, also adumbrated by Jaspers, that *any* act cuts off possibilities and denies the perfection sought for.

This is the dark side of the eiron principle and the rejection of singleness, the values of romantic comedy. In *Hamlet* they are still values, but they are placed in mortal conflict with the imperatives of filial duty, moral judgment, even self-definition. To choose and actualize only one potential is to deny wholeness. But not to choose and actualize threatens sanity itself.

Johnson assures us that among his contemporaries "the pretended madness of Hamlet causes much mirth."[38] Is it only because modern productions usually play down the zany side of Hamlet's antic disposition that our laughter in the "mad" scenes is tinged with unease? That straightforward mirth of the eighteenth century requires that the audience be certain that Hamlet's madness *is* entirely pretended; but this certainty, like so many others, the play denies us. Hamlet is a trapped eiron. Insofar as the antic disposition is a role he can consciously put on and off, it offers an escape of sorts from the constrictions that press in so heavily on him. Like the comic disguise, it allows a certain freedom—in this case the freedom of the fool who cannot be held accountable for his jibes at the mighty.[39] We should remember, though, that in comedy a disguise "put on" like a costume often goes beyond simple deception to call up in the disguiser an alternate identity. When Rosalind poses as a page, she does more than conceal her sex. She becomes a new creature, Rosalind-Ganymede. On several occasions Hamlet's mad pose similarly seems to acquire a life of its own, pushing him into extravagant railing irrelevant to his auditor, as in his tirade to Ophelia against "you" painted, lisping wantons (III.i.142–145), or into obsessive repetitions: "You cannot, sir, take from me anything that I will more willingly part withal—except my life, except my life, except my life" (II.ii.214–216). But madness cannot fill out and complete a personality the way Ganymede completes Rosalind. Unworkable, through its lack of structure, as an alternate self, the antic disposition instead points to the ultimate in conflicting, unresolved possibilities. "Man's mind breaks down . . . ."

The graveyard scene requires separate treatment. It uses comedy in a quite distinctive way, as an element within the tragic vision rather than as a contrasting ethos or a value to be turned inside out. As its impact is best approached through dramatic structure, we must at this point step back to survey the dynamics that lead up to the graveside encounter between Hamlet and the nameless clown. Of the many ways that one can look at structure in *Hamlet*, three are useful here: as fluctuation, as deflection, and as the quest for pattern.

Fluctuation dominates the early acts, with Hamlet pulled back and forth between what I have called his Horatio side and his Laertes side. He is torn in the struggle between "conscience," in the sense of consciousness, and the inner compulsions of disgust, hatred, and wounded honor. At times he allies himself with conscience, looking before and after, wishing to see his act whole, wishing to be sure. At other times reason and doubt are submerged in the need for passionate action. We have seen in the "O, what a rogue" soliloquy not only the two contrary states but the actual movement from one to the other, from bloodthirsty images of Claudius fatting the kites to "grounds more relative than this." The pattern has in fact begun much earlier, as soon as the Ghost has laid his command on Hamlet. I have already suggested that *Hamlet* departs from the usual tragic pattern of alternatives denied and possibilities narrowed into a single inevitable course, that here the tragic point is the hero's inability to achieve such narrowing even though he wants to and swears to. The desire is clear in his first reponse to the Ghost: "Haste me to know 't, that I, with wings as swift / As meditation or the thoughts of love, / May sweep to my revenge" (I.v.29–31). What until now have been his chief preoccupations—philosophical reflection and courtship—he immediately reduces to metaphors for his new devotion. Later he vows to forget everything but the Ghost's command (97–104). Yet immediately afterward this committed hero is suddenly diverging into mad comedy, "wild and whirling words," and quite literally running away from the omnipresent Ghost. The whole cellarage business is very slenderly motivated in terms of plot. There needs no ghost come from the grave to persuade Horatio and Marcellus to swear secrecy. Rather, the Ghost is reintroduced so that we may see Hamlet seeking to escape the commitment he has just made, physically backing off from the spirit to whom he has made it, and trying with comic nicknames to put distance between himself and that "hic et ubique" presence.

Fluctuation continues through Act II and the first part of Act III, the poles getting stronger and the struggle more intense. The

Mousetrap scene stretches Hamlet's inner tension almost to the breaking point: it seals his emotional conviction of Claudius's guilt while denying him the desired objective confirmation of that guilt. The scene points to crisis in other ways. Hamlet and Claudius confront each other directly for the first time since I.ii, and from this ominous start tension rises as the Gonzago action comes closer and closer to the actual murder and Hamlet's commentary reveals his own mounting excitement. The dramatic peak, Claudius's disordered exit, is striking but ambiguous. We expect something more definitive structurally, and we get it in the double climax that follows: Hamlet's two meetings, an unplanned one with the King and a planned one with the Queen.

In the prayer scene Hamlet acts out his Horatio side in its fullest implications. Presented by accident with the chance for unimpeded, perhaps even unperilous revenge, Hamlet nevertheless rejects the act because he wants to see and control all its ramifications and consequences, even into the next world. Looking before and after, he recalls his father's unsanctified death, considers the King at his prayers, calculates the future, and concludes that a murderer who may be in a state of grace is not adequate payment for a good man condemned to purgatory for his unexpiated sins. And so he takes no action. "Conscience" is triumphant—not in the ethical sense, certainly, for Hamlet's desire to make sure of Claudius's damnation is appallingly savage— but in the sense of superawareness, of thinking too precisely on the event.

Perhaps because of what has just happened, or has not happened, Hamlet soon acts all too quickly. Excitedly rebuking his mother, he hears a noise behind the arras, strikes without making sure ("Is it the King?")—and kills the wrong man. Rashness in the style of Laertes and Fortinbras has followed Horatian hesitation, and neither has worked. Narrowing to one possibility for action or nonaction has been no more effective than trying to cope with all possibilities.[40] Polonius is dead and Claudius is not. These two facts will determine the play's tragic conclusion.

After these climactic scenes the fluctuation pattern ceases to dominate, although Hamlet's "How all occasions" soliloquy in IV.iv looks back at it in the manner of a musical reprise. Hamlet himself is offstage for much of Act IV, and when he returns in

Act V, the inner conflict is no longer evident. To understand its disappearance we must turn to the other aspects of structure that I have called deflection and the quest for pattern. The climactic scenes just examined provide a useful focus for these two related movements. Both event and nonevent will ultimately be decisive, the killing of Polonius and the not-killing of Claudius, but at the time they seem meaningless. Hamlet's revenge against his mighty opposite is mistakenly, absurdly deflected onto the irrelevant Polonius. There is in fact an order into which these things fit, but between happening and meaning intervenes the large-scale deflection of Act IV. The whole thrust of the first three acts, Hamlet's dilemma and the resulting fluctuations, is dropped; he himself is apparently deflected from his purpose by being ordered off to England; and he physically leaves the action after scene iv. For the rest of the act, our attention is preempted by the pathos of Ophelia, the rebellion of Laertes, the new schemes of Claudius. Of Hamlet we learn only that he is returning, after some strange experiences. What they have to do with his earlier state we must wait for Act V to reveal.

Various critics have in one way or another singled out deflection as a *theme* of the play and have shown how the general course of the action is illuminated by such statements as Ophelia's "Lord, we know what we are, but know not what we may be" (IV.v.41–42), Claudius's reflections on goodness dying in its own too-much (IV.vii.114–118), and most of all the Player King's conclusion:

> But, orderly to end where I begun,
> Our wills and fates do so contrary run
> That our devices still are overthrown;
> Our thoughts are ours, their ends none of our own.
>   (III.ii.205–208)

What has not been emphasized is how thoroughly the structure of *Hamlet* embodies this notion of deflection: something always intervenes between purpose and act, expectation and result.

"Deflection" in this sense may describe the same process that I have called "fluctuation," in this case thought of in terms of line and deviation rather than of pendulum swings back and forth. It also applies to the series of attempted escapes that begins with Hamlet's request to leave Elsinore for Wittenberg and continues through his consideration of suicide, his wild and whirling words in the cellarage scene, and the antic disposition itself. From one point of view, indeed, the whole play is a form of deflection, between the imposition of the revenge task in I.v and its final accomplishment in V.ii. Deflection is also the key to the ordering of parts, notably in II.ii and III.i. In the First Quarto memorial reconstruction, the order of events is as follows:

1. Polonius announces his theory that Hamlet is mad for love; he and Claudius plan to test the theory by eavesdropping on an encounter between Hamlet and Ophelia.
2. Hamlet enters and speaks his "To be or not to be" soliloquy; the Ophelia encounter follows.
3. Rosencrantz and Guildenstern seek the cause of Hamlet's madness.
4. The players arrive, one performs the Pyrrhus speech, and Hamlet plans the Mousetrap.
5. Rosencrantz and Guildenstern report their failure but announce that Hamlet wants a play performed.
6. The play is performed.

This is a simpler ordering than that of the Second Quarto and the Folio, and a more "natural" one: plots are conceived and then carried out without delay. This is the way one might mistake the sequence of events in memory, or simplify it for provincial performance.[41] In the authoritative texts, however, some break *always* comes between plan and execution. Claudius's first plot to spy out Hamlet's mystery, which will employ Rosencrantz and Guildenstern, is followed by a second plot based on Polonius's theory of frustrated love, which will involve the "loosing" of Ophelia. Then the first plan is enacted, after which the players come on and Hamlet initiates a plan of his own. Before we see it executed, Claudius's second plot is put into action and found unsatisfactory ("Love! His affections do not that way tend"), and he proposes yet another one, dispatching Hamlet to England. Only then is Hamlet's own plot fulfilled in the Mousetrap scene. Always there is that intervention, like Eliot's "Shadow" that falls "between the idea / And the reality / Between the motion / And the Act."[42]

The unexpected break between cause and result is akin to the evitability of comedy. But in this case as with multiple truths and the superiority of the eiron, the comic notion serves tragic ends. Outside the safely bounded comic universe, discontinuous structure is not so much freeing as unsettling. It suggests a kind of cosmic irrelevance that interferes with expected patterns. Each plan in this sequence does work out, to be sure, but never very definitively. Instead, one scheme gives way to another, and the sense of displacement persists. In his chapter on *Hamlet* in *Shakespeare and the Energies of Drama*, Michael Goldman has shown several ways in which "we are regularly invited to complete an action—to consider what it means, to anticipate where it may lead—only to have our response blocked, distracted, or diverted, compromised in some way."[43] Booth remarks that all through the play "the audience gets information or sees action it once wanted only after a new interest has superseded the old."[44] But Booth, unlike Goldman, sees even in the ending of *Hamlet* "an impossible coherence of truths that are both undeniably incompatible and undeniably coexistent."[45] Does this in fact match our experience at the end of *Hamlet*? In my view Shakespeare is being more directive than Booth will allow, first creating in the audience a need to find purpose and pattern in events and then satisfying that need in the play's final phase.

We arrive thus at my third structural approach to the comic encounter of Hamlet and the gravedigger in Act V. Although the formula "quest for a pattern" mainly describes the way an audience experiences the action of *Hamlet*, that quest also enters into the action itself. Various interpreting characters, as I have noted, shape the events they see to fit their own subjective reality. Meanwhile Hamlet tries to find the stance that will permit him, like the magician-manipulators of comedy, to set fully to rights his out-of-joint time. The interpretations of Polonius and the others are tried and found wanting. Hamlet himself in larger style tries both the Horatian withholder from action and the Laertean rash doer, only to find both inadequate. He does indeed set up a show in the manipulator tradition, but without the traditional results. The Mousetrap fails to provide the public clarification for which it was designed. Claudius, no mean manipulator himself, refuses the role of pawn in that he does not let loose his occulted guilt on cue, "in one speech." Nor does Claudius in the following scene conform any better to Hamlet's master-pattern, which requires that revenge be taken when the usurper is found in some characteristic grossness, not in prayer. And the next scene finds Polonius, yet another would-be manipulator, where Claudius ought to be. Claudius in fact is back in the manipulator-position, ordering an unfree Hamlet on a journey to England apparently irrelevant to any princely pattern of revenge. The order Hamlet tries to impose thus fails, short-circuited by rival craft and the waywardness of events.

When he returns from the abortive journey to England, his goal is no longer governing control. What he seeks now, and finds, is readiness as an agent, as part of a pattern he may perceive but did not create: "If it be now, 'tis not to come; if it be not to come, it will be now; if it be not now, yet it will come—the readiness is all" (V.ii.212–215). The returned prince is changed, as many critics have observed. While the nature of the change is subject for debate, most see in him a new calmness, an acceptance of life and death. Certainly there is no further expression of the struggle I have seen as informing the early part of the play, between emotional conviction and the need for external validation. Even when Hamlet seems to appeal once more for Horatio's confirmation ("Does it not, think thee, stand me now upon . . . / . . . is't not perfect conscience / To quit him with this arm?"), the question is really rhetorical. Hamlet is not asking any more; he is telling.[46]

What has happened to Hamlet at sea? By a chance indiscretion he discovered that Rosencrantz and Guildenstern carried a warrant for his execution. He responded by substituting a new order commanding the death of his former friends instead, and by another chance he had with him his father's signet to imprint the royal seal. The next day chance intervened again when pirates attacked the ship. Hamlet led the defense, was taken prisoner, found his new captors more accommodating than the old, and returned to Denmark. That is, to this man who felt impelled to impose significant moral order on his own time but was unable to manipulate people and events to his own pattern, comes a series of events which he has not initiated but which displays the kind of clarity and sureness of effect he had lacked before. His friends have betrayed him, and so he is given the opportunity to serve them in the same way. His duel with Claudius is unfinished, and so circumstances cut off his journey to England and bring him back to Denmark. In telling his tale, Hamlet keeps interpreting it in terms of providential order: "Our indiscretion sometime serves us well, / When our deep plots do pall . . . / There's a divinity that shapes our ends"; "even in that was heaven ordinant" (V.ii.8–10, 48). It is this perception of what *has* happened that decides his approach to what *will*. In spite of his "gaingiving" about the projected duel, he defies augury and trusts in the special providence that governs even the fall of the sparrow (V.ii.210–211). He has found an objective truth outside himself, a pattern not subject to his distortion, with which the subjective element cooperates, knowingly or not. This order of things has saved his life and brought him home; he trusts it to bring about the final movement of his destiny.

The terms in which Hamlet describes this order have Christian resonance—divinity, heaven, the fall of a sparrow—but I doubt that they are meant to evoke Christian values full force. Such an emphasis would completely skew our view of Hamlet's duty of revenge, which the play never really questions.[47] Shakespeare used these Christian references, I suspect, because in their familiarity they would most easily call up for his audience the general sense of a plan in human existence. Those who see only a "desperate stoicism" in Hamlet's words before the duel miss this all-important conviction of purpose and pattern. The phrase belongs to Donald Stauffer, who concludes: "Augury is defied, destiny is bitterly acknowledged, and a passive readiness is all."[48] But in the context of Hamlet's positive affirmations that heaven is ordinant and divinity shapes our ends, why should his acknowledgment be bitter? And his readiness is passive only in that he will respond to opportunity rather than create it—respond actively, as he has already done with Rosencrantz and Guildenstern and the pirates.

Nevertheless, before Hamlet tells us that the universe, however mysterious, is not without plan, we have the graveyard scene suggesting something quite different. The reader may think I have taken much too long to arrive at it, but I hope that as Shakespeare's deflections of plot ultimately justify their place in the play's dynamic, so my own windlasses and assays will allow a fuller interpretation of this strange venture into radical comedy.

The graveyard scene is the last and most striking of the play's displacements. As in the earlier movement of plot and counterplot, the order of scenes and their revelations is significant here. In IV.vi, Hamlet's return is signaled by a letter to Horatio which, while it alludes to the events that brought about his new vision, says nothing of what that vision is. He raises expectations with "I have words to speak in thine ear . . . too light for the bore of the matter" (IV.vi.21–23). The words, however, are not spoken until V.ii. In between, the last scene of Act IV keeps Hamlet's unexplained return in our minds, with more hints in his letter to Claudius of revelations to come; but the dramatic emphasis passes back to Claudius himself as he plans his most deadly plot against Hamlet. It seems like a reprise of the structural pattern of Acts II and III. We would expect, when Hamlet finally does appear, to find him plotting in his turn, or in any case making the great disclosures prepared for by his letters. Instead we get a pair of clowns digging a grave and Hamlet's long conversation with one of them, which is quite apart from his supposed preoccupations. There is a link, indeed, for the grave is Ophelia's; but Hamlet does not know it.

Structurally, though not tonally, the graveyard scene is the counterpart of Hamlet's "To be or not to be" soliloquy. There, too, against expectation, we step aside from the turmoil of plot and counterplot into a kind of reflective middle distance, where the hero speculates in general terms on the human condition. Before that entrance in III.i, Hamlet has been asking questions about his immediate problem—Am I a coward? Is the Ghost really a devil?—but now the questioning extends to everything: Why live? Why not die? The speech gives no real answer. Even the negative one Hamlet had advanced in his first soliloquy, God's prohibition of self-slaughter, fades into uncertainty here. Is there perhaps a divine tribunal that rewards and punishes, and thus makes sense out of life's grinding indignities and inequities? Hamlet's doubt comes through in his phrasing: *"perchance* to dream," *"something* after death." The shadowy sanction against suicide, even if it exists, imparts no positive meaning to the mortal coil. It simply paralyzes men in the action of shuffling it off. The soliloquy breaks off on a note indeterminate and ironic, as Hamlet hails Ophelia and her "orisons," which we know are not real prayers but window dressing for spying. The questions hang unresolved. What if there is no justice in the undiscovered country, after all? What if there is no undiscovered country? What if the fear of it exists only to prevent us from the one negatively significant act of ending life? In such a void, where is the validity of revenge or of anything else?

For a few moments Hamlet's anxiety is that of the modern existentialist, seeking a direction in life and finding only fear of the unknown and hints of absurdity. Caught up again in the climactic action of Act III, he moves into other moods, but the note struck here anticipates the graveyard meditations. The substance of those meditations is also anticipated, verbally at least, by Hamlet's preoccupation with Polonius's corpse.

> *Ham.* A certain convocation of politic worms are e'en at him. Your worm is your only emperor for diet: we fat all creatures else to fat us, and we fat ourselves for maggots; your fat king and your lean beggar is but variable service—two dishes, but to one table. That's the end.
> *King.* Alas, alas!
> *Ham.* A man may fish with the worm that hath eat of a king, and eat of the fish that hath fed of that worm.
> *King.* What dost thou mean by this?
> *Ham.* Nothing but to show you how a king may go a progress through the guts of a beggar.
>
> (IV.iii.20–31)

At this point, Hamlet's image of worms reducing royalty to the level of beggary is mainly a thrust at Claudius, the bloat king. Yet death works in the same way on the good as on the guilty, on princes as well as on kings. Among the graves, accepting the cheerful impersonality of the gravedigger, Hamlet will have to include himself and all men in the vision of universal decay.

What we have not been prepared for is the peculiar tone of the graveyard scene, the spirit of *play* that infuses its contemplation of death. The two gravediggers in their discussion of Ophelia's doubtful death strike a note of comic questioning that does not change with the entrance of the tragic hero. The clown who remains to gossip with the incognito Prince is not the usual "other voice" of tragedy introduced to challenge but ultimately ratify the heroic posture. Here it is rather the hero who seems to be ratifying the clown's view of things. Mack notes that the case the gravedigger makes for the "bread and cheese" of common life is not overborne by Hamlet.[49] We are, I think, invited to go further than this, to feel a whole new impact of the comic in a serious context as it bores to the heart of the tragic vision and questions the very notion of the heroic, irreplaceable self. Their talk is not of common life but of common death, which comes not only to the ordinary butts of satire like politicians and fine ladies but to Alexander and Caesar. It is all one to the clown and to the figure that looms behind him, Death the Leveler casting down indifferently the skull of a jester and the dust of an emperor. In this setting human choice seems no more than a bad joke. If Caesar ends up patching a wall, why strive to be Caesar? He is just as dead as Yorick. The equation of fool and world conqueror pushes us to the limits of comic relativism. No person or thing has any more value than any other. Points of honor have no more meaning than the niceties of the law which are here reduced to absurdity in the clowns' discussion of suicide. Ophelia is dead, whether "se offendendo" or not. Death is the only reality here. In the "To be or not to be" soliloquy it was at least a significant reality, at once fearsome and desirable. Now the comic perspective calls even that significance into question. Death just comes, whether you suffer nobly or take arms against your troubles; it is the end of life that makes every life equally absurd.

In that earlier soliloquy Hamlet asked his own questions about life's meaning or lack of it. Here he becomes part of the question put to the audience, which is posed through his own musings and, most tellingly, by the persistent use of comedy's alien perspective in this place of death. It is not just the jokes and incongruities, though these are plentiful: Alexander stops up a beer barrel, Hamlet's madness will not be noticed in England where everyone is as mad as he. It is Hamlet's satiric wit playing freely with the futile activities of politicians and lawyers, piling up puns and "quillets" in a burst of linguistic vitality, and the clown's cheerful literalism: "A tanner will last you nine year" (163). The clown has the habit of his comic brotherhood of reducing everything, including death, to the physical. The question for him is not whether the individual self survives death but how long the bodily remains will last in the earth. Nor do the great events of Claudius's Denmark take up much space on this man's broad horizon. He, after all, looks all the way back to Adam, the first gentleman, and forward to the end of the world, when his graves will open. Specifically, he recalls the day Hamlet was born, and almost in the next breath prophesies that Hamlet's dead body will not last in the ground more than eight or nine years. Perhaps the references to Adam and Doomsday bring in some notion of a great sequence in the universe, but the dominant sense is just that men have been getting born and dying through countless ages and will go on doing so. This is the matter-of-fact comic voice: there will always be more bodies to bury. Shakespeare has in earlier plays pictured Death as an "antic," laughing heroes and kings to scorn.[50] Yet even this image, which suggests malice directed at a specific individual ("scoffing *his* state and grinning at *his* pomp" in the imagination of Richard II), is a less radical threat to the irreplaceable "I" of tragedy than the gravedigger's good-humored impartiality. He and his milieu make a direct address to the tragic fact of death, but an address that emphasizes its *commonness* rather than the quenching of a unique spirit. Hamlet's life is a mere "one" in a long panorama. The whole tendency of the play, in which the other comic characters have participated, has been to set Hamlet off from and above the mass of common humanity. Now, for a time, that movement is reversed.

It is in terms of this comic-absurd challenge to heroic individuality that we should see the actions that conclude this scene. As in III.i, the entrance of Ophelia returns Hamlet from his meditative distance. Reduced from roselike beauty to rotting flesh, she might well call forth some wry speculation in the vein of "imperious Caesar." Instead, Hamlet hurls himself into a series of self-affirmations.

> This is I,
> Hamlet the Dane
> . . . .
> Why, I will fight with him upon this theme
> Until my eyelids will no longer wag.
> . . . .
> I lov'd Ophelia: forty thousand brothers
> Could not, with all their quantity of love,
> Make up my sum. . . .
> . . . .
> I lov'd you ever.

> (V.i.251–284)

In all this, as in his dramatic leap to (or into) the grave, there is a strong element of hyperbole. The contest of grief with Laertes feels overdone: Hamlet himself says, "I'll rant as well as thou." But this extra assertive force is dramatically justified if Hamlet is defying not just Laertes but the whole foregoing perception of a senseless universe. Against that threat and his own acquiescence in it, his affirmations and commitments have a special dimension of the heroic, suggesting a willed self-creation out of nothingness rather than a simple return to tragic hyperbole. It is an important effect to grasp, especially for those readers and spectators who find the Hamlet of the next scene diminished by his willingness to give up the initiative, to be a mere pawn and not the master-manipulator. The unsupported, self-engendered heroism here should condition our reaction to the state Hamlet achieves at the last and prevent us from seeing in it no more than passive fatalism.

It is important that we are made to confront absurdity here only to learn in the next scene that Hamlet has in fact found a meaning and pattern in human existence. Why have Hamlet accede to the gravedigger rather than counter him with new-found apprehensions of providential plan? Why have the grave-yard conversation at all, troubling the audience with nihilistic intimations when the problem has "already" been solved for the hero? The point, I think, is that we do not know about that "already" until afterwards, in retrospect. Shakespeare exploits this gap between logical time and stage time, between happening and revelation, to pursue his theme of multiple possibility right to the edge of the void. In terms of Hamlet's own consciousness, we can see in retrospect that the ordering of scenes—IV.vi and vii and V.ii surrounding V.i on either side—has contained uncertainty in certainty. But the audience is made to apprehend in time, to experience the extremest need for pattern by contemplating the complete absence of it, and thus to find special satisfaction in Hamlet's self-definition and his subsequent assertions of the divinity that shapes our ends.

Hamlet's words, of course, are not enough by themselves to create a sense of pattern. The whole ending does that. By the time Fortinbras arrives, the stage is littered with bodies, yet the deaths are handled so as to suggest order rather than senseless carnage. Each seems to define the life it ends in some significant way. Sometimes the significance is stated for us, as in Laertes' "I am justly kill'd with mine own treachery" (V.ii.299). Laertes also comments on Claudius after Hamlet has returned both poisons, of foil and of cup, back to the source of all poison: "He is justly serv'd" (319). There is a richer, though more indirect comment in Hamlet's furious pun on "union."

> Here, thou incestuous, murd'rous, damned Dane,
> Drink off this potion. Is thy union here?
> Follow my mother.
>
> (317–319)

The union, as Bradley pointed out, is at once the rich pearl that Claudius said he was throwing into the cup, the poison that he did throw, and the incestuous marriage "which must not be broken by his remaining alive now that his partner is dead."[51] It thus subsumes everything Claudius could not let go ("my crown, mine own ambition, and my queen"), now turned to poison and choking him to death. It has already killed Gertrude. But while this death from the same cup alludes to her guilty union with Claudius, it also defines Gertrude's peculiar tragic position, caught between love for her husband and love for her son: she drinks in defiance of Claudius, to honor Hamlet.

Seen from this vantage point, the earlier deaths also show a defining fitness. Polonius mistook and was mistaken. The destruction of Rosencrantz and Guildenstern "[did] by their own insinuation grow" (V.ii.59). All three were still acting out their partial perspectives in death, Polonius caught in the classic comic role of eavesdropper and Rosencrantz and Guildenstern respecting the royal seal. Even poor Ophelia finds an appropriate death in pliant water, weighed down by the garments of convention.[52]

Hamlet's own life, as it has unfolded before us in this hero-centered play, is far too complex to receive any satisfying definition in his death. Certainly it is fitting that Claudius should be the prime mover and Laertes the instrument, that Hamlet's end should stem both from the "original sin" of the play, the murder of King Hamlet, and from his own disastrous plunge into action, the murder of Polonius. It accords with our dual perception of Hamlet as one who both suffers evil and causes it.[53] Beyond this, Shakespeare wisely attempts no further explanation. Instead of the summings-up that accompany the other deaths, we have only hints at insights never spoken: "Had I but time, as this fell sergeant Death / Is strict in his arrest, O, I could tell you— / But let it be. . . . / . . . the rest is silence."

Hamlet, the play as well as the hero, has been asking persistently, "What is real?" Act V responds to the question in two ways: it brings Claudius's villainy into the open, and it adumbrates some order in human affairs. The double response is more effective than a single one—the exposure of Claudius—which would simply conduct Hamlet to his delayed revenge without illuminating the larger effects of the King's crime. Shakespeare has not, of course, solved the mystery of existence in *Hamlet*. Dramatic rather than philosophical means achieve the sense of pattern at the play's end, and its truth is one of emotions, not metaphysics.[54] It must be emphasized again that the providence Hamlet acknowledges has little to do with nicely adjusted rewards and punishments. The deaths of the major figures link character and deed to final end, but they are not weighted according to moral culpability. Ophelia suffers as much as Claudius. If we feel a principle of poetic justice operating in them, it is with a very heavy accent on *poetic*.

Comedy in *Hamlet* is at once more obvious and more deeply embedded than in *Romeo and Juliet* and *Othello*. Once again, as in *Romeo*, our awareness of a tragic situation is sharpened by the presence of characters who do not understand it. Polonius and Osric, all cheerful bustle, are good examples of what I have called the principle of irrelevance. They direct us to dark and depth by their bright, ordinary unawareness. So, in a lesser way, do Rosencrantz and Guildenstern, by their demonstration of the complete political creature. All of these characters present some version of the antitragic view, only to be discredited. Like other idealized modes, tragedy is the more compelling if it can incorporate and somehow disarm emotions and attitudes outside its realm rather than ignore them completely. In *Romeo* the Nurse's earthy practicality and Mercutio's mockery express two perspectives antithetical to the absolutes of love, but the Nurse is undercut through exaggeration and Mercutio is silenced. Emilia in *Othello* objectifies our potential for cynicism but then discredits it by her death, in which she chooses truth and loyalty over the pragmatic self-interest she once defended. With Polonius and Osric, Rosencrantz and Guildenstern, the point is made not so much through death, though three of the four do die, as through their whole stage existence: little, limited, constantly bested by the hero, they at once present and denigrate a possible critique of Hamlet's hyperawareness.

Below this level, Shakespeare projects a special kind of tragic disillusion in *Hamlet* by bringing into play an extraordinary amount of comic machinery only to subvert it. In *Romeo* the borrowings from comedy included a manipulator, the kind of friar-healer who had traditionally acted as an agent of comedy's natural law and had saved the situation by his cleverness and magic skill. Friar Laurence failed, caught in the tragic acceleration of time, but we were not invited to blame him or to question his assumption of control. In *Hamlet*, however, the comic devices of manipulation—the deceptions, masks, espials, diversions, plots, and play-acting of Hamlet himself and of Claudius and Polonius— beg basic questions about human power and benevolence. All three characters fail as manipulators because they are *not* above human passion and blindness and because, often concealed behind the apparently erratic relation between purpose and result, a slow process is working out the poison of Denmark according to its own inexorable rules. However satisfying in some ways is Hamlet's final submission to the dimly perceived larger order, there is nonetheless an accompanying sense of human impotence. *Hamlet* is like Shakespeare's other plays of this period (the early years of the new century) in its pessimism about man's ability to alter events by his mind and will. It is not simply a matter of genre. *All's Well* and *Measure for Measure* have the traditional happy endings of comedy, but their erring, unattractive heroes have to be dragged into grace against their wills, and the successful manipulating of Helena and Duke Vincentio carries strong overtones of miracle and power beyond the human. When left to their purely human devices, as in *Troilus and Cressida*, men achieve only their own devaluation and destruction. It is this disheartening vision that links the so-called problem plays, I think; and it is a vision that affects *Hamlet* and *Othello* as well, for all the magnetic force of their central figures. *Othello* offers the stronger countering affirmation, but the transmutation of the manipulator-figure into Iago is a tragic comment on the disjunction of goodness and power.

In Iago the awareness of the eiron, his traditional source of power in the comedies, is put in the service of destruction; in *Hamlet* that awareness itself threatens self-destruction. Multiple being, after all, is very close to nonbeing. Well before Shakespeare, in Erasmus's masterpiece of multiple vision, Folly had joked that wisdom's full awareness would get in the way of any action at all—except suicide.[55] In our own time, Jaspers has seen in Folly's paradox the essence of Hamlet's tragedy.

> All life-force stems from blindness. It grows from imagined knowledge, in myth taken for faith, and in the substitute myths; in unquestioning acceptance, and in mind-narrowing untruths. Within the human predicament the quest for truth presents an impossible task.
>
> If totally manifest, truth paralyzes.... Reflective thought—rational consciousness—enfeebles man, unless the unbroken drive of a personality gathers even more strength in the clear light of knowledge. But such a drive consumes itself without concrete fulfillment, leaving an impression of greatness superhuman—not inhuman—in its failure.[56]

The uncommitted life is no life, for human beings define, even create themselves by choice; yet any choice represents the closing off of other alternatives, an inevitable narrowing as multiple possibility gives way to a single commitment. This tragic fact emerges in almost every aspect of *Hamlet*: the play's unusual variety that Johnson noted, Hamlet's brilliantly versatile address to the world, his peculiar anguish under the Ghost's command, his attempted escapes, the balancing of Horatio against Laertes and Fortinbras, the paired, opposing climaxes of Act III, the revenge motive itself. Any proposed action may be seen as tragic in that it cuts off other possibilities and reduces multiple selves into one, yet a revenge plot offers a specially dramatic example. The significant action is difficult and dangerous, a matter solely of individual initiative apart from the normal supports of law and society, and it is also imperative, dictated by the closest human tie: "If thou didst ever thy dear father love. . . ."[57]

So comprehensive is Hamlet's consciousness of plural meanings that it finally takes in even the absence of meaning. In the graveyard scene comedy approaches the tragic hero in a radical new way, not as contrast to his fate or material for his diversion but as a potential *part* of his fate, joining him at least hypothetically to his own butts Polonius, Rosencrantz and Guildenstern, as the object of a cosmic joke. In the gravediggers' matter-of-fact, undifferentiating view no individual is irreplaceable, no commitment more significant than any other. Horatio acts the foil role for the last time when he fails to see the full joke of Alexander stopping a beer-barrel: " 'Twere to consider too curiously to consider so." It is Hamlet's peculiar heroism that he can see the joke very clearly indeed and still in the face of absurdity assert the meaning of his own life, as lover, friend, son of the royal line. In the revelations about the voyage to England that follow the graveyard scene, we may feel that Hamlet has not simply been given his intuition of providential pattern, he has earned it.

Nevertheless, that intuition does follow and thus enclose safely the brief vision of absurdity in *Hamlet*. When Shakespeare next mingled comic with tragic in this radical way, he observed no such bounds of safety. *King Lear* is in a way the obverse of *Hamlet*, for there, order is enclosed in chaos and moral pattern in amoral patternlessness.

NOTES

1. Bradley, *Shakespearean Tragedy*, p. 131; on the other side see, for example, J. Dover Wilson, *What Happens in "Hamlet"*, 3rd ed. (Cambridge, 1951), pp. 73–75.

2. See Bernard Spivack, *Shakespeare and the Allegory of Evil* (New York, 1958), pp. 24–27. Spivack supports Schücking's assertion, "It must be made a principle to deny that Shakespeare makes any character in a monologue state reasons for his actions that are not meant to be substantially correct and sufficient." Levin L. Schücking, *Character Problems in Shakespeare's Plays* (London, 1922), p. 212.

3. *Shakespearean Tragedy*, p. 175.

4. Maynard Mack observes that, unlike the committed Othello, Hamlet is "partly an *eiron* figure," and that "disengagement is in a sense his problem." "Engagement and Detachment in Shakespeare's Plays," in *Essays on Shakespeare and Elizabethan Drama in Honor of Hardin Craig*, ed. Richard Hosley (Columbia, Mo., 1962), pp. 286–287.

5. II.ii. 242–250, 294–309; my italics.

6. *The Dream of Learning* (Oxford, 1951), pp. 41–42.

7. *Shakespeare's Living Art* (Princeton, 1974), p. 216.

8. *Montaigne's Essays*, tr. John Florio, ed. J. I. M. Stewart (London, 1931), I, 646.

9. Bernard McElroy similarly connects Hamlet's speech to his mother with the first soliloquy: see *Shakespeare's Mature Tragedies* (Princeton, 1973), pp. 48–49. Although his study of *Hamlet* takes a direction different from mine, McElroy also finds central Hamlet's multiple viewpoint, his capacity for "believing simultaneously two or more things which logically should cancel each other out" (p. 38).

10. Cf. Karl Jaspers on Hamlet, *Tragedy Is Not Enough*, tr. Harald A. T. Reiche, Harry T. Moore, and Karl W. Deutsch (London, 1953): "It is not his character that paralyzes him. Only the predicament of a man who knows—with a sovereign command of penetrating vision—yet does not know, makes him linger. . . . He is, as it were, caught up in his knowledge, and in the knowledge of his ignorance" (pp. 64–65).

11. Wilson and Greg both thought that the Folio omission of "How all occasions" and its preamble represented playhouse practice. *The Manuscript of Shakespeare's "Hamlet"* (Cambridge, 1934), I, 30; and *The Editorial Problem in Shakespeare* (Oxford, 1942), p. 65. Empson suggests in *"Hamlet When New"* (*Sewanee Review*, 61 [1953], 41) that "How all occasions" was reserved as an encore speech, to use when the performance went well. In any case, the speech seems detachable from its situation in a way that other soliloquies are not detachable from theirs. Eleanor Prosser speculates that Shakespeare intended to use the speech earlier in the play, later found it redundant, tried it in IV.iv, and finally cut it completely. *Hamlet and Revenge* (Stanford, 1967), p. 206.

12. I.ii.23–25; I.i.80–95.

13.   For thou hast been
As one, in suff'ring all, that suffers nothing;
A man that Fortune's buffets and rewards
Hast ta'en with equal thanks.

14. Harold Skulsky makes this point in considering Claudius's less than clear reaction to the Mousetrap. "'I Know My Course': Hamlet's Confidence," *PMLA*, 89 (1974), 484.

15. Horatio's opinion is no less ambiguous in the briefer exchange of Q1: he says only: "The king is moved, my lord."

16. *What Happens in "Hamlet"*, pp. 52–86.

17. I.i.130–131, 127, 46–49.

18. I.v. 92–93. Wilson sees "And shall I couple hell?" as a returning doubt about the Ghost's origin, immediately stifled in a self-rebuking "O, fie!" *Hamlet*, New Cambridge ed. (Cambridge, 1936), p. lii.

19. In his British Academy Shakespeare Lecture *Hamlet: The Prince or the Poem* (London, 1942), pp. 11–12, C. S. Lewis describes well this sense of the Ghost as "permanently ambiguous." His statement that Hamlet is convinced when in the Ghost's presence and doubtful in its absence brings out an important element in the situation but does not account for assertions of certainty when the Ghost is not there, such as the first part of "O what a rogue."

20. *What Happens in "Hamlet"*, pp. 26–44.

21. Marriage to the brother's widow was proposed for Charles IX of France and Mary Queen of Scots after the death of Mary's husband François II. And, of course, it was carried out in the case of Henry VIII and Catherine of Aragon, widow of Henry's elder brother Arthur.

22. J. P. Malleson, *Times Literary Supplement*, 4 January 1936, p. 15, and 25 January 1936, p. 75; cf. E. A. J. Honigmann, "The Politics in *Hamlet* and 'The World of the Play,'" in *Hamlet*, ed. J. Russell Brown and Bernard Harris, Stratford-upon-Avon Studies, 5 (London, 1963), pp. 129–47.

23. It might be argued that at least some of the audience would have known the Hamlet story through an earlier version—that of Saxo Grammaticus, Belleforest, or the old play—and thus could not have doubted the Ghost's authenticity and Claudius's guilt. It is possible; but the likeliest source of their expectation, the Ur-*Hamlet*, is not extant, and we know nothing about it except that it featured a ghost and the tag line "Hamlet, revenge!" Compared with the sources available, Shakespeare's play consistently makes the clear unclear. In the Latin and French narratives, the characters know from the start who killed the king, no problematic ghost troubles the night, and there is no question about the incestuous nature of the new king's marriage. With these certainties muddled into ambiguities—the murder secret, the Ghost suspect, etc.—even a spectator who knew the old story could not be sure it would proceed in the usual way.

24. "On the Value of *Hamlet*," in *Reinterpretations of Elizabethan Drama*, ed. Norman Rabkin (New York, 1969), p. 152.

25. *Style in "Hamlet"* (Princeton, 1969), p. 36; see Charney's discussion following, pp. 36–39.

26. III.i.51; III.iv.147–149; IV.i.21–23; IV.iii.35–37; I.ii.256–257; V.ii.312.

27. Coleridge's image of Hamlet comes through most clearly in the 1818 *Lectures* ("a great, an almost enormous, intellectual activity, and a proportionate aversion to real action") and in the *Table Talk* comment of 24 June 1827 ("Hamlet's character is the prevalence of the abstracting and generalizing habit over the practical. . . . I have a smack of Hamlet myself"). Quoted in *Hamlet: A Casebook*, ed. John Jump

(London, 1968), pp. 30–31. Freud's attribution of Hamlet's troubles to an unresolved Oedipus complex appeared at the height of his interest in that pattern, in *The Interpretation of Dreams* (first published 1900). *Basic Writings of Sigmund Freud*, tr. A. A. Brill (New York, 1938), pp. 309–10. In the library scene of Joyce's *Ulysses*, Stephen Dedalus interprets *Hamlet* in terms of his own dilemmas as son and artist. *Ulysses* (New York, 1934), pp. 182–215. For Eliot's Prufrock, Hamlet is not a projection of himself but rather everything he wishes he were and fears to be. This Hamlet, quite opposite to that of Coleridge, is active and powerful like the other Renaissance figures in the poem, but Prufrock himself is "not Prince Hamlet, nor was meant to be." Instead he identifies with the supporting character, an "attendant lord" who is a composite of Polonius, Osric, Horatio, Rosencrantz and Guildenstern.

In *Some Shakespearean Themes* (London, 1959), L. C. Knights points out how consistently Shakespeare's plays of this period concern themselves with subjective illusion. In addition to *Hamlet*, he cites *Troilus and Cressida, Much Ado, Othello,* and *Julius Caesar*: "In all these plays . . . we find we are pondering questions of a kind that are prompted by Blake's dictum, 'As a man is, so he sees'" (p. 171).

28. Frye (*Anatomy*, pp. 174–175) links Polonius with another comic type, the older authority figure who retreats from the action to see how the young will behave in his absence. Other examples are Knowell in *Every Man in His Humour* and Duke Vincentio in *Measure for Measure*.

29. III.ii.36–42. Hamlet's epitaph of "fool" for Polonius anticipates Antony's for one of Polonius's direct descendants: "Fool Lepidus!" (*Ant.* III.v.17). Like Polonius a commonplace, well-meaning go-between, Lepidus too is caught in the conflict of mighty opposites, "half to half the world oppos'd" (III.xiii.9). When he gets in the way, he is eliminated from the arena of power as irrelevant.

30. Fergusson, *The Idea of a Theatre* (Princeton, 1949), pp. 108–09.

31. *La folle de Chaillot*, ed. Mary E. Storer (New York, 1955), p. 20.

32. *The Question of "Hamlet"* (New York, 1959), pp. 51–52.

33. For Thomas McFarland, Rosencrantz and Guildenstern lose their identities *because* they reject the responsibilities of *Existenz*—in this case friendship. *Tragic Meanings in Shakespeare* (New York, 1966), pp. 40–41.

34. *Cor.* II.i.31. Against the political, accommodating *we* of Brutus and Sicinius is set the heroic, individual *I* of Coriolanus: "If you have writ your annals true, 'tis there / That, like an eagle in a dove-cote, I / Flutter'd your Volscians in Corioli: / Alone I did it" (V.vi.114–117).

35. "Why then, your ambition makes it one; 'tis too narrow for your mind" (II.ii.251–252). Both Wilson in the New Cambridge edition

and Kittredge in his annotated *Hamlet* (Boston, 1940) see in these lines a veiled reference to the fact that Hamlet has not succeeded his father as king.

36. *Wilhelm Meisters Lehrjahre*, Book 5, cited in the New Variorum *Hamlet*, ed. H. H. Furness, reissue (New York, 1965), II, 274.

37. *Tragedy Is Not Enough*, p. 42.

38. *Johnson on Shakespeare*, VIII, 1011.

39. See Levin's discussion of the "antic disposition" in *Question of "Hamlet*," pp. 111–28.

40. "If Hamlet spares Claudius because he considers the matter too closely, he stabs Polonius because he does not consider the matter at all." McElroy, *Mature Tragedies*, p. 77.

41. Chambers argues for memorial reconstruction (*William Shakespeare: A Study of Facts and Problems* [Oxford, 1930], pp. 415–20); Greg prefers the provincial performance theory (*Editorial Problem*, p. 67).

42. "The Hollow Men" (1925). Here, as in *Hamlet*, form expresses meaning: in each phrase, beginning is separated from conclusion by a line ending, and in each stanza a second phrase intervenes before we are given the result of the first.
      Michael Goldman also finds the Q1 ordering unsatisfactory on the grounds that "the break in our expectations, the resistance to interpretation, is vital." *Shakespeare and the Energies of Drama* (Princeton, 1972), pp. 87–88.

43. *Shakespeare and the Energies of Drama*, pp. 76–88.

44. "On the Value of *Hamlet*," p. 143.

45. Ibid., p. 171. Norman Rabkin in the stimulating discussion of *Hamlet* that opens his *Shakespeare and the Common Understanding* (New York, 1967) takes a similar position: "The experience of *Hamlet*, then, culminates in a set of questions to which there are no answers" (p. 9). Tillyard's parallel conclusion, reached by a different path, that *Hamlet* presents problems rather than solutions and significant ordering, led him to place it with the problem plays rather than with the tragedies. *Shakespeare's Problem Plays* (London, 1950), p. 31.

46. V.ii.63–68. Cf. A. J. A. Waldock, *"Hamlet": A Study in Critical Method* (Cambridge, 1931), p. 26: "Horatio does not answer the question, simply because he knows that Hamlet is not seriously asking it."

47. See below, n. 57.

48. Stauffer, *Shakespeare's World of Images* (New York, 1949), p. 126. Cf. Bradley, *Shakespearean Tragedy*, p. 145; Schücking, *The Meaning of "Hamlet"* (London, 1937), p. 167; H. B. Charlton, *Shakespearian Tragedy* (Cambridge, 1944), p. 103.

49. "The Jacobean Shakespeare," in *Jacobean Theatre*, ed. J. Russell Brown and Bernard Harris (London, 1960), p. 22.

50. In *I Henry VI* IV.vii.18, the two heroic Talbots, father and son, are mocked. Richard II sees Death as a jester at the King's court (*Richard II* III.ii.160–170).

51. *Shakespearean Tragedy*, p. 151.

52. Maynard Mack, Jr., comments: "At first her clothes, trappings of the court, hold her up, like her obedience to Polonius, but before long the same courtly trappings pull her to her death." *Killing the King* (New Haven and London, 1973), p. 99.

53. "He, like the others, is inevitably engulfed by the evil that has been set in motion. . . . he himself becomes the cause of further ruin." H. D. F. Kitto, *Form and Meaning in Drama* (London, 1956), p. 330.

54. Janet Adelman reaches a similar conclusion after observing that, like Hamlet at sea, the audience in Act V is "taken over by events, by the plot itself. Like Hamlet, we lose the leisure for questions and seem to be guided by something outside ourselves. . . . All the earlier questions of will and purpose that are posed intellectually are now answered, but not intellectually; in place of conceptual answers, we are given the *feeling* that they have been answered by the very movement of the plot." *The Common Liar*, p. 8.

55. *The Praise of Folly*, tr. Leonard Dean (Chicago, 1946), pp. 61–69.

56. *Tragedy Is Not Enough*, pp. 70–71.

57. It has been argued that revenge was *not* an obligation. But assertions that Shakespeare, or Hamlet, or both, found revenge ethically repugnant cannot be supported from the play, which never invokes the Christian sanction against private vengeance. If Shakespeare wanted to make a central issue of the morality of revenge, he has done very strangely never to bring it out in Hamlet's self-questionings or in his talks with Horatio—that is, never to place it before us dramatically. Whatever evidence scholars may amass from other documents to show that Elizabethans were taught to repudiate revenge as a great sin, we must still trust to the guidance of the text in determining what issues are significant in *Hamlet*. Shakespeare's audience was as used to the heroic values of folk tale and legend as to the Christian ones of the catechism. Like audiences of today, they could hold in abeyance a moral reaction or bring it forth as directed by the playwright. Indeed, the success of either tragedy or comedy depends to some extent on the audience's willing suspension of a specifically Christian point of view.

Of course, in accepting the revenge obligation as a *donné*, we need not view the Ghost as a divine agent or give unqualified approval to every speech and action of Hamlet. Such black-and-white moral distinctions have no place in Shakespearean tragedy. Both of these corollaries seem to be assumed in Eleanor Prosser's *Hamlet and Re-*

venge. This is the most thorough and intelligent presentation of the case against revenge. But even Prosser, searching for dramatic expressions of the issue in the play, must resort to some indirect allusion, a very strained reading of "To be or not to be," and such dubious critical propositions as this: "The moral issue is implicit throughout the ["O what a rogue"] soliloquy, and . . . it is so subtly treated only because Shakespeare felt no need to make it explicit" (p. 155).

Marco Mincoff

From "The Structural Pattern of Shakespeare's Tragedies"

The subject of this paper is not, on the whole, one to which scholars have devoted much attention, and the results of this lack of interest have in some ways been unfortunate. Shakespeare's tragedies seem to conform outwardly to the conventional Aristotelian triangle well enough to foster on the one hand the impression that the triangular scheme is the only possible one and that playwrights such as Fletcher who have worked on other principles are lacking in form, while on the other certain un-Aristotelian tendencies, such as the frequent disappearance of the hero during the decline, or the rather abrupt episodic nature of the structure, have been overlooked and even, for instance in discussing the doubtful plays, been regarded as un-Shakespearian while in fact they are typical.

Of the four great tragedies it is *Hamlet* that seems to exhibit the Shakespearian pattern most perfectly. The opening scene is a wonderful piece of atmosphere: a solitary sentry pacing up and down, muffled in an inky cloak to suggest the dark and the cold; to him another figure, similarly muffled, a hasty snatch of conversation in muffled tones, betraying a sense of uneasiness—then more figures, more talk, and out of it, abruptly dropped, the cause of the uneasiness—"What, has this thing appear'd again to-night?" Gradually the thing begins to take shape—it is a dreaded sight, then an apparition, we are about to hear more of it, the

Reprinted from *Shakespeare Survey*, vol. 3 (1950), pp. 58–62, by permission of Cambridge University Press. Copyright © 1950 by Cambridge University Press.

atmosphere for a description is carefully prepared, and then, freezing the words on the speaker's lips, the thing itself—the ghost of the newly dead king—appears in the background. The tension rises to a peak—agitated whispers, the thing is challenged but speaks no word, vanishes again, and the muffled figures, shaken to the soul, are left to ponder the portent. Suggestions are made, suggestions that miss the true mark entirely, yet serve to introduce one of the secondary themes of the coming tragedy and underline the deep significance of the apparition, political events, war preparations, a general unrest. Then the Ghost once more, a fresh surge of horror, a more solemn challenge, and just as we hope to have our questions explained the cock crows, the apparition vanishes, and the feelings of horror are now allayed with the calm and lovely poetry of the closing speeches. The whole scene is almost a complete work of art in itself, with its introduction, climax and resolution. Its closest analogy is the overture of a modern opera. It has stirred us deeply and soothed us again, yet leaves us expecting more; it has, towards the close, mentioned the titular hero of the play, and it has introduced the Ghost, who is to start the action, but actually it has told us nothing, it has not even offered us a situation out of which dramatic action can arise, it is purely atmospheric.

And what happens now? We expect the arrival of the watchers to tell young Hamlet what they have seen. Instead a brazen flourish of trumpets shatters the calm of the early morning and the whole court, in the magnificent apparel of state ceremony, sweeps on to the stage, a magnificent effect of sheer contrast. Only the one solitary figure, accentuated by his isolation, strikes a jarring note in this gorgeous throng, awakening for the hardened playgoer, even if the story of the play were not already familiar to him, associations with the familiar theme of the melancholic revenger, awakening too perhaps a vague sense of unfitness—why is the place on the throne not occupied by the young prince, the dead king's son, rather than this man who might in years be his father? But there is no time to think of these matters, we are swept at once into the political complications that have been exercising the watchers on the battlements with the King's clear explanation of events; we are introduced indirectly to Fortinbras and directly to Laertes, who are to play an important part as contrast figures, to Polonius too, and the memory of last night's watch sinks more and more into the background; it has been made to seem more than ever the prelude to the coming war. And now at last the attention turns to the hero, the listless figure in black, and already the contrast with Laertes is stressed— Laertes has had leave to continue his studies abroad, Hamlet must stay at home; and even in the seat of their studies—Paris and Wittenberg—a typical contrast is stressed. And now, with the prince's sardonic comments, his evident hostility towards his uncle's advances, the emotional tension begins to rise. It reaches its peak with the hero's first monologue, while at the same time we are given a marvellous glimpse into the inner man; we feel his disgust and bitterness, his frayed nerves, his desire for death. And when the watchers, whom by now we have almost forgotten, arrive, his sardonic humour and almost hysterical excitement come into play. But there is still no dramatic situation, no germ of action. If the first scene was a piece of static atmosphere, this is static portraiture. The hero is fully introduced to us before the action begins to modify his character. But now the news that the watchers bring cuts across the prince's overwrought tension, and again the scene ebbs away emotionally to its end. The need for a decision imposes restraint, Hamlet becomes collected, a little abstracted perhaps, but the decision is made as it should be, and the scene seems to be leading over to a return to the battlements.

Instead of that, however, what follows is another strong contrast—simple domestic interior, the introduction of the last of the more important figures of the tragedy and some fresh light on Hamlet, even something that might develop into a theme for action, but action which is only to play a subordinate part. The scene serves also to mark the passage of time till night shall fall again, but that interval scarcely needed stressing in itself. The importance of the scene is more intrinsic as the beginning of a minor action and as a point of contrast, a relaxation of the tension, leading in its turn to tension of another kind. The result is that when we return to Hamlet the atmosphere of the battlements has to be built up anew with a fresh introduction.

We are now approaching an important point, the inception of the action, and here at this crucial moment Shakespeare makes a clear statement of the theme of his tragedy—

> So, oft it chances in particular men,
> That for some vicious mole of nature in them—

a fine piece of dramatic irony that the hero, just as the action is about to start, the conflict about to be defined, points already to the flaw in his own character out of which the real tragedy will grow. Thereupon follows in two scenes, which are in reality but one, the disclosure of the Ghost; the hero is at last precipitated into a really dramatic situation with all the latent possibilities of a development of conflicts, and we are present at the very creation of that situation. But the act does not close at that moment of extreme tension—the cellarage scene brings a gradual relaxation of the tension, a cooling off of Hamlet's wild and whirling words and of his hysterical excitement down to collected thought and decision, and finally to the melancholic lethargy of his generalization "the time is out of joint."

This analysis already brings out some of the most salient features of Shakespeare's structural methods. Each scene tends to follow in itself a pyramidal structure, beginning on a low note with a deliberate introduction even, rising to high tension and dropping once more towards the end, forming thus a separate unit, and these units are carefully played off against one another to produce a maximum of contrast. Contrast plays its part, too, in the grouping of the characters within the scenes. Much care is given to a gradual preparation and building up of effects, some of which will not actually be made use of till the later acts. Hints that can only be taken up by one familiar with the play as a whole are introduced, hints that do not in themselves rouse curiosity or anticipation but which will rather serve as an unconscious preparation for what is to come, making things drop into place as parts of an inevitable pattern. The action is slow in getting under way, yet, although the scenes might almost be termed static, at least by comparison with Shakespeare's more baroque successors, the emotional tension is extremely high. There is throughout the act scarcely any action really connected with the central conflict, indeed that conflict does not even exist until the very close, yet there is an effect of action, of forward motion, which is on the whole spurious if closely examined. Practically every scene ends on a note which seems to be leading over to the next, but what follows is in sharp contrast, and generally starts us off along a new path—the transitions are in fact made purposely abrupt. There is a constant holding back of the point to which we wish to come, which results in a great increase of the tension, but also in a very steady rhythmical pulsation.

From the inception onwards the tension rises fairly steadily in the main but with the same rhythmic movement in a series of separate units up to the climax. The main tendency of the next two acts is to present Hamlet in a series of separate encounters, carefully graduated, with Polonius, with his old friends Rosencrantz and Guildenstern, with Ophelia, with the King (in the play-scene) and finally with his mother. It can hardly be said that any of these encounters advances the action, though that is largely due to the theme of delay, which naturally excludes any true action. Nor do they rise naturally out of one another in a chain of cause and effect, producing a clear flow. What they do is rather to illuminate the hero and the situation in which he finds himself in a series of static glimpses which only by their steadily increasing tension give an effect of progess. It is, in fact, the structure of *Tamburlaine*, a series of semi-independent, episodic units held together by a certain parallelism (in the play-scene the parts are reversed, it is the King who is being probed, not Hamlet) and by the personality of the hero, but not by any interdependence or running line of action. Artistically any other order would of course be unthinkable, but as far as mere logic is concerned the position of any of the encounters in the series—except the last— might easily be altered. Even the play-scene might logically head the list and provide a stronger motive for the King's attempts to pierce Hamlet's disguise.

One may note, too, the careful preparation of events, and their delay and interruption. The series sets in with the Reynaldo-scene, a scene unique in Shakespeare in that its main purpose is to underline a time gap, a gap, too, caused not by any necessity of the action but introduced for the sake of the portraiture, to make clear the objective nature of Hamlet's procrastination. Ophelia's disclosures start a train of action, but this action does not move forward smoothly. The transition to the palace is what we expect, but instead of a short introduction leading up to Polonius's entry we have the preparation for a later unit of the series with Rosen-

crantz and Guildenstern, and even the purposeful delay with the
business of the embassy, before Polonius can bring out his news,
and the train is laid actually for a third encounter before even the
first has taken place. The first two encounters follow then in
quick succession, but with the arrival of the players the series is
interrupted to prepare for the fourth, and then, and not till then,
are we allowed the peep into Hamlet's mind for which by now we
have begun to feel impatient. With his soliloquy the emotional
tension, which has already shown two marked pulsations of increasing strength, shoots up to a peak and ebbs even more swiftly
with the final resolution to action, a clearly marked peroration
cutting the action short for the moment. In the third act the
pulsations are considerably stronger—hectic almost. The thread,
as usual, is not taken up where the preceding scene left it, but
harks back to Rosencrantz and Guildenstern, and the tension
rises slowly at first. Hamlet's new soliloquy is subdued in tone,
and it is not until the Ophelia-scene that a sharper rise occurs,
followed by a slackening as the eavesdroppers exchange their
impressions. The opening of the play-scene drops even further,
then rises in a steady crescendo to Hamlet's moment of wild
exultation, and slowly ebbs again, closing with his preparations to
face his mother. And again that forward movement at the close of
the scene with the introduction of a new theme is not carried
through—the scene in the King's closet interrupts it sharply and
is woven into the main movement only by Hamlet's rather illogical appearance. But the comparatively low tone in which the
whole scene, including its own distinct apex, is pitched serves as a
breathing space and contrast before we reach the last lap of the
ascent. In fact every turn of the action is anticipated long ahead,
but the sequence of cause and effect is consistently interrupted.
We have several episodes running concurrently, overlapping and
interrupting one another while the plot threads its way between
them. The plot is in fact a network of separate elements.

   With the bedroom-scene the highest peak of the action is past,
and it is noteworthy that here at the apex of the action the Ghost
is reintroduced, recalling its inception. Hamlet has played his
cards almost as badly as he could, and failed, and the counterplot
of the King now takes the centre of the stage while Hamlet is
eliminated during the greater part of the fourth act—even his

appearance in IV, iv was apparently cut out of the final version. Instead, the two "contrast"—or rather "reflector"—figures of Fortinbras and Laertes, introduced directly or indirectly already in the first act, are developed, each with a father to revenge, and each in his way solving his problem more successfully than Hamlet. This naturally produces a more obviously episodic effect than the actually equally episodic rise of the action, an effect still further increased by the episode of Ophelia's madness

Even after Hamlet's return, the whole churchyard-scene with its comic interlude is still a markedly separate unit and more evidently static than any of the others. And then, with the final scene, the various threads are drawn together—and there are more of them than one might be inclined to admit off-hand. Hamlet has both achieved his revenge and failed, the sub-plot of Ophelia's love, its disaster and her brother's revenge—almost a separate tragedy in itself—has also worked itself out, and Fortinbras's ambitious energy, which throughout has been more spoken of than represented in action, is also satisfied. And yet these three sequences during the play do not stand out as clearly defined strands, because each step in their development has at the same time been made an element of the main plot too. Ophelia's love has been used as a means of probing Hamlet's disguise, the murder of her father is an essential part of the main plot, only her resulting madness and death break apart as an unconnected episode until they are worked into the main theme by employing Laertes's thirst for revenge to bring about the catastrophe, while her burial serves as an effective setting for Hamlet's reappearance. And in the same way each mention of the Fortinbras theme has its part to play in the main plot. It is first introduced as a red herring to explain the Ghost's appearance, in II, ii it is made use of to stress the time gap—the embassy has had time to go and return—it serves as the subject of one of Hamlet's soliloquies, and finally it rounds the play off on a note of triumph. The result is still further to increase the effect of a closely woven network rather than a clear, bold line of action. Indeed, one could put it better the other way about and say that each element of the plot, each episode, has the tendency to become a centre of its own, to send out filaments which catch hold of the secondary characters too, and force them into prominence. Each person is in fact a separate entity, the centre of a little world of his own, with his own individuality and his own fate, developed far beyond the limits of what the mere plot demands, and there is a certain struggle between the desire to portray, to dwell on the separate personality, on the separate situation, and the need to proceed with the action. Hence the abruptness of the transitions from scene to scene, from episode to episode, hence even a certain diffuseness which does not make itself unpleasantly felt only because each scene or episode is given a centre of interest of its own, a rise and fall of tension and succeeds in capturing the imagination.

Noteworthy, however, is it that the play is given a definite apex, and that the tensions are graduated so as to lead up to and down again from that peak, and this, though we may be inclined to regard the Aristotelian analysis of the parts of a drama as universal in its application, is by no means true either of Shakespeare's predecessors, like Marlowe and Kyd, who on the whole left the pattern of the play to take care of itself, or at least paid small attention to a centring climax or definite turn of the action and still less to making such a turn coincide with the maximum of emotional tension, or his successors from Fletcher down to Dryden, who preferred, not a single climax but a whole series with a corresponding number of turns, but who insisted on the other hand on a flowing, uninterrupted line to join them.

PART 2:
Hamlet
the Character

R. A. Foakes (ed.)

From Coleridge on Shakespeare

The first question was, what did Shakespeare mean when he drew the character of Hamlet? Coleridge's belief was that a poet regarded his story before he began to write in much the same light that a painter looked at his canvas before he began to paint. What was the point to which Shakespeare directed himself? He meant to portray a person in whose view the external world, and all its incidents and objects, were comparatively dim and of no interest in themselves, and which began to interest only when they were reflected in the mirror of his mind. Hamlet beheld external objects in the same way that a man of vivid imagination, who shuts his eyes, sees what has previously made an impression upon his organs.

Shakespeare places him in the most stimulating circumstances that a human being can be placed in: he is the heir apparent of the throne; his father dies suspiciously; his mother excludes him from the throne by marrying his uncle. This was not enough, but the Ghost of the murdered father is introduced to assure the son that he was put to death by his own brother. What is the result? Endless reasoning and urging—perpetual solicitation of the mind to act, but as constant an escape from action—ceaseless reproaches of himself for his sloth, while the whole energy of his resolution passes away in those reproaches. This, too, not from cowardice, for he is made one of the bravest of his time—not

Reprinted from *Coleridge on Shakespeare: The Text of the Lectures of 1811–12*, ed. R. A. Foakes (The University Press of Virginia for the Folger Shakespeare Library, 1971, pp. 124–28), by permission of Routledge and Kegan Paul PLC (London).

from want of forethought or quickness of apprehension, for he sees through the very souls of all who surround him,—but merely from that aversion to action which prevails among such as have a world within themselves.

How admirable is the judgment of the poet! Hamlet's own fancy has not conjured up the Ghost of his father; it has been seen by others; he is by them prepared to witness its appearance, and when he does see it he is not brought forward as having long brooded on the subject. The moment before the Ghost enters, Hamlet speaks of other matters in order to relieve the weight on his mind; he speaks of the coldness of the night, and observes that he has not heard the clock strike, adding, in reference to the custom of drinking, that it is

> More honour'd in the breach, than the observance.

From the tranquil state of his mind he indulges in moral reflections. Afterwards the Ghost suddenly enters:

Hor.   Look, my lord, it comes.
Ham. Angels and Ministers of grace defend us!

The same thing occurs in *Macbeth*: in the dagger scene, the moment before he sees it, he has his mind drawn to some indifferent matters: thus the appearance has all the effect of abruptness, and the reader is totally divested of the notion that the vision is a figure in the highly wrought imagination.

Here Shakespeare adapts himself to the situation so admirably, and as it were puts himself into the situation, that through poetry, his language is the language of nature: no words, associated with such feelings, can occur to us but those which he has employed, especially the highest, the most august, and the most awful subject that can interest a human being in this sentient world. That this is no mere fancy, Coleridge undertook to show from Shakespeare himself. No character he has drawn could so properly express himself as in the language put into his mouth.

There was no indecision about Hamlet; he knew well what he ought to do, and over and over again he made up his mind to do it: the moment the Players, and the two spies set upon him, have withdrawn, of whom he takes leave with the line, so expressive of his contempt,

> Ay so; good bye you.—Now I am alone,

he breaks out into a delirium of rage against himself for neglecting to perform the solemn duty he had undertaken, and contrasts
the artificial feelings of the player with his own apparent indifference:

> What's Hecuba to him, or he to Hecuba,
> That he should weep for her?

Yet the player did weep for her, and was in an agony of grief at
her sufferings, while Hamlet could not rouse himself to action
that he might do the bidding of his Father, who had come from
the grave to incite him to revenge:

> This is most brave,
> That I, the son of a dear father murdered,
> Prompted to my revenge by heaven and hell,
> Must, like a whore, unpack my heart with words
> And fall a cursing, like a very drab,
> A scullion.

It is the same feeling, the same conviction of what is his duty,
that makes Hamlet exclaim in a subsequent part of the tragedy:

> How all occasions do inform against me,
> And spur my dull revenge! What is a man,
> If his chief good and market of his time
> *Be but to sleep and feed?* A beast, no more . . .
>   . . . I do not know
> Why yet live I to say—"this thing's to do,"
> Sith I have cause and will and strength and means
> To do't.

Yet with all this sense of duty, this resolution arising out of
conviction, nothing is done: this admirable and consistent character, deeply acquainted with his own feelings, painting them with
such wonderful power and accuracy, and just as strongly convinced of the fitness of executing the solemn charge committed to
him, still yields to the same retiring from all reality, which is the
result of having what we express by the term "a world within
himself."

> Such a mind as this is near akin to madness: Dryden has
> said,[1]

> Great wit to madness, nearly is allied

and he was right; for he means by wit that greatness of genius, which led Hamlet to the perfect knowledge of his own character, which with all strength of motive was so weak as to be unable to carry into effect his most obvious duty.

Still, with all this, he has a sense of imperfectness, which becomes obvious while he is moralising on the skull in the church-yard: something is wanted to make it complete—something is deficient, and he is therefore described as attached to Ophelia. His madness is assumed when he discovers that witnesses have been placed behind the arras to listen to what passes, and when the heroine has been thrown in his way as a decoy.

Another objection has been taken by Dr. Johnson,[2] and has been treated by him very severely. I refer to the scene in the third act, where Hamlet enters and finds his Uncle praying, and refuses to assail him excepting when he is in the height of his iniquity: to take the King's life at such a moment of repentance and confession, Hamlet declares,

> Why this is hire and salary, not revenge.

He therefore forbears, and postpones his Uncle's death until he can take him in some act

> That has no relish of salvation in't.

This sentiment Dr. Johnson has pronounced to be so atrocious and horrible as to be unfit to be put into the mouth of a human being (See Malone's Shakespeare, vii. 382).[3] The fact is that the determination to allow the King to escape at such a moment was only part of the same irresoluteness of character. Hamlet seizes hold of a pretext for not acting, when he might have acted so effectually. Therefore he again defers the revenge he sought, and declares his resolution to accomplish it at some time

> When he is drunk, asleep, or in his rage,
> Or in th'incestuous pleasures of his bed.

This, as Coleridge repeated, was merely the excuse Hamlet made to himself for not taking advantage of this particular moment to accomplish his revenge.

Dr. Johnson[4] further states that, in the voyage to England, Shakespeare merely followed the novel as he found it, as if he had no other motive for adhering to his original; but Shakespeare never followed a novel but where he saw the story contributed to tell or explain some great and general truth inherent in human nature. It was unquestionably an incident in the old story, and there it is used merely as an incident, but Shakespeare saw how it could be applied to his own great purpose, and how it was consistent with the character of Hamlet, that after still resolving, and still refusing, still determining to execute, and still postponing the execution, he should finally give himself up to his destiny, and, in the infirmity of his nature, at last hopelessly place himself in the power and at the mercy of his enemies.

Even after the scene with Osrick, we see Hamlet still indulging in reflection, and thinking little of the new task he has just undertaken; he is all meditation, all resolution as far as words are concerned, but all hesitation and irresolution when called upon to act; so that, resolving to do everything, he in fact does nothing. He is full of purpose, but void of that quality of mind which would lead him at the proper time to carry his purpose into effect.

Anything finer than this conception and working out of a character is merely impossible: Shakespeare wished to impress upon us the truth that action is the great end of existence—that no faculties of intellect, however brilliant, can be considered valuable, or otherwise than as misfortune, if they withdraw us from or render us repugnant to action, and lead us to think and think of doing, until the time had escaped when we ought to have acted. In enforcing this truth, Shakespeare has shown the fulness and force of his powers: all that is amiable and excellent in nature is combined in Hamlet, with the exception of this one quality: he is a man living in meditation, called upon to act by every motive, human and divine, but the great purpose of life [is] defeated by continually resolving to do, yet doing nothing but resolve.

NOTES

1. *Dryden has said*] 'Great Wits are sure to madness near alli'd,' *Absalom and Achitophel*, I, 163 (so Raysor).

2. *Dr. Johnson*] see *Johnson on Shakespeare*, ed. Sherbo, VIII, 990; Johnson said the speech "is too horrible to be read or to be uttered."

3. The reference in brackets is interlined, and must have been added after 1821, when Malone's edition of Shakespeare in 21 volumes was published. The page reference fits this edition.

4. *Dr. Johnson*] Johnson says nothing of the kind, but a note in Reed's edition of 1803, which Coleridge was apparently using (see above, p. 121 and n.), XVIII, 270, on the speech of Claudius at the end of IV, iii, states "The circumstances mentioned as including the King to send the prince to England, rather than elsewhere, are likewise found in the *Hystory of Hamblet.*" See also Raysor, II, 197 (154).

William Hazlitt

From *Characters of Shakespeare's Plays*

The feint is so close to nature, and there is underlying it withal so undeniable a substratum of morbid feeling, that in spite of ourselves, in opposition to our full knowledge that in his antic disposition Hamlet is putting on a part, we cannot from the first dispossess ourselves of the idea, that a mind fallen, if not from the sovereignty of reason, at least from the balance of its faculties, is presented to us. So much is undirection of mind blended with pregnant sense and apprehension, both however perverted from the obvious line of sane thought; so much is the universal and caustic irony tinged with melancholic self-depreciation, and that longing for death which in itself alone constitutes a form of mental disease. In the various forms of partial insanity, it is a question of intricate science to distinguish between the portions of a man's conduct which result from the sound operations of mind, and those which result from disease. Hamlet's own assertion, "I am but mad north-north-west: when the wind is southerly I know a hawk from a hand-saw," is pregnant with a psychological truth which has often engaged the most skilful and laborious investigation both of medical men and of lawyers. It has often been a question of life or death, of wealth or poverty, whether a criminal act was done, or a civil one performed, by a half-madman, when the mental wind was in the north-west of disease, or blowing from the sanatory south.

That in his actual unfeigned mental condition Hamlet is far from being in a healthy state of mind, he is himself keenly conscious, and acknowledges it to himself in his soliloquy upon the players:

> The spirit that I have seen
> May be a devil: and the devil hath power
> To assume a pleasing shape; yea, and perhaps
> *Out of my weakness and my melancholy,*
> As he is very potent with such spirits,
> Abuses me to damn me.

Upon this actual weakness of mind and suicidal melancholy, combined with native humour and the biting irony into which his view of the world has sharpened it, is added the feigned form of insanity, the antic disposition wilfully put on, the dishevelled habiliments of person and wild converse. The characteristics of this feigned form are those of mania, not indeed violent, acute, and demonstrative, but mischievous, reckless, and wayward, and so mingled with flashes of native wit, and disguised by the ground colour of real melancholy, shewing through the transparency of the feigned state, that Hamlet's character becomes one of the most interesting and complicated subjects of psychological study anywhere to be met with.

He is first introduced to us in his feigning condition with a fine touch to excite pity:

> *Queen.* But, look, where sadly the poor wretch comes reading.
> *Polonius.* Do you know me, my lord?
> *Hamlet.* Excellent well; you are a fishmonger.

Coleridge and others remark upon this, that Hamlet's meaning is, You are sent to fish out this secret. But we are not aware that fishmongers are in the habit of catching their fish. May it not rather be that a fishmonger was referred to as a dealer in perishable goods, and notoriously dishonest; and thus to give point to the rejoinder—

> Then I would you were so honest a man.

The writers who insist upon a profound meaning, even in Hamlet's most hurling words, have been mightily puzzled with the lines: "For if the sun breed maggots in a dead dog, being a god kissing carrion," etc.

Coleridge refers to "some thought in Hamlet's mind, contrasting Ophelia with the tedious old fool her father." Is it not rather a wild taunt upon the old man's jealous suspicion of his daughter, as if he had said, since the sun causes conception in such vile bodies, "let not your precious daughter walk in the sun."

Perhaps he only intended to convey to Polonius, by a contemptuous simile, the intimation that he cared not for the daughter, and thus to throw him off the scent of his quest. The intention to offend the tedious old fool, and thus to disembarrass himself of his presence, becomes still more obvious in the description of old age which immediately follows, "Slanders, sir," etc.

The point of the satire, and the absence of unreason, strikes Polonius.

> *Polonius.* Though this be madness, yet there is method in't. Will you walk out of the air, my lord?
> *Hamlet.* Into my grave.
> *Pol.* Indeed, that is out o' the air. How pregnant sometimes his replies are! a happiness that often madness hits on, which reason and sanity could not so prosperously be delivered of.

In this, again, the old man shews that though his wits may be somewhat superannuated, yet, either from reading or observation, he has no slight knowledge of mental disease.

What depth of melancholy and life-weariness is there not apparent in the conclusion of the interview.

> *Pol.* I will most humbly take my leave of you.
> *Ham.* You cannot, sir, take from me anything that I will more willingly part withal: except my life, except my life, except my life!

But when his old schoolfellows arrive, how frank and hearty his greeting; how entirely is all disguise for the moment thrown aside! The noble and generous native nature is nowhere made more manifest than in his reception of these friends of his youth, men to whom he once adhered, neighbours to his youth and humour. Until his keen eye discovers that they have been "sent for," and are mean instruments, if not spies, in the hands of the king, he throws off all dissimulation with them, greeting them with right hearty and cheerful welcome. Yet how soon his melancholy peers through the real but transient cheerfulness. The world is a prison, "in which there are many confines, wards, and dungeons; Denmark being one of the worst." If it is not so to his friend, yet is it so to him from thinking it so, for "there is nothing either good or bad, but thinking makes it so: to him it is a prison." The real prison, then, is his own mind, as, in the contrary mental state, a prison is no prison, for

> Stone walls do not a prison make,
> Nor iron bars a cage.

Hamlet feels that he could possess perfect independence of circumstance if the mind were free.

> *Rosencrantz.* Why then, your ambition makes it one; 'tis too narrow for your mind.
> *Hamlet.* O God, I could be bounded in a nutshell and count myself a king of infinite space, were it not that I have bad dreams.

The spies sound him further on the subject of ambition, thinking that disappointment at losing the succession to the crown may be the true cause of his morbid state. In this intention they decry ambition: "it is but a shadow's shadow." Hamlet replies logically enough, that if ambition is but a shadow, something beyond ambition must be the substance from which it is thrown. If ambition represented by a King is a shadow, the antitype of ambition represented by a beggar must be the opposite of the shadow, that is, the substance. "Then are our beggars, bodies; and our monarchs, and outstretch'd heroes, the beggars' shadows." He reduces the sophistry of his false friends to an absurdity, and closes the argument by declining to carry it further: "By my fay, I cannot reason." But Mr. Coleridge declares the passage to be unintelligible, and perhaps this interpretation of it may be too simple.

So far from being able to examine and recover the wind of Hamlet, his old schoolfellows are put by him to a course of questioning as to the motives of their presence, as to whether it is a free visitation of their own inclining, or whether they have been "sent for." Their want of skill in dissemblance and their weaker natures submit to him the secret that they had been "sent for," and the old "rights of fellowship," "the obligations of ever-preserved love," are immediately clouded by distrust: "Nay, then, I'll have an eye of you," he says. Yet notwithstanding he freely discloses to them the morbid state of his mind; and, be it remarked, that in this exquisite picture of life-weariness, in which no image could be altered, no word omitted or changed, without obvious damage to its grand effect, he does not describe the maniacal state, the semblance of which he has put on before Ophelia and Polonius, but that morbid state of weakness and melancholy which he really suffers, of which he is thoroughly self-conscious, and which he avows in his first speech, before he has seen the Ghost:

> I have of late—but wherefore I know not—lost all my mirth, foregone all custom of exercise; and indeed it goes so heavily with my disposition that this goodly frame, the earth, seems to me a sterile promontory, this most excellent canopy, the air, look you, this brave o'erhanging firmament, this majestical roof fretted with golden fire, why, it appears no other thing to me than a foul and pestilent congregation of vapours. What a piece of work is a man! how noble in reason! how infinite in faculty! in form and moving how express and admirable! in action how like an angel! in apprehension how like a god! the beauty of the world! the paragon of animals! And yet, to me, what is this quintessence of dust? man delights not me: no, nor woman neither, though by your smiling you seem to say so.

How exquisitely is here portrayed the state of the reasoning melancholiac, (melancholia without delusion,) who sees all things as they are, but feels them as they are not. All cheerfulness fled, all motive for action lost, he becomes listless and inert. He still recognises the beauty of the earth and the magnificence of the heavens, but the one is a tomb, and the other a funereal pall. His reason still shews him the place of man, a little lower than the angels, but the sources of sentiment are dried up, and, although no man-hater, he no longer derives pleasure from kindly affections. The waters of emotion are stagnant; the pleasant places of the soul are sterile and desert.

Hamlet is not slow to confess his melancholy, and indeed it is the peculiarity of this mental state, that those suffering from it seldom or never attempt to conceal it. A man will conceal his delusions, will deny and veil the excitement of mania, but the melancholiac is almost always readily confidential on the subject of his feelings. In this he resembles the hypochondriac, though not perhaps from exactly the same motive. The hypochondriac seeks for sympathy and pity; the melancholiac frequently admits others to the sight of his mental wretchedness from mere despair of relief and contempt of pity.

Although Hamlet is ready to shew to his friends the mirror of his mind, he jealously hides the cause of its distortion. "But wherefore I know not" is scarcely consistent with the truth. In his first soliloquy, which we take to be the key-note of his real mental state, he clearly enough indicates the source of his wretchedness, which the Queen also, with a mother's insight, has not been slow to perceive:

> His father's death, and our o'erhasty marriage.

He is jealous that his friends should not refer his melancholy to love-sickness. The opinion propounded by Polonius, that he was mad for love, could not have escaped him; a theory, of his malady, which would be likely to wound his pride severely. Polonius had already made, in his presence, sundry aside observations on this point; and the significant smile of Rosencrantz at his observation, "Man delights not me," would be likely to stimulate the sleeping suspicion that he was set down as a brain-sick, rejected lover; and some annoyance at an attempt to explain his madness as the result of his rejection by Ophelia, may combine with the suspicion that he is watched to explain his harshness towards her in his subsequent interview with her.

How are we to understand his confession to the men he already distrusts, that in the appearance of his madness the King and Queen are deceived, except by his contempt for their discrimination, and his dislike to wear his antic disposition before all company?

When Polonius returns, he immediately puts on the full disguise, playing upon the old man's infirmities with the ironical nonsense about Jephtha, king of Israel, who had a daughter, etc., and skilfully leading Polonius by the nose on the scent of his own theory, "Still on my daughter."

When the players enter, however, he thoroughly throws off not only the antic counterfeit, but the melancholy reality of his disposition: he shakes his faculties together, and becomes perfectly master of himself in courtesy, scholarship, and solid sense. His retort to Polonius, who objects to the speech of the player as too long, seems a valuable hint of Shakespeare's own opinion respecting the bad necessity he felt to introduce ribald scenes into his plays: "It shall to the barber's, with your beard. Prithee, say on: he's for a jig or a tale of bawdry, or he sleeps." A noble sentiment in homely phrase is that in which he marks the right motive of behaviour towards inferiors, and indeed towards all men. To Polonius's assurance that he will use the players according to their desert, the princely reply is—

> God's bodykins, man, much better: use every man after
> his desert, and who should 'scape whipping? Use them after
> your own honour and dignity: the less they deserve, the
> more merit is in your bounty.

Although he freely mocks the old lord chamberlain himself, he will not permit others to do so. His injunction to the player, "Follow that lord, and look you mock him not," not only indicates that the absurdities of Polonius are glaring, but that there is less real malice in Hamlet's heart towards the old man than he assumes the appearance of.

Hamlet decides upon the use he will make of the players with a promptitude that shews that his resolve, "sicklied o'er with the pale cast of thought," is but the inactivity of an over-reflective melancholic mind, and that there is energy enough in him to seize some forms of opportunity.

Hamlet's soliloquy, "O, what a rogue and peasant slave am I!" resembles, with a difference, the one following his interview with the Captain: "How all occasions do inform against me." The latter one, after he has obtained satisfactory proof of his uncle's guilt, is by far the least passionate and vehement, justifying in some degree the remark of Schlegel, that "in the last scenes the main action either stands still or appears to retrograde." There is, however, an important distinction between these two soliloquies. The passionate outburst of the first has been stimulated by emotional imitation. The feigned passion of the player has touched the most sensitive chord of feeling, and given occasion to the vehemence of his angry self-rebuke. The account of the soldier's temper, "greatly to find quarrel in a straw when honour's at the stake," sets him calmly to reflect and philosophize upon the motives of action. In these two soliloquies we have to some extent Shakespeare's own exposition of Hamlet's natural character, and the motives of his conduct.

"The whole," says Schlegel, "was intended to shew that a consideration which would exhaust all the relations and possible consequences of a deed to the very limits of human foresight, cripples the power of acting." In this tragedy of thought we have delineated a highly sensitive, reflecting, self-introspective mind, weak and melancholic, sorrow-stricken and life-weary. In a manner so awful that it might shake the soundest mind, this man is called upon to take away the life of a king and a relative for a crime of which there exists no actual proof. Surely Hamlet is justified in pausing to weigh his motives and his evidence, in concluding not to act upon the sole dictation of a shadowy appearance, who may be the devil tempting his "weakness and his melancholy"; of resolving to "have grounds more relative than this," before he deliberately commits himself to an act of revenge which, even had the proof of his uncle's crime been conclusive and irrefragable, would have been repulsive to his inmost nature. Hamlet's indecision to act, and his over-readiness to reflect, are placed beyond the reach of critical discovery by his own analytical motive-hunting, so eloquently expressed in the abstruse reasoning in which he indulges. Anger and hatred against his uncle, self-contempt for his own irresolution, inconsistent as he feels it with the courage of which he is conscious; disgust at his own angry excitement, and doubts of the testimony upon which he is yet dissatisfied that he has not acted, present a state of intellectual and emotional conflict perfectly consistent with the character and the circumstances. If Hamlet had had as much faith in the Ghost as Macbeth had in the Weird Sisters, he would have struck without needing further evidence. If he had been a man of action, whose firstlings of the heart are those of the hand, he would have struck in the earliest heat of his revenge. He feels while he questions, that it is not true that he is "pigeon-liver'd, and lacks gall to make oppression bitter"; but he does lack that resolution which "makes mouths at the invisible event"; he does make "I would, wait upon, I will": he does hesitate and procrastinate, and examine his motives, and make sure to his own mind of his justification, and allow us to see the painful labour of a noble and sensitive being struggling to gain an unquestionable conviction of the right thing to do, in circumstances most awry and difficult; he does feel balancing motives, and painfully hear the ring of the yes and no in his head.

Che sì, e nò nel capo mi tenzona.

Shall we think the less nobly of him because his hand is not ready to shed kindred blood; because, gifted with God-like discourse of reason, he does not look before and after; because he does not take the law in his own hands upon his oppressor until he has obtained conclusive evidence of his guilt; that he seeks to make sure he is the natural justiciar of his murdered father, and not an assassin instigated by hatred and selfish revenge?

Augustus Schlegel

From *Course of Lectures on Dramatic Art and Literature*

Hamlet is singular in its kind: a tragedy of thought inspired by continual and never-satisfied meditation on human destiny and the dark perplexity of the events of this world, and calculated to call forth the very same meditation in the minds of the spectators. This enigmatical work resembles those irrational equations in which a fraction of unknown magnitude always remains, that will in no way admit of solution. Much has been said, much written, on this piece, and yet no thinking head who anew expresses himself on it, will (in his view of the connexion and the signification of all the parts) entirely coincide with his predecessors. What naturally most astonishes us, is the fact that with such hidden purposes, with a foundation laid in such unfathomable depth, the whole should, at a first view, exhibit an extremely popular appearance. The dread appearance of the Ghost takes possession of the mind and the imagination almost at the very commencement; then the play within the play, in which, as in a glass, we see reflected the crime, whose fruitlessly attempted punishment constitutes the subject-matter of the piece; the alarm with which it fills the King; Hamlet's pretended and Ophelia's real madness; her death and burial; the meeting of Hamlet and Laertes at her grave; their combat, and the grand determination; lastly, the appearance of the young hero Fortinbras, who, with warlike pomp, pays the last honours to an extinct family of kings; the interspersion of comic characteristic scenes with Polonius, the courtiers, and the grave-diggers, which have all of them their signification,—all this fills the stage with an animated and varied movement. The only circumstance from which this piece might be judged to be less theatrical than other tragedies of Shakspeare is, that in the last scenes the main action either stands still or appears to retrograde. This, however, was inevitable, and lay in the nature of the subject. The whole is intended to show that a calculating consideration, which exhausts all the relations and possible consequences of a deed, must cripple the power of acting; as Hamlet himself expresses it:—

> And thus the native hue of resolution
> Is sicklied o'er with the pale cast of thought;
> And enterprises of great pith and moment,
> With this regard, their currents turn awry,
> And lose the name of action.

With respect to Hamlet's character: I cannot, as I understand the poet's views, pronounce altogether so favourable a sentence upon it as Goethe does. He is, it is true, of a highly cultivated mind, a prince of royal manners, endowed with the finest sense of propriety, susceptible of noble ambition, and open in the highest degree to an enthusiastic admiration of that excellence in others of which he himself is deficient. He acts the part of madness with unrivalled power, convincing the persons who are sent to examine into his supposed loss of reason, merely by telling them unwelcome truths, and rallying them with the most caustic wit. But in the resolutions which he so often embraces and always leaves unexecuted, his weakness is too apparent: he does himself only justice when he implies that there is no greater dissimilarity than between himself and Hercules. He is not solely impelled by necessity to artifice and dissimulation, he has a natural inclination for crooked ways; he is a hypocrite towards himself; his far-fetched scruples are often mere pretexts to cover his want of determination: thoughts, as he says on a different occasion, which have

> —but one part wisdom
> And ever three parts coward.—

He has been chiefly condemned both for his harshness in repulsing the love of Ophelia, which he himself had cherished, and for his insensibility at her death. But he is too much overwhelmed with his own sorrow to have any compassion to spare for others;

besides his outward indifference gives us by no means the measure of his internal perturbation. On the other hand, we evidently perceive in him a malicious joy, when he has succeeded in getting rid of his enemies, more through necessity and accident, which alone are able to impel him to quick and decisive measures, than by the merit of his own courage, as he himself confesses after the murder of Polonius, and with respect to Rosencrantz and Guildenstern. Hamlet has no firm belief either in himself or in anything else: from expressions of religious confidence he passes over to sceptical doubts; he believes in the Ghost of his father as long as he sees it, but as soon as it has disappeared, it appears to him almost in the light of a deception.* He has even gone so far as to say, "there is nothing either good or bad, but thinking makes it so"; with him the poet loses himself here in labyrinths of thought, in which neither end nor beginning is discoverable. The stars themselves, from the course of events, afford no answer to the question so urgently proposed to them. A voice from another world, commissioned it would appear, by heaven, demands vengeance for a monstrous enormity, and the demand remains without effect; the criminals are at last punished, but, as it were, by an accidental blow, and not in the solemn way requisite to convey to the world a warning example of justice; irresolute foresight, cunning treachery, and impetuous rage, hurry on to a common destruction; the less guilty and the innocent are equally involved in the general ruin. The destiny of humanity is there exhibited as a gigantic Sphinx, which threatens to precipitate into the abyss of scepticism all who are unable to solve her dreadful enigmas.

NOTE

*It has been censured as a contradiction, that Hamlet in the soliloquy on self-murder should say,

> The undiscover'd country, from whose bourn
> No traveller returns—

For was not the Ghost a returned traveller? Shakspeare, however, purposely wished to show, that Hamlet could not fix himself in any conviction of any kind whatever.

A. C. Bradley

From *Shakespearean Tragedy*

"Melancholy," I said, not dejection, nor yet insanity. That Hamlet was not far from insanity is very probable. His adoption of the pretence of madness may well have been due in part to fear of the reality; to an instinct of self-preservation, a fore-feeling that the pretence would enable him to give some utterance to the load that pressed on his heart and brain, and a fear that he would be unable altogether to repress such utterance. And if the pathologist calls his state melancholia, and even proceeds to determine its species, I see nothing to object to in that; I am grateful to him for emphasising the fact that Hamlet's melancholy was no mere common depression of spirits; and I have no doubt that many readers of the play would understand it better if they read an account of melancholia in a work on mental diseases. If we like to use the word "disease" loosely, Hamlet's condition may truly be called diseased. No exertion of will could have dispelled it. Even if he had been able at once to do the bidding of the Ghost he would doubtless have still remained for some time under the cloud. It would be absurdly unjust to call *Hamlet* a study of melancholy, but it contains such a study.

But this melancholy is something very different from insanity, in anything like the usual meaning of that word. No doubt it might develop into insanity. The longing for death might become an irresistible impulse to self-destruction; the disorder of feeling and will might extend to sense and intellect; delusions might arise; and the man might become, as we say, incapable and irresponsible. But Hamlet's melancholy is some way from this condition. It is a totally different thing from the madness which he feigns; and he never, when alone or in company with Horatio alone, exhibits the signs of that madness. Nor is the dramatic use of this melancholy, again, open to the objections which would justly be made to the portrayal of an insanity which brought the hero to a tragic end. The man who suffers as Hamlet suffers—and thousands go about their business suffering thus in greater or less degree—is considered irresponsible neither by other people nor by himself: he is only too keenly conscious of his responsibility. He is therefore, so far, quite capable of being a tragic agent, which an insane person, at any rate according to Shakespeare's practice, is not. And, finally, Hamlet's state is not one which a healthy mind is unable sufficiently to imagine. It is probably not further from average experience, nor more difficult to realise, than the great tragic passions of Othello, Antony or Macbeth.

Let me try to show now, briefly, how much this melancholy accounts for.

It accounts for the main fact, Hamlet's inaction. For the *immediate* cause of that is simply that his habitual feeling is one of disgust at life and everything in it, himself included,—a disgust which varies in intensity, rising at times into a longing for death, sinking often into weary apathy, but is never dispelled for more than brief intervals. Such a state of feeling is inevitably adverse to *any* kind of decided action; the body is inert, the mind indifferent or worse; its response is, "it does not matter," "it is not worth while," "it is no good." And the action required of Hamlet is very exceptional. It is violent, dangerous, difficult to accomplish perfectly, on one side repulsive to a man of honour and sensitive feeling, on another side involved in a certain mystery (here come in thus, in their subordinate place, various causes of inaction assigned by various theories). These obstacles would not suffice to prevent Hamlet from acting, if his state were normal; and against them there operate, even in his morbid state, healthy and positive feelings, love of his father, loathing of his uncle, desire of revenge, desire to do duty. But the retarding motives acquire an unnatural strength because they have an ally in something far stronger than themselves, the melancholic disgust and apathy; while the healthy motives, emerging with difficulty from the central mass of diseased feeling, rapidly sink back into it and "lose the name of action." We *see* them doing so; and sometimes the process is quite simple, no analytical reflection on the deed intervening between the outburst of passion and the relapse into melancholy.[1] But this melancholy is perfectly consistent also with that incessant dissection of the task assigned, of which the Schlegel-Coleridge theory makes so much. For those endless questions (as we may imagine them), "Was I deceived by the Ghost? How am I to do the deed? When? Where? What will be the consequence of attempting it—success, my death, utter misunderstanding, mere mischief to the State? Can it be right to do it, or noble to kill a defenceless man? What is the good of doing it in such a world as this?"—all this, and whatever else passed in a sickening round through Hamlet's mind, was not the healthy and right deliberation of a man with such a task, but otiose thinking hardly deserving the name of thought, an unconscious weaving of pretexts for inaction, aimless tossings on a sick bed, symptoms of melancholy which only increased it by deepening self-contempt.

Again, (a) this state accounts for Hamlet's energy as well as for his lassitude, those quick decided actions of his being the outcome of a nature normally far from passive, now suddenly stimulated, and producing healthy impulses which work themselves out before they have time to subside. (b) It accounts for the evidently keen satisfaction which some of these actions give to him. He arranges the play-scene with lively interest, and exults in its success, not really because it brings him nearer to his goal, but partly because it has hurt his enemy and partly because it has demonstrated his own skill (III. ii. 286–304). He looks forward almost with glee to countermining the King's designs in sending him away (III. iv. 209), and looks back with obvious satisfaction, even with pride, to the address and vigour he displayed on the voyage (V. ii. 1–55). These were not *the* action on which his morbid self-feeling had centred; he feels in them his old force, and escapes in them from his disgust. (c) It accounts for the pleasure with which he meets old acquaintances, like his "school-fellows" or the actors. The former observed (and we can observe) in him a "kind of joy" at first, though it is followed by "much forcing of his disposition" as he attempts to keep this joy and his courtesy alive in spite of the misery which so soon returns upon him and the suspicion he is forced to feel. (d) It accounts no less for the painful features of his character as seen in the play, his almost savage irritability on the one hand, and on the other his self-absorption, his callousness, his insensibility to the fates of those whom he despises, and to the feelings even of those whom he loves. These are frequent symptoms of such melancholy, and (e) they sometimes alternate, as they do in Hamlet, with bursts of transitory, almost hysterical, and quite fruitless emotion. It is to these last (of which a part of the soliloquy, "O what a rogue," gives a good example) that Hamlet alludes when, to the Ghost, he speaks of himself as "lapsed in *passion*," and it is doubtless partly his conscious weakness in regard to them that inspires his praise of Horatio as a man who is not "passion's slave."[2]

Finally, Hamlet's melancholy accounts for two things which seem to be explained by nothing else. The first of these is his apathy or "lethargy." We are bound to consider the evidence which the text supplies of this, though it is usual to ignore it. When Hamlet mentions, as one possible cause of his inaction, his "thinking too precisely on the event," he mentions another, "bestial oblivion"; and the thing against which he inveighs in the greater part of that soliloquy (IV. iv.) is not the excess or the misuse of reason (which for him here and always is god-like), but this *bestial* oblivion or "*dullness*," this "letting all *sleep*," this allowing of heaven-sent reason to "fust unused":

> What is a man,
> If his chief good and market of his time
> Be but to *sleep* and feed? a *beast*, no more.*

So, in the soliloquy in II. ii. he accuses himself of being "a *dull* and muddy-mettled rascal," who "peaks [mopes] like John-a-dreams, unpregnant of his cause," dully indifferent to his cause.[3] So, when the Ghost appears to him the second time, he accuses himself of being tardy and lapsed in *time*; and the Ghost speaks of his purpose being almost *blunted*, and bids him not to *forget* (cf. "oblivion"). And so, what is emphasised in those undramatic but significant speeches of the player-king and of Claudius is the mere dying away of purpose or of love.[4] Surely what all this points to is not a condition of excessive but useless mental activity (indeed there is, in reality, curiously little about that in the text), but rather one of dull, apathetic, brooding gloom, in which Hamlet, so far from

---

*(italics added here and elsewhere)

analysing his duty, is not thinking of it at all, but for the time literally *forgets* it. It seems to me we are driven to think of Hamlet *chiefly* thus during the long time which elapsed between the appearance of the Ghost and the events presented in the Second Act. The Ghost, in fact, had more reason than we suppose at first for leaving with Hamlet as his parting injunction the command, "Remember me," and for greeting him, on re-appearing, with the command, "Do not forget."[5] These little things in Shakespeare are not accidents.

The second trait which is fully explained only by Hamlet's melancholy is his own inability to understand why he delays. This emerges in a marked degree when an occasion like the player's emotion or the sight of Fortinbras's army stings Hamlet into shame at his inaction. "*Why*," he asks himself in genuine bewilderment, "do I linger? Can the cause be cowardice? Can it be sloth? Can it be thinking too precisely of the event? And does *that* again mean cowardice? What is it that makes me sit idle when I feel it is shameful to do so, and when I have *cause, and will, and strength, and means*, to act?" A man irresolute merely because he was considering a proposed action too minutely would not feel this bewilderment. A man might feel it whose conscience secretly condemned the act which his explicit consciousness approved; but we have seen that there is no sufficient evidence to justify us in conceiving Hamlet thus. These are the questions of a man stimulated for the moment to shake off the weight of his melancholy, and, because for the moment he is free from it, unable to understand the paralysing pressure which it exerts at other times.

I have dwelt thus at length on Hamlet's melancholy because, from the psychological point of view, it is the centre of the tragedy, and to omit it from consideration or to underrate its intensity is to make Shakespeare's story unintelligible. But the psychological point of view is not equivalent to the tragic; and, having once given its due weight to the fact of Hamlet's melancholy, we may freely admit, or rather may be anxious to insist, that this pathological condition would excite but little, if any, tragic interest if it were not the condition of a nature distinguished by that speculative genius on which the Schlegel-Coleridge type of theory lays stress. Such theories misinterpret the connection between that genius and Hamlet's failure, but still it is this connection which gives to his story its peculiar fascination and makes it appear (if the phrase may be allowed) as the symbol of a tragic mystery inherent in human nature. Wherever this mystery touches us, wherever we are forced to feel the wonder and awe of man's godlike "apprehension" and his "thoughts that wander through eternity," and at the same time are forced to see him powerless in his petty sphere of action, and powerless (it would appear) from the very divinity of his thought, we remember Hamlet. And this is the reason why, in the great ideal movement which began towards the close of the eighteenth century, this tragedy acquired a position unique among Shakespeare's dramas, and shared only by Goethe's *Faust*. It was not that *Hamlet* is Shakespeare's greatest tragedy or most perfect work of art; it was that *Hamlet* most brings home to us at once the sense of the soul's infinity, and the sense of the doom which not only circumscribes that infinity but appears to be its offspring.

NOTES

1. *E.g.* in the transition, referred to above, from desire for vengeance into the wish never to have been born; in the soliloquy, "O what a rogue"; in the scene at Ophelia's grave. The Schlegel-Coleridge theory does not account for the psychological movement in those passages.
2. Hamlet's violence at Ophelia's grave, though probably intentionally exaggerated, is another example of this want of self-control. The Queen's description of him (V. i. 307),

> This is mere madness;
> And thus awhile the fit will work on him;
> Anon, as patient as the female dove,
> When that her golden couplets are disclosed,
> His silence will sit drooping,

may be true to life, though it is evidently prompted by anxiety to excuse his violence on the ground of his insanity.
3. Cf. *Measure for Measure*, IV.iv.23, "This deed . . . makes me unpregnant and dull to all proceedings."
4. III. ii. 196 ff., IV. vii. III ff.: *e.g.*,

> Purpose is but the slave to *memory*,
> Of violent birth but poor validity.

5. So, before, he had said to him:

> And duller should'st thou be than the fat weed
> That roots itself in ease on Lethe wharf,
> Would'st thou not stir in this.

Levin Schücking

From *Character Problems in Shakespeare's Plays*

In [his] new treatment of the subject and partial revision of the old play Shakespeare worked out the character in accordance with a plan which in a simpler form, as has been shown, was in all likelihood already contained in the play, viz., the *idea of melancholy.*[1] When Shakespeare wrote *Hamlet*—in 1601—the "melancholy type" was almost a fashionable figure, the word "melancholy" itself a favourite expression. At that time anyone who wished to cut a really distinguished and aristocratic figure pulled his black hat with the long black plume far over his face, wore a long black cloak, and posed, wherever possible, with his arms crossed over his chest. Those wishing to appear as "coming of a noble family" not only adopted, like the visitors in Auerbach's cellar, a "proud and discontented" mien, but also spread round themselves the sublime and sombre halo which surrounds the victim of melancholy. "Why so melancholy?" was the fashionable question if people wished to be particularly polite. In a contemporaneous play, *Thomas Lord Cromwell* (III, ii), a gentleman of rank changes places with his servant and asks him how he now feels. The answer is:

> My nobility is wonderful melancholy. Is it not most gentlemanlike to be melancholy?

This kind of jest is not unfrequent, especially in the comedy of manners of that period.

Among the serious melancholy types upon the stage we notice especially the melancholy lover, handed down by the literature of fiction, with certain conventional features which still preserved something of the rigidity of the Provençal theories of love in the twelfth century. The melancholy lover is in a kind of fever, alternately hot and cold, pale and flushed, consumed by impatience, full of fears and forebodings, sighing, weeping, uttering complaints in solitude which he sometimes puts into sentimental verses; he is indifferent to all demands of social life and physical nature; he can live without eating and sleeping; all he needs is a little music and his private sorrow. The melancholy of love, however, is only a mood, a transitory state, which vanishes again together with its cause, and apparently is not supposed to be due to any particular natural tendency. Quite another thing is that melancholy which, though appearing only under the influence of certain proximate causes, rests on the firm ground of a clearly defined temperament. It is true that the manifestations of both kinds are in some respects very similar, but they are so only in appearance. The second type is evolved from the medieval doctrine of temperaments. Shakespeare's age had an idea of this type of temperament which is very strikingly differentiated. It is not at all impossible that the essential part of it is derived from the very play before us, viz., Kyd's *Urhamlet*. A little later an attempt is made to analyse its peculiar nature by Sir Thomas Overbury in his work entitled *Characters* (1614), which cleverly presents a number of various types of human individuals and professions. According to him the melancholy person is a whimsical fellow who goes his own ways, remote from other men. He takes a completely pessimistic view of the world, and finds satisfaction only in continually spinning out his destructive and suicidal fancies. Strange visions haunt his mind. "He thinks business, but never does any; he is all contemplation, no action." The neglect and disorder of his outward appearance agree with his mental disharmony. He is an enemy to sun and warmth, eats little, and sighs a lot.

In this portrait some features of the melancholy type stand out in bold relief, especially the unwholesome, diseased, and overexcited state of his mind, manifested in his distrust of and aversion to people, in his inability to concentrate himself, to get rid of tormenting ideas, to pull himself together. All this we should nowadays declare to be a sign of neurasthenia. What surprises us, however, is the fact that the Elizabethan author considers an

unnaturally strong activity of the imagination to be an inseparable accompaniment of melancholy. "Straggling thoughts are his
content, they make him dreame waking, there's his pleasure. His
imagination is never idle, it keeps his mind in a continuall motion,
as the poise the clocke: he winds up his thoughts often, and as
often unwinds them; Penelope's web thrives faster."

When we look for an incarnation of this type on the stage in
the time previous to Hamlet, in addition to Hieronimo in *The
Spanish Tragedy* we are particularly struck by the hero of Marston's
revenge-tragedies, Antonio. With his sleeplessness, his many
sighs and sudden outbursts of passionate complaints, his tardi-
ness of action, his pessimistic reflections, his slight tendency to
dissimulation, his high culture and intelligence, his excessive irritability, and his abrupt spasms of fury—things of which Overbury says nothing—he would remind us vividly of Hamlet even if
he did not, like the latter, come upon the stage dressed in black
garments and reading a book.

Still more striking in certain traits is the resemblance to the
portrait drawn by Overbury on the one hand, and Hamlet on the
other, of a certain melancholy figure which was probably meant
to be a caricature—perhaps of the *Urhamlet*. This is young Lord
Dowsecer in Chapman's comedy, *A Humorous Day's Mirth* (1597),
who is expressly designated as suffering from the "humour" of
melancholy. The King and his Court divert themselves with placing a few objects of everyday use in the way of this queer fellow,
who is introduced as a highly cultured pessimist and misanthrope.
He promptly takes up these things and, to the amusement of the
listeners, makes them the subjects of a monologue and proceeds
from them, just as Hamlet does from the skull, to pessimistic
reflections, castigating the vanities, abuses, and annoyances of
the world, and now and then demanding their abolition with a
rhetorical gesture. Very characteristic are the aversion and disgust with which he refers to procreation and his exaggerated and
almost ludicrous cynicism. His father says to him: "I wish thou
wouldst confess to marry," and he answers:

> To marry, father? why, we shall have children.
> *Father.* Why, that's the end of marriage, and the joy of men.
> *Dowsecer.* Oh, how you are deceived! You have but me, and
>   what a trouble am I to your joy! But, father, if you long to

have some fruit of me, see, father, I will creep into this
stubborn earth and mix my flesh with it, and they shall
breed grass, to fat oxen, asses, and such-like, and when
they in the grass the spring converts into beasts' nourish-
ment, then comes the fruit of this my body forth; then
may you well say, seeing my race is so profitably increased, that good fat ox and that same large-eared ass are
my son's sons, that calf with a white face is his fair
daughter; with which, when your fields are richly filled,
then will my race content you; but for the joys of children,
tush, 'tis gone—children will not deserve, nor parents take
it: wealth is the only father and the child, and but in
wealth no man hath any joy.[2]

The additional traits we find in this figure of melancholy
complete the representation of the type. Here also we note as
characteristic features a high degree of education—he enters
meditating on a quotation from Cicero (the melancholy man of
Overbury likewise is given to intellectual pursuits)—a whimsical
depreciation of and turning away from life, a kind of pessimism
which in this case leads to occasional lapses into extreme philosophical materialism, but is also found combined with rigorous
moral principles. The most significant traits, however, are, as
elsewhere, the eternal persistence in the train of gloomy reflections on men and the world, fantastical ideas which that period
considered such essential constituents of the melancholy nature
that Ben Jonson once in an enumeration of the temperaments
contrasts the slow-phlegmatic with the fantastic-melancholy.
Moreover, though this character is to a certain extent a caricature, it is not regarded exclusively as comical, and it is very
characteristic that the King, after listening to him, refuses to
identify his behaviour with madness and prefers to speak of it as
"a holy fury," even acknowledging that "he is more humane than
all we are."

The same type, in a slightly different shape, turns up again in
Shakespeare's Jaques in *As You Like It*, who actually styles himself a
melancholy man. He loves solitude, is "compact of jars," as the
Duke says of him, a pessimist, a wit, knows the ways of the world,
and is an unfailing judge of its abuses, has a great power of self-
criticism, an inclination to brooding and laziness, no interest in

women, and a decided love of music. His vocation in life seems to be discovering bitter truths and cleverly formulating them. His character further resembles that of Dowsecer in being moved by a sense of critical superiority to attempt a reformation of the world. He says:

> give me leave
> To speak my mind, and I will through and through
> Cleanse the foul body of the infected world.
>
> II, vii

The examples adduced will suffice to enable us to recognize this type which, embodied in a variety of figures, but fundamentally unchanged, lives on in the dramatic literature of the time. Its most fascinating representative is Hamlet. It is true that we have to distinguish in his character the mask from the original face. Hamlet, as we know, declares after the appearance of the ghost that he is going to take on "an antic disposition," yet those scenes in which there is no necessity for the mask sufficiently inform us about his true nature.[3]

It is indeed impossible to throw Hamlet's character more strongly into relief than is done in the opening scenes. The very first words the King addresses to him in the First Quarto give us the decisive cue: "What meanes these sad and melancholy moods?" This remark directs the eyes of all the spectators toward him. They must, however, have been struck by his appearance before, because in the glittering and sumptuous assembly where the King, attended by his train, is giving audience Hamlet alone, among gorgeously dressed courtiers, wears an "inky cloak" and "solemn black." He has put it on as sign of mourning, but no one else is still in mourning, and therefore all the onlookers, from the boxes to the end of the pit, at once are sure that this is the "melancholy gentleman." The stage types of the time are each distinguished by a peculiar costume—the steward by his chain and velvet coat, the harlot by a glaring "loose-bodied" satin gown, the king by a long beard and red robe, the fool by his motley, and so the melancholy gentleman also reveals himself by his dress and bearing. This first impression is not deceptive, because it is confirmed by what the spectators see and hear. Evidently he sits on his chair "with veiled lids," as his mother says, and bears in his expression, in his sighs and tears, as he himself informs us, "The trappings and the suits of woe." The somewhat snappy retort to his mother's question, "Seems, madam! nay, it is; I know not 'seems,'" the surprisingly laconic answers, the outbreak of despair after the Court have retired: "O! that this too too solid flesh would melt . . . ," which reveals a degree of pessimism, a disgust of the world, incapable of being surpassed, all confirm this impression. We see that he is in a condition reminding us of the neurasthenic type of Overbury. Horatio enters and accosts him: "Hail to your lordship," and he replies mechanically, absorbed in thought: "I am glad to see you well," then, recollecting himself and looking up, adds: "Horatio, or I do forget myself." "Speak to him," says Overbury of the melancholy man; "he hears with his eyes, eares follow his mind, and that's not at leysure." The idea of his father comes into his mind and instantly his irritated brain reacts so powerfully that he sees him standing before him: "My father—methinks I see my father," whereupon his friend, puzzled, but impressed by the apparition of the preceding night, asks him: "O where, my lord?" receiving the reassuring answer: "In my mind's eye, Horatio." All this takes place before the ghost has yet revealed to him his dreadful secret and laid upon him the arduous task.

The key to the figure of Hamlet is to be found at once in the impression of this first scene. Here we see yet another instance of Shakespeare's commonest technical device, which he applies more consistently than any other artistic process, viz., to give a clearly marked outline of the characters in the exposition and to make their first appearance more especially yield as much information as possible. The definition given by Overbury of this type of character and so faithfully followed by Shakespeare in this scene is observed throughout the rest of the play. In several passages the external symptoms of his condition, his sighs, his sleeplessness, his habit of walking up and down in solitude, are especially emphasized. It is interesting to note that Hippolito in Dekker's *Honest Whore*, after becoming melancholy, also paces restlessly up and down his room: ("He sups up a draught of as much aire at once as would serve at thrice," Overbury says; "he denies nature her due in sleep.") He complains of bad dreams. The actor that wishes to represent him properly ought therefore to adopt from the very beginning an air of being languid and exhausted by lack of sleep, exhibit a strong trait of morbidity, give clear signs of the inward unrest which makes him cross and recross his room, and put an expression into his eyes as though they were afraid of broad daylight, like those of the melancholy Vindici in *The Revenger's Tragedy.* If, then, we are asked to define the first principle of Hamlet's nature, we must reply, disregarding entirely the apparent violence of his passion, that it is *weakness and irritability.* His abnormal irritability clearly appears on several occasions, especially in the scene at Ophelia's grave, where the fact of Laertes loudly lamenting his dead sister drives Hamlet into that "fit" for which he afterward apologizes to Horatio, pleading his inability to control himself ("His madness is poor Hamlet's enemy"). To this fit there are exact parallels in the cases of two other melancholy characters, Hieronimo and Marston's Antonio, who too are unable to bear the idea of another person daring to suffer more under misfortunes than themselves.[4] This irritability is also the cause of Hamlet's extraordinary *intolerance,* which he manifests, *e.g.,* in his meetings with Polonius. If we require any further proof we may find it in Hamlet's self-characterization, in which he speaks twice of this weakness, once plainly styling it his "weakness and melancholy," the other time characterizing himself as the counter-pole to Hercules.

Now the objection might be raised that weakness and irritability or a clearly defined temperament are not, properly speaking, the ultimate foundation of character. "Temperament," says Kuno Fischer (*Hamlet,* p. 79), "is the musical mode in which our feelings are expressed, but not the music itself; it is the rhythm of life, not its theme." It might seem that from the kind of description indicated above no conclusion can be reached as to whether a character is noble or mean, whether a mind is well stored or poorly equipped, whether the reasoning faculty is keen or blunt. People have even gone so far as to see in the whole melancholy disposition of Hamlet merely a derivative quality proceeding as a necessary consequence from his wounded moral idealism, the strength of that emotion being only a symptom and measure of this deeper principle. This conclusion, however, must be challenged. Though we admit that the outbreak of Hamlet's melancholy is evidently caused by his great disappointment at the marriage of his mother, yet we maintain that this circumstance might have affected another kind of character, possessing maybe as much or even more moral idealism, quite differently. It is a well-known fact that the extent and degree of the reaction is determined by the emotional susceptibility, not by the moral idealism. Now Hamlet possesses this emotional susceptibility and irritability in a highly morbid degree. Moreover, if Shakespeare had seen in the fact that Hamlet allows his constitution to be so utterly ruined by his sad emotional experiences a sign of a particularly noble disposition he would assuredly have put this idea into the mouth of some other person. In reality, however, he holds precisely the opposite view; he is an unreserved advocate of resistance against the evils of life, and therefore sees the greatest merit in not allowing, to use his own expressions, the "judgment" to be overcome by the "blood."

Now if the Elizabethan spectator regarded Hamlet as a "melancholy man," *i.e.*, as an *imaginative, brooding intellectualist with morbid traits*, we can see how explanations that assign an undue weight to accidental phenomena must necessarily co-operate with distortions of the text in order to achieve their end. The melancholy type, as we have seen already in Overbury, is incapable of any concentrated systematic activity. Hamlet too is unable to pursue a plan. The melancholy person always sinks back into his reverie and must be pushed from without. This is true, *e.g.*, of Hieronimo, the avenger in *The Spanish Tragedy*, an early specimen of the type, who, despite the tremendous passion of revenge that devours him, must in the end receive an energetic impulse from Bellimperia, in order to achieve his purpose. But the melancholy person is not in the least afraid of bloodshed, and does not shrink from murder as being in itself a frightful deed. Here comes in the error of a great many critics, who conceive Hamlet as having far too delicate a mental organization to be capable of committing murder in pursuance of a revenge demanded of him. In ever new forms this explanation of Hamlet is brought forward, which in many respects might appear as the most natural solution of the problem. The reader sympathizes with Hamlet and says to himself: Here is a delicately constituted creature of brain and nerves, with modern ways of thinking and feeling, just like yourself, in the midst of people whom he has left far behind in respect of mental development. Would you not, in his position, act precisely as he does? This conception, which is fundamentally wrong, is founded upon certain traits which are especially apparent at the beginning. There can be no doubt that Shakespeare refined and ennobled the feelings of his hero in many directions in an unprecedented manner, though leaving intact his fundamental character. In many passages he represents him as imbued with the spirit of purest humanity. His words about his dead father are full of that piteous tenderness which tell of a wound still unhealed— we must remember that Shakespeare's father had died in the year which saw the production of *Hamlet*—they breathe the aspiration of a noble heart to offer the deceased in his thoughts a kind of compensation, by means of his passionate admiration, for the wrong done to his memory by the indifference of his widow and the speedy forgetfulness of the others. A most distinguished and sympathetic trait is the way in which the innermost depths of his soul are cruelly affected by this purely spiritual and unselfish disappointment. A fine manly friendship, setting aside all considerations of rank, unites him to Horatio, whom he entreats to style himself not his servant but his friend—a genuine affection like that entertained by Schiller's young Don Carlos for his beloved Posa. How hearty and courteous is his first reception of his old companions, Rosencrantz and Guildenstern; how noble and truly generous his acknowledgment of the good qualities possessed by Laertes, his enemy; how strongly pronounced is his preference for what is simple and natural, and his dislike, even his hatred, of affectation and pretence!

All these are beautiful traits, unmistakable signs of rare humanity and exquisite tact; hence they have been taken as revealing the poet's own personality. His behaviour toward Ophelia and Polonius, however, shows no trace of them. The cause of this contradiction is not to be sought in the conflict between the character and the action. Rümelin's idea is that the same Hamlet in whom Shakespeare has put so much of himself is no longer fit to be the hero of the Northern legend, the bloody avenger and fivefold murderer. He thinks that Shakespeare ought to have remoulded the material and given the theme a more humane and symbolic aspect, as Goethe did in his *Iphigenie*. By making, says Rümelin, this man of delicate feeling, who is so sensitive to the

moral deficiencies of others and the depravity of the world, able
to kill, incidentally as it were, three innocent people and then
behave as if nothing had happened, he produces an impression
upon us comparable to that which we should receive if Goethe's
Iphigenie in an *entr'acte* were to immolate a number of captives on
the altar of Diana, whose priestess she is. In this criticism there is
a certain amount of truth, but it misses the fact that Hamlet—at
least in the condition in which we see him—is just as little the
male ideal of the Elizabethan Age as he is that of our modern
times.

Some momentary flashes of irony and cynicism, certain harsh
and cutting remarks ("We shall obey, were she ten times our
mother,"), his occasional manifestations of a certain malignity, a
pleasure in unmasking evildoers, which especially appears in his
fierce joy at the self-betrayal of the King, may be explained as a
reaction against the tremendous emotional tension, which finds
relief in this way. Very likely, however, this interpretation would
be wrong, for other melancholy personalities also, in quite different situations, show the same trait, which is closely connected
with their morbid weakness, though Hamlet alone vents his excitement in that hilarity which is demanded by the peculiar exi-
gencies of the situation. A good actor ought strongly to emphasize this trait.

The neurotic condition of Hamlet should never be lost sight
of. It is not necessary to make him express it by such external
means as, according to a trustworthy description, were once
employed by Sarah Bernhardt in Berlin. In the play-scene she
climbed up the balustrade behind which the royal murderer was
sitting with his consort and "grinned in his face with distorted
features like a malignant ape showing his teeth." The fundamental idea, however, of her rendering, viz., to represent Hamlet as a
man suffering from nervous disorder and being haunted by hallucinations, doubtless rests on a sound historical basis. The diseased quality of this nature is best expressed by the actor alter-
nating between the one extreme of morbid self-absorption and
the other of absolutely unrestrained exaltation.

His incredibly excited manner is described by Queen Gertrude
in the First Quarto, where she says of his behaviour in the
interview which leads to the killing of Polonius, "He throws and

tosses me about." Further, a curious passage in a contemporaneous poem written about a person who has been made half mad by
love runs as follows:

> Puts off his cloathes, his shirt he onely wears,
> Much like mad Hamlet,

thus giving some idea of the remarkably odd way in which the
character was at that time represented!⁵

Only by keeping all this in mind shall we be able to comprehend Hamlet's treatment of the body of Polonius. It again shows
the morbid traits, purposely elaborated, of the melancholy character who, according to the opinion of the period (as we find also in
Burton's *Anatomy of Melancholy*), may occasionally create the impression of being morally irresponsible. The same morbidity of
mind is shown in his behaviour toward his mother. These things,
i.e., Hamlet's luxuriating in the minute description of the sexual
relations between his mother and his stepfather, the warning he
gives her not to

> Let the bloat king tempt you again to bed;
> Pinch wanton on your cheek . . .

are either passed over by critics of Hamlet in silence as unfit for
treatment, or made the pivot of the whole problem. Both conceptions are equally wrong. The indulging in erotic imaginations and
the interest taken in procreation and the peculiar qualities of
women, due to a feeling of disgust, are regular traits of the
melancholy character. We find this note sounded already in the
case of young Lord Dowsecer, and again and again it enters as a
component part, in the most varied forms, into the delineation of
melancholy. As late as 1603, in Marston's *Malcontent*, the further
development of the type, we have in the central figure this preoccupation with immorality and similar furious attacks delivered
upon it.

The melancholy character, feeding his discontent with constant brooding and proudly fond of his loneliness, inevitably develops into a censor of morals, a function which he can, of course,
exercise only if he takes a high ethical standpoint. It is true, no
doubt, that the melancholy character's moral censure was not
taken quite seriously by his age; his utterances appeared to some

as extravagant,[6] and were certainly received with laughter by the ordinary Elizabethan audience, which never took a very advanced view of ethical questions. In all these things the moral standards have become very much changed during the last few centuries, so that the statements made then no longer appear in quite the same light. We can therefore apply to many of Hamlet's sayings Shakespeare's own word: "This was sometime a paradox, but now the time gives it proof." Fortunately for the work of exposition, Hamlet by his utterances gives plenty of unmistakable proofs of his melancholy; but such pessimistic opinions as that the world "is an unweeded garden that grows to seed" were also, we may be sure, taken merely as expressions of an almost insane mind by a period which was firmly convinced that everything is most excellently arranged by a wise providence. Such sayings are estimated like the famous passage in *Lear*:

> As flies to wanton boys are we to the gods,
> They kill us for their sport,

> IV, i, 36

and like the wonderful words about the nature of life spoken by Macbeth after his breakdown:

> It is a tale
> Told by an idiot, full of sound and fury,
> Signifying nothing.

> V, v, 26

It remained for a later century to construct a philosophy on the foundation of pessimism, and then, of course, the expression of melancholy was taken much more seriously than by the period to which it was addressed.

NOTES

1. That Hamlet is to be conceived as a melancholy character has often been asserted by earlier Shakespearean scholars, one of the first being the Scottish critic Henry Mackenzie, in the *Mirror*, No. 99 (1780). An exhaustive scholarly discussion of this view has also been contributed by Löning in his work entitled *Shakespeares Hamlet-Tragödie*, Stuttgart, 1893. Since, however, the knowledge which English and American scholars have of German Shakespearean research rarely reaches far-

ther than the extracts given in the Variorum edition of Furness, the same discovery has recently been made once more by Bradley in his excellent book, *Shakespearean Tragedy*, London, 1904. Neither Löning nor Bradley, however, has treated the problem from the purely literary point of view, *i.e.*, cleared up its genetic connexions. *Cf.* on this point the author's article in the *Germ. Roman. Monatschr.*, iv, 1912, No. 6; E. E. Stoll, *Mod. Philology* iii ("Shakespeare, Marston, and the Malcontent Type"); Bieber, *loc. cit.*; and Radebrecht, *Shakespeares Abhängigkeit von Marston* (Schücking and Deutschbein's "Neue Anglistische Arbeiten," No. 3, 1918).

2. Compare the similar remarks of Hamlet: "How a king may go a progress through the guts of a beggar."

3. If we fix our attention on the manifestations of his character from the very beginning of the play, we shall be better able to recognize it than by investigating minutely what Hamlet was *before* the events related in the play. This point of view, which is taken, *e.g.*, by Kuno Fischer, Bradley, etc., must be regarded as quite erroneous, if only for the reason that it always comes perilously near confounding art and reality. Only what has been present in the poet's consciousness can be adduced for the purpose of explaining artistic creations. In the case of an imagined figure we cannot speak of its past unless the poet himself does so. To attempt its reconstruction from the given facts is ridiculous. As well might we look under the frame of a picture for a continuation of the scene represented on the canvas. Hence it is amazing that even a great and serious critic like Dowden should think it worth while to reflect on the probability of Hamlet's having been influenced by the fact that during the reign of the strong-willed elder Hamlet his introspective son was not compelled to take an active part in affairs. This would be an ingenious inference in the case of a real person, but it is comical if we are dealing with a fictitious character, whose nature can obviously not be determined by such reflections, since it is conceived in the mind of its creator in the state demanded by the dramatic action. It is ridiculous of Kuno Fischer to maintain that "Claudius is elected king probably for economic reasons," and of Thümmel to connect the skull of Yorick, the jester, in the last act with the personality of the deceased King and assert that the warlike and ever active father of Hamlet had felt the need of creating a kind of artistic relief to the tragedy of life. This is to transfer the methods of historical research to the realm of fancy, which is subject to quite different laws. Critics like these resemble the farmer in the Drury Lane gallery who upon hearing Richard III cry out "a kingdom for a horse" offered him a two-year-old brown gelding: they confound appearance and reality.

4. *Cf.* Radebrecht, p. 71 ff.

5. *Cf.* the poem in Munro, *Shakespeare Allusion Book*, London, 1909, p. 133. It is interesting to note that King Lear too when overwhelmed by madness begins to throw off his clothes.

6. When Lord Dowsecer, speaking of the usual relation between men and women, indignantly says,

> But to admire them as our gallants do,
> "Oh, what an eye she hath! O! dainty hand,
> Rare foot and leg!" and leave the mind respectless,
> This is a plague that in both men and women
> Makes such pollution of our earthly being . . .

one may be in doubt whether the author is quite serious. When, however, the hero finds a sword laid in his way and angrily exclaims: ". . . as if there were not ways enough to die by natural and casual accidents, diseases, surfeits, brave carouses, old aqua-vitae, and too base wives, and thousands more: hence with this art of murder!" the audience certainly received these "pacifist" utterances with laughter.

Ernest Jones

From *Hamlet and Oedipus*

That Hamlet is suffering from an internal conflict the essential nature of which is inaccessible to his introspection is evidenced by the following considerations. Throughout the play we have the clearest picture of a man who sees his duty plain before him, but who shirks it at every opportunity and suffers in consequence the most intense remorse. To paraphrase Sir James Paget's well-known description of hysterical paralysis: Hamlet's advocates say he cannot do his duty, his detractors say he will not, whereas the truth is that he cannot will. Further than this, the deficient will-power is localized to the one question of killing his uncle; it is what may be termed a *specific aboulia*. Now instances of such specific aboulias in real life invariably prove, when analysed, to be due to an unconscious repulsion against the act that cannot be performed (or else against something closely associated with the act, so that the idea of the act becomes also involved in the repulsion). In other words, whenever a person cannot bring himself to do something that every conscious consideration tells him he should do—and which he may have the strongest conscious desire to do—it is always because there is some hidden reason why a part of him doesn't want to do it; this reason he will not own to himself and is only dimly if at all aware of. That is exactly the case with Hamlet. Time and again he works himself up, points out to himself his obvious duty, with the cruellest self-reproaches lashes himself to agonies of remorse—and once more falls away into inaction. He eagerly seizes at every excuse for occupying

Reprinted from *Hamlet and Oedipus*, pp. 54–79, by Ernest Jones (1976), by permission of W. W. Norton and Company.

himself with any other matter than the performance of his duty—even in the last scene of the last act entering on the distraction of a quite irrelevant fencing-match with a man who he must know wants to kill him, an eventuality that would put an end to all hope of fulfilling his task: just as on a lesser plane a person faced with a distasteful task, e.g. writing a difficult letter, will whittle away his time in arranging, tidying, and fidgeting with any little occupation that may serve as a pretext for procrastination. Bradley[1] even goes as far as to make out a case for the view that Hamlet's self-accusation of "bestial oblivion" is to be taken in a literal sense, his unconscious detestation of his task being so intense as to enable him actually to forget it for periods.

Highly significant is the fact that the grounds Hamlet gives for his hesitancy are grounds none of which will stand any serious consideration, and which continually change from one time to another. One moment he pretends he is too cowardly to perform the deed, at another he questions the truthfulness of the ghost, at another—when the opportunity presents itself in its naked form—he thinks the time is unsuited, it would be better to wait till the King was at some evil act and then to kill him, and so on. They have each of them, it is true, a certain plausibility—so much so that some writers have accepted them at face value; but surely no pretext would be of any use if it were not plausible. As Madariaga[2] truly says: "The argument that the reasons given by Hamlet not to kill the king at prayers are cogent is irrelevant. For the man who wants to procrastinate cogent arguments are more valuable than mere pretexts." Take, for instance, the matter of the credibility of the ghost. There exists an extensive and very interesting literature concerning Elizabethan beliefs in supernatural visitation. It was doubtless a burning topic, a focal point of the controversies about the conflicting theologies of the age, and moreover, affecting the practical question of how to treat witches. But there is no evidence of Hamlet (or Shakespeare!) being specially interested in theology, and from the moment when the ghost confirms the slumbering suspicion in his mind ("O, my prophetic soul! My uncle!") his intuition must indubitably have convinced him of the ghost's veridical nature. He never really doubted the villainy of his uncle.

When a man gives at different times a different reason for his conduct it is safe to infer that, whether consciously or not, he is concealing the true reason. Wetz,[3] discussing a similar problem in reference to Iago, truly observes: "Nothing proves so well how false are the motives with which Iago tries to persuade himself as *the constant change in these motives.*" We can therefore safely dismiss all the alleged motives that Hamlet propounds, as being more or less successful attempts on his part to blind himself with self-deception. Leoning's[4] summing-up of them is not too emphatic when he says: "They are all mutually contradictory; *they are one and all false pretexts.*" The alleged motives excellently illustrate the psychological mechanisms of evasion and rationalization I have elsewhere described.[5] It is not necessary, however, to discuss them here individually, for Loening has with the greatest perspicacity done this in full detail and has effectually demonstrated how utterly untenable they all are.[6]

Still, in his moments of self-reproach Hamlet sees clearly enough the recalcitrancy of his conduct and renews his efforts to achieve action. It is noticeable how his outbursts of remorse are evoked by external happenings which bring back to his mind that which he would so gladly forget, and which, according to Bradley, he does at times forget: particularly effective in this respect are incidents that contrast with his own conduct, as when the player is so moved over the fate of Hecuba or when Fortinbras takes the field and "finds quarrel in a straw when honour's at the stake." On the former occasion, stung by the monstrous way in which the player pours out his feeling at the thought of Hecuba, he arraigns himself in words which surely should effectually dispose of the view that he has any doubt where his duty lies.

> What's Hecuba to him, or he to Hecuba,
> That he should weep for her? What would he do,
> Had he the motive and the cue for passion
> That I have? He would drown the stage with tears
> And cleave the general ear with horrid speech,
> Make mad the guilty and appal the free,
> Confound the ignorant, and amaze indeed
> The very faculties of eyes and ears; yet I,
> A dull and muddy-mettled rascal, peak
> Like John-a-dreams, unpregnant of my cause.[7]
> And can say nothing; no, not for a king,
> Upon whose property and most dear life
> A damn'd defeat was made: Am I a coward?

> Who calls me villain, breaks my pate across,
> Plucks off my beard and blows it in my face,
> Tweaks me by the nose, gives me the lie i' the throat
> As deep as to the lungs? Who does me this?
> Ha, 'swounds, I should take it: for it cannot be
> But I am pigeon-liver'd, and lack gall
> To make oppression bitter, or ere this
> I should ha' fatted all the region kites
> With this slave's offal. Bloody, bawdy villain!
> Remorseless, treacherous, lecherous, kindless villain!
> O, vengeance!
> Why, what an ass am I! This is most brave,
> That I, the son of a dear father murder'd,
> *Prompted to my revenge by heaven and hell,*
> Must like a whore unpack my heart with words,
> And fall a-cursing like a very drab;
> A scullion![8]

The readiness with which his guilty conscience is stirred into activity is again evidenced on the second appearance of the Ghost, when Hamlet cries,

> Do you not come your tardy son to chide,
> That lapsed in time and passion lets go by
> Th'important acting of your dread command?
> O, say!

The Ghost at once confirms this misgiving by answering,

> Do not forget! this visitation
> Is but to whet thy almost blunted purpose.

In short, the whole picture presented by Hamlet, his deep depression, the hopeless note in his attitude towards the world and towards the value of life, his dread of death,[9] his repeated reference to bad dreams, his self-accusations, his desperate efforts to get away from the thoughts of his duty, and his vain attempts to find an excuse for his procrastination: all this unequivocally points to a *tortured conscience*, to some hidden ground for shirking his task, a ground which he dare not or cannot avow to himself. We have, therefore, to take up the argument again at this point, and to seek for some evidence that may serve to bring to light the hidden counter-motive.

The extensive experience of the psycho-analytic researches carried out by Freud and his school during the past half-century has amply demonstrated that certain kinds of mental process show a greater tendency to be inaccessible to consciousness (put technically, to be "repressed") than others. In other words, it is harder for a person to realize the existence in his mind of some mental trends than it is of others. In order therefore to gain a proper perspective it is necessary briefly to inquire into the relative frequency with which various sets of mental processes are "repressed." Experience shows that this can be correlated with the degree of compatibility of these various sets with the ideals and standards accepted by the conscious ego; the less compatible they are with these the more likely are they to be "repressed." As the standards acceptable to consciousness are in considerable measure derived from the immediate environment, one may formulate the following generalization: those processes are most likely to be "repressed" by the individual which are most disapproved of by the particular circle of society to whose influence he has chiefly been subjected during the period when his character was being formed. Biologically stated, this law would run: "That which is unacceptable to the herd becomes unacceptable to the individual member," it being understood that the term herd is intended here in the sense of the particular circle defined above, which is by no means necessarily the community at large. It is for this reason that moral, social, ethical, or religious tendencies are seldom "repressed," for, since the individual originally received them from his herd, they can hardly ever come into conflict with the dicta of the latter. This merely says that a man cannot be ashamed of that which he respects; the apparent exceptions to this rule need not be here explained.

The language used in the previous paragraph will have indicated that by the term "repression" we denote an active dynamic process. Thoughts that are "repressed" are actively kept from consciousness by a definite force and with the expenditure of more or less mental effort, though the person concerned is rarely aware of this. Further, what is thus kept from consciousness typically possesses an energy of its own; hence our frequent use of such expressions as "trend," "tendency," etc. A little consideration of the genetic aspects of the matter will make it comprehensi-

ble that the trends most likely to be "repressed" are those belonging to what are called the innate impulses, as contrasted with
secondarily acquired ones. Loening[10] seems very discerningly to
have grasped this, for, in commenting on a remark of Kohler's to
the effect that "where a feeling impels us to action or to omission,
it is replete with a hundred reasons—with reasons that are as
light as soap-bubbles, but which through self-deception appear to
us as highly respectable and compelling motives, because they are
hugely magnified in the (concave) mirror of our own feeling," he
writes: "But this does not hold good, as Kohler and others believe,
when we are impelled by *moral* feelings of which reason *approves*
(for these we admit to ourselves, they need no excuse), only for
feelings that arise from our *natural man*, those the gratification of
which is *opposed by our reason*." It only remains to add the obvious
corollary that, as the herd unquestionably selects from the "natural" instincts the sexual one on which to lay its heaviest ban, so it
is the various psycho-sexual trends that are most often "repressed" by the individual. We have here the explanation of the
clinical experience that the more intense and the more obscure is
a given case of deep mental conflict the more certainly will it be
found on adequate analysis to centre about a sexual problem. On
the surface, of course, this does not appear so, for, by means of
various psychological defensive mechanisms, the depression,
doubt, despair, and other manifestations of the conflicts are trans-
ferred on to more tolerable and permissible topics, such as anxiety
about worldly success or failure, about immortality and the salvation of the soul, philosophical considerations about the value of
life, the future of the world, and so on.

Bearing these considerations in mind, let us return to Hamlet.
It should now be evident that the conflict hypotheses discussed
above, which see Hamlet's conscious impulse towards revenge
inhibited by an unconscious misgiving of a highly ethical kind, are
based on ignorance of what actually happens in real life, since
misgivings of this order belong in fact to the more conscious
layers of the mind rather than to the deeper, unconscious ones.
Hamlet's intense self-study would speedily have made him aware
of any such misgivings and, although he might subsequently have
ignored them, it would almost certainly have been by the aid of
some process of rationalization which would have enabled him to

deceive himself into believing that they were ill-founded; he would in any case have remained conscious of the nature of them. We have therefore to invert these hypotheses and realize—as his words so often indicate—that the positive striving for vengeance, the pious task laid on him by his father, was to him the moral and social one, the one approved of by his consciousness, and that the "repressed" inhibiting striving against the act of vengeance arose in some hidden source connected with his more personal, natural instincts. The former striving has already been considered, and indeed is manifest in every speech in which Hamlet debates the matter: the second is, from its nature, more obscure and has next to be investigated.

This is perhaps most easily done by inquiring more intently into Hamlet's precise attitude towards the object of his vengeance, Claudius, and towards the crimes that have to be avenged. These are two: Claudius' incest with the Queen,[11] and his murder of his brother. Now it is of great importance to note the profound difference in Hamlet's attitude towards these two crimes. Intellectually of course he abhors both, but there can be no question as to which arouses in him the deeper loathing. Whereas the murder of his father evokes in him indignation and a plain recognition of his obvious duty to avenge it, his mother's guilty conduct awakes in him the intensest horror. Furnivall[12] remarks, in speaking of the Queen, "Her disgraceful adultery and incest, and treason to his noble father's memory, Hamlet has felt in his inmost soul. Compared to their ingrain die, Claudius' murder of his father—notwithstanding all his protestations—is only a skin-deep stain."

Now, in trying to define Hamlet's attitude towards his uncle we have to guard against assuming off-hand that this is a simple one of mere execration, for there is a possibility of complexity arising in the following way: The uncle has not merely committed *each* crime, he has committed *both* crimes, a distinction of considerable importance, since the *combination* of crimes allows the admittance of a new factor, produced by the possible inter-relation of the two, which may prevent the result from being simply one of summation. In addition, it has to be borne in mind that the perpetrator of the crimes is a relative, and an exceedingly near relative. The possible inter-relationship of the crimes, and the fact that the author of them is an actual member of the family, give scope for a confusion in their influence on Hamlet's mind which may be the cause of the very obscurity we are seeking to clarify.

Let us first pursue further the effect on Hamlet of his mother's misconduct. Before he even knows with any certitude, however much he may suspect it, that his father has been murdered he is in the deepest depression, and evidently on account of this misconduct. The connection between the two is unmistakable in the monologue in Act I, Sc. 2, in reference to which Furnivall[13] writes: "One must insist on this, that before any revelation of his father's murder is made to Hamlet, before any burden of revenging that murder is laid upon him, he thinks of suicide as a welcome means of escape from this fair world of God's, made abominable to his diseased and weak imagination by his mother's lust, and the dishonour done by her to his father's memory."

> O that this too too solid[14] flesh would melt,
> Thaw and resolve itself into a dew,
> Or that the Everlasting had not fix'd
> His canon 'gainst self-slaughter, O God, God,
> How weary, stale, flat, and unprofitable
> Seem to me all the uses of this world!
> Fie on 't, O fie, 'tis an unweeded garden
> That grows to seed, things rank and gross in nature
> Possess it merely, that it should come to this,
> But two months dead, nay, not so much, not two,
> So excellent a king; that was to this
> Hyperion to a satyr, so loving to my mother,
> That he might not beteem the winds of heaven
> Visit her face too roughly—heaven and earth
> Must I remember? why, she would hang on him
> As if increase of appetite had grown
> By what it fed on, and yet within a month,
> Let me not think on 't; frailty thy name is woman!
> A little month or ere those shoes were old
> With which she follow'd my poor father's body
> Like Niobe all tears, why she, even she—
> O God, a beast that wants discourse of reason
> Would have mourn'd longer—married with my uncle,
> My father's brother, but no more like my father
> Than I to Hercules, within a month,

> Ere yet the salt of most unrighteous tears
> Had left the flushing in her galled eyes,
> She married. O most wicked speed . . . to post
> With such dexterity to incestuous sheets!
> It is not, nor it cannot come to good,
> But break my heart, for I must hold my tongue.

According to Bradley,[15] Hamlet's melancholic disgust at life was the cause of his aversion from "any kind of decided action." His explanation of the whole problem of Hamlet is "the moral shock of the sudden ghastly disclosure of his mother's true nature,"[16] and he regards the effect of this shock, as depicted in the play, as fully comprehensible. He says,[17] "Is it possible to conceive an experience more desolating to a man such as we have seen Hamlet to be; and is its result anything but perfectly natural? It brings bewildered horror, then loathing, then despair of human nature. His whole mind is poisoned. . . . A nature morally blunter would have felt even so dreadful a revelation less keenly. A slower and more limited and positive mind might not have extended so widely through the world the disgust and disbelief that have entered it."

But we can rest satisfied with this seemingly adequate explanation of Hamlet's weariness of life only if we accept unquestioningly the conventional standards of the causes of deep emotion. Many years ago Connolly,[18] a well-known psychiatrist, pointed out the disproportion here existing between cause and effect, and gave as his opinion that Hamlet's reaction to his mother's marriage indicated in itself a mental instability, "a predisposition to actual unsoundness"; he writes: "The circumstances are not such as would at once turn a healthy mind to the contemplation of suicide, the last resource of those whose reason has been overwhelmed by calamity and despair." In T. S. Eliot's[19] opinion, also, Hamlet's emotion is in excess of the facts as they appear, and he specially contrasts it with Gertrude's negative and insignificant personality. Wihan[20] attributes the exaggerated effect of his misfortunes to Hamlet's "Masslosigkeit" (lack of moderation), which is displayed in every direction. We have unveiled only the exciting cause, not the predisposing cause. The very fact that Hamlet is apparently content with the explanation arouses our misgiving, for, as will presently be expounded, from the very nature of the emotion he cannot be aware of the true cause of it. If we ask, not what ought to produce such soul-paralysing grief and distaste for life, but what in actual fact does produce it, we are compelled to go beyond this explanation and seek for some deeper cause. In real life speedy second marriages occur commonly enough without leading to any such result as is here depicted, and when we see them followed by this result we invariably find, if the opportunity for an analysis of the subject's mind presents itself, that there is some other and more hidden reason why the event is followed by this inordinately great effect. The reason always is that the event has awakened to increased activity mental processes that have been "repressed" from the subject's consciousness. His mind has been specially prepared for the catastrophe by previous mental processes with which those directly resulting from the event have entered into association. This is perhaps what Furnivall means when he speaks of the world being made abominable to Hamlet's "diseased imagination." In short, the special nature of the reaction presupposes some special feature in the mental predisposition. Bradley himself has to qualify his hypothesis by inserting the words "to a man such as we have seen Hamlet to be."

We come at this point to the vexed question of Hamlet's sanity, about which so many controversies have raged. Dover Wilson[21] authoritatively writes: "I agree with Loening, Bradley and others that Shakespeare meant us to imagine Hamlet as suffering from some kind of mental disorder throughout the play." The question is what kind of mental disorder and what is its significance dramatically and psychologically. The matter is complicated by Hamlet's frequently displaying simulation (the Antic Disposition)[22] and it has been asked whether this is to conceal his real mental disturbance or cunningly to conceal his purposes in coping with the practical problems of this task? This is a topic that presently will be considered at some length, but there can be few who regard it as a comprehensive statement of Hamlet's mental state. As T. S. Eliot[23] has neatly expressed it, "Hamlet's 'madness' is less than madness and more than feigned."

But what of the mental disorder itself? In the past this little problem in clinical diagnosis seems to have greatly exercised psychiatrists. Some of them, e.g. Thierisch,[24] Sigismund,[25] Stenger,[26] and many others, have simply held that Hamlet was insane, without particularizing the form of insanity. Rosner[27] labelled Hamlet as a hystero-neurasthenic, an opinion contradicted by Rubinstein[28] and Landmann.[29] Most, however, including Kellog,[30] de Boismon,[31] Heuse,[32] Nicholson,[33] and others, have committed themselves to the view that Hamlet was suffering from melancholia, though there are not failing psychiatrists, e.g. Ominus,[34] who reject this. Schücking[35] attributes the delay in his action to Hamlet's being paralysed by melancholia. Laehr[36] has a particularly ingenious hypothesis which maintains that Shakespeare, having taken over the Ghost episode from the earlier play, was obliged to depict Hamlet as a melancholiac because this was theatrically the most presentable form of insanity in which hallucinations occur. Long ago Dowden made it seem probable that Shakespeare had made use of an important study of melancholia by Timothe Bright,[37] but, although he may have adapted a few phrases to his own use, the clinical picture of Hamlet differs notably from that delineated by Bright.

More to the point is the actual account given in the play by the King, the Queen, Ophelia, and above all, Polonius.[38] In his description, for example, we note—if the Elizabethan language is translated into modern English—the symptoms of dejection, refusal of food, insomnia, crazy behaviour, fits of delirium, and finally of raving madness; Hamlet's poignant parting words to Polonius ("except my life," etc.) cannot mean other than a craving for death. These are undoubtedly suggestive of certain forms of melancholia, and the likeness to manic-depressive insanity, of which melancholia is now known to be but a part, is completed by the occurrence of attacks of great excitement that would nowadays be called "hypomanic," of which Dover Wilson[39] counts no fewer than eight. This modern diagnosis has indeed been suggested, e.g. by Brock,[40] Somerville,[41] and others. Nevertheless, the rapid and startling oscillations between intense excitement and profound depression do not accord with the accepted picture of this disorder, and if I had to describe such a condition as Hamlet's in clinical terms—which I am not particularly inclined to—it would have to be as a severe case of hysteria on a cyclothymic basis.

All this, however, is of academic interest only. What we are essentially concerned with is the psychological understanding of the dramatic effect produced by Hamlet's personality and behaviour. That effect would be quite other were the central figure in the play to represent merely a "case of insanity." When that happens, as with Ophelia, such a person passes beyond our ken, is in a sense no more human, whereas Hamlet successfully claims our interest and sympathy to the very end. Shakespeare certainly never intended us to regard Hamlet as insane, so that the "mind o'erthrown" must have some other meaning than its literal one. Robert Bridges[42] has described the matter with exquisite delicacy:

> Hamlet himself would never have been aught to us, or we
> To Hamlet, wer't not for the artful balance whereby
> Shakespeare so gingerly put his sanity in doubt
> Without the while confounding his Reason.

I would suggest that in this Shakespeare's extraordinary powers of observation and penetration granted him a degree of insight that it has taken the world three subsequent centuries to reach. Until our generation (and even now in the juristic sphere) a dividing line separated the sane and responsible from the irresponsible insane. It is now becoming more and more widely recognized that much of mankind lives in an intermediate and unhappy state charged with what Dover Wilson[43] well calls "that sense of frustration, futility and human inadequacy which is the burden of the whole symphony" and of which Hamlet is the supreme example in literature. This intermediate plight, in the toils of which perhaps the greater part of mankind struggles and suffers, is given the name of psychoneurosis, and long ago the genius of Shakespeare depicted it for us with faultless insight.

Extensive studies of the past half century, inspired by Freud, have taught us that a psychoneurosis means a state of mind where the person is unduly, and often painfully, driven or thwarted by the "unconscious" part of his mind, that buried part that was once the infant's mind and still lives on side by side with the adult mentality that has developed out of it and should have taken its place. It signifies *internal* mental conflict. We have here the reason why it is impossible to discuss intelligently the state of mind of anyone suffering from a psychoneurosis, whether the description is of a living person or an imagined one, without correlating the manifestations with what must have operated in his infancy and is *still operating*. That is what I propose to attempt here.

For some deep-seated reason, which is to him unacceptable, Hamlet is plunged into anguish at the thought of his father being replaced in his mother's affections by someone else. It is as if his devotion to his mother had made him so jealous for her affection that he had found it hard enough to share this even with his father and could not endure to share it with still another man. Against this thought, however, suggestive as it is, may be urged three objections. First, if it were in itself a full statement of the matter, Hamlet would have been aware of the jealousy, whereas we have concluded that the mental process we are seeking is hidden from him. Secondly, we see in it no evidence of the arousing of an old and forgotten memory. And, thirdly, Hamlet is being deprived by Claudius of no greater share in the Queen's affection than he had been by his own father, for the two brothers made exactly similar claims in this respect—namely, those of a loved husband. The last-named objection, however, leads us to the heart of the situation. How if, in fact, Hamlet had in years gone by, as a child, bitterly resented having had to share his mother's affection even with his own father, had regarded him as a rival, and had secretly wished him out of the way so that he might enjoy undisputed and undisturbed the monopoly of that affection? If such thoughts had been present in his mind in childhood days they evidently would have been "repressed," and all traces of them obliterated, by filial piety and other educative influences. The actual realization of his early wish in the death of his father at the hands of a jealous rival would then have stimulated into activity these "repressed" memories, which would have produced, in the form of depression and other suffering, an obscure aftermath of his childhood's conflict. This is at all events the mechanism that is actually found in the real Hamlets who are investigated psychologically.[44]

The explanation, therefore, of the delay and self-frustration exhibited in the endeavour to fulfil his father's demand for vengeance is that to Hamlet the thought of incest and parricide combined is too intolerable to be borne. One part of him tries to carry out the task, the other flinches inexorably from the thought of it. How fain would he blot it out in that "bestial oblivion" which unfortunately for him his conscience contemns. He is torn and tortured in an insoluble inner conflict.

NOTES

1. Bradley, *Shakespearean Tragedy*, pp. 125, 126, 410, 411.
2. Madariaga, *On Hamlet*, p. 98.
3. Wetz: Shakespeare vom Standpunkt der vergleichenden Litteratur-geschichte, 1890, Bd. I, S. 186.
4. Loening, *Die Hamlet-Tragödie Shakespeares*, S. 245.
5. *Journal of Abnormal Psychology*, 1908, p. 161.
6. See especially his analysis of Hamlet's pretext for non-action in the prayer scene: op. cit., S. 240-2.
7. How the essence of the situation is conveyed in these four words.
8. Dover Wilson considers this a misprint for "stallion."
9. Tieck (Dramaturgische Blätter, II, 1826) saw in Hamlet's cowardly fear of death a chief reason for his hesitancy in executing his vengeance. How well Shakespeare understood what this fear was like may be inferred from Claudio's words in "Measure for Measure":

    > The weariest and most loathed worldly life
    > That age, ache, penury and imprisonment
    > Can lay on nature is a paradise
    > To what we fear of death.

10. Loening, S. 245, 246.
11. Had this relationship not counted as incestuous, then Queen Elizabeth would have had no right to the throne; she would have been a bastard, Katherine of Aragon being still alive at her birth.
12. Furnivall: Introduction to the "Leopold" Shakespeare, p. 72.
13. Furnivall, p. 70.
14. Dover Wilson (*Times Literary Supplement*, May 16, 1918) brings forward excellent reasons for thinking that this word is a misprint for "sullied." I use the Shakespearean punctuation he has restored.
15. Bradley, p. 122.
16. Ibid., p. 117.
17. Ibid., p. 119.
18. Connolly, *A Study of Hamlet*, 1863, pp. 22, 23.
19. T. S. Eliot, *The Sacred Wood*, 1920.
20. J. Wihan: "Die Hamletfrage," in Leipziger Beiträge zur englischen Philologie, 1921, S. 89.
21. Dover Wilson, *What Happens* etc., p. 217.
22. Cp. R. Alexander, "Hamlet, the Classical Malingerer," *Medical Journal and Record*, Sept. 4, 1929, p. 287.

23. T. S. Eliot, *Selected Essays*, 1932, p. 146.
24. Thierisch, *Nord und Süd*, 1878, Bd. VI.
25. Sigismund, *Jahrbuch der Deutschen Shakespeare-Gesellschaft*, 1879, Jahrg. XVI.
26. E. Stenger, *"Der Hamlet Charakter," Eine psychiatrische Shakespeare-Studie*, 1883.
27. Rosner, *Shakespeare's Hamlet im Lichte der Neuropathologie*, 1895.
28. Rubinstein, *Hamlet als Neurastheniker*, 1896.
29. Landmann, *Zeitschrift für Psychologie*, 1896, Bd. XI.
30. Kellog, *Shakespeare's Delineation of Insanity*, 1868.
31. De Boismon, *Annales médico-psychologiques*, 1868, 4e série, 12e fasc.
32. Heuse, *Jahrbuch der deutschen Shakespeare-Gesellschaft*, 1876, Jahrg. XIII.
33. Nicholson, *Transactions of the New Shakespeare Society*, 1880-5, Part II.
34. Ominus, *Revue des Deux Mondes*, 1876, 3e sér., 14e fasc.
35. Schücking, *Character Problems in Shakespeare's Plays*, 1922, p. 162.
36. Laehr, *Die Darstellung krankhafter Geisteszustände in Shakespeare's Dramas*, 1898, S. 179, etc.
37. Timothe Bright, *A Treatise of Melancholia*, 1586.
38. Act 2, Sc. 2. "Fell into a sadness," etc.
39. Dover Wilson, p. 213.
40. J. H. E. Brock, *The Dramatic Purpose of Hamlet*, 1935.
41. H. Somerville, *Madness in Shakespearean Tragedy*, 1929.
42. Robert Bridges, *The Testament of Beauty*, I, 577.
43. Dover Wilson, p. 261.
44. See, for instance, Wulf Sachs, *Black Hamlet*, 1937.

A. J. Waldock

From *Hamlet: A Study in Critical Method*

It was inevitable that Hamlet, sooner or later, should be psy-cho-analysed, for he is a perfect subject. It is, indeed, very inter-esting to note what the new psychology has to say about him.

We owe the major elucidation of him from this point of view to Dr. Ernest Jones (*Essays in Applied Psycho-Analysis*). Jones first of all posits the impression which Hamlet makes as that of "a strong man tortured by some mysterious inhibition." Our business, then, is to discover the nature of this inhibition. Bradley's account is judged inadequate, for it is based on rather conventional ideas of the causes of deep emotion: it is not, according to Dr. Jones, psychologically up-to-date: nor does it quite recognise that certain disproportion between cause and effect which appears in Ham-let's responses to his mother's re-marriage. Hamlet's sufferings (Jones rightly points out) have struck many people as being, even when all allowances are made for the idealism of his character, a good deal in excess of the occasion. We may grant that the marriage was offensive then as it would not be now: it was not only indecently hasty; it was incestuous. The point still remains that Hamlet is shocked in a way and to a degree that we can hardly help thinking abnormal. The question is, what does really produce this abnormal effect?

Jones then plunges in. With care and industry, and much shrewdness of observation, he collects the relevant data, assumes for his purpose that they have precisely the validity that would attach to a case in real life, and works out his solution. There are admittedly some difficulties, but they are for the most part only such as would occur to laymen. Thus, we must begin, of course, by assuming that Hamlet did not understand the nature of his inhibition: if he had understood it, it would not have been one. The ordinary person, accordingly, might feel some qualms about the practicability of penetrating to it. Jones, however, denounces this at once as a "pessimistic thought" and smiles at the simplicity of such a doubter. "Fortunately for our investigation, psychoanalytic studies have demonstrated beyond doubt that mental trends hidden from the subject himself may come to external expression in ways that reveal their nature to the trained observer." Nor is that all. It is equally possible that Shakespeare himself did not understand the nature of the inhibition that was stopping Hamlet. We reach in the end the startling, but to Jones only "apparent" paradox, that "the hero, the poet, and the audience are all profoundly moved by feelings due to a conflict of the source of which they are unaware."

But the audience, at least, if it will follow Jones, is not condemned to remain in unawareness and may presently understand the case far better than the dramatist. Let us consider it again. Hamlet does not know why he cannot act. He *can* act, in other matters, but not in this. His trouble is *specific aboulia*, his will power is restricted in one direction. He tries to explain his inability to himself, but his explanations differ and are therefore and for other reasons untenable. The real explanation is this. The mother's second marriage awakes into activity a slumbering memory. Hamlet, as a child, had had a passion for his mother. He had resented sharing this passion with his father. He had regarded this father as a rival and had secretly wished him out of the way, so that he might enjoy the monopoly of his mother's affection. The point is that such thoughts had been repressed. Now, in the murder of the father, these old repressed desires find their realisation; the stifled memories are rekindled; and the result is this terrible disturbance of soul, the cause of which Hamlet is far from knowing, but which we see as the "obscure aftermath of his childhood's conflict." And why cannot he kill his uncle? Because his uncle, the slayer of his father, is the symbol of his own repressed desires become victorious. His uncle is his buried self: to kill his uncle is to kill himself. He is only released from the mysterious band, set free to fulfil his duty, when himself brought to the door of death.

Here is realism in interpretation with a vengeance. But Jones does not let the matter rest quite there. He eludes our obvious comments by suddenly shifting his explanation a stage farther back. All this conflict in Hamlet is neither more nor less than the echo of a similar one in Shakespeare himself. Ultimately, it was Shakespeare who had the Oedipus complex, who hated his father as a rival, and would, in similar circumstances, have found it impossible to kill his uncle.

Two comments still seem relevant. In the first place one wonders where this principle, of an author's unconsciousness of his own purposes, might eventually lead us. Indeed, it has led us far in the present case. Jones makes light of such a perplexity, or rather, proclaims his creed with bravado. It is, he asserts, actually beside the point to enquire into Shakespeare's conscious intentions. So it is, he thinks, with the work of most great creative artists. The play is simply the form in which Shakespeare's deepest, unconscious feelings find their spontaneous expression. Now that there is some truth in such a view we may readily grant. We can easily think of writers to whom such phrases might seem to apply with greater aptness. But it is surely not going too far to feel with Jones that much of the stuff of *Hamlet* came from inspirations that took their origin in the "deepest and darkest regions" of Shakespeare's mind. No one would suggest at least that a writer needs to be able to supply a coherent psychological analysis, with terms complete, of the characters he creates: his business is rather to feel his characters very intensely. We can have no doubt, for all the perplexities of the play, that if ever Shakespeare did feel a character intensely, it was Hamlet. Nor does there seem a reason to refuse the suggestion, which Jones (after Bradley) makes, that the behaviour of Hamlet might well represent Shakespeare's sense of what his own behaviour in such circumstances could have been. There is no harm in having the notion, if we like it, that Shakespeare, while he would have extricated himself from Othello's difficulties with the greatest ease, could not have coped with Hamlet's problem. All this we may let pass. It is still a good deal to ask us to believe that not this or that touch, not an intimation here, a suggestion there, but the central plot of this play, depends on, *is*, a complex of the author's, the nature of which, the existence of which, were of course quite hidden from his conscious mind. One wonders what Shakespeare himself thought of Hamlet's symptoms; and seeing that, when he had produced them, he could gain no glimmer of an idea of what they meant (as of course by hypothesis he could not), why he did not become anxious about them. Even Jones will admit that, in all probability, Shakespeare was "not only inspired from the personal and intimate sources we have indicated, but was also influenced by his actual conscious experiences." It is conceded that there is something "conscious" in the play. And although, according to Jones, Shakespeare's Oedipus complex is rampant in other works, still it must surely be allowed that in many of his plays he seems to be writing in some considerable state of awareness. Why, in *Hamlet*, he should have departed from what seems to have been his usual practice (namely, of working as a more or less conscious artist) and have suddenly decided to abandon himself to the whims of his subconscious nature, is hard to see.

But even supposing it were so; even supposing that Shakespeare did try here to portray something which he could not himself understand; that the play, as Mr. T. S. Eliot puts it, is "full of some stuff that the writer could not drag to light, contemplate, or manipulate into art"; plainly in such a case our own understandings cannot be of much use. The point, as Mr. Eliot says, is that the stuff is not dragged to light, is *not* manipulated into art. If Hamlet has a complex, what business is it of ours? When a complex is made into dramatic material it becomes our business, not before. And even to speak of Hamlet's complex is to speak of something in another dimension: it is a thing that has no being in the world of our play. With as much reason might we set about explaining Macbeth's crime by an investigation of the medical history of his grandfather. The reply, in short, to all such attempts is that, whatever illumination they may shed by the way, they are in bulk devoid of all dramatic relevance.

Dr. Jones *does* shed illumination by the way. It seems to me that few investigators have laid emphasis so valuably on an aspect of the play strangely ignored or underestimated in *Hamlet* criticism: I mean, using the term in a rather special sense, its sexual quality. Goethe and Coleridge, as we have seen, do not recognise the existence of such a quality in the play, and Bradley scarcely seems to grant it the importance it deserves. Let us return to that first soliloquy. Really, "moral shock" hardly seems adequate to the impression this soliloquy conveys. There is in some of the lines almost a physical nausea. Hamlet is sick with disgust. He could retch with the thought of the things his mother has been doing. Now this impression seems of very great importance indeed. There is, if we like, something abnormal in the quality of Hamlet's feeling. But, above all, it is no *abstract* feeling (although, as we know, the despair does universalise itself). The feeling is in its essential nature exceedingly intimate. And it does, surely, put us in mind strongly of the things on which Jones fixes his attention. There is a suggestion that Hamlet has received damage of a kind analogous to the damage sometimes revealed by the procedures of psycho-analysis. I see no possibility, in a dramatic appreciation of the play, of going much farther than this. That Hamlet seems to have been hurt in that most intimate relationship, the relationship between mother and son; that his trouble derives, in a narrower sense than is usually understood, from this source: we may surely go so far.

We may go farther. What is the play of *Hamlet* really about? It is, of course, about many things; we understand how various are its appeals. But what is it most deeply about? Irresolution? Surely there is something in the play deeper than that. If we answer the question by asking ourselves another one, What is it that Hamlet himself is most deeply concerned about?—What is it that above all other things dominates his soul?—we can have no doubt what we must say. It would be too much to affirm that, compared with his horror at his mother, the shock of the murder is a trifle: yet it is nearly true. If the centre of the equilibrium of the play is the centre of the equilibrium of Hamlet's soul, then it is clear where it must lie. He forgets his vengeance; but he remembers this other thing. How he remembers it! It is strange that so vital a strain in the play should not have received more attention: it is impossible not to feel it. The first soliloquy brings it home to us; it is from then onwards the underlying theme. With Hamlet the feeling is an obsession and we are never left for long without an indication of its presence. We hear from Ophelia presently (II, i, 88) how he came to her, grasped her wrist, and, with his hand o'er his brow, fell to such perusal of her face as he would draw it; then, after the soul-searching scrutiny, raised a sigh that seemed

> to shatter all his bulk
> And end his being.

It is as if already all womanhood has become suspect of the corruption he has discovered in his mother. A little later is the bitter gibing of the speech with Polonius (II, ii, 182): "Have you a daughter? . . . . Let her not walk i' the sun: conception is a blessing; but as your daughter may conceive. . . ." It is the same when next he meets Ophelia: the cruel harping on "honesty" (III, i, 103), the savage cynicism of "for wise men know well enough what monsters you make of them" (III, i, 143), the anguish that suddenly starts into his voice and makes us glimpse the abyss in his soul: "Go to, I'll no more on't; it hath made me mad" (III, i, 153). Here too is that same spreading and deepening of the disgust to include all life: "What should such fellows as I do crawling between heaven and earth?" (III, i, 129). We see him again soon in the play-scene. He and Horatio are supposed to be watching every movement of the King's features. How does he occupy himself? We remember how he lies down at Ophelia's feet and with what manner of jesting he passes the time. And then, the troubled Ophelia calling him "merry," instantaneously, and, as it were, automatically, comes the sarcastic rejoinder: "What should a man do but be merry? for, look you, how cheerfully my mother looks, and my father died within's two hours." Presently, " 'Tis brief, my lord," comments Ophelia, of the play; the response is inevitable: "as woman's love." It is as if his experience has become woven into the very texture of his mind; he thinks of nothing else. The very word "mother" has become an instrument of torture to him and he invents ways of using it on himself: puns, innuendoes, cryptic jests (III, ii, 343):

> *Rosencrantz.* She desires to speak with you in her closet, ere
>   you go to bed.
> *Hamlet.* We shall obey, were she ten times our mother.

His good-bye to the King is a grotesque conundrum (IV, iii, 51):

> Farewell, dear mother.
> *King.* Thy loving father, Hamlet.
> *Hamlet.* My mother: father and mother is man and wife; man
> and wife is one flesh, and so, my mother.

The climax is reached in the scene in Gertrude's room, where his tormented spirit relieves itself in those bitter upbraidings. But what is most interesting to note is the quality of the dark thoughts and images that now gush forth. The loathsome broodings that had made his mind a hell now appear in all their hideousness in the light of day. It is a terrible and wonderful scene and in figure after figure ("batten," "compulsive ardour," frost that burns, "rank sweat," "stew'd in corruption," "sty," "compost") we are made to see with what thoughts, what pictures, Hamlet had been living. We need not wonder much further about what came to him in the bad dreams. Perhaps most terrible, most touching of all, is that strangely intimate, urgent, pleading with the mother, that she should not return to the marriage-bed. He can scarcely relinquish this subject; it is as if it had fastened on his very soul.

It seems certain, too, that we must understand the mystery of his relations with Ophelia (so far as we can understand it) in the light of all this trouble. It is indeed rather a question of guessing than of understanding. The whole matter is left, perhaps with some deliberation, enigmatic. We seem justified in assuming that Hamlet loved Ophelia once, though even there we are given little chance of doing more than speculate on the quality and intensity of his love. It seems clear that the love, as we see it in the play, has been poisoned by some strange resentment, suspicion or hatred. The rest is left undetermined. But we do seem warranted, at least, in connecting this change with that other experience. All women fall under the ban. Perhaps we may go even farther. Those jeering allusions of Hamlet's to "conception"; those pitiful songs of Ophelia in madness; do such hints amount to anything? Is it suggested that Hamlet savagely tried Ophelia, to see if she was of the selfsame metal as his mother? It would at least have been natural, in this wreckage of his world, to turn and experiment bitterly on

this last piece of seeming innocence, testing if it also were wrecka-
ble. If it were so, we can imagine what her death meant to him
and gain, as Professor Allardyce Nicoll suggests, a new comprehension of the "It is no matter." mood of Act V. But we cannot
pursue this. We are left with the conclusion that Shakespeare did
not trouble or did not wish to make the Hamlet-Ophelia story
plainer, and in face of his refusal are helpless.

Paul Gottschalk

From *The Meanings of Hamlet*

Psychoanalysis is based largely on the principle that "mental trends hidden from the subject himself may come to external expression in ways that reveal their nature to a trained observer."[1] Accordingly, Jones's interpretation assigns to Hamlet feelings and motives that are never directly expressed in the play. Thus, there is no mimetic evidence that to Hamlet Polonius is a modified father figure or Ophelia a mother figure, no immediate evidence of Hamlet's incestuous attraction to his mother or of hidden antagonism toward his father; even his identification with Claudius, though perhaps inferable from the text, is not indisputably oedipal.[2] Indeed, Hamlet expresses nothing but love for his father and nothing but contempt and hate for Claudius. These facts do not in themselves contradict the psychoanalytic interpretation, for presumably Hamlet's conscience would not only demand that his guilty emotions be utterly repressed, but that his conscious mind avow only their direct opposites. The text, of course, contains only these avowals of his conscious mind. Yet all of Hamlet's hidden emotions, particularly those involving his mother, his father, and Claudius, are central to any Freudian interpretation of the play, and their absence from the text provides the critics of Freud their chief weapon and his friends their main stumbling block. F. L. Lucas, who accepts psychoanalytic interpretation in principle, nevertheless boggles at the assumption of Hamlet's hostility to his father: "If we are to speak in terms of the Oedipus-complex, we can only say that its mother-

Reprinted from *The Meanings of Hamlet*, pp. 87–97, by Paul Gottschalk (1972), by permission of University of New Mexico Press.

love is conspicuously present in the play, but its father-hatred concentrated wholly upon the new step-father, Claudius."[3] But if we are to speak in terms of the Oedipus complex, then we must accept that complex in its entirety, and that entirety includes antagonism toward the father. That Hamlet should conceive, *ex nihilo*, an oedipal dislike of Claudius may seem more true to the text, but it makes nonsense of Freud.

Morris Weitz, indeed, makes Hamlet's hostility to his father the issue on which the Freudian interpretation must stand or fall:

> In *Hamlet* there is no textual evidence that Hamlet is lying or even deceiving himself, consciously or unconsciously, about his love for his father. . . . In real-life situations, I suppose, we are prepared to accept explanations of emotions that convert them into something else, even into their very opposites. . . . But in Shakespeare's *Hamlet* we must accept what may in real life appear strange and implausible. We have no alternative except to open up the possibility of reading any datum of any text in any way that we like. And, clearly, that way lies chaos, not criticism.[4]

This is a very serious charge, and we should examine what psychoanalysis can bring to its defense—especially since the defense may clarify the principles of this unusual mode of interpretation.

Even if, as I think, the Freudian interpretation does not contradict the text it does go beyond the textually explicit, and once more the problem lies in the limited evidence that Shakespeare has provided us. In an actual therapeutic situation, the analyst might hypothesize hostility underlying the patient's extreme praise of his father, as Jones does with Hamlet. But in actual analysis the therapist can verify his hypothesis with the data that further analysis may uncover—and, ultimately, with the cure of the patient. Such verification, of course, is denied us in *Hamlet*. We are not told the precise contents of Hamlet's bad dreams. The question, then, is whether psychoanalysis can offer any supplementary evidence to verify its interpretation.

In fact, Jones offers two such supplementary verifications. The first of these is a biographical study of Shakespeare himself: "It has been found," he says, "that with poetic creations this critical procedure [of intellectual appreciation] cannot halt at the work of art itself: to isolate this from its creator is to impose artificial limits to our understanding of it."[5] This passage makes it sound as if Jones is in the critical tradition of Taine and Carlyle, but that is not quite so. The psychoanalytic correspondence between artist and artifact, as we shall see, ultimately involves an entirely new way of "understanding" a poetical text, as well as a new variation on the old theme of the "artist's intentions" in creating this text. In any case, to Jones it seems likely that *Hamlet* expresses the state of Shakespeare's own soul at the turn of the sixteenth century: that it marks a revival in him of his own oedipal problems, which the writing of the play alone could purge.

The evidence that Jones adduces for this revival is threefold. To begin with, there is the celebrated "strain of sex-nausea" that appears in the plays that Shakespeare wrote after 1600, beginning in *Hamlet*.[6] Secondly, in 1601 occurred the deaths of Essex and, more important, of Shakespeare's father,[7] so that *Hamlet* may have been written, as Freud suggests, "under the immediate impact of his bereavement and, as we may well assume, while his childhood feelings about his father had been freshly revived."[8] Finally, Jones surmises that Shakespeare was under the influence of his betrayal, described in the Sonnets, by his mistress and his closest friend, a betrayal analogous to what Hamlet felt and to what Shakespeare presumably felt as a child towards his parents, for it is the feelings of childhood that determine the relationships of the adult.[9] (Whether the Sonnets are truly autobiographical is, as Jones admits, impossible to determine. Nevertheless, what the poet imagines himself as doing may be as much a fact of his personality as what he actually does.)

This biographical argument, though not entirely implausible, is scarcely convincing. There is simply not enough evidence, and such evidence as we have might be contradicted by facts of which no evidence has survived. It is debatable, moreover, that the so-called "sex-nausea" of the middle plays is autobiographical, and the death of Shakespeare's father (September, 1601) may well have occurred after the composition of *Hamlet*, although, as Jones suggests, he might have suffered long from a fatal illness.[10] Moreover, Otto Rank has found the same oedipal themes in *Julius Caesar* as in *Hamlet*, and also in other plays composed long before

the death of John Shakespeare.[11] It is true that the oedipal situation seems more overt in *Hamlet* than in other plays; however, as
Jones himself admits, "the dates and circumstances . . . are too
indeterminate to allow us to regard Freud's supposition from
being any more than an inspired guess, which, however, may be
greatly inspired."[12] In any case, even though some biographical
information does seem to support a Freudian interpretation of
Hamlet, Jones would certainly not have undertaken to psychoanalyze one of his own patients on the basis of such slight evidence.

This biographical approach, we may note in passing, obviously
does not consider the creative process to spring from deliberate
artistic intent; rather, it stresses the artist's "unawareness of the
ultimate source of creation."[13] The poet's primal purpose in creation may be personal and preconscious, his consideration of the
audience secondary. Thus, for instance, Ella Sharpe can state:
"The poet is not Hamlet. Hamlet is what he might have been if he
had not written the play of *Hamlet*. The characters are all introjec-
tions thrown out again from his mind. . . . He has ejected all of
them symbolically and remains a sane man, through a sublima-
tion that satisfies the demands of the super-ego and the impulses
of the id."[14] There is, of course, no reason why the final form this
catharsis takes cannot be a popular drama. Indeed, as we shall see,
personal catharsis and popularity may go hand in hand.

If the biographical interpretation is inadequate, Jones's other
extra-textual approach to the play stands on firmer ground. This
approach is to explore the psychological relationship of *Hamlet* and
the Hamlet legend with other myths. Indeed, Jones says, "to
anyone familiar with the modern interpretation, based on psychoanalytic researches, of myths and legends, that [psychoanalytic]
explanation of the Hamlet problem would immediately occur on
the first reading of the play."[15] According to this comparative
mythology, *Hamlet* is a latter-day, highly elaborate variation of
that group of myths whose main theme is the displacement of the
rival father by the young hero, with a correspondent intimacy,
actual or symbolic, between hero and mother—a particularly significant theme when we consider the Freudian view of myths as
derived from infantile fantasy.[16] A common feature of this group
of myths is the "repression" of the actual fratricide: the hero kills
a father figure, not his real father. (The psychological mechanism

here is essentially the same as that which disguises the meaning of a dream that might otherwise offend the conscience). Thus, the father is "decomposed" into two persons—commonly, the real and tender father and the cruel tyrant. Frequently, these two are related, so that the villain is the hero's grandfather, grand-uncle, or—less often—uncle, as in the Hamlet legend. But, unlike the legendary Amleth, Shakespeare's hero shrinks even from killing the father symbol: "Shakespeare's marvelous intuition has, quite unconsciously, penetrated beneath the surface of the smooth Amleth version. He lifts for us at least one layer of the concealing 'repression' and reveals something of the tumult below."[17] Moreover, in the various relations between Hamlet and the Polonius family (as well as between Claudius and Laertes, and also in the entire Fortinbras situation) we see simply further manifestations of this same myth.[18]

This comparative mythology is based on much the same sort of hypothesis that permits the psychoanalyst to detect Hamlet's unexpressed emotions. If comparative mythology does permit us to state with some assurance that "repressed" forms of the myth are closely related to overt forms of the oedipal theme, and if, furthermore, psychoanalysts have found it useful to employ in actual therapy concepts derived from study of these myths, then we have a large body of independently derived knowledge that links life and literature (including Shakespeare's ultimate sources) and serves to corroborate the Freudian interpretation of Hamlet, to make it appear less arbitrary than it may seem at first.

The answer to Weitz's question of textual evidence, then, is that under certain circumstances it may be legitimate to regard *Hamlet* as more than simply a text. To the psychoanalyst it is, in fact, the center of a theoretical nexus that includes Shakespeare, the Elizabethan audience, and the modern reader—for what Shakespeare created, so, in its essentials, have we. *Hamlet* moves us, Jones can assert, only

> because the hero's conflict finds its echo in a similar inner conflict in the mind of the hearer, and the more intense is this already present conflict the greater is the effect of the drama. Again, it is certain that the hearer himself does not know the inner cause of the conflict in his own mind, but experiences only the outward manifestations of it. So we

reach the apparent paradox that the hero, the poet, and the audience are all profoundly moved by feelings due to a conflict of the source of which they are unaware.[19]

The Freudian interpretation is not simply an interpretation of the play, but also an interpretation of mankind's reaction to it. To confute or verify Jones we must turn from the text to psychoanalytic introspection. The question psychoanalysis ultimately poses is not whether the psychological facts that the analyst describes are present in the text, nor even whether they were present in Shakespeare's mind, but rather, whether the text provides an effective vehicle for the projection from our own personalities of the same problems and emotions that the analyst detects in *Hamlet*.[20] Comparative mythology, in linking the Hamlet myth with universal fantasies, indicates that the text does indeed serve this function. Jones has moved the interpretation of *Hamlet* into the social sciences. The professional aesthetician may limit his own approach to a rational analysis of a text by itself; recent criticism, at least, has tended to do so.[21] Jones is not, I think, as violently "antitextual" as Weitz says, but even if he were, it does not follow that "that way lies chaos"—especially if the putative misreading of the textual data is not so arbitrary but that many or most people "misread" the text in exactly the same way. Jones has tacitly raised the possibility that subjectivity, if universal, is a legitimate basis of interpretation—perhaps, with *Hamlet*, the only one. However distasteful such an approach may be to most critics, to insist too stringently on overt textual data is to beg an important question.

We are now in a position to observe how, in seeking the roots of the play in myth and fantasy, psychoanalysis suggests a resolution of the paradox that *Hamlet* is at once popular and profound. Thus, before continuing with further problems to which psychoanalytic criticism gives rise, we might look at this paradox. To my knowledge, Schlegel was the first to notice it: "*Hamlet* is singular in its kind: a tragedy of thought inspired by continual and never-satisfied meditation on human destiny and the dark perplexity of the events of this world, and calculated to call forth the very same meditation in the minds of the spectators. . . . What naturally most astonishes us, is the fact that with such hidden purposes, with a foundation laid in such unfathomable depth, the whole should, at a first view, exhibit an extremely popular appearance."[22] But the evolutionists have since stressed that *Hamlet* was, after all, a popular stage drama, and that the theatergoer could not possibly perform the sort of criticism that Schlegel at once describes and exemplifies: "This enigmatical work resembles those irrational equations in which a fraction of unknown magnitude always remains, that will in no way admit of solution."[23] The thoroughness of a Coleridgean reading, the subtlety of a Bradleian analysis, or the medical erudition of an Adams would be beyond the grasp of the average spectator as he sat in the theater, and we are left with a dilemma: if *Hamlet* is as psychologically and morally subtle as the main-line critics have found it, then its great popularity on the stage must be irrelevant to its true significance. Schlegel appeared quite willing to accept this conclusion, but, with our growing respect for the Elizabethan stage, we are liable to find it unpalatable today.[24]

Our dilemma exists because former critics have tacitly equated "understanding" the play with conscious understanding, and on the conscious level it will appear impossible to reconcile the play's complexity with its melodrama. Jones, however, posits a subconscious comprehension on the part of the audience, a comprehension of which each member of the audience is immediately capable—to which, indeed, each is compelled. Thus, the play is at once subconsciously understandable to the popular audience and yet profound in that it deals with experiences at the hidden core of human nature. To the psychoanalyst *Hamlet* is popular precisely because it is profound.

Psychoanalytic criticism also offers a solution to another aspect of Schlegel's dilemma: if the play is profound, why does it also contain so many elements of the melodramatic? It is one of the bloodiest of dramas, and it has its source in the violence of Scandinavian fable, a violence that would hardly have been played down by Kyd and evidently suffered little at the hands of Shakespeare. What is Shakespeare's subtlest character doing in such a work? Critics have long seemed to be tacitly aware of this problem and have proposed, like Coleridge, to ignore the plot and treat the play as a portrait of the hero or, like Stoll, to ignore the hero as a separate entity and treat the play as a vehicle for the melodrama inherent in the plot. From Jones, however, comes a new suggestion: the plot, the basic Hamlet story, is a mythical expression of the very problem that besets Hamlet. Both plot and character reflect a single psychological conflict, and both have the same effect—not diverse ones, as critics had tacitly assumed—on the minds of the audience.

Finally, psychoanalysis suggests that *Hamlet* is a unified whole. The evolutionists—and particularly Robertson—charged that Shakespeare failed to assimilate his material perfectly and that the signs of this failure were the "excrescences" on the plot, comprised primarily of the episodes dealing with Polonius and Fortinbras. Rank and Jones, however, treat Polonius and Fortinbras as variations in the changes that Shakespeare rings on the oedipal theme. The "superfluous" scenes show rebellion against the father or father figure and, conversely, the father trying to stem the "licentious" behavior of his son or keeping the hero's beloved from him.[25]

Another important charge often leveled at psychological criticism in general is that a dramatic character is purely fictional and, having no independent existence, cannot be explained the way one explains a real person.[26] John Dover Wilson applies this rule specifically to psychoanalytic criticism: "Apart from the play, apart from his actions, from what he tells us about himself, and what other characters tell us about him, there is no Hamlet. . . . [Those who] attribute his conduct to a mother-complex acquired in infancy, are merely cutting the figure out of canvas and sticking it in the doll's-house of their own invention."[27] This rule, if applied too stringently, would of course render almost any interpretation impossible—including that of Dover Wilson, who assumes that Hamlet has doubts during his two-month delay about the honesty of the Ghost, whereas by Dover Wilson's own dictum Hamlet ceases to exist during this hiatus. A certain amount of inference beyond the text is inevitable. The question, of course, is how much.

In fact, a fictional character is quite likely to have an independent existence in the mind of his creator, and even against the creator's will—a fact attested to by E. M. Forster among others. "I wonder what will happen with Pendennis and Fanny Bolton?" Thackeray wrote to Mrs. Brookfield about his own creations. "Writing it and sending it to you somehow it seems as if it were true—I shall know more about them tomorrow. . . ."[28] That some such process went on in Shakespeare's mind is, of course, impossible to say, but it is scarcely an incredible hypothesis. Do the same unconscious forces that affect the author's creation also affect the audience's reaction? Psychoanalytic criticism assumes that they do.

The character's independence of the text may in fact be quite great if, as psychoanalysis suggests of Hamlet, he exists not simply on paper but also in the minds of the author and audience. Hamlet's "mother-complex acquired in infancy," is really our own. T. S. Eliot makes much the same objection as Dover Wilson when he says that *Hamlet* is an artistic failure because the Prince "is dominated by an emotion which is in *excess* of the facts as they appear." Eliot apparently accepts the psychoanalytic suggestion that there is a hidden, repressed meaning in *Hamlet*, but he ignores the corollary that this meaning is common human property, and Jones can answer: "As they appear, yes, but not as they actually exist in Hamlet's soul. His emotions are inexpressible not for that reason, but because there are thoughts and wishes that no one dares to express even to himself."[29] "As they actually exist": the psychoanalyst sees literature as a part of life, Hamlet as a part of ourselves.[30]

Because it is so much centered in universal audience reaction, the psychoanalyst's interpretation may go far beyond what is overt in the text, often to the dismay of more conventional critics. "If Hamlet has a complex," complains A. J. A. Waldock, "what business is it of ours? When a complex is made into dramatic material it becomes our business, not before"[31]—the tacit assumptions being that artistic creation is a wholly conscious process, that the artist puts into the play no more than the anti-impressionistic critic perceives, and that the audience's view of the work is essentially the same as the critic's, only perhaps not quite so perceptive. But if art can be largely unconscious both in its conception and its communication, then perhaps we cannot keep Hamlet's complex from being our business. Freud even suggests that if Hamlet's complex *is* to be our business, then it cannot be shaped too explicitly into dramatic material:

> It appears as a necessary precondition of this form of art [i.e.,
> the sympathetic portrayal of the highly neurotic character,

such as Hamlet] that the impulse that is struggling into consciousness, however clearly it is recognizable, is never given a name; so that in the spectator too the process is carried through with his attention averted, and he is in the grip of his emotions instead of taking stock of what is happening. A certain amount of resistance [i.e., to forbidden impulses] is no doubt saved in this way. . . . It would seem to be the dramatist's business to induce the same illness [as the hero's] in us.[32]

In short, Freud raises the paradoxical possibility that, in order to communicate Hamlet's complex, Shakespeare had to avoid any overt explanation, had to avoid making the complex into explicit dramatic material for the very sake of the audience's sympathetic comprehension. Otherwise, Freud says, the audience's reaction would be either to dismiss Hamlet as incomprehensible or, if the neurosis is too explicit, to suggest sending for the doctor.

The current critical disavowal of character studies, if carried to extremes, becomes as extravagant as the subtlest nineteenth-century motive hunting that it reacts against. Of course Hamlet is merely ink on paper—but if it comes to that, a real person (to anyone but himself) is merely an aggregate of sound and light waves. In either instance the perceiver, from long human habit, shapes his sense impressions into some more or less coherent pattern in his own mind. Provided that he remain true to these impressions, the one action may be no more reprehensible than the other. When someone speaks of Hamlet as if he were a real person (or about a real person as if he were a real person), he is not making a statement about objective fact but about subjective reaction—his own and, in the case of the psychoanalyst talking about Hamlet, ours.

There are limits. In an earlier treatment of *Hamlet*, for example, Jones amazingly suggests that Hamlet's attraction to Ophelia never flowers "because Hamlet's unconscious only partly desires her; in part Ophelia is felt to be a permitted substitute for the desired relationship with Laertes."[33] Evidently such veiled homosexuality may occur in real-life cases that resemble Hamlet's. Jones has simply made a statement about analytical theory disguised as a statement about Hamlet, one scarcely required by the Freudian theory and leading nowhere in the play itself, however far it may sometimes lead on the couch.

Of course, a fictional character when viewed from the stand-point of the consciously shaping artist—or, more to the point, of the structural critic—will be seen as a mere part of the artistic organism. But that is not the standpoint of the theater audience. (Aristotle, we should remember, says that dramatic action must determine character only that it may appear to the audience that the character determines the action.) The artist gives his charac-ter no alternatives, but the audience must, if only to comprehend the moral significance of the character's deeds. As artifact, Mac-beth has no free will, but when Macbeth kills Duncan, the man in the gallery will not say that the choice was Shakespeare's. If a stage character *seems* real to us, we cannot keep responding to him as if he *were* real.

That is a big "if," of course. A character does exist in his own artistic world, and often (some critics will say always) this world obviates our responding to him as if he were real. No one, I suppose, has ever tried to psychoanalyze Everyman. And, to be sure, virtually everyone recognizes that what he sees in the theater is not reality but a highly formalized representation of reality, one that makes its own rules and establishes its own probabilities.[34] This is a problem that many psychoanalytic critics have ignored, often to the detriment of their work, but it has not always gone unheeded. We have already seen, for instance, that Jones seeks to bridge the gap between realism and the internal logic of the artistic universe when he says that Shakespeare's contribution to the Oedipus myth was to subject the hero himself to the same inner conflicts that the basic story expresses. Here, not only does *mythos* determine character but the two indepen-dently express the same thing. Legend and psychological realism are brought face-to-face, to the enrichment of both. Jones may not be right, of course, but at least he is not a naïve character-monger.

NOTES

1. Jones, *Hamlet and Oedipus*, p. 50.
2. The evidence for this identification is the association of himself with Claudius in the first soliloquy (I. ii. 152–53) and with his designation of Lucianus, the regicide in *The Murther of Gonzago*, as "nephew of the King" (III. ii. 254). But the evidence of the first soliloquy may indi-

cate no more than mere self-contempt, and while the identification with Lucianus might be seen as a Freudian slip, it might just as well be seen, for instance, as a deliberate, desperate taunting of the King to make him drop his mask, or as a moment of spontaneous insolence. (See Harley Granville-Barker's account, in *Prefaces to Shakespeare* [Princeton: Princeton University Press, 1946], I:91.)

3. F. L. Lucas, *Literature and Psychology* (London, 1951), p. 52.
4. Morris Weitz, *Hamlet and the Philosophy of Literary Criticism* (Chicago: University of Chicago Press, 1964), pp. 24–25. "I find it incredible," Weitz states, "that Jones does not even *mention* this fact of the text, i.e., Hamlet's own words concerning his father" (p. 23). It would be incredible if it were true. But see Jones, *Hamlet and Oedipus*, p. 79:

> If . . . the "repression" [of the son's hostility towards the father] is considerable, then the hostility towards the father will be correspondingly concealed from consciousness; this is often accompanied by the development of the opposite sentiment, namely of an exaggerated regard and respect for him.

and p. 87:

> It is here [in Hamlet's treatment of Polonius] that we see his fundamental attitude towards moralizing elders who use their power to thwart the happiness of the young, and not in the overdrawn and melodramatic portrait in which he delineates his father: "A combination and a form indeed, where every god did seem to set his seal to give the world assurance of a man."

See also ibid., 122–24. We need not accept Jones's judgment of Hamlet's poetry as melodramatic to accept his major point: even if Hamlet's love for his father is genuine and profound, it need not negate the possibility of a coexistent jealousy and hostility, which, because of that very love, must be repressed. Finally, the apparent disrespect Hamlet shows the Ghost in the cellarage scene can be taken as textual evidence that Hamlet's attitude toward his father is ambivalent (see K. R. Eissler, *Discourse on Hamlet and "Hamlet"* (New York, 1971), p. 104, n. 84)—providing one assumes that the Ghost is indeed Hamlet's father.

5. Jones, *Hamlet and Oedipus*, p. 11.
6. Ibid., p. 104.
7. Ibid., pp. 112–13.
8. Freud, *Interpretation of Dreams*, Edited by James Strachey (London, 1953), p. 265.
9. Jones, *Hamlet and Oedipus*, pp. 114–18.
10. Ibid., p. 113.
11. Otto Rank, *Inzest-Motiv*, cited in Jones, *Hamlet and Oedipus*, pp. 121–26.

12. Jones, *Hamlet and Oedipus*, p. 113. Of course, Rank's detection of recurring incest themes in Shakespeare's earlier works itself supports the oedipal interpretation of *Hamlet*, though it makes it less plausible to connect *Hamlet* with specific events in Shakespeare's adult life.

13. Ibid., p. 14.

14. Ella Sharpe, "The Impatience of Hamlet," *International Journal of Psycho-Analysis*, 10 (1929), 270–79. On the other hand, Kenneth Muir, in an otherwise sympathetic account, thinks otherwise:

> Shakespeare, being a dramatist to his finger tips, was able to utilise and magnify the infantile Oedipus wishes which are common to us all. In real life and in an ordinary man such repressed wishes would doubtless reflect an unresolved Oedipus complex; but as they have been segregated and intensified by the poet for the purposes of his play, we cannot assume that he himself suffered from the neurosis he depicted in his hero. There are other plays as great as *Hamlet*, though Jones regards it as his masterpiece; and it is clear that *Macbeth*, *Othello*, *King Lear* cannot be explained in terms of the Oedipus complex, and would give us no hint that Shakespeare suffered from it. (Kenneth Muir, "Some Freudian Interpretations of Shakespeare," *Proceedings of the Leeds Philosophical and Literary Society* [Literary and Historical Section], 7 [1952]:44)

15. Jones, *Hamlet and Oedipus*, p. 127.

16. Ibid., pp. 128–29. Jones here draws heavily on Rank's *Der Mythus von der Geburt des Helden* (Leipzig and Vienna: Franz Deuticke, 1909). Oedipus, incidentally, is a good example of this form.

17. Ibid., p. 135.

18. Ibid., pp. 137–42.

19. Ibid., pp. 50–51.

20. See ibid., p. 68: "What we are essentially concerned with is the psychological understanding of the dramatic effect produced by Hamlet's personality and behaviour."

21. D. A. Traversi echoes anti-Bradleian critics such as Dover Wilson and A. J. A. Waldock when he claims:

> We all know . . . that to discuss Hamlet's life *outside* the limits of the play, to attempt to deduce the manner of his upbringing to account for his behavior on the stage, is an illegitimate extension of the critic's proper function. (*An Approach to Shakespeare*, 2nd ed. rev. [Garden City: Doubleday Anchor Books, 1956], p. 2).

22. August Wilhelm von Schlegel, *A Course of Lectures on Dramatic Art and Literature* [1808], trans. John Black, rev. A. J. W. Morrison (London: Henry G. Bohn, 1861), p. 404.

23. Ibid.

24. At least one modern psychological critic has vitiated his interpreta-

tion by insisting that Hamlet's motives are hidden and yet that no interpretation is valid that would not be immediately clear to the theater audience; see Arthur Clutton-Brock, *Shakespeare's "Hamlet"* (London: Methuen and Co., 1922). Connoisseurs of literary mayhem will enjoy J. M. Robertson's rebuttal of Clutton-Brock in *"Hamlet" Once More* (London: Richard Cobden-Sanderson, 1923).

25. Such subthemes would be quite in keeping with Elizabethan dramaturgical practice, in which the theme of the main plot was commonly reflected in the themes of the subplots. See Bernard Beckerman, *Shakespeare at the Globe* (New York: Macmillan Co., 1962), pp. 45–48. See also below, chap. 6.

26. This position, highly influential since its adoption by the evolutionists, has its *locus classicus* in A. B. Walkley, "Professor Bradley's *Hamlet*," in *Drama and Life* (London: Methuen and Co., 1907), pp. 148–55.

27. John Dover Wilson, Introduction to his edition of *Hamlet* (Cambridge: Cambridge University Press, 1934), p. xlv.

28. Letter of 18–20 March, 1850 in Gordon N. Ray, ed., *The Letters and Private Papers of William Makepeace Thackeray* (Cambridge, Mass.: Harvard University Press, 1945–1946), 2:652, item 690. "I have been surprised at the observations made by some of my characters," Thackeray remarked elsewhere. "It seems as if an occult Power was moving the pen. The Personage does or says something, and I ask, how the dickens did he come to think of that?" ("De Finibus," *Roundabout Papers*, in *Miscellanies* [Boston: James R. Osgood, 1873], 4:354). A French novelist gives a particularly vivid account of the experience, which with him takes the form of an "alter-ego" beyond his control: "Pour vous donner un example: tout récemment, lors d'un événement qui a ébranlé la conscience du monde, au lieu de se revolter, l''autre' s'est mis à écrire une nouvelle, intitulée: 'Un tremblement de terre.' C'est l'histoire d'un personnage louche que continue à jouer aux cartes pendant que la maison s'écroule. El de surcroît, il triche. Quant [sic] j'ai fait des reproches à l'autre' pour son attitude insensible et égoiste, il s'est contenté de hausser les épaules" (Ladislas Dormandi, "La genèse d'un roman," *Revue du Ciné-Photo-Club de l'Éducation Nationale*, Nouvelle Série, Nos. 32–33 [Octobre 1958–Mars 1959], pp. 9–18).

29. Jones, *Hamlet and Oedipus*, p. 100.

30. See Norman Holland, *Psychoanalysis and Shakespeare* (New York, 1966), p. 321: "To talk about the character's mind is to talk about the audience's; to talk about the audience's is to give the character a mind."

31. A. J. A. Waldock, *Hamlet, A Study in Critical Method* (Cambridge: Cambridge University Press, 1931), p. 55.

32. Sigmund Freud, "Psychopathic Characters on the Stage" (1904–05?), in *Works*, ed. Strachey, 7:309–10. Thus, too, Eissler maintains that "while the action that takes place on the stage is extremely realistic, it is nevertheless so loose and wide-framed that nearly all of man's major, typical unconscious fantasies can be projected onto it" (*Discourse*, p. 132). On the other hand, Eissler also maintains that "even if it could be shown that a psychoanalytic interpretation of a character has never yet found an equivalent process in a member of an audience, that interpretation could still be correct" (p. 18)—but it is not clear what he means by "correct," if not simply that the interpretation provides explanation for the mimetic data of the text without being contradicted by them. But whereas such adequacy is suitable for other modes of interpretaion, which function by asking us to consider the literary work under the aspect of theory, Freud here suggests that such rational consideration will seriously distort our aesthetic reaction—that, in fact, the ontological locus of psychoanalytical interpretation is, precisely, in the unconscious. If so, then the mode of psychoanalytical interpretation Eissler defends may be of great academic or clinical interest, but it is of no aesthetic value whatever. Eissler's own study moves somewhat disconcertingly, I think, from apt consideration of audience response (as when he describes Shakespeare's technique in creating an emotional climate "that conveys a feeling [about the relationships of women and castration] such as could not have been easily reproduced by direct verbalization" [p. 114]) to theorization whose appeal is not to any conceivable aesthetic response but rather, one senses, to actual case history. ("My guess is that if Gertrude had been brought to the point of being forced to choose between Claudius's welfare and Hamlet's she would under all circumstances have decided in favor of the latter" [p. 87]).

33. Ernest Jones, Introduction to Vision Press edition of *Hamlet* (London, 1947), p. 20. Fortunately, the suggestion is dropped in *Hamlet and Oedipus*, and the whole discussion of which it formed a part is relegated to a footnote.

34. For a fuller account of this problem in relation to psychoanalysis, see Holland, *Psychoanalysis*, chaps. 10–11.

PART 3:
Scenes
and Characters

Samuel Johnson

Note to "To Be or Not To Be"

Act III. Scene iii. (III. i. 56 foll.) *To be, or not to be?*

Of this celebrated soliloquy, which bursting from a man distracted with contrariety of desires, and overwhelmed with the magnitude of his own purposes, is connected rather in the speaker's mind, than on his tongue, I shall endeavour to discover the train, and to shew how one sentiment produces another.

Hamlet, knowing himself injured in the most enormous and atrocious degree, and seeing no means of redress, but such as must expose him to the extremity of hazard, meditates on his situation in this manner: *Before I can form any rational scheme of action under this pressure of distress*, it is necessary to decide, whether, *after our present state, we are* to be or not to be. That is the question, which, as it shall be answered, will determine, *whether 'tis nobler*, and more suitable to the dignity of reason, *to suffer the outrages of fortune* patiently, or to take arms against *them*, and by opposing end them, *though perhaps* with the loss of life. If *to die*, were *to sleep, no more, and by a sleep to end* the miseries of our nature, such a sleep were *devoutly to be wished*; but if *to sleep* in death, be *to dream*, to retain our powers of sensibility, we must *pause* to consider, *in that sleep of death what dreams may come*. This consideration *makes calamity* so long endured; *for who would bear* the vexations of life, which might be ended *by a bare bodkin*, but that he is afraid of something in unknown futurity? This fear it is that gives efficacy to conscience, which, by turning the mind upon *this regard*, chills the ardour of *resolution*, checks the vigour of *enterprise*, and makes the *current* of desire stagnate in inactivity.

We may suppose that he would have applied these general observations to his own case, but that he discovered *Ophelia*.

[Francis Gentleman]

From Hamlet, Prince of Denmark, A Tragedy, by Shakespeare As Performed at the Theatre-Royal, Covent Garden . . . An Introduction, and Notes Critical and Illustrative, are added by the Authors of the Dramatic Censor. 1777

To Be or Not to Be

There never was so much philosophical reasoning expressed so nervously, in so narrow a compass by any author, as in this excellent, we may say unparalleled, soliloquy, which gives a good orator great latitude for the exertion of his abilities—the thought of death being a desirable consummation; the doubts arising from that transition; the picture of life, which our uncertainty forces us to bear, are admirably conceived and expressed.

Harley Granville-Barker

From *Prefaces to Shakespeare*

One scene, we have just been told [in the play], is to "come near the circumstance" of the old King's murder, and we shall more vaguely remember that Hamlet meant to write "a speech of some dozen or sixteen lines"—presumably to point the likeness. We are prepared for such a climax to the business. But before the play proper can begin:

> *Hoboyes play. The dumbe shewe enters.*
>
> *Enter a King and Queene, very lovingly; the Queene embracing him. She kneeles, and makes shew of Protestation unto him. He takes her up, and declines his head upon her neck. Layes him downe upon a Banke of Flowers. She seeing him a-sleepe, leaves him. Anon comes in a Fellow, takes off his Crowne, kisses it, and powres poyson in the King's eares, and Exits. The Queene returnes, findes the King dead, and makes passionate Action. The Poysoner, with some two or three Mutes, comes in againe, seeming to lament with her. The dead body is carried away: The Poysoner Wooes the Queene with Gifts, she seemes loath and unwilling awhile, but in the end accepts his love. Exeunt.*[1]

Does not this fatally anticipate the promised critical scene? Will Claudius not "blench" at so close a picturing—though a picturing only—of his crime? Let him do so, and is not Hamlet's purpose at once served, but Shakespeare's (so to say) aborted, the rest of the scene being then superfluous? Or, if Claudius manages to control himself, will he not, since "this show imports the argument of the play," stop the proceedings then and there? These questions have fomented controversy enough about the

Reprinted from *Prefaces to Shakespeare*, Vol. 1, pp. 86–92, by Harley Granville-Barker (1946), by permission of Princeton University Press.

Dumb Show. Editors have answered them variously, producers in the main by omitting it. One editorial answer is that the King is at the moment talking to the Queen or Polonius, and does not see it. That can hardly be. Shakespeare does not leave such crucial matters in the air. Failing plain indication to the contrary, we must assume, I think, that whatever there is to be seen the King sees. Another answer is that while he sees the Show he does not suppose it to "import the argument," and is content to let it pass for an unlucky coincidence which no one can remark but he; for dumb shows are apt to be, as Hamlet says, "inexplicable," and the likeness may not be striking. This is more tenable; the Folio's labeling of the murderer as *a Fellow* does, in fact, suggest no such figure as the King's. And it is likely, I think, that the method of acting a dumb show differed greatly from that developed by this time for the acting of a play. It must inevitably have had more of the formal mime in it, which we commonly associate with ballet and the *Commedia dell'Arte*.[2] But the right answer will emerge from the text and the situation involved in it; we have only straightforwardly to work this out, instead of dodging or shirking the issue.

When the King sees the Dumb Show he is at once alert. Though here may be a coincidence and no more, whatever Hamlet has a hand in will now be matter for suspicion. But what should he do? If the thing is mere coincidence, nothing. If it is a trap laid, he is not the man to walk straight into it—as he would by stopping the play for no reason he could give before it had well begun. He must wait and be wary. Ophelia (the acting of the Dumb Show has let her recover herself a little) voices the question for him:

> What means this, my lord? . . . Belike this show imports
> the argument of the play?

And Hamlet's answer:

> Marry, this is miching mallecho; it means mischief.

and his comment on the Prologue:

> the players cannot keep counsel: they'll tell all.

point disquietingly away from coincidence. "Miching mallecho . . . mischief . . . tell all"; Claudius must be wary indeed.

Here, then, is the battle joined at once, between the watcher and the watched. On the defensive is the King, whose best tactics, without doubt, are to brave the business out, calmly, smilingly, giving no slightest sign that he sees anything extraordinary in it; for the attack, Horatio, whose steady eye—he has assured us— nothing will escape, and Hamlet, a-quiver with suppressed excitement, who after a while will try—still vainly—by mocking look and word, to pierce that admirable composure. But for a long first round, from the entry of the player King and Queen, it is a still and silent battle. Its background is the line after line of their smoothly flowing verse, which we hear but need not greatly heed. Our attention is for the three: for Claudius, conscious that he is being watched, and Hamlet and Horatio, their eyes riveted to his face.

The Dumb Show falls quite pertinently into Hamlet's—and Shakespeare's—scheme. The mimic play as a whole is a calculated insult both to King and Queen. The "one scene" which "comes near the circumstance" of the old King's death, and into which Hamlet has inserted his "dozen or sixteen lines," is to be the finishing stroke merely. Were it a single one, Claudius might outface it. It is the prolonged preliminary ordeal which is to wear him down. Upon the point of dramatic technique, too, if the test of his guilt is to be limited to the one scrambled and excited moment of the

Thoughts black, hands apt, drugs fit . . .

—when our eyes and ears are everywhere at once, upon Hamlet, Lucianus and the King, upon the Queen and the courtiers, too— the play's most vital crisis must be half lost in confusion. What Shakespeare means, surely, is to make this simply the culmination of a long, tense, deliberate struggle to break down the King's composure, on his part to maintain it. Treat it thus and the confusion, when at last it comes, makes its true effect. And the eighty lines of the spineless verse of *The Murder of Gonzago* are all they should be as a placid accompaniment to a silent and enthralling struggle. If the struggle is not the salient thing, if the ambling of the verse is made so instead, it must lower the tension of the scene disastrously.[3] And we may, I think, acquit Shakespeare of meaning to do that.

But there is a minor theme for them to accompany, besides. After twenty-five lines the intention of the dialogue sharpens— in the Player Queen's

> In second husband let me be accurst!
> None wed the second but who killed the first . . . .
> The instances that second marriage move
> Are base respects of thrift, but none of love;
> A second time I kill my husband dead,
> When second husband kisses me in bed.

—to a glancing attack upon the Queen herself as she sits there. She, unlike Claudius, winces at once; and Hamlet, with his

> That's wormwood, wormwood!

rashly endorsing this petty, superfluous triumph, encourages thereby the King's growing certitude that here *is* a trap laid for him, no mere coincidence.

This baiting of Gertrude will also set the whole Court agog, will, on the other hand, prevent both her and them from remarking the sterner struggle proceeding. She outfaces the mockery as best she may. They glance aside at her from their watching of the play, scandalized, suppressing their smiles. They glance, apprehensively, at the King; what has he to say to the outrage? He is caught between the obligation to resent it and the need to keep calm under the deadlier and secret accusation. To this enrichment of the foreground picture the background of the mimic play will prove none too ample.

Upon the Player Queen's oath:

> Nor earth to me give food, nor Heaven light!
> Sport and repose lock from me day and night! . . .
> Both here and hence pursue me lasting strife,
> If, once a widow, ever I be wife!

Hamlet seals his complicity by the satiric, audibly muttered:

> If she should break it now!

It is like him that he cannot even now, when his purpose is at least well afoot, pursue it single-mindedly, must endanger it by these sinister diversions. For endanger it he plainly does. Horatio we see sticking to the task set him, steadily watching the King.

But here is Hamlet, yielded to the old obsession of his mother's guilt, veritably provoking interference—and upon another count—before the critical scene, the finally revealing moment, is reached. To taunt the Queen to her face; and before Claudius, before the Court, to challenge her with that

> Madam, how like you this play?

is to jeopardize his whole plan. The plan does still succeed; but here also is the seed of his own subsequent failure to exploit its success. Did not the Ghost warn him:

> Taint not thy mind, nor let thy soul contrive
> Against thy mother aught . . . .

But this chance of wounding and publicly shaming her he cannot bear to miss. And later, when she sends for him, the thought of scourging her with reproaches will dominate all else; and he will spare the King at his prayers, because of his unlikeness to a lustful, guilty lover; and, lost in the sating of his wrath against her, he will kill Polonius, and so deliver himself into his enemy's hands.

But, for the time, the tide is with him. The Queen does not appeal to Claudius to stop the play; she puts up no better defense than the wryly merry:

> The lady doth protest too much, methinks.

And Claudius dare not stop it, lest that should prove him guilty upon the graver count. He is reduced to demanding, lamely:

> Have you heard the argument? is there no offence in't?

No offense!—when already his Queen and his marriage have been publicly insulted by these hired and abetted players. Hamlet, seeing that the courage is out of him, lashes him, stingingly, pointedly, casting, for the first time, the one fatal word full in his face:

> No, no, they do but jest, *poison* in jest; no offence i' the world!

—mockingly dares him to unmask, knowing he dare not; and, upon the still supiner

> What do you call the play?

himself unmasks, scornfully sure now of victory. His savagely comic impromptu title labels his enemy mere vermin:

> The Mouse-trap. Marry, how? Tropically. This play is the image of a murder done in Vienna: Gonzago is the duke's name; his wife, Baptista. You shall see anon; 'tis a knavish piece of work: but what of that? your majesty, and we that have free souls, it touches us not: let the galled jade wince, our withers are unwrung.
> *Enter Lucianus. . . .*

The critical scene has come. Again, how like Hamlet to have forestalled it and discounted its value by giving Claudius such open warning of what was coming! But a sense of triumph possesses him. By the outflung

> This is one Lucianus, nephew to the king.

(to the king, to King Hamlet, not Duke Gonzago) he avows himself master of these puppets. It is with a sort of insolent confidence that he momentarily turns for another bout of bawdry with Ophelia, and then back for his firing of the mine:

> Begin, murderer; pox, leave thy damnable faces, and begin. . . .

He seems indeed to have Claudius beaten. And with the

> He poisons him i' the garden for 's estate. His name's Gonzago; the story is extant, and written in very choice Italian. You shall see anon how the murderer gets the love of Gonzago's wife.

he scourges him from the field.

But it is a barren victory, lacking its conclusive stroke, and to be turned against the victor. Hamlet—all forgetful of the promised joining of judgments with Horatio—was, it would seem, about to bridge fiction to fact, tax Claudius with the murder to his face and before the world, and take his revenge, if it might be, then and there. But, failing to do this, it is a fatal error to unmask. For Claudius, in the safe retreat he gains, will turn that now useless "madness" to his own protection and profit, leaving his enemy meanwhile to vaunt his triumph in sounding words.[4]

King, Queen, Court, attendants and Players all vanish clamorously. At this point, and with this help, the actor of Hamlet is accustomed to lift his part in the scene to such a high pitch of emotion that descent from it is most difficult, and transition into the key of what follows must seem forced. Hamlet is, of course, intensely excited; but it is an intellectual excitement and one not beyond his control. Hence Shakespeare's use of the light and inconsequent lyric:

> Why, let the stricken deer go weep,
>   The hart ungalled play;
> For some must watch, while some must sleep:
>   So runs the world away . . . .

and the ironically fanciful:

> Would not this, sir, and a forest of feathers, if the rest of
> my fortunes turn Turk with me, with two Provincial roses
> on my razed shoes, get me a fellowship in a cry of players,
> sir?

instead of such verse—into which emotion more naturally flows—as follows the Ghost's disappearance, or as we shall find in the scene to come with his mother, or of such hammering phrases as those he leveled at Ophelia when she denied that her father was spying on them. And the fantasy and banter serve to relieve the strain of what has gone before.

NOTES

1. Thus F1, which does not vary substantially from Q2, though it is worth noting that "a Fellow" replaces "another man."
2. In the 1932 revival by the *Comédie Française*, the Dumb Show was acted in this fashion, fantastically and swiftly, and the King's ignoring it did not seem very strange.
3. As producers of the play discover. They cut the Dumb Show and with it the cue for the silent struggle with the King. Then there is nothing much left to do but listen to those rather dreary lines and wait for Lucianus. Quite justifiably, that being so, as many of the lines as possible are cut. But Shakespeare did not put them in for nothing.
4. Since I owe so much to Dr. Dover Wilson's latest editing of the play, it is perhaps only right to record my total disagreement with his interpretation of the play-scene.

    He thinks the King does not see the Dumb Show. I have already given my reasons against that. But the Dumb Show is also, he holds, a deliberate betrayal by the Players of Hamlet's plan; the fact that the King does not see it is a providential stroke of luck; Hamlet's "miching mallecho" is an expression of anger at the mishap, his "the players cannot keep counsel . . ." an apprehension of more trouble to come. The "posy-prologue" is another offense and Lucianus' "damnable faces" and this speaking of "thoughts black . . ." yet another, a willful disregard of the advice to speak the speech "trippingly," not to "strut and bellow." The scene, by this reading of it, faces, so to speak, two ways. There is the effect of the play upon the King and Queen (duplicate already in itself) and there will be the effect upon Hamlet of the jeopardy of his plan.

I might argue that with the material Dr. Dover Wilson selects no actor of Hamlet could convey to an audience all this extra and very different kind of anxiety. Nor do I see how the actors of *The Murder of Gonzago* could help him much. But the proof of that pudding, it might be answered, is in the eating; who is to decide that the thing cannot be done? I prefer to plead that it is, in itself, a thing which Shakespeare would never try to do. He would never dissipate the force of such a scene by so dividing its interest, or handicap Hamlet at this juncture with a quite extraneous difficulty. Besides, there is literally nothing in the play which is not, in some way or another, germane to its story or illustrative of Hamlet's character, or a consequence, direct or indirect, of what he does or leaves undone. Such an irrelevancy as this betrayal of his plan by the Players, springing from nothing, leading nowhere, would be a rift in the fabric, and dramatically meaningless.

John Dover Wilson

From *What Happens in Hamlet*

THE PLAY SCENE RESTORED

Before attempting to interpret a scene in Shakespeare there is one question which it is well to deal with first: In what mood are the principal characters when it begins?

It is not difficult to guess the mood of Gertrude. She is possessed by that indomitable placidity which seldom deserts her. She is, of course, distressed at the madness of her son, which she steadfastly attributes, whatever her husband or Polonius may say, to "his father's death and our o'er-hasty marriage"; but she comes to the play with a glad heart, for she sees hopes of Hamlet's recovery in his interest in such amusements. She is therefore entirely unsuspicious of his intentions, and little guesses what he has particularly in store for herself. Claudius also looks with favour on the idea of the play. He is as delighted as the Queen when in the preceding scene he hears from Rosencrantz and Guildenstern that Hamlet proposes to entertain them all, for it pleases him to learn that his nephew's mind is occupied with anything so healthy and innocent. He has no suspicions of the *diplomatic* play, and no interest in it; he attends it simply to give Hamlet encouragement, "and drive his purpose into these delights." Moreover, he is thinking of other things. Hamlet's talk with Ophelia, which he has just overheard from his place of spying, has finally convinced him that the Prince is suffering from the disease of *paranoia* ambition, and that the disease may prove dangerous to the reign-

Reprinted from *What Happens in Hamlet*, pp. 174–197, by John Dover Wilson, by permission of Cambridge University Press. Copyright © 1935 by Cambridge University Press.

ing monarch. He determines therefore to watch, not the play, but Hamlet, narrowly. With him enters Polonius, the champion of the rival theory, who is not in the least satisfied that the King is right, and has insisted on a second seance behind the arras, in which Gertrude shall take the place of Ophelia as decoy.

Next of the train appears Ophelia herself, "of ladies most deject and wretched," with the pallor caused by her recent terrible experience still in her cheeks. All she knows is that Hamlet, her lover, her idol, her god, is mad. After his outrageous conduct to her in the lobby, she is prepared for anything. Her task is to endure patiently, and to do what she can by soothing words to calm the ravings of that once "noble and most sovereign reason." Behind her walk Rosencrantz and Guildenstern, commissioned no doubt by his majesty to keep a watchful eye upon the Prince. At any rate, in regard to Hamlet's "madness" they share Claudius's theory.

And Hamlet himself? His mood seems calm and self-controlled. He has just given the players the most precise instructions about the delivery of his speech, instructions which prove him to be for the time clear-headed and collected. In the exquisite and touching conversation that follows with Horatio, a conversation in which Hamlet carries on and develops the doctrine of μηδὲν ἄγαν already enjoined upon the First Player, he is at his very best. It is his one perfectly serene and untroubled moment in the whole play. Note, too, the apparent deliberation of his plans for the interlude. He entrusts Horatio with the task of fixing his eyes upon the King's face during the play, and agrees with him to compare notes afterwards. The trumpets and kettledrums (Claudius cannot do without these heralds) cut short their talk, and Hamlet adds in a hurried whisper: "They are coming to the play. I must be idle. Get you a place." It is Shakespeare's final clue as to his state of mind. Horatio and he must separate, so as not to appear to be in collusion. Moreoever he has a part to play in this scene: "I must be idle," that is to say "crazy." Hamlet is assuming his "antic disposition" consciously and of set purpose.

Indeed, he has much to do and to think of. Would his all-important lines be spoken clearly and incisively? Would the players perform the interlude as he had directed? If the play passed off well he has no anxiety about Claudius; for, had the Ghost spoken truth, there was no escape for the "conscience of the king." But "the play's the thing" for Hamlet, chiefly because it ministers to one of the cravings of his nature, his delight in plots and counter-plots. Claudius calls him "most generous and free from all contriving"; and he is so as regards men whom he trusts, like Horatio, or admires, like Laertes. But with men he hates he is very different. He takes a malicious delight in hoodwinking, fooling, and tripping up his enemies, and his love of such employment accounts in part for his delay in killing the King. He wants to play with him as a cat plays with a mouse. All this being so, how excellent a contrivance the Gonzago-play is! It will feed to the full his lust for delving a yard below Claudius's mines; it will hoist the King with his own petar. I have little doubt that Hamlet desires not merely to convict Claudius by means of the play but to put him on the rack and watch him writhing.

Claudius, however, is not his only objective. He knows the Gonzago-play and knows that it ought to catch the conscience of his mother also. He is not certain whether she is an accomplice in the crime or not. That must be tested. He will tent her to the quick, too, about her second marriage. Incest and adultery are ignored; it would be dangerous to hint at these before the assembled court, and he will have an opportunity of dealing with the matter privately afterwards. This fits in admirably with the design of making the whole thing a mouse-trap for his uncle. The King must not realise until the last moment what the play is about. He must therefore be led off the scent in the earlier part, which will deal exclusively with Gertrude. But others must be put off the scent also; the court must guess nothing of what is really afoot. How that is to be managed he does not yet know; but some device will suggest itself to his active brain.

Lastly, this interlude is his show. He is master of the revels; he has selected the scene to be played, and has even written a speech, the critical speech of the evening. He will be exceedingly anxious that the whole thing should go off well—anxious from the purely artistic point of view. Hamlet is greatly interested in drama. The players are his old friends, and he welcomes them with delight before he has even begun to think of the Gonzago scheme. He is thoroughly at home with them, and has found in their advent "a kind of joy" greater than anything he has experienced since we first saw him in his "nighted colour" at the beginning of his history. Hamlet is a patron of the stage, like Southampton, Essex, and other of Shakespeare's friends at Elizabeth's court. But he is more than this. He is an actor himself, and never so much at ease as when playing a part. Throughout almost the whole play we see him in some rôle or other. The part of madman is, of course, his main disguise, but it has many varieties: the distracted-lover variety, in two sorts at least, if not more; the variety for "tedious old fools"; and the variety of a subtler kind for his two schoolfellows, the sponges.

Nor can we doubt that this play-acting gives him intense satisfaction. It keeps his mind off that

> something in his soul,
> O'er which his melancholy sits on brood—

and which comes uppermost whenever he is left alone. It also aids him in his delving operations against Claudius and his myrmidons. And never does he obtain a more magnificent opportunity than in the play scene of displaying his great histrionic gifts, and such dramatic talent as he possessed; for since all his dupes are now gathered together watching him, he has to act all his parts at once. He "must be idle," of course—that is his habitual mask in the presence of the enemy; but he will use his madness to deadly purpose. He will shoot his poisoned arrows now at his mother, now at his uncle. He will fool Polonius, be love-distraught with Ophelia, while Rosencrantz, Guildenstern, and the rest of the court have to be hoodwinked. There is his part, too, in the play itself to be considered; here he must be "chorus," driving home the points so that not one of the varying impressions he desires to create shall miss its mark. It is a complicated and difficult task he has set himself, needing a clear head and a steady pulse.

To imagine Hamlet thinking thus helps us to disentangle the issues for ourselves; and at one time or other, no doubt, all these matters are present to his mind. But that mind does not really move in this pedestrian fashion at all. Had Shakespeare chosen to give us a glimpse of it between the nunnery scene and the play scene, in the act—shall we say?—of composing the "dozen or sixteen lines," we may be sure that it would not have been "casting beyond" itself, like the brain of Polonius, into what was about to happen or what it ought to do in the coming crisis. It would dispatch the speech for Lucianus, with the speed it later pens the "changeling letter," and would then turn to something quite remote from the purpose, something we should never have expected. Hamlet's brilliant handling of the successive situations in the play scene must be set down to genius not calculation.

The court enters for the play, and Hamlet and Horatio hurriedly break off their colloquy, Horatio taking up a place close to the seat in which Ophelia will afterwards sit, Hamlet remaining in the centre of the stage to receive the King and Queen, as befits the host. The King, Queen and Polonius enter first of the train, and Claudius, polite as ever to his "chiefest courtier, cousin and his son," enquires how he fares, eyeing him cautiously the while for further evidence of his attitude towards him. He has not long to wait. Hamlet deftly catches up the word "fares" by the wrong end, and replies: "Excellent i'faith, of the Chameleon's dish, I eat the air, Promise-crammed, you cannot feed Capons so." The commas and capitals come from the Second Quarto, and they indicate emphatic and deliberate utterance. The speech is one of those right-and-left double-barrelled shots so dear to the heart of sportsmen, hitting both marks. "Promise-crammed" and the pun upon "air" persuade Claudius that the rightful heir is still brooding over his wrongs; while "capon" has a meaning for the King also, which he misses, though we shall understand it at the end of the scene. On the other hand, the shot pierces the centre of the Polonius target, for "promise" can be taken as referring to Ophelia's broken troth, and "capon" denotes a young cock who is deprived of all capacity of love-making, or (as the popular jest of the time had it) a pullet stuffed with *billets-doux*; either way the speech points to thwarted love, and the lady's father might take his choice. Altogether, it was a good beginning to the evening.

The King parries the thrust at him by affecting not to understand it, and Hamlet with an air of contempt turns from him to his other quarry. But it is only to strike at Claudius once again; for, why, as he fools the "capital calf" about his prowess as an actor, does he lead him to speak of the scene in the Capitol, if not to remind his uncle and the court of a famous precedent for the assassination of tyrants? Nor must we miss Shakespeare's tragic irony here. Polonius will play the part of Caesar in real life, a few scenes later, when the "brute part" is Hamlet's. Rosencrantz and Guildenstern, we are also to remember, are listening intently to all this, and will recall it in the light of subsequent events. The thwarted-ambition theory is well afoot as the King moodily seats himself in his chair of state. But Hamlet has many parts to play in this strange eventful history, and it amuses him now to give the old councillor a good run for his money. To enter fully into the business, and all which it involves, we must consider for a moment how the actors are arranging themselves upon the stage.

The courtiers come in; and at once break into two groups, flanking the entrance to the inner-stage, so that the real audience may see the play properly. Claudius advances with his party, which includes Gertrude, Polonius, Rosencrantz and Guildenstern, and takes his seat right on the front of the stage, to allow the audience to watch his face carefully throughout the scene. On his inner side sits the Queen, like him half-face to the audience, while a little behind him on the outer side stands or sits Polonius. The chief of the group on the other side of the stage, which includes Horatio, is at present Ophelia, who sits opposite the King, because Hamlet is to sit at her feet, and the audience will want to watch *his* face also. Thus the characters of the play are drawn up in two confronting camps, as it were, at the beginning of this, the crisis of their history. For a moment, however, Hamlet is left standing between them, with kin on the one hand and kind on the other; and, seeing him without a seat, his mother says: "Come hither, my dear Hamlet, sit by me." She is in a tender mood; her dear boy seems mending, and she wants to pat his hand and affect an interest in this play with which he is diverting himself. But Hamlet's place is with Horatio, opposite the King and keenly on the watch. He therefore refuses her offer in words which give the thwarted-love theory an innings. "No, good mother," he says, making for Ophelia, "here's metal more attractive." The dramatic contrast between the two parties is complete; the anti-Claudius group now has its rightful leader. But the action and the words accompanying it give Polonius, the champion of the thwarted-love theory, his opportunity. "O ho!" he chuckles exultantly to the King, "do you mark that?" Claudius is strangely obtuse in regard to this matter; Polonius had been ready to wager his head upon the truth of his own theory;[1] the nunnery

scene had just confirmed it; and, if further evidence were necessary, here it is in absolutely unmistakable form.

Hamlet continues to play up to Jephthah in the conversation
with his daughter. His language to Ophelia, outrageous as it is, is
in keeping with the part of a love-distraught swain; and her gentle
forbearance of his conduct shows that she regards him as a
madman and sees nothing strange in the form which his demen-
tia takes. Her father, too, so far from being shocked, is actually
gleeful, for every word that is uttered in this strain establishes his
theory upon a firmer basis.[2] And, as the conversation proceeds,
the old man winks and nods in triumph to the King.

Hamlet, however, has yet another hare to start before the play
begins, hare number three, the theory of his good mother. He lets
it slip, partly to enjoy throwing the enemy into still greater
confusion, partly to lead up to the dialogue of the Player King and
Queen, which he imagines is just about to begin. This dialogue is
to deal with the "o'er-hasty marriage" motive, and Hamlet wants
to point the moral clearly beforehand, for he is prologue as well as
chorus. "Look you," he cries, "how cheerfully my mother looks,
and my father died within's two hours"; and he continues fiddling
on the same string for ten or a dozen lines. It is a fine piece of
prologue work.

But Hamlet's "look you" is a direction, not merely to Ophelia
and the court, but also to the audience in the theatre. At this point
all eyes turn naturally and inevitably to the Claudius, Gertrude,
and Polonius group, to see how they will take the ruthless sally. In
other words, beneath Hamlet's purpose there lurks another purpose of which he is completely unconscious, since it is the purpose
of his creator, of the showman who is pulling the strings of the
greatest puppet-play in all literature. It is essential to Shakespeare
that his audience should be fully aware of what Claudius is doing
at this critical moment, *because it is the moment before the dumb-show
appears.* And what is he doing? Polonius and he have been watching Hamlet for several minutes past, but this last sally complicates
the matter in dispute between them, and drags in the Queen also.
For it is natural to suppose that Gertrude's cheerfulness will be
not a little dashed by Hamlet's words and that, as he continues in
the same strain, she should, affecting not to hear him, turn away
and join in the whispered conversation between her husband and

Polonius. So when Hamlet invites the audience to gaze at them, they see the three with their heads together in discussion, a discussion that perhaps grows half-audible as soon as he ceases speaking. Each is arguing in support of his favourite theory; each is eager to follow up the false trail which most flatters his judgment. It is matter for an hour's talk, especially with Polonius taking the lead. Thus they are not watching the inner-stage at all; the play is nothing to them; their whole attention is concentrated upon the problem of Hamlet's madness. The dumb-show enters, performs its brief pantomime—a matter of a few moments only—and passes out entirely unnoticed by the disputants; and when the audience turn again to see how this silent representation of his crime has affected the King, they find him still closely engaged with Gertrude and Polonius. Shakespeare's directions to his actors have gone beyond recall, and we cannot therefore be certain how he arranged this stage-business. But I am convinced that the foregoing comes near to his intentions. Halliwell's theory that Claudius was whispering to his wife during the dumb-show is unsatisfactory, because it does not go far enough; but it contains the kernel of the truth.[3]

The chief danger-spot being successfully past, it remained for Shakespeare to round off the business by explaining how the dumb-show came to be there and by preventing the audience from pondering upon it. This he does in the conversation between Hamlet and Ophelia which immediately follows.

In his talk with the First Player, barely half an hour before, Hamlet had made it quite clear that he had as little patience with "inexplicable dumb-shows" as he had with the struttings and bellowings of the average actor. The appearance of the dumb-show, therefore, just when he had been carefully prologuing the play itself, was exceedingly annoying to him. But annoyance gives place to consternation when he sees that the pantomime is likely to divulge the whole plot of the play before it even commences. He glances anxiously at the King as the thing proceeds (glances which are not lost upon the audience), and observes to his relief that it has passed by him unnoticed. He fumes, however, at the stupidity of it all, and, when Ophelia asks him what the inexplicable show means, he replies in an exasperated tone: "Marry, this is miching mallecho, it means mischief." She notes his anger, attributes it and the cryptic remark which accompanies it to a sudden freak of madness, and soothingly suggests: "Belike this show imports the argument of the play." Ophelia has a double part to perform in this scene. As Hamlet's lover she has to do what she can to calm his troubled spirit, to lend her small assistance in nursing it back to sanity. As Shakespeare's puppet she has to provide the audience with clues. This remark exhibits her in both rôles.

As for "mischief," there is mischief enough. The situation has been saved for the moment by the King's unwatchfulness; but what may not the actors do next? For, as Hamlet guesses, there is worse behind. Yet, here comes a presenter, who confirms his blackest fears. He is on tenter-hooks. A *dumb*-show may slip by unobserved, but the spoken words of a presenter, who will present the mouse-trap all too carefully, cannot fail to reach the ears of Claudius. "We shall know by this fellow," he cries in an anguished voice; "The players *cannot* keep counsel, they'll tell all." But wondering Ophelia, all unwitting of the true state of affairs, cannot leave Hamlet alone. "Will a' tell us what this show meant?" she persists, innocently touching him on the raw. "Ay, or any show that you will show him," retorts Hamlet savagely, breaking out into ribaldry, this time with too serious an intention, as she feels. "You are naught, you are naught," she reproves, hurt though still gentle; "I'll mark the play." But Master Presenter helps her not a whit towards the meaning of the show. To her surprise, Hamlet's joy, and the spectators' delighted amusement, he turns out to be—a prologue! And his three lines of silly jingle leave the cat still in the bag. Hamlet is safe, and he relapses into jocularity. "Is this a prologue, or the posy of a ring?" he enquires with mingled feelings of intense relief and an outraged sense of dramatic propriety. " 'Tis brief, my lord," assents Ophelia, taking him back into her favour, as she notices, with relief on her side, that the storm-cloud has passed away from his mind as suddenly as it had come.

The subtlety of this is masterly in the extreme, but all the points would be readily grasped by the judicious among the audience, if the dialogue were acted as Shakespeare intended it should be. Hamlet's face of dismay at the appearance of the dumb-show, his furtive glances at the King as the pantomime is being played, the exasperation in the tone of his comment upon it, his despair when the presenter enters, his savagery as Ophelia rubs it in, and finally his relief as the presenter turns out to be nothing but a posy-prologue—all this, together with Ophelia's part therein, is actable enough. And Shakespeare's boldness is the equal of his subtlety. For he makes all his dramatic capital out of his principal difficulty, the difficulty of rendering the unconscious-ness of Claudius natural and obvious. The whole business re-volves round that, and the breathless question in the minds of the spectators throughout is: Will the King find out the plot too soon? The vicissitudes of Hamlet's mood are mirrored in theirs. Their anxiety is great until the dumb-show goes off, and the appearance of the presenter revives it in full force. And, when the tension is relaxed, the dumb-show has fallen naturally into its place in the scene, the stupidity of the players is fully appreciated, and the episode is so exciting in its doubled suspense that, while taking in the complete identity which the show reveals, the spec-tators bother no more about it, since all their thoughts are con-centrated upon Claudius. Finally, this obsession with Claudius's doings drives still deeper into their minds the fact that he has not seen anything, so that by building upon his difficulty Shakespeare has completed his triumph over it.

The interlude itself now begins, opening with the seventy lines of dialogue between the Player King and Queen upon the subject of widowhood and second marriage, lines written in a deliberately archaic style in order to distinguish them from the rest of *Hamlet*. They are deliberately commonplace also, so as to provide a rest for the audience after the excitement connected with the dumb-show and the prologue. They are not devoid of interest because they support the o'er-hasty-marriage theory and reflect upon the Queen. But the interest is a secondary one, and Shakespeare has moderated the tempo, according to his invariable custom, in order that his spectators may get, as it were, a second wind before the murderer enters and the pace becomes hot again. Moreover, after the dumb-show, which has told them just what to expect, the length and emptiness of the interlude add greatly to the tension.[4] Yet the lines give them something to think about, something unconnected with the immediate action. For the Player King concludes with a long disquisition on the subject of human instability. It is leitmotiv once more and reflects on the problem of Hamlet's character, though at this stage the audience will be hardly conscious of it. And, as so often happens in Shakespeare, what serves the purpose of dramatic irony has its direct dramatic point also, a point for Hamlet and Claudius. The name of the play is "The Mousetrap," and a mouse-trap is no use without bait. The spring of the machine lies in the speech of Lucianus at the end, but the problem is how to get the victim up to it and nosing round, so that when the trap is released he will be caught fast and squealing in its jaws. Somehow the interest of the King must be arrested and secured before Lucianus appears, must be secured by an object quite unconnected with the poisoning, since a glimpse of the spring will frighten away the game. Claudius missed the dumb-show; he must not be allowed to miss the play; he must be lured into the trap by a savoury bait. The second-marriage theme is the cheese for his majesty the mouse. Let us watch how Hamlet pushes it under his nose, how the victim sniffs at it, and finally how he swallows it.

"'Tis brief, my lord," says Ophelia. "As woman's love," caps Hamlet; and his retort, which may be taken as a reflection upon her jilting of him, as one more prop to the thwarted-love theory, is also and primarily intended as an introduction to the interlude which is now, at last, about to begin. Before that wretched dumb-show usurped the stage upon which Hamlet had expected to see the Player King and Queen, he had carefully pointed the moral in two finely apt speeches on the cheerfulness of his mother's looks. But the villainous players had spoilt all that, and, now the dialogue of the play is ready to commence, he must be brief—like the superfluous Prologue who has helped to make his own prologue ineffective. Yet he tries to make up in pitch and articulation for what the phrase lacks in length, and the words go well home, to stick in the memory and be pondered upon as the dialogue progresses.

The first twenty lines afford plenty of opportunity for this pondering, since they contain nothing to interest either Claudius or anyone else. But the nine that follow, with two snap-couplets on marrying second husbands and killing first ones, spoken, we must suppose, with all the passion which the Player Queen should give them, ought to arrest attention. The reference is carefully confined to the Queen; it is wives, and not second husbands, which are hinted at as possible murderers. Hamlet is testing his mother as to her complicity in the murder; and his aside "That's wormwood, wormwood" suggests a start or a flinching on her part which would seem to him evidence of guilt. But Claudius also begins to sniff at this; for a faint aroma of the cheese is now perceptible. A long gnomic passage follows, in which the interest is again relaxed, though it has its point, just noted, for the audience. But the scent grows strong once more in the last two lines of the speech, and the Player Queen's violent oath of fidelity, together with Hamlet's comment, "If she should break it now!" brings the game right up to the bait. Player King sleeps, Player Queen leaves him, and Hamlet turns—not to Claudius, that would never do—but to Gertrude, with "Madam, how like you this play?" The inference is glaringly obvious, and she stammers "The lady doth protest too much methinks," trying to put the best face she can upon it, conscious that the eyes of the court are looking at her. Hamlet, who is almost as anxious that she should see it as that Claudius should, does his utmost to drive the point home. "O, but *she'll* keep her word," he mocks wickedly. This brings uncle-mouse fairly into the trap with the cheese in his mouth. The suspicions of Claudius are fully aroused, not about the murder—he has no inkling of that as yet—but about the second-marriage theme. What new mad prank is Hamlet up to? He arranged this play, and must be held accountable for it. "Have you heard the argument?" he asks his nephew sharply. "Is there no offence in't?" His attention is thoroughly secured; he will now watch the play out. The bait has been swallowed whole; and the first part of Hamlet's task is accomplished.

Too much "o'er-hasty marriage" business, however, may frighten the mouse before the spring is released, and if so the trap will be empty after all. Hamlet must both soothe the King and give a fresh turn to his thoughts. The chorus-talk becomes here extraordinarily brilliant and audacious, for it rivets the victim's attention by dazzling him with glints of steel—the steel of the spring itself! "No, no," replies Hamlet to his uncle's last question, stroking his prey with a gentleness which conceals exquisite malice, "*they do but jest*, poison in jest, no offence i'th'world." "Poison!" the word grates harshly on the ear of Claudius, as it was meant to do. Hamlet is playing prologue again; he is preparing the King's mind for Lucianus and his vial; he is flashing the vial in his face, but so swiftly that he cannot see what it is. The flash is disconcerting, but Claudius has no suspicion of the truth, and his thoughts are still occupied with second husbands as he asks for more information: "What do you call the play?" The answer is rapped out suddenly: "The Mouse-trap, marry how trapically."[5] Hamlet knows the quarry is caught, and he cannot resist the temptation to give vent to his glee, to cry "marry trap" like a boy who has won the game.[6] "The Mouse-trap" makes the King start, he knows not why; perhaps there is something in Hamlet's manner to cause it; a strange being, this nephew of his! "Marry how trapically" he does not catch, or, if he does, Hamlet hastily covers it up by giving it a "tropical" twist in the context that follows.

The rest of the speech, with its talk of Vienna, Gonzago and Baptista, is reassuring enough, and contains nothing more about second marriages. It is prologue work again, however, though King Mouse is unaware of the claws in the soft paw which is caressing him, oh! so gently. "'Tis a knavish piece of work, but what of that? your majesty, and we that have free souls, it touches us not—let the galled jade wince, our withers are un-wrung." How sweet these words and this moment must be to Hamlet! The bait is swallowed; the mouse sits, still unconscious, in the very jaws of the trap; and the spring is about to go off! Nothing now can save the King.

Yet the Prince keeps his head admirably through it all. He has others to catch as well as Claudius; and as the murderer enters he realises how they may be caught. In a loud voice, so that all can hear, he suddenly announces: "This is one Lucianus, Nephew to the King." I give the sentence from the text of the Second Quarto, which with its comma, denoting a slight pause, and its emphasis-capital for the essential word, beautifully exhibits the force which Shakespeare intended the actor to throw into his pronunciation of the all-important "Nephew." By this time the courtiers are as keenly intent upon the play as Claudius himself. The attacks upon the Queen have not escaped their notice; the cause of Hamlet's madness is, we must suppose, as hotly dis-cussed among them as by their principals; and Rosencrantz and

Guildenstern have doubtless whispered the word "ambition."
When, therefore, a new character enters and is described by the
master of the ceremonies as the nephew of the King, they ask
whether he may not be intended for Hamlet himself. And they
watch the doings of this actor with bated breath; for it is now
clear to all that the interlude has a direct bearing upon the royal
house, and has been selected by the mad Prince for that very
reason. "You are as good as a chorus, my lord," breathes Ophelia.
She speaks truth; it is the acme of his chorus-work.

Lucianus has a little business to perform before the speech; he
has to take off the King's crown, kiss it, and place it on his own
head.[7] Hamlet knows this, and occupies the interval with "idle"
love-talk with Ophelia, in which his scorn for "presenters" is once
again evident. They are his last words to her before they separate
for ever. His mind is completely at ease. All his game are now in
the trap—all except the Queen perhaps, and he can deal with her
later. It only remains to begin those lines of his, those precious
lines of which he is so proud, and the gin will go off, the jaws will
snap, and the imprisoned prey will writhe in the anguish that
Hamlet longs to see.

But Shakespeare has his master-stroke to play in this scene.
There must be a hitch, at the eleventh hour, to raise the excitement of the audience to the highest possible point. The actor is
very long with his crown-business. What in Heaven's name is he
doing? Hamlet looks up, and the sight he sees freezes a half-
spoken sentence to Ophelia on his lips.[8] This First Player, in
whom after the Pyrrhus speech he had put his confidence—
confidence grossly abused by the insertion of the dumb-show and
the prologue—has once again flown straight in the face of his
express commands. He is strutting and fretting about the stage,
making the ludicrous grins of the conventional murderer, and
sawing the air with the hand which holds the vial. He has caught,
actor-like, the electric feeling of his audience, and is determined to
make the most of his opportunity. All Hamlet's irritability is
revived. Is this periwig-pated ruffian going to ruin everything
after all, as he so nearly ruined it at the beginning of the play? Is
he going to tear the passion to tatters, to the very rags, to split the
ears of all present, so that the very point of the whole evening
may be missed, and the Mouse-trap fail to catch its prey? The

situation is intolerable; something must be done, and that quickly, to bring the rogue and peasant slave to his senses. After a brief moment of speechless indignation, Hamlet bursts into bitter sarcasm. " 'Begin, murderer!' " he shouts at him—"murderer of the Play, and now about to murder my lines. 'Pox! leave thy damnable faces and begin.' Come, tear the speech to tatters in your own sweet style. O'er-do Termagant and out-herod Herod! Let's have it in the fashion of the good old ranting chronicle plays. Quick, fellow: 'the croaking raven doth bellow for revenge'; that's your mark!"

The audience has had its third moment of breathless suspense. But all is well. Whether subconsciously or unconsciously, "revenge" is more prologue-work in Hamlet's mouth, and sounds ominously in the ears of both Claudius and the court. Hamlet, however, is not thinking of anything but the play, and the speech to the player is mock-prologue this time. Lucianus pulls himself together; the quotation from the old chronicle reminds him of Hamlet's words half an hour before; and he speaks the lines clearly and trippingly on the tongue, so that their full effect is felt. The court sees the point of the drama at last: the Player King is Claudius, and crazy Hamlet is threatening to murder his uncle and seize the crown. Claudius also sees the point, *his* point. The jaws of the deadly trap hold him in a vice. The words "mixture rank, of midnight weeds collected" bring back to his vision in dreadful detail that scene four months before, when he too was bending over a sleeping king, about to poison him with "cursed hebona in a vial." His face grows livid, he clutches the arms of his seat, his eyes start from his head. He has forgotten everything, everyone, except the hideous spectacle before him. Yes, the murderer is pouring the poison into the ears of the sleeper. The secure hour, the kind of poison, the flowery bank, the dozing king are the same. Just so, that is the way it should be done, that is how he poisoned his brother on that afternoon in the palace garden. It takes the voice of Hamlet to bring him slowly back to his senses. At first he can hardly follow the words. But he must force himself to listen; it is vital to hear what this incomprehensible, this fearful, this omniscient nephew of his is saying: "Gonzago . . . story extant . . . Italian." The words are meaningless, pointless, in their bland sauvity. But what follows is not: "You shall see anon how the murderer gets the love of Gonzago's wife." Murderer, wife! wife, murderer! second husband, poison! The thing is clear. The plot of the interlude is his life's history. *Hamlet knows all!* Claudius is not safe; anything may happen. He pulls himself to his feet, and, squealing for light, he totters as fast as his trembling knees will carry him from the terrible, the threatening room. King Mouse has become a shambling, blinking paddock.

The play has made mad the guilty, but it has also appalled the free. As the murderer, the nephew, begins to administer his sham poison, a murmur of horror and indignation runs round the assembled court. Hamlet affects surprise at this and the now visible distemperature of his uncle. His cue is still "our withers are unwrung." His urbanity is imperturbable. "You are mistaken, gentlemen," he seems to protest. "'His name's Gonzago,' as I told you before. 'The story is extant, and written in very choice Italian.' It has nothing whatever to do with Claudius or Denmark. Why all this fuss? You are spoiling the play. There is more to follow. 'You shall see anon how the murderer gets the love of Gonzago's wife.'" But courtiers as well as King have had enough. As their master rises at the outrage—quite properly, as they think—they break up in confusion. Hamlet sees all his enemies in full flight, a panic-stricken mob. He no longer conceals his malice, as he hurls his last shaft into the midst of them. "What! frighted with false fire!" he shouts through the clamour, though still his meaning is a double one. The Queen, good lady, ever sympathetic with those in distress, convinced like the rest that her son has "much offended" the King, sees that he is ill, and follows him out with the solicitous enquiry: "How fares my lord?" It is the very question which Claudius had asked Hamlet at the beginning of the scene. Hamlet may "eat the air" chameleon-like, but capon-Claudius is stuffed now and ready for the carving: he has had a bellyful of "fare." Polonius also has eaten of strange meat. But he is a politician, and has at last grasped the intentions of Hamlet. His daughter has been made a screen; the thwarted-love pose was a cloak for ambition; Claudius was right all the time. He sternly commands the play to stop, and hurries after the royal pair to consult with them, Rosencrantz and Guildenstern as to the steps to be taken in view of this menace to the throne. Ophelia too, like a frightened bird, has fluttered off with the throng.

And so at last Hamlet is left alone with Horatio. He throws himself exultantly into his uncle's state seat, and chants a wild ballad snatch. Oh! the relief, the triumph, the infinite glee of that moment! He is back in the green-room of his mind, with the friend of his heart to praise him, and behind him a marvellously successful performance of histrionic art. All his disguises, his complicated and interwoven parts, drop from him. He is free, free to revel in the retrospect and to give full vent to his feelings of rapture: "Would not this, sir, and a forest of feathers—if the rest of my fortunes turn Turk with me—with two Provincial roses on my razed shoes, get me a fellowship in a cry of players, sir?" He is thinking of his acting, his lines, his admirable stage-management which saved the situation when all seemed lost. It is a characteristic outburst. Hamlet's first thoughts are of his amazing dramatic success, exceeding his wildest dreams. It is only afterwards that he remembers his uncle.

NOTES

1. 2.2.156: "Take this from this, if this be otherwise."
2. How much of Hamlet's talk with Ophelia is meant to be overheard by others is a disputable point; I think Hamlet certainly intends his mother to hear it all and does not care who else does.
3. In performance, as Mr. George Rylands suggests to me, the three figures will actually remain still and without by-play while the dumb-show is proceeding; since the whole attention of the audience must be concentrated upon *that*.
4. This important point, which lends additional support to my theory of the dumb-show, I owe to Mr. George Rylands.
5. "Trapically" is the reading of Q1; Q2 and F1 give us "tropically." But in the pronunciation of the time the two words were much alike; cf. G. D. Willcock, "Shakespeare and Elizabethan English," *A Companion to Shakespeare Studies*, p. 119. Cf. also note in my *Hamlet*.
6. Cf. *The Merry Wives of Windsor*, 1.1.155–6: "I will say 'marry trap' with you," i.e. I will give you tit for tat.
7. This is what the murderer does in the dumb-show and Lucianus should, I suppose, go through the same performance, only more elaborately.
8. The punctuation of the Second Quarto, which marks a long pause after "husbands," again brings out the point delightfully.

John C. Bucknill

From *The Mad Folk of Shakespeare*

In the interview with his mother, the idea of Hamlet's profound affection for her has been most skilfully conveyed in the painful effort with which he endeavours to make her conscious of her position, to set before her a glass where she may see her inmost part, to speak daggers to her, to be cruel, but not unnatural. From the speech,

> A bloody deed! almost as bad, good mother,
> As kill a king, and marry with his brother,

it would appear that he entertained some suspicions of his mother's complicity in the murder of his father, and that these words were tentative to ascertain whether her conscience was sore on that side. From what follows we must suppose this suspicion allayed. The readiness with which Hamlet seizes the opportunity to strike the blow which kills Polonius, under the belief that he strikes the King, is of a piece with a character too meditative to frame and follow a course of action, yet sometimes sudden and rash in action when the opportunity presents itself. The rapid action with which he utilizes the players, with which he circumvents his treacherous schoolfellows, with which he at last kills the King, resembles the quick blow which sends to his account "the wretched, rash, intruding fool," whom he mistakes for his betters. So long as resolution can be "sicklied o'er with the pale cast of thought," so long as time is allowed for any scruple to be listened to, he thinks too precisely on the event, and lives to say the thing's to do. But let the opportunity of action present itself, and he is quick to seize it, as he would have been dilatory in seeking it. It is the meditative, inactive man, who often seizes opportunities for action, or what he takes for such, with the greatest eagerness. Unable to form and follow a deliberate course of action, he is too ready to lend his hand to circumstances, as they arise without his intervention. Sometimes he fails miserably, as in the death of Polonius; sometimes he succeeds, as when he finds occasion to praise that rashness, which too often stands him in the place of steady purpose.

> Rashly,
> And praised be rashness for it, let us know,
> Our indiscretion sometimes serves us well,
> When our deep plots do pall: and that should teach us
> There's a divinity that shapes our ends,
> Rough-hew them how we will.

The comments of Hamlet upon the death of Polonius, if they had been calmly spoken by a man holding the even tenor of his way through life, would have deserved the moralist's reprobation quite as much as his speech over the praying King. To us they tell of that groundwork of unsound emotion upon which the almost superhuman intellectual activity of the character is founded. In Hamlet's life-weary, melancholy state, with his attention fixed elsewhere, such an event as the death of Polonius would have a very different effect to that which it would have had upon so sensitive and noble a mind, if its condition were healthy. His attention at the time is concentrated upon one train of ideas, his feelings are preoccupied, his sympathies somewhat indurated to the sufferings of others, and his comments upon them are likely, therefore, to appear unfeeling.

The Queen indeed, with affectionate invention, represents to the King the very opposite view. She says "he weeps for what he's done," his natural grief shewing itself pure in his very madness, like a precious ore in a base mineral. It is, however, not thus that Hamlet is represented "to draw toward an end" with the father of his mistress, and to deposit "the carrion."

The ideas which almost exclude from Hamlet's thoughts the wrong he has done Polonius now become expressed with a vehemence inconsistent with sound mind. The manner in which he dallies with the idea of his mother's incest, using images of the grossest kind—the blighting comparison of that mildewed ear, his uncle, with his warrior father—the vehement denunciation of his uncle—"a murderer and a villain, a slave," "a vice of kings, a cutpurse of the empire and the rule," "a king of shreds and patches," "a toad," "a bat, a gib,"—all this verifies his own sneer on himself, that while he cannot act he can curse "like a very drab." Although he succeeds in his purpose of turning the Queen's eyes into her very soul, and shewing black and grained spots there, it must be admitted that this excessive vehemence is not merely so much out of the belt of rule as might be justified by the circumstances, but that it indicates a morbid state of emotion; and never does Hamlet appear less sane than when he is declaring

> That I essentially am not in madness,
> But mad in craft.

Hamlet's behaviour in the second Ghost scene is more excited and terrified than in the former one. The apparition comes upon him when in a less firm and prepared mood. The first interview is expected, and each petty artery is knit to hardihood. The second is wholly unexpected, and comes upon him at a time when his mind is wrought to passionate excitement; and it is far easier for the mind to pass from one state of emotional excitement to the opposite, than from a state of self-possessed tranquillity to one of excitement. It is thus with Hamlet's rapid transition from the passionate vehemence, with which he is describing his uncle's crimes and qualities, to the ecstasy of fear, which seizes him when his father's shade once more stands before him. The sting of conscience also adds force to the emotion of awe. He has neglected the dread command, the sacred behest, of the buried majesty of Denmark. With unworthy doubts and laggard procrastination, his purpose has become almost blunted. His doubts, however, have now vanished; he no longer entertains the thought that "the spirit he has seen may be the devil"; he no longer questions whether it is "a spirit of health, or goblin damned," but accepts the appearance implicitly as the gracious figure of his father. Since the first appearance of the unearthly visitant he has caught the conscience of the fratricide King, and unkenneled the dark secret of his guilt; therefore it is that at this second visitation the feeling of awe is unmixed with doubt and that touch of defiance which is so perceptible on the former one.

Since then, moreover, his nerves have been rudely shaken; he has lived in the torture of extreme anxiety and profound grief, and the same cause naturally produces upon him a greater effect. Even while he is vehemently railing at the criminal whom he had been called upon to punish, the Ghost appears.

> Hamlet.   How is it with you, lady?
> Queen. Alas, how is't with you,
>   That you do bend your eye on vacancy
>   And with the incorporal air do hold discourse?
>   Forth at your eyes your spirits wildly peep;
>   And, as the sleeping soldiers in the alarm,
>   Your bedded hair, like life in excrements,
>   Starts up, and stands an end. O gentle son,
>   Upon the heat and flame of thy distemper
>   Sprinkle cool patience.
>
> Queen. This is the very coinage of your brain:
>   This bodiless creation ecstasy
>   Is very cunning in.
> Ham. Ecstasy!
>   My pulse, as yours, doth temperately keep time,
>   And makes as healthful music: it is not madness
>   That I have utter'd: bring me to the test,
>   And I the matter will re-word; which madness
>   Would gambol from. Mother, for love of grace,
>   Lay not that flattering unction to your soul,
>   That not your trespass, but my madness speaks:
>   It will but skin and film the ulcerous place,
>   Whilst rank corruption, mining all within,
>   Infects unseen.

It is in this agony of awe that he calls upon the heavenly guards to save and protect him, that his eyes wildly indicate alarm, that his bedded hairs stand on end, that the heat and flame of his distemper appear to lack all patience. It is in this agony of awe that he feels himself so unnerved, that he entreats his father not to look upon him, lest he should be thus rendered incapable of all action, and only live to weep. During the brief space of the Ghost's second appearance, Hamlet's extremity of fear can scarcely be overrated. Still it is the sentiment of awe, not of that horror which petrifies Macbeth in the banquet scene. Moreover, in Hamlet the reaction tends to tears, in Macbeth it is to rage.

There is something exquisitely touching in the regard which the poor Ghost shews towards the frail partner of his earthly state. The former injunction

> Taint not thy mind, nor let thy soul contrive
> Against thy mother aught

had scarcely been obeyed; and now the entreaty

> O, step between her and her fighting soul

is a fine touch of the warrior's heart, whose rough and simple silhouette is thrown upon the page in those two lines of unsurpassable descriptive terseness,

> So frowned he once, when in an angry parle
> He smote the sleded Polack on the ice.

The Ghost, indeed, is a character as never ghost was before. So far from being a neutral *it*, a *thing*, the buried majesty of Denmark is now highly personal in his simple Sclavonic majesty. Though he instigates revenge in the old viking, rather than in the Christian spirit, though he protests against the luxury and damned incest which defiles his royal bed, yet is he nobly pitiful to the wretched woman through whose frailty the transgression arises; and it is worthy of remark that after the intercession of the Ghost, Hamlet's manner to his mother entirely changes. In his former reference to the incest he makes her a full partner of the crime. In his subsequent one he represents the King as the tempter, and supposes her future conduct as that of "a queen fair, sober, wise" and to the end he gives her his affection and confidence.

That the apparition is not an hallucination, as the Queen thought, a bodiless creation caused by the diseased brain, is known to Hamlet and the reader of the play by its previous appearance, and by its reference to the disclosure then made. Its use of speech distinguishes it from the silent ghost of Banquo. It seems an error to put the Ghost on the stage clad in armour on this second occasion.

> My father, in his *habit* as he lived!

indicates that this time the design of the poet was to represent the dead king in the weeds of peace. The quarto edition, indeed, gives as a stage direction, "Enter the Ghost, in his night-gown." The appearance in this form would be suited to the place, even as the *cap-à-pie* armament to the place of warlike guard. Unlike the appearance on the battery, which is seen by all who were present, on this occasion it is only visible to Hamlet, and invisible to his mother. Ghosts were supposed to have the power to make themselves visible and invisible to whom they chose; and the dramatic effect of the Queen's surprise at Hamlet's behaviour was well worth the poetic exercise of this privilege. The Queen, indeed, must have been thoroughly convinced of her son's madness, in despite of his own disclaimer, and of the remorseless energy with which he wrings her own remorseful heart. Her exclamation, "Alas, he's mad!" is thoroughly sincere; and though her assurance that she has "no life to breathe" the secret that he is "but mad in craft" seems to imply her assent to the fact, Hamlet's language and demeanour are certainly not such as are calculated to convince her of the truth of this avowal. She is therefore likely to have spoken not falsely, but according to her convictions, when she immediately afterwards says that her son is

> Mad as the sea and wind, when both contend
> Which is the mightier.

The Queen in this ghost scene, and Lady Macbeth in the banquet scene, are placed in very similar circumstances. They both refer the appearances, by which the son of the one and the husband of the other are so terribly moved, to a morbid state of the brain; they both, but in very different degrees, are endeavouring to conceal remorse. But the Danish Queen is affrighted at the behaviour of her son; the Scottish Queen, incapable of fear, is mainly anxious about the effect which her husband's conduct will have upon the bystanders. The one gives free expression to her alarm,—she allows amazement to sit visible in her expression and attitude; the other, firm and self-possessed, is the ruling spirit of the hour. The one is a middle-aged voluptuary who, incestuously married to a drunkard of degraded appearance, has feelings so little refined that, until her son holds up the mirror to her soul, she is barely sensible of her own shameless position; the other, a great criminal, is as self-conscious as she is outwardly confident. The one is animated with the spirit of Belial, the other with that of Satan.

Hamlet finds that his assumed madness, which he puts on and off rather capricously, is likely to become an impediment to a right understanding with his mother. He sees her ready to deny the reality of her own trespass, because it is mirrored to her with the demeanour and, in some sort, with the words of ecstasy. He therefore offers as tests of his sanity, that his pulse is temperate, that his attention is under command, and his memory faithful; tests which we are bound to pronounce about as fallacious as could well be offered, and which could only apply to febrile delirium and mania. The pulse in mania averages about fifteen beats above that of health; that of the insane generally, including maniacs, only averages nine beats above the healthy standard: the pulse of melancholia and monomania is not above the average. That a maniac would gambol from reproducing in the same words any statement he had made, is true enough in the acute forms of the disease; but it is not so in numberless instances of chronic mania, nor in melancholia or partial insanity. The dramatic representations which are in vogue in some asylums prove the power of attention and memory preserved by many patients; indeed, the possessor of the most brilliant memory we ever met with was a violent and mischievous maniac. He would quote page after page from the Greek, Latin, and French classics. The Iliad, and the best plays of Molière in particular, he seemed to have at his fingers' ends. In raving madness, however, the two symptoms referred to by Hamlet are as a rule present. The pulse is accelerated, and the attention is so distracted by thick-flowing fancies, that an account can scarcely be given of the same matter in the same words. It is, therefore, to this form alone that the test of verbal memory applies.

A. C. Bradley

From *Shakespearean Tragedy*

Hamlet's return to Denmark is due partly to his own action, partly to accident. On the voyage he secretly possesses himself of the royal commission, and substitutes for it another, which he himself writes and seals, and in which the King of England is ordered to put to death, not Hamlet, but Rosencrantz and Guildenstern. Then the ship is attacked by a pirate, which, apparently, finds its intended prize too strong for it, and makes off. But as Hamlet "in the grapple," eager for fighting, has boarded the assailant, he is carried off in it, and by promises induces the pirates to put him ashore in Denmark.

In what spirit does he return? Unquestionably, I think, we can observe a certain change, though it is not great. First, we notice here and there what seems to be a consciousness of power, due probably to his success in counter-mining Claudius and blowing the courtiers to the moon, and to his vigorous action in the sea-fight. But I doubt if this sense of power is more marked than it was in the scenes following the success of the "Murder of Gonzago." Secondly, we nowhere find any direct expression of that weariness of life and that longing for death which were so marked in the first soliloquy and in the speech "To be or not to be." This may be a mere accident, and it must be remembered that in the Fifth Act we have no soliloquy. But in the earlier Acts the feelings referred to do not appear *merely* in soliloquy, and I incline to think that Shakespeare means to show in the Hamlet of the Fifth Act a slight thinning of the dark cloud of melancholy, and means us to feel it tragic that this change comes too late. And, in the third place, there is a trait about which doubt is impossible,—a sense in Hamlet that he is in the hands of Providence. This had, indeed, already shown itself at the death of Polonius,[1] and perhaps at Hamlet's farewell to the King,[2] but the idea seems now to be constantly present in his mind. "There's a divinity that shapes our ends," he declares to Horatio in speaking of the fighting in his heart that would not let him sleep, and of his rashness in groping his way to the courtiers to find their commission. How was he able, Horatio asks, to seal the substituted commission?

Why, even in that was heaven ordinant,

Hamlet answers; he had his father's signet in his purse. And though he has a presentiment of evil about the fencing-match he refuses to yield to it: "we defy augury: there is special providence in the fall of a sparrow . . . the readiness is all."

Though these passages strike us more when put together thus than when they come upon us at intervals in reading the play, they have a marked effect on our feeling about Hamlet's character and still more about the events of the action. But I find it impossible to believe, with some critics, that they indicate any material change in his general condition, or the formation of any effective resolution to fulfil the appointed duty. On the contrary, they seem to express that kind of religious resignation which, however beautiful in one aspect, really deserves the name of fatalism rather than that of faith in Providence, because it is not united to any determination to do what is believed to be the will of Providence. In place of this determination, the Hamlet of the Fifth Act shows a kind of sad or indifferent self-abandonment, as if he secretly despaired of forcing himself to action, and were ready to leave his duty to some other power than his own. *This* is really the main change which appears in him after his return to Denmark, and which had begun to show itself before he went,— this, and not a determination to act, nor even an anxiety to do so.

For when he returns he stands in a most perilous position. On one side of him is the King, whose safety depends on his death, and who has done his best to murder him; on the other, Laertes, whose father and sister he has sent to their graves, and of whose behaviour and probable attitude he must surely be informed by Horatio. What is required of him, therefore, if he is not to perish with his duty undone, is the utmost wariness and the swiftest resolution. Yet it is not too much to say that, except when Horatio forces the matter on his attention, he shows no consciousness of this position. He muses in the graveyard on the nothingness of life and fame, and the base uses to which our dust returns, whether it be a court-jester's or a world-conqueror's. He learns that the open grave over which he muses has been dug for the woman he loved; and he suffers one terrible pang, from which he gains relief in frenzied words and frenzied action,—action which must needs intensify, if that were possible, the fury of the man whom he has, however unwittingly, so cruelly injured. Yet he appears utterly unconscious that he has injured Laertes at all, and asks him:

> What is the reason that you use me thus?

And as the sharpness of the first pang passes, the old weary misery returns, and he might almost say to Ophelia, as he does to her brother:

> I loved you ever: but it is no matter.

"It is no matter": *nothing* matters.

The last scene opens. He narrates to Horatio the events of the voyage and his uncle's attempt to murder him. But the conclusion of the story is no plan of action, but the old fatal question, "Ought I not to act?"[3] And, while he asks it, his enemies have acted. Osric enters with an invitation to him to take part in a fencing-match with Laertes. This match—he is expressly told so—has been arranged by his deadly enemy the King; and his antagonist is a man whose hands but a few hours ago were at his throat, and whose voice he had heard shouting "The devil take thy soul!" But he does not think of that. To fence is to show a courtesy, and to himself it is a relief,—action, and not the one hateful action. There is something noble in his carelessness, and also in his refusal to attend to the presentiment which he suddenly feels (and of which he says, not only "the readiness is all," but also "it is no matter"). Something noble; and yet, when a sacred duty is still undone, ought one to be so ready to die? With the same careless-ness, and with that trustfulness which makes us love him, but which is here so fatally misplaced, he picks up the first foil that comes to his hand, asks indifferently, "These foils have all a length?" and begins. And Fate descends upon his enemies, and his mother, and himself.

But he is not left in utter defeat. Not only is his task at last accomplished, but Shakespeare seems to have determined that his hero should exhibit in his latest hour all the glorious power and all the nobility and sweetness of his nature. Of the first, the power, I spoke before, but there is a wonderful beauty in the revelation of the second. His body already labouring in the pangs of death, his mind soars above them. He forgives Laertes; he remembers his wretched mother and bids her adieu, ignorant that she has preceded him. We hear now no word of lamentation or self-reproach. He has will, and just time, to think, not of the past or of what might have been, but of the future; to forbid his friend's death in words more pathetic in their sadness than even his agony of spirit had been; and to take care, so far as in him lies, for the welfare of the State which he himself should have guided. Then in spite of shipwreck he reaches the haven of silence where he would be. What else could his world-wearied flesh desire?

But *we* desire more; and we receive it. As those mysterious words, "The rest is silence," die upon Hamlet's lips, Horatio answers:

> Now cracks a noble heart. Good night, sweet prince,
> And flights of angels sing thee to thy rest.

Why did Shakespeare here, so much against his custom, introduce this reference to another life? Did he remember that Hamlet is the only one of his tragic heroes whom he has not allowed us to see in the days when this life smiled on him? Did he feel that, while for the others we might be content to imagine after life's fitful fever nothing more than release and silence, we must ask more for one whose "godlike reason" and passionate love of goodness have only gleamed upon us through the heavy clouds of melancholy, and yet have left us murmuring, as we bow our heads, "This was the noblest spirit of them all"?

NOTES

1. III. iv. 172:

> For this same lord,
> I do repent: but heaven hath pleased it so,

> To punish me with this and this with me,
> That I must be their scourge and minister:

i.e. the scourge and minister of 'heaven,' which has a plural sense elsewhere also in Shakespeare.

2. IV. iii. 48:

> *Ham.* For England!
> *King.*   Ay, Hamlet.
> *Ham.*   Good.
> *King.* So is it, if thou knew'st our purposes.
> *Ham.* I see a cherub that sees them.

3. Hamlet's reply to Horatio's warning sounds, no doubt, determined;
   but so did "I know my course." And is it not significant that, having
   given it, he abruptly changes the subject?

Harold Jenkins

From *The Arden Shakespeare: Hamlet*

Why, then, does Hamlet delay? After more than two centuries
of debate on this celebrated question one detects in some quarters
a critical weariness with it as intrinsically less important than it
has been made to seem[1] But a problem does not diminish because
it becomes familiar; and Hamlet himself was of course the first to
raise it, and to be defeated by it:

> I do not know
> Why yet I live to say this thing's to do.

It is true that there are some who deny that Hamlet procrastinates. They point out that to kill a king surrounded by guards is
not a simple matter, or that once Hamlet has dispelled a reasonable doubt of the Ghost's story he is given no opportunity.[2] But
that is not Hamlet's view. What he says is:

> I have cause, and will, and strength, and means
> To do't.

And I think we must conclude that it is not Shakespeare's view
either. Prominent in the centre of the play, the fact of delay,
whatever may be said about the reason for it, is not so easily
escaped.[3]

There have, however, been attempts to minimize the effect of
the soliloquies in which Hamlet reproaches himself for what he
has not done. Stoll is the chief of those who insist that delay is
simply inherent in the story.[4] The axiom "No delay, no play" is

Reprinted from *The Arden Shakespeare: Hamlet*, pp. 136–42, by Harold
Jenkins (1982), by permission of Methuen and Company.

ultimately incontestable, but it need mean little more than that the course of revenge, like that of true love, must not run smooth too soon. In Saxo and Belleforest an interval of many years before revenge is finally achieved suggests not procrastination but sustained determination and calls for no accusing comment. So long as a hero is thought to be planning something it is unlikely to strike us that he ought by now to have done it. It is often remarked that through all the excitements of Shakespeare's unfolding drama it would never occur to us that Hamlet was neglecting his revenge if he refrained from saying so himself. Stoll finds that the charges Hamlet brings against himself are not substantiated in the action of the play. He maintains that Shakespeare, necessarily deferring the achievement of revenge until the end, "slurred over" the delay, and that the soliloquies which draw attention to it serve to reassure the audience that what the hero has not done yet he ultimately will.[5] I doubt if this explanation would occur to anyone who had not read *The Spanish Tragedy*, to which it is more appropriate; it is hardly necessary to remark that the soliloquies stress much more what is not done than what will be.

A different explanation is given by Waldock, who, in his brilliant little book on the critical reactions to *Hamlet*, holds that the self-reproach of these soliloquies, although indicative of delay, is only a minor motif of the play. The Player weeping for Hecuba, Fortinbras leading an army to capture a mere eggshell—these, he says, are little curiosities of life which happen to strike Hamlet's imagination and prompt him to consider his own conduct as he might not spontaneously have done, so that the notion of delay which they give rise to, although admittedly in the play, is not "a prominent feature of the design."[6] But the answer to this, I think, is that the doings of Fortinbras and the Player are more than interesting curiosities, because Hamlet's encounters with them are not chance encounters such as might occur in life. They occur in a dramatic composition; and why should they occur at all except to elicit from Hamlet the reflections which we have seen they do? And if the play without them would not give the impression of delay, may that not be the reason why the dramatist, so pointedly as it seems, has brought them in?

A closer look at these two soliloquies of self-reproach seems desirable. For all their matching reflections, they have an air of naturalness rather than contrivance. Characteristically there is no formal or stylistic correspondence: indeed the ruminations on the "delicate and tender prince" are very different from the passionate outburst on "this player here." But there are detailed analogies of thought which reach below the surface and suggest an underlying dramatic purpose. The Player is moved to tears by a "fiction," Fortinbras finds quarrel in a "straw," in each case something of no substance. The one has his "dream" of passion, the other his "fantasy" of fame. Hamlet by contrast has a powerful and genuine incitement—"a dear father murder'd" as the one soliloquy puts it, "a father kill'd, a mother stain'd" as the other—yet according to the first soliloquy "can say nothing," according to the second lets "all sleep." Each soliloquy asks whether he is therefore a "coward"; and each works to a climax of self-accusation, which leads to a resolve in terms appropriate to it. The speech on the Player ends:

> The play's the thing,
> Wherein I'll catch the conscience of the King,

that on the soldier:

> From this time forth
> My thoughts be bloody or be nothing worth.

In addition to such parallels there is also an unobtrusive but significant verbal link which joins the two soliloquies in a larger composition which embraces both. That a contrast between Fortinbras and Hamlet was in mind from the outset I hope I have shown; and how the contrast was to go can be seen with a little hindsight from the description of "young Fortinbras" in the first scene as being of "*mettle* hot and full." But Hamlet does not wait to meet Fortinbras in order to call himself "a *dull* and muddy-*mettled* rascal." In this phrase from the soliloquy on the Player one epithet contrasts with what we remember Fortinbras was and the other with what he still will be when the actual encounter with him spurs Hamlet's "*dull* revenge." This repeated word *dull* shows

Hamlet aware of having become what the Ghost had specially warned him not to be:

> I find thee apt.
> And *duller* shouldst thou be than the fat weed
> That roots itself in ease on Lethe wharf,
> Wouldst thou not stir in this.

It is when he becomes "dull" that the Ghost returns. The play has manifestly been preparing from the first for the moment when Hamlet beside Fortinbras would be shown as "dull," and it is as though the Player has slipped in to take Fortinbras's turn. Yet Fortinbras, although no longer the revenger we expected, still enters in his own turn, so that a design duplicates itself to produce two soliloquies, which achieve a natural symmetry. One preceding and one succeeding the reappearance of the Ghost, they unite in confirming by their "dull" motif the "almost *blunted* purpose" which occasions it. The "dull" revenge reveals itself as a creative element in a developing pattern.

Hence a consideration of the two soliloquies makes it impossible to agree with Stoll that Hamlet's delay is in any way "slurred over" or with Waldock that it is not prominent in the play's design. *Hamlet* is not simply a tragedy of revenge in which the crucial deed has to be deferred until the end: it is a play about a man with a deed to do who for most of the time conspicuously fails to do it.

Nor can we accept that delay is more talked about than exhibited. Why else do we have the prayer scene directly upon the play scene? Partly of course to show the King's conscience duly caught; but as he kneels, we see the revenger, like Pyrrhus, with drawn sword arrested and his enemy at his mercy; and when, unlike Pyrrhus, he puts his sword up, whatever we choose to think of his reasons, the tableau of an opportunity let slip is unforgettable.[7]

Moreover, the theme of purpose unfulfilled, of which Hamlet here presents a vivid and particular example, has its reflection in general terms elsewhere. Later in the play the King reminds another revenger how the human will is subject to "abatements and delays." Hamlet, in between the two soliloquies which lament his own inaction, has another soliloquy in which, looking beyond his own case to the case of humanity at large, he muses upon "resolution" which is weakened by "thought" until "enterprises of great pitch and moment . . . lose the name of action." The Player King, in those gnomic couplets which reduce large truths to truisms, plants the same thought like a motto in the centre of the play:

> What to ourselves in passion we propose,
> The passion ending, doth the purpose lose.

THE CENTRAL ACT

This speech of the Player King is but one of many things which, in the shaping of *Hamlet*, demand and receive a central place. The soliloquies of self-reproach for a deed undone, one at the end of the second act and the other near the beginning of the fourth,[8] have made themselves into a kind of frame for a sequence of crucial scenes which Shakespeare's easy mastery of the constructive art accommodates within the middle act. At the centre of all, with the nutshell truths inside it, is the play-within-the-play which re-enacts the murder. This also contains an image of the Queen as an inconstant wife. It is followed by the tableau of the inactive revenger, the "pictures" of the Queen's two husbands, and the startling reappearance of the Ghost. The King is shown confessing, if not repenting, his sin, the Queen taxed with hers. Hamlet's verbal onslaught on his mother after the play balances his denunciation of Ophelia before it: revulsion from marriage is exhibited both in effect and cause. In and around these highly dramatic scenes a seemingly unhurried amplitude persists in many brief encounters which are always liable to give some fresh perspective while sustaining the impression of natural court activity. Even as we prepare for the murder play, room is found for Hamlet to lecture the actors on their art, after it to mock Guildenstern with the recorder: we are reminded that art holds a mirror up to nature, but that the heart of a man's mystery is not easily plucked out. Polonius continues as a butt for Hamlet's wit, and the jest about the "brute part" of killing him in a play is another of the little previews of what will later happen in earnest.

Between the play scene which strengthens Hamlet's resolve to kill the King and the prayer scene which gives him his opportunity, Rosencrantz and Guildenstern, in reflections on "the cess of majesty," remind us of what killing a king may mean. The necessary participation of Horatio in Hamlet's plot to catch the King permits a vignette of the man who, rising above fortune, is not "passion's slave," and who thus contrasts with the revenger as well as with others with whom the revenger is himself contrasted. (The weeping Player, the time-serving Rosencrantz and Guildenstern immediately come to mind.) More than Horatio is of course involved here: indeed the character is not obviously correspondent, though equally not incompatible, with what we see of him elsewhere; but it brings a sketch of one kind of ideal man into the centre of the play. Most significantly perhaps, preluding the whole sequence is the soliloquy on "To be or not to be," in which Hamlet's personal plight is transcended in the plight of being man suffering all the "natural shocks that flesh is heir to," and he debates what will reveal itself as the basic issue of the play, whether this is better escaped from or endured.

In Shakespeare's art of construction here thematic expansion does not weaken, but combines with, concentration in the plot. In this central sequence the movement of events intertwines the two actions of revenge and marriage and brings them to their crises together. The meeting between Hamlet and Ophelia, now that we come to it, not only disappoints Polonius's plan but simultaneously tells Ophelia that Hamlet will not marry, the King that he *will* revenge:

> I say we will have no mo marriage. Those that are married already—all but one—shall live; the rest shall keep as they are.

This is still the gist of what Hamlet says to each of them in his excited comments as they watch the acting of the play. What one crisis means for Ophelia a later act will show. In the other, just when revenge brings its threat to a climax as the King is confronted with his guilt, it begins to recoil upon itself. Hamlet has his moment of triumph, which strengths his grim resolve ("Now could I drink hot blood"), but his eagerness to kill the King is first paralysed in the prayer scene and then in the Queen's chamber frustrated by his killing Polonius instead. When the Ghost now suddenly returns and Hamlet stands convicted of neglect, the corpse of Polonius lies before them and the second revenge action is ready to begin.

NOTES

1. "It is not fashionable to consider Hamlet as a man who delays" (*EC*, XXIII, 1973, p. 232). "The issue of Hamlet's delay . . . is, on the whole, a pretty boring one by now" (*Hudson Rev.*, 26, 1973, p. 518). Philip Brockbank calls it "the question that academic courtesy should perhaps never again allow" (*SS 30*, 1977, p. 109); Ruth Nevo dismisses it as "misconceived" (*Tragic Form in Shakespeare*, 1972, pp. 129–30). Both of these, however, see Shakespeare exploiting delay and would probably agree with the writer in the *Hudson Review* (p. 520) that "we should not be looking for an objective correlative that will explain Hamlet's motives but for an aesthetic one that might explain Shakespeare's."
2. E.g. G. L. Kittredge (ed.), *Hamlet*, pp. xi–xvi, making, notably, no reference to Hamlet's self-reproaches or his confession to the Ghost; Hazelton Spencer, *The Art and Life of William Shakespeare*, pp. 313–17.
3. Cf. D. G. James, *The Dream of Learning*, p. 47: "Few of us will deny that Hamlet's procrastination is the major fact in the play and that it was intended by Shakespeare to be so." The word *delay*, never used by or of Hamlet in the play but traditional in criticism, is in some respects an unfortunate one: unlike *procrastination* it may apply to either the agent or the event, and the ambiguity has occasioned some critical confusion. Neither word is entirely satisfactory, for although they correspond to Hamlet's *tardy*, by putting the emphasis on postponement they diminish the impression of neglect.
4. The point was trenchantly put by an 18th-century critic (said by Rawlinson to be George Stubbes) in *Some Remarks on the Tragedy of Hamlet*, 1736, p. 34: "The poet was obliged to delay his hero's revenge; but then he should have contrived some good reason for it." The romantic critics, of course, and their successors thought he gave ample reason for it in the character of his hero. An obvious fact often overlooked is that as determinants plot and character are not mutually exclusive. It is hard to see why Stoll (see next note) should be so anxious to relieve the hero of all responsibility.
5. *Hamlet: an Historical and Comparative Study*, 1919, pp. 16–25, 70. See also *Art and Artifice in Shakespeare*, 1933, pp. 94–101.

6. *Hamlet*, pp. 30, 85–86, 91–95. It is strange that Waldock should here slip into that confusion between life and art which, under the term "documentary fallacy," he discusses with such beautiful lucidity elsewhere.

7. Cf. P. Alexander, *Shakespeare's Life and Art*, p. 157: "Here Shakespeare has reduced almost to visual terms the whole of Hamlet's problem." See III. iii. 89–95 LN (end).

8. In what we call IV. iv. But apart from the fact that the first three scenes are short (140 lines altogether), it is frequently observed that the traditional beginning of Act IV, first marked in the 1676 quarto, is unsatisfactory. (See IV. i n.) The phase of the action which culminates in the slaying of Polonius is not concluded when Hamlet lugs off the body but continues for three more scenes of aftermath. The link scene of Fortinbras would more suitably be the first of Act IV or, as some would have it, even the last of Act III.

Samuel Johnson

Note to Polonius

Polonius is a man bred in courts, exercised in business, stored with observation, confident of his knowledge, proud of his eloquence, and declining into dotage. His mode of oratory is truly represented as designed to ridicule the practice of those times, of prefaces that made no introduction, and of method that embarrassed rather than explained. This part of his character is accidental, the rest is natural. Such a man is positive and confident, because he knows that his mind was once strong, and knows not that it is become weak. Such a man excels in general principles, but fails in the particular application. He is knowing in retrospect, and ignorant in foresight. While he depends upon his memory, and can draw from his repositories of knowledge, he utters weighty sentences, and gives useful counsel; but as the mind in its enfeebled state cannot be kept long busy and intent, the old man is subject to sudden dereliction of his faculties, he loses the order of his ideas, and entangles himself in his own thoughts, till he recovers the leading principle, and falls again into his former train. This idea of dotage encroaching upon wisdom, will solve all the phænomena of the character of *Polonius*.

G. L. Kittredge

From "Introduction," *Hamlet*

King Claudius is a superb figure—almost as great a dramatic creation as Hamlet himself. His intellectual powers are of the highest order. He is eloquent—formal when formality is appropriate (as in the speech from the throne), graciously familiar when famliarity is in place (as in his treatment of the family of Polonius), persuasive to an almost superhuman degree (as in his manipulation of the insurgent Laertes)—always and everywhere a model of royal dignity. His courage is manifested, under the most terrifying circumstances, when the mob breaks into the palace. His self-control when the dumb show enacts his secret crime before his eyes is nothing less than marvellous.[1] It was no accident that Shakespeare gave him that phrase which has become the ultimate pronouncement of the divine right of monarchy: "Such divinity doth hedge a king."

Intellectually, then, we must admit Claudius to as high a rank as Hamlet himself.[2] What are we to say of him morally? On this point there is danger of misinterpretation. Claudius is often regarded as a moral monster—selfish, calculating, passionless—subtle and cold as a serpent. From such an error we are rescued by one of the supreme passages in all Shakespeare—the King's soliloquy after 'The Mousetrap' has caught his conscience:

> O, my offence is rank, it smells to heaven;
> It hath the primal eldest curse upon't,
> A brother's murther!

In this soliloquy Claudius unlocks his soul. It reveals him not only as passionately remorseful—with a heart in no wise cauterized by crime[3]—but as so clear-sighted, so pitiless in the analysis of his

own offences and of the motives that actuated them, that he
cannot juggle with his conscience.

> What form of prayer
> Can serve my turn? 'Forgive me my foul murther'?
> That cannot be; since I am still possess'd
> Of those effects for which I did the murther—
> My crown, mine own ambition, and my queen.

His crime was a crime of passion. "My queen" is the acme of the
climax. So she was in the Ghost's revelation to Hamlet:

> Thus was I, sleeping, by a brother's hand
> Of life, of crown, of queen, at once dispatch'd.

To neglect or undervalue Claudius destroys the balance of the
tragedy. On the stage, for generations, his lines were cut unmer-
cifully, and his rôle was assigned to an inferior actor, so that he
became the typical melodramatic villain, who frowns and mouths
and struts and beats the air. And Hamlet has suffered accordingly, and has too often been conceived as a pathetic creature of
high imagination but feeble will. Otherwise, why did he not
abolish this ineffectual obstacle with a sweep of the arm? Of late,
however, managers and actors have done better in this regard,
but the prejudice lingers. Of Shakespeare's intent there can be no
doubt. The play is a contest between two great opponents. This
Hamlet understands; and he expresses the truth in his words to
Horatio, which might well be a summarizing motto for the play:

> The pass and fell incensed points
> Of mighty opposites.

NOTES

1. Cf. W. W. Lawrence, *Journal of English and Germanic Philology*, 18 (1919),
   7 ff.; Pearn, *Review of English Studies*, 11 (1935), 403; Granville-Barker,
   Prefaces to Hamlet, 3d Series, 1937, pp. 89 ff. For Wilson's theory, which
   differs *toto caelo*, see his *What Happens in Hamlet*, 2d ed., 1937, pp. 144 ff.
2. The testimony of the Ghost is well deserved: "with witchcraft of his
   wit" (I, 5, 43). "Thou know'st," says Iago, "we work by wit, and not by
   witchcraft"; but Claudius's wit *is* witchcraft. He has bewitched both
   Queen and state.
3. Compare the King's "aside" in III, 1, 49–54, which prepares us for the
   soliloquy.

Nigel Alexander

From *Poison, Play, and Duel*

After the play, the killing begins. The first death among the characters is not the revenge-killing predicted in the inner-play's double image of death. It is, however, a logical although unforeseen development of that action. From a dramatic point of view the play scene has built up so much tension that some kind of release of passion on the stage is essential. The mouse-trap therefore snaps shut. Only when it has done so is it discovered that it has killed a "wretched, rash, intruding fool" (3 iv 31:2413) instead of the hoped for "rat" (3 iv 23:2404).

With the death of Polonius the plot of *Hamlet* assumes a new and violent velocity. The sudden sword-thrust through the arras of Gertrude's closet transforms Hamlet from a man who has been training himself to perform the role of avenger into a homicide who falls victim to a pursuing and implacable vengeance. This sudden metamorphosis may be "accidental" as far as Hamlet's own intentions are concerned, but it represents a clear and deliberate choice on the part of the dramatist which has decisive consequences for the orientation of the entire play.

Its dramatic purpose is clear. The theme of violence, and the reaction and response to violence, is suddenly viewed in a different perspective. The use of Pyrrhus and Lucianus allows Shakespeare to demonstrate the kind of man who would be capable of killing the King without thinking about it. The death of Polonius allows Shakespeare to investigate what might have happened if Hamlet had killed the King without thinking about it.

Reprinted from *Poison, Play, and Duel*, pp. 119–52, by Nigel Alexander (1971), by permission of University of Nebraska Press and Routledge and Kegan Paul PLC (London).

The way in which Laertes and Ophelia react to their father's death with the full capacity of their passionate natures supplies the answer. The chain of disaster and sudden death would continue. Shakespeare makes Hamlet use a comparison from painting in order to draw the audience's attention to this change in perspective (5 ii 75:3579):

> But I am very sorry, good Horatio,
> That to Laertes I forgot myself;
> For by the image of my cause I see
> The portraiture of his.

It is not only the stage play which holds a mirror up to nature. Individuals, or even their pictures, may serve the same purpose.

Hamlet actually describes Laertes as a mirror in conversation with Osric before the "play" with foils (5 ii 112:3610 Q 6):

> Sir, his definement suffers no perdition in you; though I know, to divide him inventorially would dozy th'arithmetic of memory, and yet but yaw neither in respect of his quick sail. But, in the verity of extolment, I take him to be a soul of great article, and his infusion of such dearth and rareness as, to make true diction of him, his semblable is his mirror, and who else would trace him, his umbrage, nothing more.

According to this ironic account, the only person capable of acting as a "mirror" or model for the qualities of Laertes is his own reflection seen in a glass. Anyone who attempts to use Laertes as a "mirror" and to model himself upon him will achieve only the distinction of becoming like his shadow, not his reflection.

Osric's praise of Laertes as the perfect gentleman thus provokes the reply that his perfection is beyond imitation. Laertes, however, is also the "mirror" of the perfect avenger. Hamlet feels that he ought to imitate this part, but has not done so. The different perspective with which Hamlet's cause is painted or reflected in Laertes casts new light on it for the audience.

The imagery of painting and reflection thus draws attention to the new system that is being introduced into the great series of reflecting "mirrors" which forms the play of *Hamlet*. In this fashion Hamlet reverses roles with Claudius, and becomes a pursued killer, without actually playing the part of Lucianus. The graveyard scene and the duel scene are both the direct outcome of the death of Polonius. The conduct of Ophelia and Laertes shapes the second half of the play.

This repetition of the revenge theme alters the balance of the action. The fate of Polonius and his family is inextricably linked with the court of Denmark. The story of how that family is overwhelmed by disaster is also a history of the court's destruction. The grief of Ophelia and the anger of Laertes are contrasted with Hamlet's conduct. These comparisons do more than suggest other answers to the questions asked at the beginning of the play. They change the nature of the questions.

Ophelia and Laertes actually pursue the courses of action considered by Hamlet in soliloquy. Laertes chooses to be a violent avenger of blood. Ophelia follows a different course which leads her "not to be" (3 i 56:1710). After the death of her father Ophelia suffers from what the King calls "the poison of deep grief" (4 v 73:2813). This drives her to madness and the despair which so poisons her memory, understanding, and will that it leads to her death. This death may be accidental or suicidal. In both cases it has strong overtones of self-destruction.

Laertes, enraged at the death of his father, is plunged into a deep and equally poisonous grief by the madness and sudden end of his sister. Intent upon vengeance, Laertes is soon involved in the "madness" of the King's plot against Hamlet. This leads to his own independent proposal for the use of poison upon his unbated rapier—a suggestion that leads to his own destruction and the death of the King.

Hamlet is subject to exactly the same passions as Ophelia and Laertes. Grief, hate, madness, revenge, and self-destruction are the great themes of the soliloquies. Ophelia and Laertes are both ignorant of the murder of King Hamlet. Their conduct thus provides what appears to be independent testimony about the central situation. The King may exhort Hamlet to accept his father's death as "natural." He does not expect Laertes or Ophelia to respond to the killing of Polonius in a calm or reasonable fashion.

The way in which Laertes and Ophelia plunge passionately to murder and self-destruction allows the audience to measure the force of the passions which Hamlet is struggling to control. The aggressive and passionate feelings of ambition, revenge, and self-destruction are all "natural" reactions. Only Hamlet attempts to control these passions by an uncommon awareness, consciousness, and intelligence. This control is not lightly acquired. The sudden reversal of roles in which Hamlet becomes a killer turned prey for a new and vengeful hunter allows Shakespeare to examine these involved emotions and passions on a psychological as well as a physical level.

The idea that the hunter is also hunted in his turn may be safely traced back to mankind's earliest experiences. The Renaissance, however, was particularly interested in the psychological development of the idea expressed in Ovid's *Metamorphoses*, iii. The hunter Acteon, who lost his way in the forest and saw Diana naked, was changed into a stag by the goddess and pursued and killed by his own hounds.

The medieval and Renaissance commentators who had moralized Ovid in a tradition which stretches from John of Garland's *Integumenta* (*c.* 1234) through the French *Ovide Moralisé* and the work of Petrus Berchorius to George Sandy's *Ovid's Metamorphosis, Englished Mythologiz'd and Represented in Figures* (1632) had frequently interpreted Acteon as a man pursued and destroyed by the hounds of his own passion. An engraving of Acteon is used as an emblem of *Voluptas aerumnosa* in Geoffrey Whitney's *A Choice of Emblems* (1586).

That Shakespeare was perfectly familiar with such an idea is clearly demonstrated by the opening of *Twelfth Night* (1 i 16:20):

> *Curio.* Will you go hunt, my lord?
> *Duke.*   What, Curio?
> *Curio.* The hart.
> *Duke.* Why, so I do, the noblest that I have.
> O, when mine eyes did see Olivia first,
> Methought she purg'd the air of pestilence!
> That instant was I turn'd into a hart
> And my desires, like fell and cruel hounds,
> E'er since pursue me.

When Fortinbras surveys the corpses on the stage at the end of *Hamlet* he compares the sight to a display of game at the end of an unusually savage day's hunting (5 ii 356:3857):

> This quarry cries on havoc. O proud death,
> What feast is toward in thine eternal cell
> That thou so many princes at a shot
> So bloodily hast struck?

"Havoc" is a battle-cry indicating that no quarter or mercy should be shown to the enemy. Hunting which results in havoc leads to indiscriminate slaughter and thus oversteps the written and un-written laws which govern the pursuit of game. Death is a cruel sportsman.

Such a "quarry" has unquestionably been produced by the principal characters. They have released wild passions which have, in the end, "hounded" them all to death. The lust and ambition of Claudius have driven him on to seize the crown. That seizure automatically marks him as the victim of a pursuing vengeance. Yet this vengeance is itself a passion which brings further pursuit and destruction in its wake.

The search for vengeance in *Hamlet* is frequently referred to in terms of hunting. This imagery is most closely associated with the presentation of the inner-play. When Rosencrantz and Guilden-stern first report the actors' arrival they use an image from falconry to describe the children's companies whose popularity in the city has forced the actors to go on tour (2 ii 335:1387). Hamlet, in calling immediately for a speech, says: "We'll e'en to it like French falconers, fly at anything we see" (2 ii 423:1474).

By the end of *The Murder of Gonzago* the image of the hunt has become a symbol of Hamlet's success and triumph in hunting and hounding the King (3 ii 265:2143):

> Why, let the strucken deer go weep,
> The hart ungalled play;
> For some must watch, while some must sleep;
> Thus runs the world away.

Hamlet is aware, however, that the very success of his device may make the King hunt him with more urgent determination. When Rosencrantz and Guildenstern arrive to summon him to his moth-er's closet Hamlet treats them as stealthy hunters trying to keep downwind from their prey: "Why do you go about to recover the wind of me, as if you would drive me into a toil?" (3 ii 337:2216).

This image of Rosencrantz and Guildenstern as the King's hunters or dogs is realized in physical action after the death of Polonius when Hamlet escapes from his guards with the cry of "Hide fox, and all after" (4 ii 30:2659). The inner-play acts as a trap which forces the King out of cover and exposes him to the hounds of his own passions. The death of Polonius means that he can also use Rosencrantz and Guildenstern, and after them Laertes, to run down and kill Hamlet. The inner-play is an image of the destructive passions that it releases in its audience.

Within the context of tragedy it is evident that many dramatists used the theme of an avenger entirely consumed and then destroyed by his own passion for revenge. Shakespeare's use of this theme illuminates new, and unexpected, aspects of the moral and psychological questions which are the fundamental basis of *Hamlet*. Claudius, in his search for security, makes use of Laertes's passion for vengeance. Ironically he thus places in Hamlet's hands, at the most suitable occasion, the perfect instrument of vengeance. There could be no clearer demonstration of the "dream of passion" (2 ii 545:1592) pursued by the King. It is evident that the dramatic justification for the existence of Polonius is the manner of his death.

It is clear that Hamlet shares many of the passions which destroy the King and Laertes. It is easy, therefore, to assume that all passion is condemned by the play and that its moral is as commonplace as the one which Arthur Brooke prefaced to his version of *The Tragical Historye of Romeus and Juliet* (1562):

> The glorious triumphe of the continent man upon the lustes of wanton fleshe, incourageth men to honest restraynt of wyld affections, the shamefull and wretched endes of such, as have yelded their libertie thrall to fowle desires, teache men to witholde themselves from the hedlong fall of loose dishonestie.[1]

As in *Romeo and Juliet*, Shakespeare's examination of the problem is psychologically more complex and morally more profound and charitable than the simple opposition between reason and passion so well loved by authors in the tradition of *A Mirror for Magistrates*. The passion for which Romeo and Juliet sacrifice themselves cannot be dismissed as evil or even described as an undesirable development in the strife-torn and hate-ridden city of Verona. The reason which would condemn these lovers would be an instrument of little service to humanity.

The world of Elsinore is infinitely darker and more terrible than Verona. In it the torch of human passion is carried by a pair of lovers whose history is even more "star-cross'd" (*Romeo and Juliet*, Prologue 6) than that of Romeo and Juliet. Their love blazes in the language of the play with a sexuality as fierce and open as that which displays Hero naked to Leander in Marlowe's *Hero and Leander*. Shakespeare had read, or re-read, *Hero and Leander* while writing *Romeo and Juliet*. That play is filled with clear and deliberate verbal echoes of Marlowe's poem. The knowledge gained in writing *Romeo and Juliet* is now developed in the severer harmonies of *Hamlet*. The great love scene between Hamlet and Ophelia, however, is not performed on a balcony or in a bedroom. It takes place in the graveyard, when Ophelia is already beyond the reach of human love.

It is in the graveyard, and in a burst of passion, that Hamlet discovers one of the truths which has eluded him throughout the play. The imagery of hunting is concerned with the traps which are set in order to obtain information. This hunt, however, is also a search for truth on the part of the characters. Polonius expresses this when he describes the trap that he has set for Hamlet in the nunnery scene (2 ii 156:1188):

> If circumstances lead me, I will find
> Where truth is hid, though it were hid indeed
> Within the centre.

Truth, for the audience as well as for Polonius, proves to have an unexpected centre.

The truth about Denmark is that the present King murdered his brother to obtain his crown and queen. This act of love is a hunt of murderous passion in which the King and most of the court are finally pulled down and killed. The search for power and love becomes a chase in which death is the only victor—an unseen hunter whose presence is only recognized when it is too late. The search for justice and revenge relentlessly pursued by Laertes makes him, in turn, a marked victim of the hunt of death. The closer that Polonius comes to discovering the "truth" about Denmark, the nearer he is to death.

The discovery that the King is a murderer creates the problems of the play. The certain proof supplied by the inner-play does not solve the problem of *Hamlet*. The question remains, how does one deal with such a man without becoming like him? The death of Polonius, and the conduct of Laertes, make it clear that the hunt of death will never cease so long as one vengeance pursues another. The only power which can break this chain of murder is the passion of love—love which could be expressed even at this stage, as Claudius knows and reveals in the prayer scene, by repentance for the wrong he has done his brother and renunciation of the love and power gained by his crime.

It was, however, the passion of love which first drove Claudius and Gertrude to prefer the life of passion above that of wisdom and majesty. The passion which destroys the court of Denmark has the same fundamental root as the only passion that can save the state of Denmark. The play contains other mysteries, and is concerned with other truths, than the fact that Claudius murdered his brother. The conflict is not therefore simply a conflict between reason and passion. That would be a "poor concussion of positives on one side with negatives on the other."[2] The conflict is the different ways in which the same fundamental passions, based upon man's aggressive, sexual, and compassionate nature, develop in the individual. It is clear that Giordano Bruno's image of the twin peaks of Parnassus is an attempt to come to some kind of psychological understanding of the competing and apparently contradictory passions which meet in the name of love.

It must be emphasized again that while it is possible, and I believe that it is probable, that Shakespeare had read Bruno's *De gli eroici furori*, no part of this critical argument depends upon that hypothetical assumption. It is not possible to explain *Hamlet* as a dramatization of the philosophy of Bruno. They were both, however, great artists using the traditional symbolism of the Renaissance to describe and dramatize certain observable aspects of human psychology. The correspondence of their imagery—the battle within the soul, the Judgment of Paris, the hunt of passion, and the image of prudence—makes a comparison both interesting and instructive for the critic.

In this context, therefore, Bruno's treatment of the traditional figure of Acteon is particularly interesting. He does not regard him as simply the victim of his own passions. Instead he is a seeker after truth. It is not possible, in Bruno's view, for the human soul on this earth to attain a complete knowledge and understanding of the divine harmony and perfection of the universe. This harmony he symbolizes by Apollo, god of the sun. Diana, chaste huntress and goddess of the moon, then becomes the symbol of the power and beauty of the universe that may, after long search in the dark forest, finally be seen and comprehended by the human intellect.

In the Second Dialogue of the second part of *De gli eroici furori* Bruno writes:

> I say very few are the Acteons to whom destiny gives the power to contemplate Diana naked, and the power to become so enamoured of the beautiful harmony of the body of nature, so fallen beneath the gaze of these two lights of the dual splendour of goodness and beauty, that they are transformed into deer, inasmuch as they are no longer the hunters but the hunted.[3]

In this context the dogs which pursue Acteon are not simply the lusts of the flesh which destroy him. They are a desire and passion for a divine harmony which make him indifferent to the "thousand natural shocks/That flesh is heir to" (3 i 62-3:1716-17):

> The result is that the dogs, as thoughts bent upon divine things, devour this Acteon and make him dead to the vulgar, to the multitude, free him from the snares of the perturbing senses and the fleshly prison of matter, so that he no longer sees his Diana as through a glass or a window, but having thrown down the earthly walls, he sees a complete view of the whole horizon.[4]

This Diana is "the being and truth of intelligible nature, in which is infused the sun and the splendour of a superior nature." The man who has fallen in love with this Diana may truly be said to be possessed by the "heroic frenzy" of Bruno's title. The pursuit of this kind of passion is the beginning of wisdom.

It is not necessary to make Hamlet an inhabitant of Bruno's world of Pythagorean symbols and Platonic forms in order to realize that he is a man torn by conflicting passions. Bruno claimed to solve problems which Shakespeare was content to dramatize. Hamlet's love and memory of his father spur him on to revenge his death. That very act of revenge would transform him into a beast like Claudius who is bound to be destroyed by the ungoverned force of his own unleashed passions. The only method of escape is to penetrate further into the forest in order to catch a glimpse of the goodness and beauty of the naked Diana and be devoured by the dogs of love instead of the dogs of war. In order to be an avenger it is necessary to stifle such passions. Hamlet, however, catches more than a glimpse of them beside Ophelia's grave. The power and passion of human love is not dead within him, although he has failed to recognize it until that point in the play. It is, in its fashion, a heroic frenzy. It cannot save Hamlet, or lead him to the state of divine contemplation which is the goal of Bruno's search, but it does introduce a new element which has profound implications for the psychology of the whole play.

Shakespeare, therefore, uses the death of Polonius as the starting-point for a dramatization of passions which cut deep into the roots of man's social and sexual existence. The Judgment of Paris and the act of love are seen as having political as well as sexual consequences. The complex symbolism of the play makes it a carefully created and controlled fictional or dream structure which invites the audience to abandon their orthodox moral, political, and sexual certainties in order to become aware of depths of instinctual feeling which are only now being barely sounded and charted by our psychology. It is impossible to explain *Hamlet* by the metaphysics of Giordano Bruno or by the metaphysics of Sigmund Freud because the play advances beyond their principles. It is an organized system of perception for obtaining information about human psychology.

The character of Ophelia is essential to Shakespeare's dramatization of human passion in *Hamlet*. It is not surprising that her scenes carry a burden of dramatic consequence out of all proportion to their length. It is evident that the dramatist has succeeded in making them dramatically effective by filling them with intense and almost unendurable tragic emotions. Like Hamlet, Ophelia is a character whose troubled mind and consciousness have encouraged critics to seek for "real" or "historical" explanations of her conduct. The measure of Shakespeare's success is the way a critical "mythology" has grown round Ophelia.

It is extremely important to see that the dramatic character of Ophelia gathers myth and metaphysical speculation for the same reason as the dramatic character of Hamlet. Both are active centres of consciousness which mirror, and help to interpret, the events of the play for the audience. Ophelia's mind is not, perhaps, as "finely aware and richly responsible" a consciousness as Hamlet's.[5] It is a much more sensitive instrument than the minds of Laertes, Polonius, Gertrude, or even Claudius. It creates an extremely concentrated effect because it is concerned only with the passion of human love—having had its understanding in all other directions carefully limited by the dramatist.

The consciousness is necessary because, as Henry James pointed out in the preface to *The Tragic Muse*:

> No character in a play (any play not a mere monologue) has, for the right expression of the thing, a *usurping* consciousness; the consciousness of others is exhibited exactly in the same way as that of the "hero"; the prodigious consciousness of Hamlet, the most capacious and most crowded, the moral presence the most asserted, in the whole range of fiction, only takes its turn with that of the other agents of the story, no matter how occasional these may be. It is left in other words to answer for itself equally with theirs.[6]

This observation is not entirely accurate. The play is clearly designed to express the consciousness of Hamlet in a way that is denied to many of the other characters. The obvious discrepancy between the awareness of Hamlet and the dramatic ignorance of the other characters is consciously exploited for comic effect by Tom Stoppard in his play *Rosencrantz and Guildenstern Are Dead*. It is true, however, that the minds of the other characters are used in the great central scenes to help provide a searching examination of Hamlet's own role in the play. Ophelia is the most highly developed, and the most important, of these reflecting minds.

When Hamlet appears to Ophelia in her closet with his doublet unbraced, no hat upon his head, his stockings ungartered and a look (2 i 83:979):

> As if he had been loosed out of hell
> To speak of horrors,

he is behaving in the traditional fashion of distraught lovers. Ophelia and Polonius interpret this conduct as the effect of disappointment in love. The nunnery scene is devised as a "show" to convince the King of this interpretation. It fails in this purpose because Polonius has misinterpreted Hamlet's actions. The audience has had the benefit of the Ghost's information. It will therefore be able to interpret Hamlet's conduct, more correctly, as Hamlet's farewell to love in order to concentrate upon his task of revenge. He is clearing his memory, as he had sworn to do in the second soliloquy, of "all trivial fond records" (1 v 99:784).

Hamlet does not take his leave of Ophelia in this way simply because she might prove a mild distraction during the task of revenge. He believes, and this belief can be demonstrated from the imagery of the play, that to yield to his love for Ophelia would be to enter the fickle hopeless world of passionate love for a woman in which his mother and uncle wallow as if in a pigsty. It would be to commit the same Judgment of Paris and prefer passion above wisdom and power. Hamlet therefore sees Ophelia as a threat to his memory, his dedication to the task of revenge, and to his whole existence. Only when she is dead does he recognize that this view was wholly and disastrously mistaken.

Hamlet is shown as being called upon to make the traditional "choice of life" that is familiar from the literature and painting of the Middle Ages and the Renaissance. The symbolism of this choice of life is similar to the Judgment of Paris but it is not identical with it. It may be illustrated by a consideration of two paintings by Raphael, *The Dream of Scipio* in the National Gallery, London, and its companion piece, *The Three Graces*, in the Musée Condé, Chantilly. In his account of these paintings in *Pagan Mysteries in the Renaissance*, Edgar Wind draws attention to a number of recurring patterns in Classical and Renaissance imagery. These patterns are, I believe, applicable to the study of *Hamlet*, although they are not necessarily a complete and sufficient explanation of Shakespeare's imagery.

In *The Dream of Scipio*:

> The young hero lies at the foot of a laurel tree, apparently dreaming of his fame. Two women approach him. The

sterner one presents him with a sword and a book, the more gracious offers a flower. These three attributes—book, sword and flower—signify the three powers in the soul of man: intelligence, strength, and sensibility, or (as Plato called them) mind, courage, and desire. In the Platonic scheme of the "tripartite life," two gifts, the intellectual and moral, are of the spirit while the third gift (the flower) is of the senses. Together they constitute a complete man, but as they mingle in different proportions they produce different characters and dispositions.[7]

It is evident that the imagery of the book, the sword, and the flower is of great significance in the structure of *Hamlet*. It represents the choice between *contemplativa, activa,* and *voluptaria,* or the pursuit of wisdom, power, and pleasure. It has already been argued that the fall of Troy symbolizes the choice of Gertrude and Claudius as the Judgment of Paris, and that the soliloquies operate in terms of memory, understanding, and will—the Augustinian powers of the soul. These are now seen to be part of a larger series of images which present to the audience the choice of life open to the characters throughout the play.

Hamlet had attempted to follow the contemplative life when he sought to return to the University of Wittenberg. He is called to the active life of revenge by the Ghost. He attempts to follow the passionate life of hatred for the King at the same time that he rejects the passionate life of his love for Ophelia. It is clear that he has failed to understand the true nature of the passionate life of the senses. This is evidently also the situation of Claudius, Laertes, and Gertrude, for they fail to understand the flowers and herbs of healing and grace offered to them by Ophelia in the scenes of her madness.

Hamlet is twice presented as reading a book during the play. He may also be carrying one at the beginning of the nunnery scene. There he finds Ophelia, apparently the picture of chaste contemplation, reading a book which has been handed to her by her father to use as a stage property in the "show" devised for the King. In exhorting her to retire to a nunnery Hamlet is suggesting that she devote herself solely to a life of contemplation—a life that he would have preferred to follow if the King had not kept him at Elsinore.

The sword of the active life is carried by the armed figure of the dead King. The famous duel fought with Fortinbras is a paradigm of the active life of a King and a ruler. This example is kept alive in the play by the example of young Fortinbras and the presence of his army. Both Laertes and Hamlet become involved in the active life when they meet with rapiers in their hands. One of these rapiers is poisoned and it becomes plain that Claudius, too, leads an active existence, although his chosen activity is murder. The poisoned chalice is a powerful symbol of that union of action and contemplative cunning.

Ophelia carries the flower of the passionate life. The language of flowers is, in a very important sense, the language of passion in the play. The flowers may be rosemary or rue, the herbs of grace, which Ophelia carries in her scenes of madness. They may be the "mixture rank, of midnight weeds collected" (3 ii 251:2127) referred to by Lucianus and used by Claudius to poison his brother. The flowers of passion may be herbs of health, or weeds which threaten to poison the entire kingdom of Denmark. What is instructive is that Polonius and Laertes regard Hamlet as the major threat to the fair flower of Ophelia's passion.

They are unaware of Hamlet's own fierce rejection of the passion of love and the life of the senses—a rejection which causes him to treat Ophelia as if she were a bawd or a whore. Only in the graveyard does Hamlet recognize his love for Ophelia—a passion that is proclaimed in defiance of memory and understanding since it is an expression of love for a now senseless corpse. Only once he has embraced the passionate life of human love is Hamlet's union of the active, contemplative, and passionate lives complete. Only then is he ready to purge the court and kingdom of Denmark of the festering misuse of passion which threatens to poison it. It is essential to recognize that Claudius's and Gertrude's abuse of love is not intended as a condemnation of all desire. The flower is a necessary addition to the book and the sword.

Shakespeare uses only one brief scene to establish Ophelia before he calls upon her to perform some of the most difficult and important acting in the play. It is vital that all the actors should be aware of the purpose and fundamental nature of this scene. It is too often scurried through in order to permit suitable pauses and dramatic effects in the scene with the Ghost. The company must understand that there can be no *Hamlet* without Ophelia and that this scene establishes the reflecting consciousness used in the nunnery, play, and graveyard scenes.

It establishes an atmosphere of acute sexual anxiety. Ophelia has only spoken one half-line in the play when her brother starts to reprove her for recklessly exposing herself to Hamlet's advances (1 iii 5:467):

> For Hamlet, and the trifling of his favour,
> Hold it a fashion and a toy in blood,
> A violet in the youth of primy nature,
> Forward not permanent, sweet not lasting,
> The perfume and suppliance of a minute;
> No more.

The violet is an image which links the play's sexuality to the graveyard. Ophelia is unable to offer her brother violets on his return from France since "they wither'd all when my father died" (4 V 181:2936). Laertes hopes that violets may spring from her dead body.

The scene uses the complete range of the play's imagery of poison, play, and duel in order to impress upon Ophelia the danger of her sexual situation and to inform the audience of a passion that might otherwise pass unregarded. It is a passion which has important consequences for the play. Laertes begins by offering Ophelia reasons of state. If the safety, or perhaps, as the Folio reads, sanctity, of Denmark depends upon Hamlet's choice of a future queen, so the sanity and health of Ophelia depend upon her ability to realize that Hamlet's "will" in these matters is not his own. She must accordingly treat any protestations of love as dangerous to her honour and perhaps poisonous to life itself (1 iii 29:492):

> Then weigh what loss your honour may sustain,
> If with too credent ear you list his songs,
> Or lose your heart, or your chaste treasure open
> To his unmast'red importunity.
> Fear it, Ophelia, fear it, my dear sister;
> And keep you in the rear of your affection,
> Out of the shot and danger of desire.

> The chariest maid is prodigal enough
> If she unmask her beauty to the moon.
> Virtue itself scapes not calumnious strokes;
> The canker galls the infants of the spring
> Too oft before their buttons be disclos'd
> And in the morn and liquid dew of youth
> Contagious blastments are most imminent.

If Ophelia "weighs" Hamlet's greatness she must realize he is not master of his "will." She should then proceed to "weigh" the danger she will incur if she permits him to master her "will." Will is a common expression for sexual desire. It is not certain that it carries the explicit sexual sense of Sonnet 135 here, but the implications of "your chaste treasure open" are clear enough. Hamlet must approach that area through her ear and her heart. Ophelia must therefore be wary of the engagement that takes place in her own mind and urges her to yield these parts to her enemy. She must keep "in the rear" of her own passions and therefore "out of the shot and danger of desire."

The duel or military engagement between the lovers now turns into a masque or play. The end of a masque occurs when the dancers unmask. The end of the play of love is near when the lovers unmask by removing their clothes. Laertes warns Ophelia that maids must unmask when the moon is their only audience.

Roses are "the infants of the spring"—or at least the phrase describes them in *Love's Labour's Lost*, 1 i 101:110—and Laertes later calls Ophelia "rose of May" (4 v 154:2910). The flower imagery, however, carries a submerged metaphor of sexual passion. The dew of Ophelia's youth would certainly be blasted if, as a result of opening her chaste treasure to Hamlet, she should canker the rose of her chastity by giving birth to a real infant of the spring. The details of the story found in the *Danish History* of Saxo Grammaticus are thus reversed. The young woman was there used by the King as a device to entrap Amleth. Laertes and Polonius are anxious to protect Ophelia from the cunning trap for her chastity laid by the Prince—a trap which they think would poison their honour and her life.

Ophelia accepts this advice with a certain amount of irony—an irony which expresses her character but also runs deeper than

her present consciousness in the language of the play. Shakespeare is preparing the mind of his audience for later dramatic
effects (1 iii 45:508):

> I shall the effect of this good lesson keep
> As watchman to my heart. But, good my brother,
> Do not, as some ungracious pastors do,
> Show me the steep and thorny way to heaven,
> Whiles, like a puff'd and reckless libertine,
> Himself the primrose path of dalliance treads
> And recks not his own rede.

The guard set by Ophelia on her heart may find the real enemy
within. The guard upon the battlements will find themselves in
that situation in the next scene.

It will shortly be evident—from the Polonius–Reynaldo
scene—that Polonius does expect Laertes to tread the path of
dalliance at least as far as the Paris brothels. Both Polonius and
Laertes prove "ungracious" as shepherds to Ophelia. It is ironic
that Laertes should attack the Priest in the graveyard for not
following the rule of Christian charity. "The primrose path" is the
road to hell. The entire family are in danger of taking it. Polonius
follows it as a servant of the King whose whole power is based
upon such dalliance. Laertes follows it gladly when he returns to
avenge his father. In the graveyard the Priest indicates that he
regards Ophelia's death as no more than a passport to hell.
Ophelia sees more dangers in the situation than are visible to her
father and brother.

The entry of Polonius develops both the imagery and the
action. His speech of good advice is a traditional, and therefore
"memorable," genre which can be traced to a variety of possible
sources. The "wise father" tradition continues from David's advice to Solomon through Erasmus's version of Isocrates' *Letter to
Demonicus* to the versions usually cited as sources—Lord Burgh-
ley's ten precepts to his son and Euphues' advice to Philautus in
John Lyly's *Euphues* (1578). Yet, as Doris V. Falk[8] has pointed out,
the great difference is that all of these fathers begin by offering
their sons spiritual advice. Polonius gives only the prudential
maxims of the practised politician.

Like Claudius, Polonius is both rhetorician and politician. An actor must cause his audience to nod wisely at the conventional wisdom of (1 iii 78:543):

> This above all—to thine own self be true
> And it must follow as the night the day,
> Thou canst not then be false to any man

and yet cause them to doubt the context in which this advice is given. The passions of remembrance and love are hardly to be controlled by this fashion of self-regard. Polonius now makes it impossible for Ophelia to trust her own judgment, and therefore be true to herself, in the terrible transactions of the heart.

Polonius believes that Hamlet intends to deceive Ophelia. For every one of her statements about love, Polonius has a different, and discreditable, interpretation.

Polonius picks up Ophelia's phrase, "many tenders of his affection to me" (1 ii 99–100:565-6) and, in heavy sarcastic fashion, develops its meaning of "offer for contract." In the metamorphoses which follow Hamlet first seeks to pass counterfeit money and offers "tenders" which "are not sterling" (1 iii 107:573). He then becomes a man whose vows are a snare and a delusion set simply as "springes to catch woodcocks" (1 iii 115:581). Hamlet next becomes the general of a besieging army, a Machiavellian tactician who calls for a parley in order to obtain the unconditional surrender of the opposing forces. Finally he appears as an actor dressed in false clothes to utter fictitious vows (1 iii 126:592):

> In few, Ophelia,
> Do not believe his vows; for they are brokers,
> Not of that dye which their investments show
> But mere implorators of unholy suits,
> Breathing like sanctified and pious bonds,
> The better to beguile.

Hamlet's vows are "brokers"—or go-betweens—who do not possess the capital, or the powers, shown in their documents and are therefore engaged in the business of fraud. Polonius is still elaborating the "offer for contract" sense of Ophelia's original choice of "tender." One such possible contract suggested by Hamlet's vows is "a contract of eternal bond of love" (*Twelfth Night*, 5 i 150:2318). The bonds of such a ceremony would be "pious bonds" and if they breathe it is because they represent the vows spoken in the marriage service.

Hamlet's vows are "mere implorators of unholy suits" because they use the colour of the robes worn at the ceremony of marriage to give a semblance of propriety to their own fraudulent purpose—which is presumably to obtain Ophelia's "chaste treasure." Ophelia would be a fool to listen to Hamlet and would expose her father as a fool for not looking after his daughter. Like the good advice of Laertes, the tedious but bitter jokes of Polonius contain a buried metaphor. If Ophelia really took Hamlet's "tenders for true pay" she might literally "think" herself "a baby" and "tender" or give birth to a "fool" or child. An unwanted pregnancy would be a grave consequence for Ophelia.

The irony of the situation is that it is their failure to believe Hamlet's vows which makes fools of them all. The Priest regards the ceremony at the graveyard as "unholy" and would never have performed it unless the King had acted as "broker." The part that Polonius imagines Hamlet to be playing—a cunning false-seemer gratifying his lust by fraud and guile—is an accurate picture of the King of Denmark.

Polonius attempts to make Ophelia forget Hamlet in his own version of the rhetoric of oblivion. Polonius and Laertes, unaware of the poisoning of King Hamlet, identify the Prince as the source of poison. He is a threat to Ophelia's chastity and his madness endangers the stability of the entire kingdom. This initial mistake renders their triangle of affection fatal. It leads to the graveyard and the oblivion of death.

This scene indicates both the difficulty, and the immense opportunity, of the part of Ophelia. Although her reply to her brother is spirited, Ophelia's behaviour is sober, steadfast, and apparently demure. Yet in the language of the other characters she appears as an active and exciting participant in the submerged inner life of the court. The solemn warnings of her brother and father contain a strong libidinous undercurrent of sexuality. They regard her as a girl of vibrant personality who must restrain and "understand" herself in order not to ally herself with her lover.

Both speeches picture Ophelia as seduced, made pregnant, and abandoned by Hamlet.

When Hamlet encounters her in the nunnery and play scenes his language is so overtly sexual that it might be considered obscene or insulting. It is fairly evident that, at this stage of the action, Hamlet views Ophelia as he considers his mother—a passionate voluptuary whose flagrant sexuality is a poisonous and destroying force. The image of poison which Polonius and Laertes see in Hamlet, he sees in Gertrude and Ophelia. Yet his choice of language, and the very violence of his reaction, show that he is far from immune to such poison. The fantasy picture of Ophelia created by Polonius, Laertes, and Hamlet reveals their own most deeply rooted fears and acute sexual anxieties.

Their description of Ophelia is not entirely fantasy. The scenes of madness reveal, beyond all reasonable doubt, a strong-willed and passionately sexual nature which breaks out violently in thought and deed once the restraints of reason have been removed. In her songs Ophelia describes herself as seduced, made pregnant, and abandoned.

It is, therefore, hardly surprising that a character who is so variously described should cause some difference of critical opinion. It is not simply a historical accident, nor is it solely a matter of individual predilection, that Ophelia should appear to some critics as demure and to others as depraved. There are outspoken confident moral judgments, such as Rebecca West's decisive opinion that "the truth is that Ophelia was a disreputable young woman: not scandalously so, but still disreputable."[9] The continuing debate about such textual cruces as "pious bonds" (1 iii 130:596), emended by Theobald to "pious bawds" with no apparent textual justification, or the argument whether "nunnery" (3 i 121:1776) means "a community of nuns" or "a brothel" are equally all part of a passionate argument about the nature of Ophelia's character.

Since this ambiguity is not accidental, but derives from the ways in which Shakespeare has made the other characters describe her, it is hardly surprising that critics who are also psychologists should assume that Ophelia and Gertrude are different, and perhaps incompatible, aspects of the same female figure. It would be correct to say that at certain stages of the play Hamlet's attitude to Ophelia is governed by his love–hate relationship with his mother. To treat Ophelia simply as a mother-substitute, however, is to over-simplify and distort the imagery which expresses the play's unusually complex psychology.

If it is possible to categorize Ophelia beyond doubt as an injured innocent, or a sly slut, or even a "disreputable young woman," then the moral problems of the play can be simplified. Conventional attitudes can be adopted to events which, if taken seriously, must arouse in the audience a terror and a pity at the tragic possibilities of human existence which are not easily allayed by any soothing or reassuring system of metaphysics. The desire to simplify Ophelia and resolve her into components which can be classified in terms of current critical, moral, or psychological orthodoxies, is the same kind of critical simplification which attached the puritanical title of *Sacred and Profane Love* to Titian's masterpiece in the Gallery Borghese at Rome.

The paintings of Titian contain visual imagery which is as provocative, and as divisive, as the imagery of Renaissance drama. Like that drama, they make demands upon the intellect and emotions of the spectator rather than offering him comfortable reassurance. The Renaissance handled its visual imagery in exactly the same way that Picasso has claimed he treats his:

> When I paint, I always try to give an image people are not expecting and beyond that, one they reject. That's what interests me. It's in this sense that I mean I always try to be subversive. That is, I give a man an image of himself whose elements are collected from among the usual ways of seeing things in traditional painting and then reassembled in a fashion that is unexpected and disturbing enough to make it impossible for him to escape the questions it raises.[10]

It is now being claimed that Shakespeare's imagery in treating Ophelia is remarkably similar to Titian's painting. Both are unexpected and disturbing enough to make it impossible for the spectator to escape the questions raised.

Titian's painting shows two women, one clothed, the other naked except for a loin-cloth and a red cloak over one shoulder. Between them is a fountain, carved with various figures, in which Cupid appears to dip his hand. The figures carved on the fountain are scenes of chastisement. "A man is being scourged, a woman dragged by the hair, and an unbridled horse is led away by the mane."[11] Edgar Wind argues that these symbols on the fountain of love "show how animal passion must be chastened and bridled."[12]

It is possible that the figures on the fountain link the chastisement of love to the chastisement of Fortune. The woman with the flying forelock may be the figure of *Fortuna*. An unbridled horse is also listed in Cartari's *Le Imagini . . . de i dei de gli antichi* as a symbol of fortune. Wind then argues that:

> If the reliefs on the fountain thus demonstrate that animal passion has been exorcized, it would follow that the water in the fountain of love is pure, although it is gently stirred by Amor; and it follows further that the two women conversing at the fountain in the presence of the god are both representatives of a love above the "profane," their dialogue rising to those *casti misteri amorosi di Platone* which allow for two forms of chastened love, *Amore celeste e umano.* Human Love, while beautifully adorned, is the more restrained of the two because she knows her adornments to be vicarious, whereas Celestial Love, who is unadorned, is the more passionate and ardent, holding in her hand a vase from which a flame rises. Between the two, Amor is seen setting the water of the fountain in motion, an idyllic version of the "spirit moving over the face of the water," which changes chastity into love. As the movement of the group is from left to right, the three figures again illustrate the progression from *Pulchritudo* through *Amor* to *Voluptas*, with Amor playing his traditional part as a mediating or converting power. The theme of the picture is therefore exactly what the untutored eye has often suspected—an initiation of Beauty into Love.[13]

The figures on the fountain make it clear that although one may "fall in love" it requires intense effort and arduous application to reach the kind of love symbolized by the two women. The elements of the painting are part of the long attempt made by the Classical, Medieval, and Renaissance artists and philosophers to reconcile virtue with pleasure. Raphael's *Dream of Scipio* and the choice of life which must embrace wisdom, power, and pleasure is part of this tradition. So is the companion painting of *The Three Graces.* Wind believes that this painting was originally placed back to back with *The Dream of Scipio*, like the obverse and reverse of a medal.

The three graces are Chastity, Beauty, and Pleasure. They are naked, except for Chastity who has a light loin-cloth, and they are joined together in the rhythm of an eternal dance. The different qualities of these three female figures together make up the feminine principle which is also the power of pleasure or love. Just as each man must strive, in his choice of life, to be a union of wisdom, power, and pleasure, so every woman must be a combination of chastity, beauty, and passion. A woman is therefore three women, since she possesses the graces within her, and the different balance or harmony that they adopt in their dance of the spirit determines her character.

Since the three graces are also the power of pleasure they also form part of the character of every man. It is disastrous to ignore the graces and it may be equally disastrous to neglect any one of them. They must all be pursued if the individual is to acquire within his own soul the harmony of the dance which is also in tune with the music of the spheres and the divine order of the world. It is not enough to be wise, or powerful, or to be in love. It is insufficient to be as chaste as ice, or simply beautiful, or entirely devoted to pleasure. A man or woman is called to be a complete union of opposites.[14]

Wind draws attention to the extreme importance of the balance of the group in Raphael's painting:

> Not quite so abstemious as Chastity, nor so liberally adorned as Pleasure, Beauty holds the balance between them, being chaste and pleasurable in one. She touches Chastity's shoulder as she turns towards Pleasure; and so subtle is the distribution of weights that, although the group retains its classical symmetry, the emphasis is decidedly to the right.[15]

This distribution of weight creates a mathematical union of scale and proportion with its companion painting. In *The Dream of Scipio* the ratio of gifts is two to one against pleasure. In *The Three Graces* the ratio of grace is two to one in pleasure's favour:

> In offering these gifts of love, the Graces counterbalance the demands of Scipio's heroic dream. Instead of two gifts of the

spirit and one of the senses, they bring two delectable gifts
and one of restraint. While the hero is advised to adopt a rule
of action by which he subordinates his pleasure to his duties,
he is here invited to soften these severities and allow virtue
to come to fruition in joy. The discipline of Scipio is only one
side of the picture; the other is his affectionate liberality.
Virtus and *Amor* belong together.[16]

In the nunnery scene when Hamlet meets Ophelia he has just
finished an agonizing attempt to harmonize the conflicting passions in his own soul. "To be or not to be" (3 i 56:1710) demonstrates his difficulties in pursuing an active, a contemplative, or a
passionate life. When he looks up from this desperate debate
Hamlet sees the figure of a solitary girl reading a book. She
appears to be the symbol of quiet and chaste contemplation. The
language which Hamlet addresses to Ophelia in the nunnery
scene is founded on the image of the three graces.

Ophelia's first action is to deny the power of the book of
contemplation which she holds in her hand. She breaks the power
of memory by offering to return to Hamlet the remembrances of
their mutual love. To Hamlet this repudiation of memory makes
Ophelia, like his mother, the figure of *Voluptas*—but a figure of
passion who is not subject to the chastening of love or the
chastening of fortune. Hamlet sees an engrossing and forgetful
lust which makes women lower than beasts. Gertrude has broken
the harmony of the graces by her hasty marriage. Hamlet now
denies that grace can ever have existed in the female sex. He
identifies Ophelia as unrestrained and lustful passion. It is hardly
surprising that she is unable to understand him.

The terms used by Hamlet in this exchange, "honesty,"
"beauty," and a "bawd," are the names of the three graces—
except that the grace of pleasure or passion is identified as the
whore of lust (3 i 103:1758):

> *Hamlet.* Ha, ha! Are you honest?
> *Ophelia.* My lord?
> *Hamlet.* Are you fair?
> *Ophelia.* What means your lordship?
> *Hamlet.* That if you be honest and fair, your honesty should
> admit no discourse to your beauty.

> *Ophelia.* Could beauty, my lord, have better commerce than
> with honesty?
> *Hamlet.* Ay truly; for the power of beauty will sooner trans-
> form honesty from what it is to a bawd than the force of
> honesty can translate beauty into his likeness. This was
> sometime a paradox, but now the time gives it proof.

Hamlet warns Ophelia that the dance of the graces is a progression to lust rather than passion. Any contact between "honesty"
or *Castitas* and "beauty" or *Pulchritudo* must transform honesty into
a bawd. Hamlet believes that this result is the inevitable outcome
of the "discourse" of beauty and honesty since "the time gives it
proof" in the conduct of his mother.

From this belief there follows the conclusion that he is himself
tainted with this lust—since he is by birth a prisoner of the nature
that he must have inherited from the whore his mother (3 i
118:1772):

> *Hamlet.* You should not have believ'd me; for virtue cannot
> so inoculate our old stock but we shall relish of it. I loved
> you not.
> *Ophelia.* I was the more deceived.

Since all women are symbolized by the solitary figure of *Voluptas*,
mankind is entirely corrupted by the disease of lust. Marriage and
the birth of children are thus a biological confidence trick in which
a union formed without love or faith breeds "sinners" who are in
turn condemned to a wanton progress to oblivion.

The only way of breaking this endless wheel of misfortune is
to stop the process of human reproduction. This can only be
accomplished if women in general, and Ophelia, become the figure of *Castitas* and abjure marriage by retiring from the world to a
nunnery. It is important to realize that Hamlet's attack is not
directed at women alone. Hamlet regards himself as equally vicious and corrupt (2 i 124:1779):

> I am very proud, revengeful, ambitious; with more offences
> at my beck than I have thoughts to put them in, imagination
> to give them shape, or time to act them in. What should such
> fellows as I do crawling between earth and heaven? We are
> arrant knaves, all; believe none of us. Go thy ways to a
> nunnery.

Marriage is for fools. The doors should be shut upon her father that "he may play the fool nowhere but in's own house" (3 i 132:1787). Ophelia should take care to marry a fool since no married woman can escape calumny and wise men are aware that women make them "monsters."

"Monsters" in this sense probably means men with horns, or cuckolds. Since all marriage vows are contracted between a fool and a whore Hamlet now embarks upon his bitter and extraordinary attack upon the whorish art of painting the face (3 i 142:1798):

> I have heard of your paintings too, well enough; God hath given you one face, and you make yourselves another. You jig and amble, and you lisp, and nickname God's creatures, and make your wantonness your ignorance.

As a description of Ophelia this is irrelevant "madness." There is little doubt that the figure with the painted face, the provocative walk, and the transformation of God's handiwork is the traditional and powerful image of *Voluptas* in her less reputable guise of fleshly lust. The image is particularly powerful in this context since the audience are aware that Ophelia is acting as a front or "face" for the King.[17] Claudius has just used the image of a harlot's painted face to describe his own conduct (3 i 50:1702):

> How smart a lash that speech doth give my conscience!
> The harlot's cheek, beautied with plast'ring art,
> Is not more ugly to the thing that helps it
> Than is my deed to my most painted word.
> O heavy burden!

Hamlet's attack is an attack upon the court, and it is at least in part accurate.

The double sense of "nunnery" is thus extremely important for the rising tension of the scene. Since Hamlet is exhorting Ophelia to assume the attributes of *Castitas* it must mean "a community or body of nuns." Since, however, he also sees her as the painted figure of *Voluptas* it seems probable that "nunnery" could also be a blasphemous euphemism for a brothel. In making use of Ophelia to protect his lust, Claudius, and Polonius are treating her like a prostitute. This implication is sustained by the way in which Polonius has offered to "loose my daughter to him" (2 ii 161:1196), while Hamlet identifies Polonius as a "fishmonger" (2 ii 173:1211) who may also be a brothel-keeper. The King of Denmark has turned the whole court into a brothel or stews by making the royal bed "a couch for luxury and damned incest" (1 v 83:768).

Hamlet's generalizations about the nature of *Voluptas* are correct. He has rightly detected the satyr's face leering behind the painted harlot's mask of court ceremony. He is wrong, however, when he imagines that Ophelia is a particularly vicious part of this false show. This error, created by the terrible pressure of the passions which divide Hamlet, makes him appear a madman to Ophelia.

Her description of the Prince allows Shakespeare, like Raphael, to link the symbolism of the choice of life to the dance of the three graces (3 i 150:1806):

> O, what a noble mind is here o'erthrown!
> The courtier's, soldier's, scholar's, eye, tongue, sword;
> Th'expectancy and rose of the fair state,
> The glass of fashion and the mould of form,
> Th'observed of all observers—quite, quite down!

Hamlet's union of the active, contemplative and passionate life had seemed to Ophelia best expressed in his vows of love. It is this harmony which she now believes has been shattered (3 i 155:1811):

> And I, of ladies most deject and wretched,
> That suck'd the honey of his music vows,
> Now see that noble and most sovereign reason,
> Like sweet bells jangled, out of time and harsh;
> That unmatch'd form and feature of blown youth
> Blasted with ecstasy.

Ophelia's conclusion is, in part, accurate. It is unbalanced of Hamlet to assume that all women must be figures of vice and agents of corruption. Her judgment of Hamlet, however, is as mistaken as his view of her. In Denmark the harmony of the initiation of beauty into love, the harmony which informs Titian's painting of *Amor–Pulchritudo–Voluptas* and which should be the basis of the affection between Ophelia and Hamlet, has been destroyed by Claudius and Gertrude. The fierce rejection of Ophelia is a symptom of the damage done to the balance of Hamlet's affections by his mother's marriage. This very revulsion is also an indication of the intensity of the inner struggle which will eventually restore harmony to Denmark.

Ophelia's supreme importance in the play is that she reminds the audience, and eventually Hamlet, that sexual passion may be the mediating force which turns beauty into a passionate but higher love, as well as the unrestrained and degrading power which corrupts Gertrude and Claudius. The chastening of love and the chastening of fortune endured by these lovers is so severe that it destroys them both. The passion of love, however, which Hamlet at last comes to recognize in the graveyard is the only power which can prevent him from becoming, like Pyrrhus, Lucianus, Claudius, or Laertes, another black, blood-splashed figure of unrestrained and murderous passion.

Ophelia cannot know that the reason for Hamlet's bitter attack is that "the time is out of joint" (1 v 189:885), and therefore his words sound "like sweet bells jangled, out of time and harsh." The time has been lost because the sovereign of Denmark has abandoned the harmony of reason in favour of the pleasures to be gained by murder and incest. It is not Hamlet, but the court, which has really gone mad. It is this murderous passion of lust, this hidden figure of *Voluptas* behind the arras, which turns the meeting of Hamlet and Ophelia, which should have been a triumph ceremony[18] of the mutual remembrance of their love, into a bitter scene of forgetfulness, mutual incomprehension, and misdirected aggression.

In the nunnery scene Shakespeare makes the hardest demand that any dramatist can make of his principal actor. He asks him to lose the sympathy of the audience. This is different from asking him to play the part of a villain. The actor who plays Richard III or Iago is in no danger of being asked to sacrifice his emotional control over the audience. He can control the audience's sympathies and direct in what way they should be out of sympathy with the character.

The actor playing Hamlet is asked to abandon his claim upon the audience in favour of Ophelia. An actor playing Hamlet should be on his guard against mitigating the obviously mistaken cruelty of the nunnery scene.[19] Hamlet is cruel to Ophelia in order that Shakespeare may be kind to his audience. The audience reacts against Hamlet when he misjudges so totally the character of the girl he loves. This reaction may be traced and proved in detail in the history of Hamlet criticism. This natural audience reaction is part of Shakespeare's calculated demonstration that love and kindness are potent forces in human affairs even in the dark labyrinth of Elsinore. Ophelia's love, her madness, and even her death are an indication that a passionate female sexuality may exist as an intrinsic part of the three graces. Upon an acceptance of that harmony depends the safety and health of the individual and the state. Hamlet and Ophelia form part of Shakespeare's case for the dramatic defence of humanity.

The nunnery scene is one of forgetfulness and "purposes mistook" (5 ii 376:3879). The play scene, in which Ophelia also plays an important part, is a memory device designed to recall a love that has been forgotten. It is concerned with dalliance and sexual play and shows how the "primrose path" (1 iii 50:513) leads to the murder of a King. The themes of love and death, which will dominate the imagery of the graveyard, are already present in *The Murder of Gonzago*.

The mirror which Hamlet holds up to the court contains, it has already been suggested, a rather different reflection from the mirror that it holds up to the audience. The "dream of passion" (2 ii 545:1592) is only complete once the audience have taken account of Hamlet's comments upon the action. He is sitting at Ophelia's feet in the position traditionally adopted by young lovers in public. His words are concerned with the act that young lovers usually perform in private. They are of such an unexampled sexual frankness that they have provoked a general reaction of critical shock and an unusual, if uneasy, editorial silence.

Hamlet's language of bitter bawdry has often been condemned. This comdemnation, and the pall of editorial self-censorship, suggest that these words must have a very powerful effect upon an audience capable of understanding them. Hamlet's openly sexual suggestions to Ophelia are in marked contrast to the combination of fair words and foul deeds by which the King has removed all impediments to his own marriage of untrue minds. If his soothing hypocrisy seems a "normal" reaction then that is an interesting commentary upon our own sexual situation.

The sexual imagery of the three exchanges between Hamlet and Ophelia during the performance of the inner-play is neither random nor accidental. It is again based upon the image of the three graces and it develops a pattern of fantasy action that contrasts with the murderous passion being presented by the Players. It is an important expression of Hamlet's conscious and unconscious wishes and desires. It provides a possible forecast for the future of the characters that is very different from the prediction which follows from the appearance of the black figure of Lucianus.

The word games between Hamlet and Ophelia start when Hamlet rejects his mother's invitation to sit beside her. He prefers to sit beside Ophelia in order to observe the reactions of the King and Queen. The language also expresses another, and more intimate, level of action (3 ii 108:1966):

> *Hamlet.* Lady, shall I lie in your lap?
> *Ophelia.* No, my lord.
> *Hamlet.* I mean, my head upon your lap.
> *Ophelia.* Ay, my lord.
> *Hamlet.* Do you think I meant country matters?
> *Ophelia.* I think nothing, my lord.
> *Hamlet.* That's a fair thought to lie between maid's legs.
> *Ophelia.* What is, my lord?
> *Hamlet.* Nothing.

The "country matters" that are performed in a lady's lap may be fairly assumed to be the same as the act about to be enjoyed by the "country copulatives" in *As You Like It* 5 iii 54:2632. If Ophelia thinks "nothing" about such an act Hamlet suggests that she may be so chaste that she has no "thing" or sexual organ between her legs. That Shakespeare intended the pun on "no thing" is perhaps indicated by the fact that he makes Hamlet use it again of the King at 4 ii 29:2657. Hamlet explains to Rosencrantz and Guildenstern that the King is a "thing" of "no thing"—although the implications are here political as well as sexual.

It seems beyond doubt that "country matters" contains a deliberate pun on "cunt." This kind of pun is a method of sexual aggression and may well represent the siege to Ophelia's chastity feared by Polonius and Laertes. It is an expression of a desire that is never fulfilled in the play. The bed on which such an act might have been performed becomes the bridal bed of the grave where Ophelia is claimed as the bride of death.

Gertrude makes the bed-grave comparison explicit in her farewell speech (5 i 238:3436):

> I hop'd thou shouldst have been my Hamlet's wife:
> I thought thy bride-bed to have deck'd, sweet maid,
> And not have strew'd thy grave.

It was, however, the "country matters" engaged in by Gertrude with Claudius which led to the "maimed rites" (5 i 213:3408) of Ophelia's incomplete burial service. Even the unwilling Priest has to allow her "her virgin crants, her maiden strewments" (5 i 225–6:3421–2). Hamlet's suggestion that she has no "thing" between her legs is supported by this more sombre imagery. Ophelia does possess the grace of *Castitas*.

The argument is carried a stage further when Ophelia is puzzled by the dumb show and asks Hamlet for enlightenment. Hamlet changes the meaning of the word "show" and suggests that Ophelia might herself become a performer who could unmask for the benefit of the actor playing the Prologue (3 ii 138:2010):

> *Ophelia.* Will 'a tell us what this show meant?
> *Hamlet.* Ay, or any show that you will show him. Be not you asham'd to show, he'll not shame to tell you what it means.
> *Ophelia.* You are naught, you are naught. I'll mark the play.

In his original warning to Ophelia, Laertes had advised her to "unmask" her beauty only to the moon. It is this sense of unmasking or "show" that Hamlet puns upon here. He does not actually suggest that Ophelia should perform a strip-show in order to reveal her naked beauty to the actor, but the metaphor of a strip-show is buried in his words. The actor will not be ashamed to tell Ophelia the meaning of any "show" she is not ashamed to show him. She would, of course, be ashamed to show him her unmasked beauty and Hamlet is very well aware of the fact.

The pun is a further aggressive sexual advance based upon the fact that Ophelia has obeyed the caution of her father and brother and hardly showed herself to Hamlet, let alone unmasked her beauty for him. Ophelia turns the obscene joke aside, but is evidently aware of its meaning, when she describes Hamlet as "naught." It is a clear sexual recognition, for the benefit of the audience, of the beauty that lies hidden from view beneath Ophelia's clothes.

This recognition is supremely important. The inner-play is concerned with exposing the ugliness that the court has kept hidden from view. Hamlet regards this hidden ugliness as the real truth about the world. He describes the Prologue as being as brief "as woman's love" (3 ii 149:2022). The sexuality of Ophelia is a deliberate challenge to this corrupt view of the world and its passions. Hamlet has now admitted that he is sitting at the feet of a girl who combines *Castitas* and *Pulchritudo*. He can still only imagine *Voluptas* as a degrading passion. His last exchange with Ophelia suggests that this is a tragic mistake.

Hamlet is engaged in explaining the entry of Lucianus to the King when Ophelia interrupts him (3 ii 239:2113):

> *Ophelia.* You are as good as a chorus, my lord.
> *Hamlet.* I could interpret between you and your love, if I could see the puppets dallying.
> *Ophelia.* You are keen, my lord, you are keen.
> *Hamlet.* It would cost you a groaning to take off mine edge.
> *Ophelia.* Still better, and worse.
> *Hamlet.* So you mis-take your husbands.—Begin murderer; pox, leave thy damnable faces and begin.

The dallying of puppets is an action that might logically follow from the kind of show that Ophelia was invited to perform for the actor.

An interpreter is an actor who gives words to the dumb show performed by puppets. Their use is shown in Ben Jonson's *Bartholomew Fair* (5 iii 75):

> *Cokes.* These be players minors indeed. Do you call these players?
> *Leatherhead.* They are actors, sir, and as good as any, none disprais'd, for dumb shows: indeed I am the mouth of them all.

Hamlet would interpret to Ophelia the actions of the "puppets" as they performed the dalliance of love. These "puppets" may be intended to be more flesh than wood since Hamlet himself clearly intends to take part in the show. It will cost Ophelia the "groaning" of losing her virginity to take off the "edge" of his wit or sexual appetite.

Ophelia regards this display of wit as both "better," or wittier, and "worse" or even more indecent than his other suggestions. In these three exchanges Hamlet has established that she is a virgin, has suggested that she ought to remove her clothes and display her beauty, and now deliberately proposes that she might engage in the kind of passionate act which might result in the mis-take of a husband. The sexual puns and innuendoes thus lead Ophelia from *Castitas* through *Pulchritudo* to *Voluptas*. Beauty is thus initiated into Passion by Love and the harmony of the graces is completed at the level of an obscene joke.

Hamlet still clearly regards Ophelia as the kind of figure of sensual passion who makes all marriage a mis-take. In the world presented by the inner-play chastity can only be turned into a bawd by beauty. This interpretation of the world is supported by the presence on stage of the Player Queen and Gertrude. It is contradicted by the presence of Ophelia.

It has already been argued that Shakespeare controls the time scheme of *Hamlet* by dramatizing the past, present and future of his characters during the "eternal present" of the court performance. The inner-play is an image of passionate sexual love as well as a representation of murder. It is, therefore, important that it is as much an assault upon the Queen's betrayal of her love as an accusation levelled at the King.

The inner-play presents the golden world of the past, filled with the protestations of a Queen in love and moderated only by the Player King's belief that even love is subject to time and fortune. The Player Queen's protestations move even Gertrude to unfavourable criticism. The false vows of the inner-play are uttered in the presence of the woman whose own marriage vows were not proof against the assault of Claudius. He won her by appearing as the "implorator" of the unholy suit of incest disguised as the "sanctified and pious bonds" (1 iii 130:596) of a royal marriage.

As *The Murder of Gonzago* shows how the marriage that existed in the past became a "primrose path of dalliance" (1 iii 50:513), so the interaction of the play and its royal spectators demonstrates how love was turned by poison into murderous lust. The entry of the "Fellow" in the dumb show and of Lucianus in the spoken play show how the King's death shattered the remembrance of love. The past has become the present union of lust and murderous will that dare not remember how it came into existence.

As Claudius and Gertrude watch the play they are watching the growth of their own poisonous love and the birth of their incestuous marriage. They are themselves the things "rank and gross in nature" (1 ii 136:320) which now possess the "unweeded garden" (1 ii 135:319) of the present. According to the inner-play, the world of love inevitably becomes the world of lust. All human passion is either a false and hypocritical show or else an appetite that degrades men below the level of beasts. As Hamlet sits with his eyes riveted to the King's face he represents a threat of the further operation of murderous passion in the future.

The inner-play presents a prediction, or what Jan Kott calls a forecast,[20] for the future. This prediction is fulfilled in the play but it is brought about in an unexpected fashion which has not been predicted by the action of *The Murder of Gonzago*. Hamlet desires to play the part of Lucianus but does not perform it. Similarly, although Ophelia is cast for the part of *Voluptas*, in common with Gertrude and the Player Queen, she is finally destroyed because of her obsessive remembrance and love for her father rather than by an oblivious pleasure in the present. Behind the obscene jests of man's sexuality lies a grave reality. Ophelia really possesses a balance and harmony of the graces in which her beauty might have become the reality of a passionate love. This harmony is shattered by the tragic conditions of Elsinore.

At this point in the action the stage picture is of supreme importance. The three pairs of lovers on the stage present the audience with the choice of love and the comparison of the different depths and capacity for human passion that is so familiar in Shakespearean comedy. The inner-play in *A Midsummer Night's Dream* or the "show" of manhood adopted by Viola in *Twelfth Night* reveal an infinite variety within the harmony of love. The inner-play in *Hamlet* serves a similar function.

The marriage that is past, the marriage that is present, and the possible marriage that might exist in the future are present in the actors taking the parts of Players and the Characters of their stage audience. King Hamlet and Gertrude are presented by the Players in Duke Gonzago and Baptista. Claudius and Gertrude exhibit their own misalliance. The only hope for Denmark appears to lie in the future consummation of the marriage of Hamlet and Ophelia. That future, however, has already been mortgaged to pay the debts of the past.

In *Twelfth Night* the Clown, Feste, sings of the way a journey should end (*Twelfth Night* 2 iii 41:742):

> Trip no further, pretty sweeting;
> Journeys end in lovers meeting
> Every wise man's son doth know.

Journey's end for Hamlet is near when he returns to Elsinore from the voyage to England. Once he arrives he hears a love-song which is also sung by a Clown. This Clown, however, is also a gravemaker and the meeting which Hamlet at last recognizes as a lovers' meeting is also an encounter with death at the edge of a grave.

The proof of the sterility and horror of the court of Denmark is that it had no place for the passionate life of love and remembrance symbolized by Ophelia and her flowers. In this world of madness the only soil suitable for the "rose of May" (4 v 154:2910) is the earth which covers her dead body. The flowers which the Queen drops into her grave mark the defeat of love and the end of hope in the play. The graveyard scene is one of the most tragic in the play because the characters are burying the future.

The graveyard scene, which is also the scene of Hamlet's final declaration of the passionate sexual love which has blazed through his supposed obscenities, is a dramatic and logical consequence of the death of Polonius. It thus repeats, in interesting fashion, one of the patterns of *Romeo and Juliet*. Romeo, provoked by the death of Mercutio, kills Juliet's cousin Tybalt in a duel. Hamlet, provoked by his father's murder, kills Ophelia's father Polonius in a fashion that is certainly mistaken but which may still be culpable.

One of the most tragic and passionate scenes in *Romeo and Juliet* is the scene in which Juliet hears of Tybalt's death from her Nurse. Her instant reaction is hate and assent to the conventional wisdom of grief and revenge expressed by the Nurse. Slowly at first, and then more strongly, she rejects hatred and starts to fight her way back to her love for Romeo across the gulf of blood and despair that threatens to divide them. Passionate love here recreates itself by an act of remembrance and dedicates itself to a new understanding.

This leap of intelligence and love is not possible in *Hamlet*. Juliet requires all the arguments of her reason to assist the passion of her love for Romeo against the rising tide of hate. Ophelia's reason has been shattered by the death of Polonius and in madness she can find no relief except death. Juliet has the firm knowledge of a love expressed in a recent marriage with which to face the furies released by Tybalt's death. Ophelia has no more than a love expressed before the play began and since apparently denied in the bitterness of the nunnery and play scenes. The conditions which permitted the leap of love and faith in Verona do not obtain in Elsinore.

The severed and mutilated passion of Hamlet and Ophelia, darkened by all the bitterness of misunderstanding and the language of obscenity, still dignifies the power and possibility of sexual passionate human love. The consummated union of Gertrude and Claudius degrades it. The hope which the play offers its spectators is a dance of the three graces—a vision of a passionate life directed by the operation of memory and the forces of intelligence. The agony of the graveyard is the knowledge of an insupportable loss.

NOTES

1. G. Bullough (ed.), *Narrative and Dramatic Sources of Shakespeare*, i, 1957, 284.
2. Henry James, *The Art of the Novel: Critical Prefaces by Henry James*, ed. R. P. Blackmur, 1934, p. 132.
3. P. E. Memmo Jr., *Giordano Bruno's The Heroic Frenzies: A Translation with Introduction and Notes*, 1964, pp. 225–26, cf. 123.
4. Ibid.

5. Henry James, p. 62.

6. Ibid., p. 90.

7. Edgar Wind, *Pagan Mysteries in the Renaissance*, 1967, p. 81.

8. Doris V. Falk, "Proverbs and the Polonius Destiny," *Shakespeare Quarterly*, 18 (1967), pp. 23–36.

9. Rebecca West, *The Court and the Castle*, 1958, p. 17.

10. Françoise Gilot, *Life With Picasso*, 1965, p. 64.

11. Wind, pp. 141–51.

12. Ibid.

13. Ibid.

14. The Platonic concept of such a union of opposites has had a long and important influence in European thought. Its development by Montaigne, Pascal, Proust, and Sainte-Beuve is applied to *Hamlet* by Peter Alexander in *Hamlet: Father and Son*, 1955.

15. E. Wind, pp. 81–96.

16. Ibid.

17. Helen Gardner, "Lawful Espials," *Modern Language Review*, 33 (1938), 345–55; D. J. Palmer, "Stage Spectators in *Hamlet*," *English Studies*, 47 (1966), 423–30.

18. Konrad Lorenz, *On Aggression*, Bantam Books, 1967, pp. 169 ff.

19. Carol J. Carlisle, in "Hamlet's 'Cruelty' in the Nunnery Scene: The Actors' Views," *Shakespeare Quarterly*, 18 (1967), 129–40, gives an interesting account of the way in which many famous actors have tried to retain the audience's sympathy by romanticizing the action at this point.

20. Jan Kott, "Hamlet and Orestes," *Publications of the Modern Language Association of America*, 82 (1967), 303–13.

Harold Jenkins

From "Introduction," *Hamlet*

The "nunnery" scene, as it is called, and indeed Ophelia's whole part in the play, has generally been misunderstood: it is not too much to say that the failure to get Ophelia right has frustrated the interpretation of the tragedy. Bradley doubted "whether from the mere text of the play a sure interpretation" could "be drawn,"[1] and I suspect that it is still the usual view that "we are left with an unsolved puzzle."[2] Those who think that Shakespeare "deliberately" kept Ophelia's story "vague" and that the "uncertainty" contributes to the "attractiveness" of the play even try to make a virtue of defeat.[3] Yet if we grasp the implications of what Hamlet says to Ophelia and to her father about her, the reason for Hamlet's treatment of her is, I believe, clearly and powerfully given.[4]

The essential of her story is that she is the woman Hamlet might have married and did not. What we learn from the opening act is that he had wooed her with "holy vows of heaven" but that she in obedience to her father afterwards repelled his suit. The critics, confusing an Elizabethan play with life, or at least a romantic novel, assume that Hamlet must react to this and so project on to him the resentment they would feel themselves. They accuse Ophelia of rejecting him, suppose him to feel jilted or betrayed, and, all prepared for a lovers' tiff, make a problem of what happens. To assume that Hamlet's behaviour to Ophelia is due to her refusal of his love letters is to make the mistake of Polonius, whose view the play specifically repudiates. His view

Reprinted from *The Arden Shakespeare: Hamlet*, pp. 149–53, by Harold Jenkins (1982), by permission of Methuen and Company.

has its importance because the testing of it is what leads to the
nunnery scene itself; but when we reach the nunnery scene, if we
read what it says instead of what we expected it to say, we find
that it is Hamlet who rejects Ophelia's love and not she his. He
says nothing of her repelling him; he astonishes her by asking if
she is honest and, holding that honesty is incompatible with
beauty, implies that she will not be. The frailties he will later
denounce in his mother he foresees in her. He directs at her a
diatribe against face-paintings and cuckoldings and all the sins
traditional to women. Yet, though this is not always noted, the
sins he first refers to are his own:

> Nymph, in thy orisons
> Be all my sins remember'd.

And he presently goes on:

> I could accuse me of such things that it were better my
> mother had not borne me.

What things they are we are not told; for his sins, like hers, are
less actual than potential, what he calls "offences at my beck," the
sins inherent in the nature of a man "crawling between earth and
heaven." He confesses that he loved her once and then immediately denies it; and the paradox of love that is not love is, I take
it, in the nature of the lover. His heavenly vows have the satyr
lurking in them. With the example of his mother, who has made
"marriage vows as false as dicers' oaths," it is not difficult to see
why he should say to Ophelia "We will have no mo marriage." But
more than this, while he fears that Ophelia will prove false, the
greater fear is that she has valued his love, and even has returned
it. It is her confession that she believed in it that provokes the
horrified exclamation, "Wouldst thou be a breeder of sinners?"
For that is what love and marriage lead to, the propagation of
one's kind, and it explains the nature of Hamlet's recoil.

It is a recoil for which the play has prepared: for the present
dialogue with Ophelia only brings to the surface what has been in
Hamlet's mind before, as the "method" of his madness has been
used to show. He has associated Polonius's daughter with ideas of
mating and breeding and the sort of life they may bring forth. In
his mad talk he called Polonius "a fishmonger" and then suddenly

interjected "Have you a daughter?" It was believed that the daughters of fishmongers were unusually prone to breed;[5] and the thought of the daughter here comes straight upon a nauseous example:

> If the sun breed maggots in a dead dog, being a good kissing carrion . . .

With the word in a double sense, "a good kissing carrion" may be one way of describing the fair Ophelia herself, and the point of requiring her to be protected from the sun, though much obscured by critical ingenuities, should be clear. "Conception is a blessing," Hamlet goes on, "but as your daughter may conceive—" With the sun and the maggots in mind it may be better that she should not. The warning has been given. But on Polonius's next appearance Hamlet addresses him as Jephthah; and Jephthah too had a "fair daughter," as Hamlet reminds us by quoting a popular ballad while leaving us to complete her story. And what we shall, or should, recall, if Polonius does not, is that Jephthah's daughter notoriously did not breed but could only bewail her virginity before being sacrificed by her father. As between the fishmonger's daughter and Jephthah's Hamlet makes the choice for Ophelia when he consigns her to a nunnery. He cannot resist her attraction, as is shown by his behaviour at the play; but his obscene jests there make her whom he has so ambiguously loved the focus of his disgust with the whole sexual process. His last word to her is a jest about how women "mis-take" their husbands.

On her side, the pathos of Ophelia's rejection is eloquent in her memory of Hamlet's "music vows." When he has killed her father and himself been shipped away from Denmark there is little left for Ophelia but, like Jephthah's daughter, to bewail her virginity, as she does in the songs and the fantasies of her madness, which betray a frustrated love.[6] Her forsaking has its emblems in her death from the breaking of a willow[7] and the "maimed rites" this leads to, which Hamlet has to watch. But neither the "churlish priest," nor indeed the uncomprehending critics,[8] can refuse "her virgin crants, her maiden strewments" as "her fair and unpolluted flesh" is committed to the earth. It is only the most obvious of the ironies in these last words that they are spoken by the brother who began her story with a warning not to yield Hamlet her "chaste treasure." Her tragedy of course is that Hamlet has left her treasure with her; and it is also a large part of his. In the final conjunction of epithets—"fair and unpolluted"— the play allows her in her death to confute those fears of Hamlet's about honesty and beauty which were partly responsible for it; but she is buried in her maiden purity with her true love unful-filled. The beautifully imagined and beautifully wrought sub-plot of Ophelia's constant and forsaken love is one of the most poi-gnant things in Shakespeare; and the final irony of her fate is that it has been so often misconceived.

Bradley thought Shakespeare restricted his scope with Ophe-lia so that "too great an interest should not be aroused in the love-story";[9] and Schücking likewise saw it as a thing apart, with "the figure of Ophelia . . . a beautiful dramatic luxury . . . superflu-ous" to Shakespeare's main design.[10] Yet Shakespeare's more usual way was to let a sub-plot illumine, not distract from, his central theme. And that is what the story of Ophelia, once we have understood it, may be seen to do in *Hamlet*. Hamlet's revul-sion from love and marriage and from whatever would perpetu-ate a loathed life is the obverse of that wish for release from life's ills which opens his first soliloquy and has its fullest expression in the soliloquy which the meeting with Ophelia interrupts. His own nature of man, including bestial lusts and lethargies as well as godlike reason, mingles good and evil; and he is placed in a situation—his ideally virtuous father destroyed by a wicked brother who is now in possession of his kingdom and his queen— which shows evil prevailing over good. So although he sees the nobility of man, the beauty of women, the majesty of the uni-verse, what his imagination dwells on is the quintessence of dust, the reason unused, the mutiny in the matron's bones, the nasty sty, the prison. His vision of the world may be said to exemplify the process which a famous speech of his describes whereby "some vicious mole of nature" in a man extends itself in the general view till "all the noble substance" is obscured. Hamlet sees evil flourish and spread. His first soliloquy links the death-wish with his image of a world where corrupt growth is unchecked.

> 'Tis an unweeded garden
> That grows to seed; things rank and gross in nature
> Possess it merely.

Later he will exhort his mother not to

> spread the compost on the weeds
> To make them ranker.

The "mildew'd ear," the ulcer, the impostume grow and infect. Fertility manifests itself in vile forms of life; and in this teeming life of weeds, and maggots, and sinners, to which his being commits him, Hamlet wishes to have no part. He wishes he had never been born; he cannot bear to bring his love to fruition; he shuns marriage and procreation.

Thus Hamlet denies his own nature, declining to act out the part that life purposes for him. And is this not also what happens when he eagerly responds to the Ghost's "If thou hast nature in thee . . ." and then fails to fulfil what nature is demanding? It is not necessary that a turning away from love and a reluctance in revenge should be connected in the plot: below the level of explicitness a correspondence is not difficult to detect. Hamlet "importun'd" Ophelia with "holy vows" of love, and his vows to remember the Ghost palpitate all through his speech at the Ghost's departure; and then, for reasons which the drama, in respect of love, makes clear, nature is resisted and vows are unfulfilled. May we not say that the love plot gives expression to what the revenge plot too, if it stops short of articulating it, nevertheless suggests?

NOTES

1. A. C. Bradley, *Shakespearean Tragedy*, 1904, p. 153.
2. Geoffrey Bullough, *Narrative and Dramatic Sources of Shakespeare's Plays*, vol. 7, 1973, p. 52.
3. J. M. Patrick, "The Problem of Ophelia," in A. D. Matthews and C. M. Emery (eds.), *Studies in Shakespeare*, 1953, pp. 139–44; L. Kirschbaum, "Hamlet and Ophelia," *PQ*, vol. 35, pp. 376–93.
4. For fuller exposition, see my *Hamlet and Ophelia*, British Academy Shakespeare Lecture, 1963. (Proceedings of the British Academy, vol. 49, pp. 135–51.)
5. II, ii, 174. Long Note in *Arden Hamlet*.
6. See IV, v, 23, 23–40, 48–66, 184. Long Notes in *Arden Hamlet*.
7. IV, vii, 165–82. Long Note in *Arden Hamlet*
8. One would have thought the point of the virginal allusions here could not be missed. Those who assert that Ophelia "was not a

chaste young woman" (Rebecca West, *The Court and the Castle*, p. 15) and even that she had been seduced by Hamlet would appear not merely to have misunderstood earlier parts of the play but to have left the end unread.

9. Bradley, p. 160.

10. Levin L. Schücking, *Character Problems in Shakespeare's Plays*, 1922, p. 172.

PART 4:
Language

Madeleine Doran

From *Shakespeare's Dramatic Language*

What a marvel is *Hamlet*! I mean in the legerdemain by which Shakespeare fools us into thinking Hamlet is a living person, that all those stupid or complaisant or crafty characters at the Danish court are, too—puzzled by him, worried about him, scheming to get at him. With what freedom and ease the language moves, with what shifts and turns and stops! in how many different keys, responsive to all the shades of passion and mood, to the movement of thought, to the inwardness of self-examination, to the ambience of public occasion!—as well to the awful return of a spirit from Purgatory as to the excited springing of a trap to catch royal prey; as well to the sarcastic baiting of a counsellor of state as to the lucid and despairing examination of a bad conscience. So natural, so alive, it all seems that we forget the art. Shakespeare intends us to do just that.

In a passage exhibiting Polonius humorously, Shakespeare with tongue in cheek exercises his own formal training in rhetoric. Polonius offers to diagnose for the King and Queen Hamlet's apparent madness:

> My liege, and madam, to expostulate
> What majesty should be, what duty is,
> Why day is day, night night, and time is time,
> Were nothing but to waste night, day, and time;
> Therefore, since brevity is the soul of wit,
> And tediousness the limbs and outward flourishes,

Reprinted from *Shakespeare's Dramatic Language*, pp. 33–62, by Madeleine Doran (1976), by permission of University of Wisconsin Press.

> I will be brief. Your noble son is mad:
> Mad call I it, for to define true madness,
> What is't but to be nothing else but mad?
> But let that go.

(II. ii. 86–95)

Polonius has begun with a deprecatory introduction in the form of a *praeteritio*, a proposition, a rhetorical definition—all, he supposes, wittily turned. When the Queen interposes, "More matter with less art," he takes her remark for a compliment: "Madam, I swear I use no art at all"—a modest disclaimer which gives away his pride in it. The joke is, of course, that concealing his art—the aim of the best orators—is precisely what he is not doing; he cannot bear that his listeners should miss any point of his masterly skill.

> That he's mad, 'tis true, 'tis true 'tis pity,
> And pity 'tis 'tis true—a foolish figure,
> But farewell it, for I will use no art.

The reluctant farewell means nothing, for he manages a good many more foolish figures before he finally concludes his diagnosis with the "declension" of Hamlet into madness.

More seriously and subtly, Shakespeare makes use of another curious device of indirection, this time to conceal his own art. There are two places in which he affects to quote something, to bring something in from outside the play itself. He does not, of course, really bring anything in; he composes the "quotations," but he sets them off in styles quite different from any style in the body of the play.

One of these pieces is the play within the play, "The Murder of Gonzago" or "The Mouse-trap." This is how it goes:

> Full thirty times hath Phoebus' cart gone round
> Neptune's salt wash and Tellus' orbed ground,
> And thirty dozen moons with borrowed sheen
> About the world have times twelve thirties been,
> Since love our hearts and Hymen did our hands
> Unite comutual in most sacred bands.

(III. ii. 155–60)

The conceits are formal and rather labored; the riming couplets are in a monotonous rhythm. The argument is largely built on sententious commonplaces: "What to ourselves in passion we propose,/The passion ending, doth the purpose lose"; or "This world is not for aye, nor 'tis not strange/That even our loves should with our fortunes change"; or "The great man down, you mark his favorite flies,/The poor advanc'd makes friends of enemies." The points to be made, those meant to wring the withers of the King and those meant to bring a blush to Gertrude's face, are heavily, even tediously, amplified—not only so that the King and Queen will not miss them, but so that we hardly can, either, for our primary attention must be on Hamlet, and, with Hamlet's, on Claudius and Gertrude. We are not to be absorbed in "The Murder of Gonzago" for its own sake, but to get its message while we are caught up in the excitement of watching these three during the mounting tension marked by Hamlet's pointed comments—"Wormwood, wormwood!"[1] "Let the gall'd jade winch, our withers are unwrung," "Come, the croaking raven doth bellow for revenge!"—until the climax of the King's abrupt rising and the play's abrupt ending. But Shakespeare is also serving another, less evident, purpose, in the sharp differentiation between the styles of the play within the play and the play itself. The conspicuous artfulness of the one enhances the seeming naturalness of the other.

The other most important "quoted" passage is the one on the slaughter of Priam (II. ii. 450 ff.). Hamlet invites the chief player to recite a passage from a play Hamlet likes, evidently a play about Dido and Aeneas, and the speech he recalls is from Aeneas' tale to Dido on the last events in Troy before it fell. The style of this tragedy is quite different from that of "The Murder of Gonzago"; this compels attention to its positive features. Listen to the verse and the diction as Hamlet begins the recitation:

> 'The rugged Pyrrhus, he whose sable arms,
> Black as his purpose, did the night resemble
> When he lay couched in th' ominous horse,
> Hath now this dread and black complexion smear'd
> With heraldry[2] more dismal: head to foot
> Now is he total gules, horridly trick'd
> With blood of fathers, mothers, daughters, sons,
> Bak'd and impasted with the parching streets,
> That lend a tyrannous and a damned light
> To their lord's murther. Roasted in wrath and fire,

> And thus o'er-sized with coagulate gore,
> With eyes like carbuncles, the hellish Pyrrhus
> Old grandsire Priam seeks.'

The old-fashioned Senecan style had been popular twelve to fifteen years earlier than Shakespeare's *Hamlet*. The vocabulary is heavy, turgid, highly rhetorical. It is the necrophilous and Stygian vocabulary of *Thyestes*: "blood," "gules," "coagulate gore," "sable," "black," "baked," "impasted," "roasted," "dread," "dismal," "ominous," "hellish," "damned." Critics have argued a good deal about whether Shakespeare could possibly have admired this style, and whether he was not intentionally making fun of it. But Shakespeare's taste in the matter is beside the point: what matters is that he makes Hamlet admire the speech—it is "caviary to the general."

As the actor takes over from Hamlet and carries on in fine histrionic style through the description of the distraught Hecuba,[3] who bursts into clamor at the sight of Pyrrhus making "malicious sport/In mincing with his sword her husband's limbs," Shakespeare lays the groundwork for the dramatic function of the speech. Hamlet is so struck by the actor's emotion over a fiction, a dream of passion, that he is moved, after the others leave, to soliloquize on his own imagined lack of passion in a true cause:

> What's Hecuba to him, or he to Hecuba,
> That he should weep for her? What would he do
> Had he the motive and the cue for passion
> That I have? He would drown the stage with tears,
> And cleave the general ear with horrid speech,
> Make mad the guilty, and appal the free, . . .
>   Yet I,
> A dull and muddy-mettled rascal, peak
> Like John-a-dreams, unpregnant of my cause,
> And can say nothing.

The recital piece must be patently "artificial," conspicuously different from the larger piece of art, the play of *Hamlet*, in which it is set. For Hamlet's point to be made, there must be for us, the audience, only one fiction, the account of Pyrrhus' slaughter of Priam and of Hecuba's grief. The old-fashioned diction and rheto-

ric of the passage must, by contrast, make us think of the language of Hamlet as the very language of men, of Hamlet himself
as a living person—as one of us. Absorbed in his response to the
actor's recitation, we perhaps do not even notice—at least if we
are watching, not reading—that the soliloquy is phrased in the
cadences of blank verse, not in the prose of everyday speech.
Although the verse should, and probably does, give us a special
pleasure, it does not call attention to itself as art, however much it
actually is. It does not interfere with our being one with Hamlet
in his experience.

Still another short passage is used for the same effect as these
two "quotations" from plays Hamlet liked—that is, to divert our
attention from the art of *Hamlet*. This passage is a quotation from
Hamlet himself, the letter to Ophelia which Polonius reads to the
King and Queen. The verses in it startle us with their triteness:

> Doubt thou the stars are fire,
> Doubt that the sun doth move,
> Doubt truth to be a liar,
> But never doubt I love.
>
> (II. ii. 116–19)

Hamlet forstalls our criticism, however, with his own: "O dear
Ophelia, I am ill at these numbers. I have not art to reckon my
groans." For Shakespeare to exhibit Hamlet as emphatically no
poet in a play in which he is the chief speaker of lines of accomplished poetry is an even more oblique device to make us move
with Hamlet's feelings as if he were a living person, not a fictional
creature. Shakespeare had made use of a similar indirection in the
expressive Hotspur's detestation of poetry:

> I had rather hear a brazen canstick turn'd,
> Or a dry wheel grate on the axle-tree,
> And that would set my teeth nothing on edge,
> Nothing so much as mincing poetry.
>
> (*1 Henry IV*, III. i. 129–32)[4]

Thus far, except for Polonius' aborted oration and the letter to
Ophelia, I have been speaking of language outside the action. We
may now turn, in contrast, to the language within the dramatic
action of the play and notice its range.[5] The play opens with

simple, natural talk (albeit in blank verse) as the sentries change their watch:

> *Fran.* You come most carefully upon your hour.
> *Bar.* 'Tis now struck twelve. Get thee to bed, Francisco.
> *Fran.* For this relief much thanks. 'Tis bitter cold. And I am
>   sick at heart.
> *Bar.* Have you had quiet guard?
> *Fran.*   Not a mouse stirring.
> *Bar.* Well, good night.

But the fearsome awe with which the Ghost—"this dreaded sight"—must impress us is marked by language which always imparts dignity to its motion: "With martial stalk hath he gone by our watch"; "See, it stalks away"; "with solemn march/Goes slow and stately by them."

Another style in this first scene is the easy, vivid movement of Horatio's exposition on the state of things in the kingdom. First, Marcellus asks what is going on in Denmark, why there are so many preparations for war, evident in the work round the clock and round the week at the ordnance factories and shipyards: "Who is't that can inform me?" Horatio replies: "That can I,/At least the whisper goes so." He fills us in on some past history of a war between Denmark and Norway, and on the peace treaty made, then continues:

> Now, sir, young Fortinbras,
> Of unimproved mettle hot and full,
> Hath in the skirts of Norway here and there
> Shark'd up a list of lawless resolutes
> For food and diet to some enterprise
> That hath a stomach in't, which is no other,
> As it doth well appear unto our state,
> But to recover of us, by strong hand
> And terms compulsatory, those foresaid lands
> So by his father lost; and this, I take it,
> Is the main motive of our preparations,
> The source of this our watch, and the chief head
> Of this post-haste and romage in the land.

The syntax is varied, complex, generally loose, though with explanatory interruptions which make for momentary suspensions in the forward movement. Much is said in short space; there is much compression, much metaphorical suggestion, yet the lines move with speed. The homely "post-haste" and "romage" (rummage) give them naturalness and strength. This style might be called the underlying staple of the play, when it is simply moving forward, where no heightening of passion or play of wit is wanted. No special effects are intended, nor is differentiation of character necessarily in question. The same kind of language is spoken by Horatio, Claudius, Laertes, even Hamlet at times. This style is not primarily a matter of character, but of occasion or dramatic function—simply, as I said, of the play's moving forward. Compare Claudius' comment to Gertrude, late in the play, when he has just witnessed mad Ophelia's pitiful performance:

> O Gertrude, Gertrude,
> When sorrows come, they come not single spies,
> But in battalions: first, her father slain;
> Next, your son gone, and he most violent author
> Of his own just remove; the people muddied,
> Thick and unwholesome in their thoughts and whispers
> For good Polonius' death; and we have done but greenly
> In hugger-mugger to inter him.
>
> (IV. v. 77–84)

Or compare Hamlet, telling Horatio how he discovered the King's plot against his life:

> Up from my cabin,
> My sea-gown scarf'd about me, in the dark
> Grop'd I to find out them, had my desire,
> Finger'd their packet, . . .
>
> (V. ii. 12–15)

Or even the ghost of King Hamlet, describing the manner of his death when, as he was sleeping within his orchard, Hamlet's uncle stole upon him,

> With juice of cursed hebona in a vial,
> And in the porches of my ears did pour
> The leprous distillment, whose effect
> Holds such an enmity with blood of man
> That swift as quicksilver it courses through

> The natural gates and alleys of the body,
> And with a sudden vigor it doth posset
> And curd, like eager droppings into milk,
> The thin and wholesome blood. So did it mine, . . .
>
> (I. v. 62–70)

Contrast these speeches with the studied balance and antithesis in Claudius' formal opening speech from the throne:

> Though yet of Hamlet our dear brother's death
> The memory be green, and that it us befitted
> To bear our hearts in grief, and our whole kingdom
> To be contracted in one brow of woe,
> Yet so far hath discretion fought with nature
> That we with wisest sorrow think on him
> Together with remembrance of ourselves.
> Therefore our sometime sister, now our queen,
> Th' imperial jointress to this warlike state,
> Have we, as 'twere with a defeated joy,
> With an auspicious, and a dropping eye,
> With mirth in funeral, and with dirge in marriage,
> In equal scale weighing delight and dole,
> Taken to wife.
>
> (I. ii. 1–14)

This is a politician's speech. Claudius is seeking by his phrasing to make acceptable, and apparently "wise," an action about which there might be some serious questions; above all, trying to make appear harmonious what is by nature antithetical and in some way shocking—"mirth in funeral," "dirge in marriage," "a defeated joy." This figure is what the Elizabethan rhetoricians called *synoeciosis*, or composition of contraries;[6] here the contraries ought not to be composed. The strain is evident in the grotesque image of "with an auspicious, and a dropping eye."

The falsity of this nice balance between "delight" and "dole" is exposed by Hamlet's first bitter pun—"A little more than kin, and less than kind"—when Claudius tries to draw him into the family circle with his ingratiating "But now, my cousin Hamlet, and my son—." Hamlet refuses the "wisest sorrow," the equality of delight and dole.

> *King.* How is it that the clouds still hang on you?
> *Ham.* Not so, my lord, I am too much in the sun.

The hollowness beneath this composition of contraries is further exposed by Hamlet in his sarcastic reply to his mother, when she urges him to put aside this mourning for his father:

> *Queen.* Do not for ever with thy vailed lids
> Seek for thy noble father in the dust.
> Thou know'st 'tis common; all that lives must die,
> Passing through nature to eternity.
> *Ham.* Ay, madam, it is common.

(The emptiness of this truism in Gertrude's mouth is indicated by her "for ever." We are soon to learn that her husband has been dead less than two months.)

> *Ham.* Ay, madam, it is common.
> *Queen.*   If it be,
> Why seems it so particular with thee?
> *Ham.* Seems, madam? nay, it is, I know not "seems."
> 'Tis not alone my inky cloak, good mother,
> Nor customary suits of solemn black,
> Nor windy suspiration of forc'd breath,
> No, nor the fruitful river in the eye,
> Nor the dejected havior of the visage,
> Together with all forms, moods, shapes of grief,
> That can denote me truly. These indeed seem,
> For they are actions that a man might play,
> But I have that within which passes show,
> These but the trappings and the suits of woe.
>
> (I. ii. 74–86)

Note the language of this speech, how everything is exaggerated and hyperbolic; in Hamlet's phrasing, the mourning clothes and the mourning attitudes all appear slightly ridiculous. If we are puzzled by this tone of Hamlet's we are presently, in his first soliloquy, to learn the reason for it. So his mother dressed, apparently; so she sighed and wept as she followed her husband's coffin:

> That it should come to this!
> But two months dead, nay, not so much, not two. . . .
> Let me not think on't! Frailty, thy name is woman!—
> A little month, or ere those shoes were old
> With which she followed my poor father's body,

Like Niobe, all tears—why she, even she—
O God, a beast that wants discourse of reason
Would have mourn'd longer—married with my uncle, . . .
            Within a month,
Ere yet the salt of most unrighteous tears
Had left the flushing in her galled eyes,
She married.

                                                    (II. 137-56)

She cannot have meant any of her grief-stricken display, or so it seems to Hamlet. Hence his pointed, "I know not 'seems.'" His grief is real: "I have that within which passes show."

This speech gives us the key to Hamlet's central question: What is and what is not? What is the world truly like under its fine outward show? We hear echoes of the question in many places, as in Hamlet's bitter charge to Ophelia in the nunnery scene, reflecting on women generally:

God hath given you one face, and you make yourselves
another. You jig and amble, and you lisp, you nickname
God's creatures and make your wantonness your ignorance.

                                                    (III. i. 143-46)

Shakespeare makes Hamlet always alert to pretense, to false sentiment, to exaggeration, and often makes him respond in kind. By parody or exaggeration he exposes the shallowness or falsity betrayed in the speaker's manner or language. The exposure is done in a purely comic way with Osric, whose modish lingo Hamlet outdoes: "Sir, his definement suffers no perdition in you, though I know to divide him inventorially would dozy th' arithmetic of memory, and yet but yaw neither in respect of his quick sail, but in the verity of extolment . . ." and much more of the same (V. ii. 112-15).

Exposure is made in another mood, an intense and passionate mood, with Laertes in the graveyard (V. i. 246 ff.). The funeral of Ophelia, with its abbreviated rites, is going forward. Her coffin has been lowered into the grave, and the Queen has scattered flowers on the body. Laertes cries out:

            O, treble woe
Fall ten times treble on that cursed head
Whose wicked deed thy most ingenious sense

Depriv'd thee of! Hold off the earth a while,
Till I have caught her once more in mine arms.
                                    [*Leaps in the grave.*]
Now pile your dust upon the quick and dead,
Till of this flat a mountain you have made
T' o'ertop old Pelion, or the skyish head
Of blue Olympus.

The speech and the gesture draw Hamlet out of the shadows:

What is he whose grief
Bears such an emphasis, whose phrase of sorrow
Conjures the wand'ring stars and makes them stand
Like wonder-wounded hearers? This is I,
Hamlet the Dane!
                        [*Hamlet leaps in after Laertes.*]

After they have grappled, been pulled apart, and come out of the grave, Hamlet angrily outdoes Laertes in hyperbolic offers:

'Swounds, show me what thou't do.
Woo't weep, woo't fight, woo't fast, woo't tear thyself?
Woo't drink up eisel? eat a crocodile?
I'll do't. Dost thou come here to whine?
To outface me with leaping in her grave?
Be buried quick with her, and so will I.
And if thou prate of mountains, let them throw
Millions of acres on us, till our ground,
Singeing his pate against the burning zone,
Make Ossa like a wart! Nay, and thou'lt mouth,
I'll rant as well as thou.

Since Hamlet has had no quarrel with Laertes, we are startled with the violence of his outburst. We must understand, I think, that it goes hard with him to be blamed by Laertes for Ophelia's death. Moreover, it seems clear from these lines that he detects a false note in Laertes' ostentatious display of grief. We cannot suppose that Laertes would have let himself be buried as a result of his sudden impulse. Note Hamlet's pejorative verbs: "whine," "prate," "mouth," "rant." Note the precise rhetorical word, "emphasis," for the heightened language. He tells Horatio later that "the bravery" (showiness) of Laertes' grief put him into a towering passion. We are led to ask what Laertes' love for his sister amounted to. He has shown himself to be fond of her, certainly, but with no certain perception of her feelings. Like Polonius he belongs to that world of policy in which love is suspect. Such a simple possibility as Hamlet's love for Ophelia, a love without self-interest, given honestly and unconditionally, her father and her brother never seriously entertained; and hers for him did not count, for she was a green girl. Their prudential counsel to her was good enough as worldly wisdom, no doubt—Lord Hamlet was a prince, out of her star, he could not marry whom he chose, his blaze gave more light than heat, his love was

> a fashion and a toy in blood,
> A violet in the youth of primy nature,
> Forward, not permanent, sweet, not lasting,
> The perfume and suppliance of a minute—
>
>   (I. iii. 6-9)

and so on. The only trouble with the advice was that it did not speak to the truth. Polonius did indeed admit his mistake, only to fall into another error, namely, that Hamlet had gone mad for love. He and his son are shown to move on a wholly different plane of ethical perception from Hamlet's. Between them they had infected Ophelia with mistrust of Hamlet, and, however innocently, even Laertes had had a part in wrecking her life. It is no wonder that Hamlet could say, after Laertes' hyperboles at the grave, "I lov'd Ophelia. Forty thousand brothers/Could not with all their quantity of love/Make up my sum."

It is through these quick verbal responses of Hamlet's to the betraying nuances of language and manner that we are alerted to the varieties of false-seeming which surround the Prince: the faddish language of the empty-headed fop, the overblown protestations of the heedless youth, the trite moral commonplaces of the politic men and the shallow woman, the devious rhetoric of the astute politician with something to hide. Hamlet is by no means objective in his witty or passionate responses to the seemers. But though we may not always assent wholly to his judgments, we always trust his perceptions. His sensitivity to the affected or false or strained note is our touchstone of honesty.

This function of Hamlet's sensitiveness as a touchstone is important, I believe, in how we are meant to take the Ghost.

Nothing in Hamlet's response, on its first appearance to him, suggests falsity or duplicity in the Ghost. The skeptical Horatio's conviction assures us, the audience, that the apparition is to be taken as real, not as a figment of the imagination. Hamlet's reception of the Ghost's message assures us that the apparition is also to be taken precisely as the ghost of King Hamlet and that its narration is true. Had Shakespeare intended us to take the apparition otherwise—as "goblin damn'd" or spirit from hell—we should have expected signs of some sort to alert us. But the signs point all the other way. And Hamlet, always sensitive to truth, detects no false note. It is only later, with the horror and the awfulness of the burden upon him, that he is shown to be in doubt of the Ghost's honesty; at its reappearance in his mother's chamber, his immediate response is again unquestioning belief.

Through his responses to the false notes in the language of others Hamlet is established as the touchstone of truth. This function is dramatically important. For we see the world always through his eyes, and we must trust without question his own honesty of intent. He uses words himself in a great variety of ways, and we must feel, beneath all the exaggerations, the self-reproaches, the rages, the witty jibes, and the bitter taunts, the passionate earnestness in his search for the truth.

Hamlet has many voices, yet they are all Hamlet's. He has also what the rhetoricians called *energeia*—vigor or animation of style. Aristotle equates ἐνέργεια, or activity, with χίντοιζ, or movement; Quintilian speaks of that "ἐνέργεια, or vigour . . . which derives its name from action and finds its peculiar function in securing that nothing that we say is tame."[7] In Hamlet's style the range and the intensity together are the key to the extraordinary vitality we feel in him. No character in literature has more. We may distinguish in Hamlet principally the language of passion, the language of mockery, the language of reflection. There is another voice, too, which ought not to be forgotten in any analysis of Hamlet's ways of talking, though it appears less frequently. It is the normal, engaging manner of Hamlet in everyday conversation, as when he greets Horatio and Marcellus with spontaneous courtesy: "Horatio—or I do forget myself . . ." and then "Sir, my good friend—I'll change that name with you" (I. ii. 161, 163). Or as when with gracious jesting he welcomes the traveling players

to Elsinore: "You are welcome, masters, welcome all. I am glad to
see thee well. . . . O, old friend! why, thy face is valanc'd since I
saw thee last; com'st thou to beard me in Denmark? . . ." (II. ii.
421 ff.). Or as when before the duel he begs Laertes' pardon for
the accidental killing of Polonius:

> Give me your pardon, sir. I have done you wrong,
> But pardon't as you are a gentleman. . . .
> Sir, in this audience,
> Let my disclaiming from a purpos'd evil
> Free me so far in your most generous thoughts,
> That I have shot my arrow o'er the house
> And hurt my brother.
>
> (V. ii. 226–44)

(Nothing better shows up Hamlet's candor against Laertes' duplicity, for while Laertes answers,

> I am satisfied in nature,
> Whose motive in this case should stir me most
> To my revenge, . . .
> I do receive your offer'd love like love,
> And will not wrong it,

we know that he intends to fight Hamlet with an unbated foil,
anointed with a deadly poison.) This frank, normal manner of
Hamlet's is, however, rare in a tragedy concerned with his mental
turmoil. The major voices, or modes of speaking, are, then, the
voices of passion, mockery, and reflection. They are, of course,
not always separate. Mockery may enter, and often does, into the
passion (as in the speeches to Rosencrantz and Guildenstern in
the recorder episode, III. ii. 296 ff., and to Laertes in the graveyard scene, V. i. 254 ff.). And the intensity of the passion may be
expressed in close and logical argument, as in some of the persuasive speeches to his mother in the closet scene. But there are
speeches we can separate.

We may consider first the mode of passion. Our concern is
with the dramatic purpose of the speech, with Hamlet's response
to the situation in which he finds himself. One response is grief at
his father's death, shock at his mother's falsity or shallowness.
This is shown especially well in the first soliloquy (I. ii. 129 ff.),
already commented on and quoted from. Note how, as Dover

Wilson once pointed out,[8] the sentences circle round and round
the vision that he keeps trying to put out of his mind, but that
keeps returning: "That it should come to this!/But two months
dead, nay, not so much, not two./ . . . Must I remember? . . . and
yet, within a month— . . . A little month, . . . why, she, even
she— . . ." His first response to the Ghost's disclosure is passionate assent to the charge given him, and physical shock:

> O all you host of heaven! O earth! What else?
> And shall I couple hell? O fie, hold, hold, my heart,
> And you, my sinews, grow not instant old,
> But bear me stiffly up. Remember thee!
>
> (I. v. 92–95)

Another response is savage hatred of Claudius, often expressed in coarse, ugly, brutal language, as in the Hecuba soliloquy:

> Hah, 'swounds, I should take it; for it cannot be
> But I am pigeon-liver'd, and lack gall
> To make oppression bitter, or ere this
> I should 'a' fatted all the region kites
> With this slave's offal. Bloody, bawdy villain!
> Remorseless, treacherous, lecherous, kindless villain!
>
> (II. ii. 576–81)

Notice the cadences in the epithets, the falling rhythm, the chim-
ing endings. Or notice the grossly vivid images in the speech
when Hamlet comes upon the King at prayer:

> Up, sword, and know thou a more horrid hent:
> When he is drunk asleep, or in his rage,
> Or in th' incestious pleasure of his bed,
> At game a-swearing, or about some act
> That has no relish of salvation in't—
> Then trip him, that his heels may kick at heaven,
> And that his soul may be as damn'd and black
> As hell, whereto it goes.
>
> (III. iii. 88–95)

His speeches of persuasion to his mother in the closet scene
(III. iv) are also speeches of passion, intense and earnest; he paints
the enormity of her action in strong colors. She has done

> Such an act
> That blurs the grace and blush of modesty,
> Calls virtue hypocrite, takes off the rose
> From the fair forehead of an innocent love
> And sets a blister there, makes marriage vows
> As false as dicers' oaths, O, such a deed
> As from the body of contraction plucks
> The very soul, and sweet religion makes
> A rhapsody of words. Heaven's face does glow
> O'er this solidity and compound mass
> With heated visage, as against the doom;
> Is thought-sick at the act.[9]

Hamlet sees the breaking of the marriage vow as a blow struck at sacred bonds generally, hence at religion itself; he imagines the response of Heaven to such an act to be a prefiguring of Dooms-day. His charges against her of sexual grossness, or even unnaturalness, at a time when the heyday in the blood should be tame and wait upon the judgment, are likewise put in extreme terms. She cannot call it love; her sense must be apoplexed to allow her to step from her wholesome husband to this "mildewed ear," his brother:

> O shame, where is thy blush?
> Rebellious hell,
> If thou canst mutine in a matron's bones,
> To flaming youth let virtue be as wax
> And melt in her own fire. Proclaim no shame
> When the compulsive ardure gives the charge,
> Since frost itself as actively doth burn,
> And reason panders will.

Under such pressure she does indeed repent. It is just this intense conviction of Hamlet's and his power of making vivid to her the immorality of what she has done that move her to repentance; for he is able to turn her eyes into her very soul to see "such black and grained spots/As will not leave their tinct."

To make sure that her mood of repentance holds, Hamlet puts positively, for emphasis, what he is enjoining her not to do:

> Not this, by no means, that I bid you do:
> Let the bloat king tempt you again to bed,

> Pinch wanton on your cheek, call you his mouse,
> And let him, for a pair of reechy kisses,
> Or paddling in your neck with his damn'd fingers,
> Make you to ravel all this matter out,
> That I essentially am not in madness,
> But mad in craft.

This speech has the quality of *energeia*,[10] of setting something before the eyes with lively clarity—here, a disgusting clarity. Lest we take the easy way out offered us by the Freudians of reading Hamlet's reproaches as morbid love for his mother, we should remember that, in keeping with the Ghost's admonition not to contrive anything against her, he had charged himself to speak daggers to her, but to use none. The amplification in his speeches—by such methods as hyperbolic diction, exaggerated comparison, and heaping up of detail—is persuasive rhetoric of the emotional kind at its strongest. If we shift the onus of aberrant behavior from Gertrude to Hamlet, we are doing what she does in blaming Hamlet's wild behavior (at the Ghost's sudden reappearance) on his madness. "Lay not that flattering unction to your soul," Hamlet enjoins her, "That not your trespass but my madness speaks."

Hamlet can be as passionate in self-reproach as in reproach to his mother. The Hecuba or "O, what a rogue" soliloquy affords the best example:

> Yet I,
> A dull and muddy-mettled rascal, peak
> Like John-a-dreams, unpregnant of my cause,
> And can say nothing; no, not for a king,
> Upon whose property and most dear life
> A damn'd defeat was made. Am I a coward?
> Who calls me villain, breaks my pate across,
> Plucks off my beard and blows it in my face,
> Tweaks me by the nose, gives me the lie i' th' throat
> As deep as to the lungs? Who does me this?
> Ha, 'swounds, I should take it; for it cannot be
> But I am pigeon-liver'd, and lack gall
> To make oppression bitter.
>
> (II. ii. 566–78)

Again, the speech is both vigorous and vivid, because of the strong colloquial diction, the rhetorical questions, the swiftly sketched actions. These exaggerated charges against himself for lack of feeling and for cowardice are demonstrably not true. This very speech gives the lie to his own charge of dullness. Recognizing the futility of such outbursts, he makes, himself, the best comment on the quality of the speech:

> Why, what an ass am I! This is most brave,[11]
> That I, the son of a dear father murther'd,
> Prompted to my revenge by heaven and hell,
> Must like a whore unpack my heart with words
> And fall a-cursing like a very drab,
> A scullion![12]
>
> (II. 582–87)

But the outburst, in his state of "sore distraction," has been a natural enough response. These final, corrective lines are Shakespeare's artful way of helping us to interpret the speech aright.

Another place in which we are made strongly aware of Hamlet's "sore distraction" is in the "nunnery" scene (III. i), that scene in which Ophelia and Hamlet are at cross-purposes, and in which the tension mounts to an almost unbearable pitch. Here, Hamlet's distraught state is marked by prose, looser and more wayward than verse can be. Ophelia's image of Hamlet's reason as like "sweet bells jangled out of time,[13] and harsh" catches for us the discordant quality of the scene itself. In *Hamlet* Shakespeare moves easily back and forth between verse and prose according to occasion, purpose, and mood—not with an eye to limited rules of decorum, but responsive to dramatic need. So appropriate, so varied, so "natural" are both his verse and his prose in this play that in hearing the dialogue we respond to the change of tone and of nuance without always noticing the medium.

The voice of "sore distraction" sometimes takes another form, of "wild and whirling words" that suggest a release from tension, a rebound from some terrible concentration of passion. The first instance of this is in the somewhat disjointed response (I. v. 115 ff.) Hamlet makes to Horatio and Marcellus after his interview with the Ghost. We hear the strange note first when he answers Marcellus' call, "Illo, ho, ho, my lord!" with "Hillo, ho, ho, boy! Come, bird, come." We hear it again in his avoidance of direct response to their natural curiosity: "What news, my lord?"

> *Ham.* There's never a villain dwelling in all Denmark
> But he's an arrant knave.
> *Hor.* There needs no ghost, my lord, come from the grave
> To tell us this.
> *Ham.*   Why, right, you are in the right,
> And so, without more circumstance at all,
> I hold it fit that we shake hands and part,
> You, as your business and desire shall point you,
> For every man hath business and desire,
> Such as it is, and for my own poor part,
> Look you, I'll go pray.
> *Hor.* These are but wild and whirling words, my lord.
> *Ham.* I am sorry they offend you, heartily,
> Yes, faith, heartily.
>
> (I. v. 123–35)

Another example of this release from tension, though in a very different mood, is Hamlet's excitement after the play scene:

> Why, let the strooken deer go weep,
>   The hart ungalled play,
> For some must watch while some must sleep,
>   Thus runs the world away.
>
> (III. ii. 271–74)

The excitement is sustained through much of the conversation with Rosencrantz and Guildenstern that follows. But its disjointedness to them is only Hamlet's impudence; he is quite able to reword the matter, as his recorder lesson shows.

This episode brings us naturally to the mode of mockery, another mode quite as frequent as the mode of passion. It is Hamlet's protection against the spies with which he is beset; he plays up to Polonius' theory that he is mad for love and to the King's that he may be brooding on ambition. He loves to feed Polonius the bait that he takes so readily:

> *Ham.* O Jephthah, judge of Israel, what a treasure hadst
> thou!
> *Pol.* What a treasure had he, my lord?

> *Ham.* Why—
>> 'One fair daughter, and no more,
>>   The which he loved passing well.'
> *Pol.* [*Aside.*] Still on my daughter.
> *Ham.* Am I not i' th' right, old Jephthah?
>
>   (II. ii. 403–10)

And he easily shows up those "sponges" of the King, Rosencrantz and Guildenstern, whose leading questions on ambition he has turned aside:

> *Ham.* . . . Will you play upon this pipe?
> *Guild.* My lord, I cannot.
> *Ham.* I pray you.
> *Guild.* Believe me, I cannot.
> *Ham.* I do beseech you.
> *Guild.* I know no touch of it, my lord.
> *Ham.* It is as easy as lying. Govern these ventages . . .
>
>   (III. ii. 350–57)

Hamlet's wit at the expense of the politicians makes him the chorus of the play as well as the protagonist, its fool as well as its hero. These particular "seemers"—Polonius, the King, and the King's two cat's-paws—he mocks not by outdoing their language, as he does with Laertes and Osric, but by otherwise tailoring his method to the character and intelligence of the victims. Certain features of the mockery, what one might call the generic features of his assumed madness—a disconcerting waywardness, shown in his abrupt changes of subject or apparent non-sequiturs, and a perverse habit of misinterpreting his questioner's word or intent—may appear in any of his encounters. But these tricks are varied to fit the occasion and the adversary.

Towards his old schoolfellows he bears no initial ill-will, is even willing to describe to them his depressed state of mind: "I have of late . . . lost all my mirth, forgone all custom of exercises," and so on, from "this brave o'erhanging firmament" to "this quintessence of dust" (II. ii. 291–309). But when, after the play scene, he perceives that they are still serving as willing spies of the King, he minces no words in letting them know that he knows their mission. He first puts them down in jest by refusing to make them "a wholesome answer" to their message from his mother and by giving them a crumb for the King ("Sir, I lack advancement"). But then he forces them to play the uncomfortable game with the recorders. He ends it with his angry scorn at their incompetence, and at their effrontery in trying to pluck out the heart of his mystery: ". . . there is much music, excellent voice, in this little organ, yet cannot you make it speak. 'Sblood, do you think I am easier to be play'd on than a pipe? . . ." (III. ii. 296 ff.). Later, when they affect not to understand his metaphors of the nuts (or apple)[14] kept in the corner of the jaw to be first mouthed, then swallowed, and of the squeezed sponge that will be dry again, he dismisses them as of no consequence: "I am glad of it; a knavish speech sleeps in a foolish ear" (IV. ii. 12–24).

Hamlet describes Polonius to his face in terms as insulting as he uses to those two, and with more evident pleasure. No need to quote his repulsive portrait of old men, with the identifying sting in the tail of it: "all which, sir, though I most powerfully and potently believe, yet I hold it not honesty to have it thus set down, for yourself, sir, shall grow as old as I am, if like a crab you could go backward" (II. ii. 196–204). But Polonius, in his fatuous conceit of his own powers of detection, is more fun to take in than the two dullards, and Hamlet plays the game of "diseased" wit with him zestfully and often. He plays it by satisfying the self-appointed clinician's notions of how a madman should speak and act and thus draws him into ridiculous responses and situations, as when he willingly goes along with the transformation of Hamlet's imaginary cloud from camel to weasel and from weasel to whale (III. ii. 376–82). The same game is even more fun when Hamlet plays it (as in the "fishmonger" and "Jephthah" sequences, II. ii. 170–91, 403–20) so as to confirm the old man's own cherished diagnosis of the cause of Hamlet's lunacy. Hamlet's trick is to draw Polonius to the lure by a riddling pronouncement, the meaning of which he makes sure Polonius cannot miss. For example, after an opening gambit of recognizing Polonius as a fishmonger and moralizing on the word, Hamlet remarks, in two apparent non-sequiturs: "For if the sun breed maggots in a dead dog, being a good kissing carrion—Have you a daughter?" The dialogue continues:

> *Pol.* I have, my lord.
> *Ham.* Let her not walk i' th' sun. Conception is a blessing,
>   but as your daughter may conceive, friend,[15] look to't.

> *Pol.* [*Aside.*] How say you by that? still harping on my daugh-
> ter. Yet he knew me not at first, . . .

Polonius, having in his youth suffered much extremity for love, recognizes the symptoms. He has swallowed the bait, as he will do again. The fun for Hamlet and for us is in watching the man who thinks he is hunting the trail of policy so sure get caught himself, yet never know it.

The game Hamlet plays with Claudius is also a game of impudence, insults, and veiled threats, but it is a far more danger-ous, challenging, and interesting game, with a worthier opposite. Although Hamlet talks parabolically and twists meanings in the same perverse ways as with his other victims, he knows he can leave interpretation to the King, a circumstance in which he takes perceptible satisfaction. As with Polonius, he teases Claudius with hints which support the listener's own suspicions of the cause of his madness. This is the brief conversation the two have just before the play at court opens.

> *King.* How fares our cousin Hamlet?
> *Ham.* Excellent, i' faith, of the chameleon's dish: I eat the air,
> promise-cramm'd—you cannot feed capons so.
>
> (III. ii. 92–95)

But, unlike Polonius, the King does not bite: "I have nothing with this answer, Hamlet; these words are not mine." Hamlet turns away with an impertinent reply: "No, nor mine now."

After the King has been caught by "The Mouse-trap," Hamlet is bolder in mockery. In the interchange between them when Claudius demands of Hamlet where he has concealed the body of Polonius (IV. iii. 16 ff.), Hamlet again uses the parabolic form, but this time to preach a gruesome sermon on *vanitas vanitatum* and the grave-worm.

> *King.* Now, Hamlet, where's Polonius?
> *Ham.* At supper.
> *King.* At supper? where?
> *Ham.* Not where he eats, but where 'a is eaten; a certain
> convocation of politic worms are e'en at him. Your worm
> is your only emperor for diet: we fat all creatures else to
> fat us, and we fat ourselves for maggots; your fat king and

> your lean beggar is but variable service, two dishes, but to
> one table—that's the end.
> *King.* Alas, alas!
> *Ham.* A man may fish with the worm that hath eat of a king,
> and eat of the fish that hath fed of that worm.
> *King.* What dost thou mean by this?
> *Ham.* Nothing but to show you how a king may go a pro-
> gress through the guts of a beggar.

Ignoring both the threat and the impudence, Claudius tries again: "Where is Polonius?" and Hamlet's reply is even naughtier:

> In heaven. Send thither to see; if your messenger find
> him not there, seek him i' th' other place yourself. But if
> indeed you find him not within this month, you shall nose
> him as you go up the stairs into the lobby.

Again, the same disconcerting misinterpretation of the speaker's meaning as we have heard before, but with a sharper edge. The sharpest edge of all is on a piece of sophistical reasoning to which Hamlet treats the King when, later in the scene, he is being packed off to England:

> *Ham.* . . . Farewell, dear mother.
> *King.* Thy loving father, Hamlet.
> *Ham.* My mother: father and mother is man and wife, man
> and wife is one flesh—so, my mother. Come, for England!

For Hamlet this impudence is a form of relief from the intensity of his passion. It is a relief for us, too. For example, this scene with the King, with its mordant and macabre humor, follows soon after the intensely emotional scene with his mother. The exchange between Hamlet and the King in prose lowers the pitch. And normally the scenes of mockery and wit are in prose.

We come, finally, to the mode of quiet reflection. Beneath the passion, the mockery, the wit, there is something profound—the fundamental questions which the burden imposed on Hamlet have given rise to; and these questions he can sometimes face and consider in a dispassionate, objective way. He does so notably in the "What a piece of work is a man" speech, in the "To be or not to be" soliloquy, in the speech before the play scene in praise of Horatio, and in the graveyard scene before the entry of the court for the funeral of Ophelia; also to a lesser degree in the "How all occasions" soliloquy after the passage of Fortinbras' army. The questions stated or implied in his reflections are those commonplace, even trite, questions which we all must ask, yet to which there are no certain answers: What is the world? What is a man? How ought one to meet the problems of life? What is death?

The first two questions Hamlet answered pessimistically in the bitter mood of the first soliloquy ("O that this too too sallied flesh," I. ii. 129 ff.), when the world seemed to him like an unweeded garden grown to seed, possessed wholly by things rank and gross in nature. But in acknowledging to his old schoolfellows his low spirits, he returns to these questions in a low-keyed, reflective mood, with alternative possibilities expressed in prose (II. ii. 295 ff.). This "goodly frame, the earth," with its "majestical roof fretted with golden fire," seems to him "a sterile promontory," overhung with "a foul and pestilent congregation of vapors." And man, so noble in reason, so infinite in faculties, so like a god—man, the beauty of the world, the paragon of animals, is to him the quintessence of dust. Between these directly antithetical views, no attempt at reconciliation is made. The passage is an oblique way of suggesting to us, I think, Hamlet's normal idealistic view of the world before he experienced the shock of disillusion. For he puts the idealistic view objectively, as an accepted truth, the pessimistic one subjectively, as a state of his own mind.

The third question, what is the noblest way for a man to bear the burdens of life, to meet the painful obligations it thrusts upon him, is posed in the "To be or not to be" soliloquy (III. i. 55 ff.) He puts the question in the form of alternatives between patient endurance and bold action confronting danger:

> Whether 'tis nobler in the mind to suffer
> The slings and arrows of outrageous fortune,
> Or to take arms against a sea of troubles,
> And by opposing, end them.

The soliloquy is pitched low, general in its observations, not narrowly focussed on Hamlet's particular problem; and suicide, suggested by the opening proposition, "To be or not to be," comes to the surface only once, with the possibility of ending this "weary life" "with a bare bodkin." The argument moves with the naturalness of thought. Two ideas thread through the soliloquy, the burdens of life and the uncertainty of what lies beyond the bourn of death. The question of whether it is nobler to take arms against a sea of troubles, to meet them head on and hence to risk death, leads naturally to the question of what death is. For if death is like sleep, it is "a consummation devoutly to be wish'd." But if it is like sleep, who knows "what dreams may come/When we have shuffled off this mortal coil"? Who can know what lies beyond the grave? Who would ever endure the ills of life, and bear its burdens, were it not that the dread of something after death "puzzles the will,/And makes us rather bear those ills we have,/Than fly to others that we know not of"?

These are Job's questions. Job, like Hamlet, both longed for death and feared it.

> For so shulde I now have lyen and bene quiet, I shulde have slept then, and bene at rest,/ . . . The wicked have there ceased from their tyrannie, and there they that laboured valiantly, are at rest./ . . . Wherefore is the light given to him that is in miserie? and life unto them that have heavy hearts?/Which long for death, & if it come not, they wolde even search it more then treasures.
>
> (3: 13–21)

> Are not my dayes fewe? let him cease, and leave of from me, that I may take a litle comfort,/Before I go and shal not returne, even to the land of darkenes and shadowe of death:/ Into a land, I say, darke as darkenes it self, & into the shadow of death, where is none order, but the light is there as darkenes.[16]
>
> (10: 20–22)

Hamlet returns twice to the question of how one should conduct one's life. It is implied in his words to Horatio before the play scene (III. ii. 54 ff.), those words of praise in which Hamlet is at his frank and warmly generous best. This time he takes up the first of the alternate choices posed in the question he had asked in the preceding soliloquy: whether it is nobler to suffer the ills of Fortune or to take arms against them. Hamlet admires his friend for his stoical superiority to the buffets and rewards of Fortune, a man—no passion's slave—who has been "as one in suff'ring all that suffers nothing." But this tranquil indifference is a choice out of reach of Hamlet, in his own state of passionate turmoil; not open to him in any case, because of the solemn charge laid upon him by the Ghost. Hence the poignancy we feel in Hamlet's admiration for this idea of noble equanimity.

The same question is again provoked in Hamlet when he comes upon the army of Fortinbras on the way to fight the Poles (IV. iv. 32 ff.). He sees "the imminent death of twenty thousand men,/That for a fantasy and trick of fame,/Go to their graves like beds." The mood this time is not as objective as in the earlier reflections on how to meet the ills of Fortune. Because Hamlet feels shamed for his inaction by the example of Fortinbras, he puts the alternatives of passivity and of action quite differently, no longer as of equal value; on the one hand, "to sleep and feed" in bestial oblivion, allowing man's godlike reason "to fust in us unus'd"; or, on the other, to make "mouths at the invisible event" and to expose "what is mortal and unsure/To all that fortune, death, and danger dare,/Even for an egg-shell." Between such alternatives there can be only one possible choice:

> Rightly to be great
> Is not to stir without great argument,
> But greatly to find quarrel in a straw
> When honor's at the stake.

And Hamlet has far greater argument to stir for than has Fortinbras. The astonishing thing to Hamlet in this encounter is the realization that by Fortinbras and his men death goes unregarded. He once again blames himself for "thinking too precisely on th' event," and the event he is thinking on is surely death. This soliloquy has an important dramatic function. It clears the air for Hamlet by moving death as an obstacle to action out of the center of his vision.

Not that death is banished from Hamlet's consideration, or from ours. As the play draws to an end it is death, never far from the surface, which becomes the dominant motive. But Hamlet, returning from what seems to him the providential adventure with the pirates, can now look at death from an altered perspective and in a universal way. It is in a graveyard (V. i) that we first see him on his return to Denmark. He makes the skulls tossed up in the digging of a new grave the occasion for a speculative and moralizing sermon on the Dance of Death. For one thing is certain: whatever death may be, it is what we must all come to in the end, king and beggar alike. The variations on the theme are done in a vein of detached irony. The grave, the grave-worm, the stinking chapless skull that a sexton can knock about with a spade, dust—these are the common end, the end for the politician, who would circumvent God and whose pate the gravedigger over-reaches; for the courtier, who could say "Good morrow, sweet lord"; for the lawyer, with his quiddities and his quilleties; for the buyer of land, with his fines, his double vouchers, his recoveries, whose fine pate is full of fine dirt; for the lady in her chamber, who painted an inch thick; for Yorick the jester himself, who mocked at the pretensions of beauty and power, and who, chap-fallen, has not one gibe now to mock his own grinning; for Caesar and Alexander, the very types of worldly power, whose "clay/ Might stop a hole to keep the wind away."[17]

It is in a simple and thoughtful way that the truth comes to Hamlet at last—the answer to what to do about the terrible burden of revenge laid on him by the ghost of his father. The answer is spoken quietly, when Horatio urges him to heed his premonition and not to take part in the fencing-match with Laertes:

> *Hor.* If your mind dislike any thing, obey it. . . .
> *Ham.* Not a whit, we defy augury. There is special provi-
> dence in the fall of a sparrow. If it be now, 'tis not to come;
> if it be not to come, it will be now; if it be not now, yet it
> will come—the readiness is all. Since no man, of aught he
> leaves, knows what is't to leave betimes, let be.[18]
>
> (V. ii. 219-24)

The unspoken noun is, of course, "death." The language in the passage is biblical and stoical, and the speech is in prose—this time not for mockery, but for quietness. The answer is simply readi-ness for whatever may come. When Hamlet is ready, the problem disappears. The answer has been forming since his return, as his report to Horatio on his escape has shown, earlier in the scene. Confidence has come with his surrender to a larger purpose: "There's a divinity that shapes our ends,/Rough-hew them how we will" (ll. 10-11). And to Horatio's warning that the fate of Rosencrantz and Guildenstern will be shortly known from England, Hamlet has replied: "It will be short; the interim is mine,/ And a man's life's no more than to say 'one'" (ll. 73-74).

The final readiness, then, is to take death when it comes. For this is what Hamlet's coming to terms with himself and his world means, has meant from the beginning, when the Ghost returned to lay the fearful charge upon him. It means acceptance of death.[19]

Hamlet has a final great fling of passion when he is mortally wounded and discovers the treachery of the King and Laertes. He cries out, "O villainy! Ho, let the door be lock'd!/Treachery! Seek it out." And he has a final bitter pun, as he forces Claudius to swallow the poisoned drink intended for him, with the pearl, or "union," dissolved in it: "Is thy union here?"

But in spite of so many words spoken during the play, so many wild and whirling words, so much unpacking of his heart, so much bitter and witty comment on the uses of this world, so much probing and questioning of things, Hamlet's final feeling is the deeply poignant one of failure: This was not the way it was to have been at all, with so much done that should not have been done, so much unsaid that ought to be said. The final sad irony for Hamlet, so scrupulous in seeking the truth and in searching for the right thing to do, is that he should be thought a common assassin.

> Had I but time—as this fell sergeant, Death,
> Is strict in his arrest—O, I could tell you—
> But let it be. Horatio, I am dead,
> Thou livest. Report me and my cause aright
> To the unsatisfied.

Hamlet, who must himself join the Dance of Death, puts an end to words with the final poignant word for the ultimate mystery: "The rest is silence."

If, in our intense absorption, we have ceased to think of Hamlet as a character in a play, the flourish of trumpets for Fortinbras and the dead march as the body of Hamlet is carried off the stage end the illusion. They return us from Shakespeare's world of art to ours of common day.

1. Folio reading, supported by Q1 ("o wormewood, wormewood!"); Evans, following Q2, reads "That's wormwood!"
2. *heraldry* (Q1, F1); Evans, *heraldry* (Q2).
3. To write an *ethopoeia*, a speech in the "passive," or passionate mode, for the grieving Hecuba at the fall of Troy was a regular schoolbook exercise prescribed in the commonly used *Progymnasmata* of Aphthonius (as revised by Reinhard Lorich, 1542, 1546, etc.); also in Richard Rainolde's English adaptation, *The Foundacion of Rhetorike*, 1563 (ed. Francis R. Johnson in Scholars' Facsimiles and Reprints, New York, 1945), sigs. Nj-Niij (note the vocabulary of dolefulness and death).
4. See "Imagery in *Richard II* and in *1 Henry IV*," in the Appendix, p. 232.
5. For a sensitive and stimulating essay on the language of *Hamlet*, see Arthur R. Humphreys, "Style and Expression in *Hamlet*," in *Shakespeare's Art: Seven Essays*, ed. Milton Crane (Chicago, 1973), pp. 29–52.
6. Cf. John Hoskins, *Directions for Speech and Style* (1599), ed. Hoyt H. Hudson (Princeton, 1935), pp. 36–37: "This is a fine course to stir admiration in the hearer and make them think it a strange harmony which must be expressed in such discords. . . . This is an easy figure now in fashion, not like ever to be so usual."
7. *Institutio oratoria* VIII. iii. 88, 89 (trans. H. E. Butler, Loeb Classical Library); Quintilian treats *energeia* as one of several related means to attain force (*virium*); his is a less specific use of the term than Aristotle's use of it only to characterize metaphor which makes us "see things" by representing them "in a state of activity" (*Rhetoric* 1411^{b}22-1412^{a}15; W. Rhys Roberts' translation, in *Works*, ed. W. D. Ross, Vol. XI [Oxford, 1924]). Hamlet's style qualifies as "energetic" as well in its easy use of vivid metaphors as in all the other features, verbal and syntactical, of a forceful style. Sidney says in the *Defense of Poesy* that to be persuasive love poetry should betray the passions by "that same forcibleness or *energia* (as the Greeks call it) of the writer" (*Miscellaneous Prose of Sir Philip Sidney*, ed. Katherine Duncan-Jones and Jan van Dorsten [Oxford, 1973], pp. 116–17).
8. J. Dover Wilson, *What Happens in Hamlet* (Cambridge, 1936), pp. 41–42.
9. "Heaven's . . . act," Evans, following Q2; Kittredge, following F1: "Heaven's . . . glow;/ Yea, this . . . mass/ With tristful visage, . . . doom,/ Is . . . act"—one of the many difficult cruxes in *Hamlet*.
10. ἐνάργεια, distinctness, clarity, visibility; Quintilian (*Inst. orat.* IV.ii. 63–65; VIII. iii. 61–62) calls it *evidentia* (vivid illustration) or *repraesentatio* (representation), "which is something more than mere clearness

(*perspicuitas*), since the latter merely lets itself be seen, whereas the former trusts itself upon our notice."

11. *brave*, generally glossed in this passage as "fine," "noble"; but the word perhaps carries as well the common sixteenth-century sense of "showy," "splendid," as in "this brave o'erhanging firmament."

12. *scullion* (F1); Evans, *stallion* (male whore), following Q2.

13. *time*, Evans (Qq); *tune*, Kittredge and others (F1).

14. Another Hamlet crux: "as an Ape doth nuttes" (Q1), "like an apple" (Q2), "like an Ape" (F1).

15. "but as . . . conceive, friend," Evans (Q2); "but not as . . . conceive. Friend," Folio reading, followed by Kittredge and most editors.

16. Quoted from the Geneva Bible, 1560.

17. Cf. Holbein's set of woodcuts of the Dance of Death in an edition of the Old Testament printed in Lyons in 1538; reproduced in *Holbein's Dance of Death and Bible Woodcuts*, New York, 1947 (see especially VII The Emperor, X The Queen, XIX The Advocate, XXIV The Nun, XXXVI The Duchess).

18. "of . . . be," Evans (Q2); "ha's ought of what he leaves. What is't to leave betimes?" (F1); "knows aught of what he leaves, what is't to leave betimes? Let be," Kittredge, following Dr. Johnson.

19. On Hamlet's resolution, and much besides, read Maynard Mack's fine essay, "The World of Hamlet," *The Yale Review* 41 (1952), 502–23; reprinted in *Shakespeare: Modern Essays in Criticism*, ed. Leonard F. Dean (New York, 1957), 237–57.

Inga-Stina Ewbank

"Hamlet and the Power of Words"

If the first law of literary and dramatic criticism is that the approach to a work should be determined by the nature of that work, then I take courage from the fact that *Hamlet* is a play in which, in scene after scene, fools tend to rush in where angels fear to tread. That such fools also tend to come to a bad end—to be stabbed behind the arras or summarily executed in England, "not shriving-time allowed"—I prefer at this point not to consider.

The area into which I propose to rush is the language of *Hamlet*. The method of entry is eclectic. If there is any timeliness about the rush it is that—just as ten years or so ago King Lear was Our Contemporary—Hamlet is now coming to the fore as one of the inhabitants of No Man's Land. A recent book on Shakespeare's *Tragic Alphabet* speaks of the play being about "a world where words and gestures have become largely meaningless," and even as long as twenty-five years ago an article on "The Word in *Hamlet*" began by drawing attention to "the intensely critical, almost disillusionist, attitude of the play towards language itself."[1] Against these, I must confess a firm (and perhaps old-fashioned) belief that *Hamlet*, the play, belongs not so much in No Man's as in Everyman's Land: that it is a vision of the human condition realized in the whole visual and verbal language of the theatre with such intensity and gusto that from any point of view it becomes meaningless to call that language meaningless; and

Reprinted from *Shakespeare Survey*, vol. 30 (1977), pp. 85–102, by permission of Cambridge University Press. Copyright © 1977 by Cambridge University Press.

that in the play as a whole speech is something far more complex, with powers for good and ill, than the "words, words, words" of Hamlet's disillusionment. My aim is to explore the part which speech plays in the life of this play *and* the function of speech as part of Shakespeare's vision in the play. I must start with an example.

At the opening of act IV—or, as some would prefer to describe it, at the close of the closet scene—Claudius pleads with Gertrude, whom he has found in considerable distress:

> There's matter in these sighs, these profound heaves,
> You must translate; 'tis fit we understand them.

Of course he thinks he knows what the "matter" is, for he also immediately adds "Where is your son?" Gertrude has just been through the most harrowing[2] experience: Hamlet's words to her have "like daggers" entered into her "ears" and turned her "eyes into [her] very soul" where she has gained such unspeakable knowledge of her "black and grained spots" as might well have made her feel unable to comply with Claudius's request for a "translation." Indeed, in a modern play, where husbands and wives tend to find that on the whole they don't speak the same language, the shock of insight might well have led her to make some statement of non-communication—some version of the reply by Ibsen's Nora (that early non-communicating wife) to her husband's wish to "understand" her reactions:

> You don't understand me. Nor have I ever understood you.[3]

In fact, of course, Gertrude does the opposite. She provides a translation of the preceding scene which manages to avoid saying anything about herself but to describe Hamlet's madness, his killing of Polonius, and his treatment of the body. As so often in this play,[4] we have a retelling of an episode which we have already witnessed. And so we can see at once that Gertrude's translation is a mixture of three kinds of components: first, of what really happened and was said (including a direct quotation of Hamlet's cry "a rat," though she doubles it and changes it from a question to an exclamation);[5] secondly, of what she thinks, or would like to think, happened and was said. She is prepared to read into Hamlet's behaviour such motivations, and to add such details, as she would have liked to find—as Polonius suspected when he appointed himself "some more audience than a mother,/Since nature makes them partial" (III, iii, 31–2), though even he could not have foreseen that her partiality would come to extend to a fictitious description of Hamlet mourning over his corpse.[6] Thirdly, but most importantly, as it most controls both what she says and how she says it, her translation consists of what she wants the king to think did happen: that the scene demonstrated what Hamlet in a doubly ironic figure of speech had told her not to say, i.e. that he is "essentially" mad and not "mad in craft." Her emotion is released, and her verbal energy spends itself, not on the part of the recent experience which concerns herself most radically, but on convincing her husband that her son is

> Mad as the sea and wind, when both contend
> Which is the mightier.

Claudius may end the scene "full of discord and dismay," but— and this seems usually to be the most Gertrude can hope for— things are not as bad as they might have been. She has in a manner protected her son by sticking to her assurance to him that

> if words be made of breath
> And breath of life, I have no life to breathe
> What thou hast said to me;

she has at least not added to Claudius's suspicions of Hamlet's "antic disposition"; and she has paid some tribute to the victim of the game between the two, the murderer and the revenger: "the unseen good old man." I do not think that Gertrude's design is as conscious as this analysis may have suggested, but her translation has worked.

In so far as anything in this play, so full of surprises at every corner, is typical of the whole, the scene seems to me a model for how language functions within much of the play: communicating by adapting words to thought and feeling, in a process which involves strong awareness in the speaker of who is being spoken to. Of course there has not been much truth spoken and on that score, no doubt, the scene is a thematic illustration of that dreaded pair of abstracts, Appearance and Reality; and the author's attitude is "disillusionist" enough. And of course the scene in one sense speaks of non-communication between husband and wife. Gertrude has drawn apart, with her unspeakable knowledge and suspicion, much as Macbeth has when he bids his wife "Be innocent of the knowledge, dearest chuck" (*Macbeth*, III, ii, 45). But, in its dramatic context, the language does a great deal more than that. There is, as Polonius has said, "some more audience" in the theatre, and to them—to us—the language speaks eloquently of the strange complexities of human life, of motives and responses and the re-alignment of relationships under stress. It speaks of Gertrude's desperate attempt to remain loyal to her son but also (however misguidedly) to her husband and to his chief councillor. Ultimately the power of the words is Shakespeare's, not Gertrude's, and it operates even through the total muteness of Rosencrantz and Guildenstern who, like parcels, are, most Stoppard-like, sent out and in and out again in the course of the scene.

Claudius's verb for what he asks Gertrude to do is apter than he knew himself: "You must translate." Presumably (and editors do not seem to feel that annotation is needed) he simply wants her to interpret her signs of emotion in words, to change a visual language into a verbal. But, as anyone knows who has attempted translation in its now most commonly accepted sense, the processes involved in finding equivalents in one language for the signs of another are far from simple. There is a troublesome tension—indeed often an insoluble contradiction—between the demands of "interpretation" and those of "change," between original meaning and meaningfulness in another language. That Shakespeare was aware of this—although, unlike many of his fellow poets and dramatists, he was apparently not an interlingual translator—is suggested, in the first place, by the various ways in which he uses the word "translate" in his plays. Alexander Schmidt's *Shakespeare-Lexicon* separates three clearly defined meanings: 1. to transform or to change, as Bottom is "translated," or as beauty is *not* translated into honesty in the nunnery scene; 2. "to render into another language (or rather to change by rendering into another language)," as Falstaff translates Mistress Ford's inclinations "out of honesty into English," or as the Archbishop of York translates his whole being "Out of the speech of peace . . . Into the harsh and boist'rous tongue of war" (both these examples being rather demanding in the way of dictionaries); and 3. to interpret or explain, as in the Claudius line I have been discussing, or as Aeneas has translated Troilus to Ulysses.[7] Not only do Schmidt and the *OED* disagree over these definitions,[8] but, as the examples I have given indicate, meanings seem to overlap within Shakespeare's uses of the word—so that all three hover around the following lines from Sonnet 96:

> So are those errors that in thee are seen
> To truths translated and for true things deem'd.

That sonnet is in a sense about the problem of finding a language for the "grace and faults" of the beloved—a problem which haunts many of the Sonnets and can be solved, the poems show, only by fusing change and interpretation into a single poetic act. In much the same way, *Hamlet* is dominated by the hero's search for a way to translate (though Shakespeare does not use the word here) the contradictory demands of the Ghost:

> If thou hast nature in thee, bear it not;
> . . . .
> But, howsomever thou pursuest this act,
> Taint not thy mind . . .
>
> (I, v, 81, 84–5)

Claudius, we are going to see, finds that his position translates best into oxymorons; and Troilus feels the need to be bilingual— "this is, and is not, Cressid"—or simply silent: "Hector is dead; there is no more to say."

If, then, to translate means both to interpret and to change, it also usually means being particularly conscious of the words used in the process. All of us, surely, are prepared to claim with Coleridge that we have "a smack of Hamlet" in us; but those of us who have approached the English language from the outside may perhaps claim a special kind of smack. For lack of sophistication we may share that alertness to a rich, hybrid language, to latent metaphors and multiple meanings waiting to be activated, which Hamlet has by an excess of sophistication. With still fresh memories of looking up a word in the English dictionary and finding a bewildering row of possible meanings, or an equally bewildering

row of words for a supposedly given meaning, we are also peculiarly prepared to give more than local significance to Claudius's
line: "You must translate; 'tis fit we understand."

I would not indulge in these speculations if I did not believe
that they applied directly to *Hamlet*. George Steiner, in *After Babel*,
maintains that *"inside or between languages, human communication equals
translation."*[9] *Hamlet*, I think, bears out the truth of this. Hamlet
himself is throughout the play trying to find a language to express himself through, as well as languages to speak to others in;
and round him—against him and for him—the members of the
court of Elsinore are engaging in acts of translation. The first
meeting with Rosencrantz and Guildenstern, in II, ii, would be a
specific example of this general statement. Hamlet's speech on
how he has of late lost all his mirth—mounting to the much-
quoted "What a piece of work is man! . . . /And yet, to me, what is
this quintessence of dust?"—is only partly, if at all, a spontaneous
overflow of his mythical sorrows (let alone of Shakespeare's).
Partly, even mainly, it is his translation, in such terms of *fin-de-
siècle* disillusionment as clever young men will appreciate, of just as
much of his frame of mind as he wants Rosencrantz and Guildenstern to understand. And the verbal hide-and-seek of the
whole episode turns what might have been a simple spy/coun-
terspy scene into a complex study of people trying to control each
other by words. Here, and elsewhere in the play, the mystery of
human intercourse is enacted and the power of words demonstrated: what we say, and by saying do, to each other, creating
and destroying as we go along.

No one in the play seems to regret that it is words they "gotta
use" when they speak to each other. Hamlet, unlike Coriolanus,
never holds his mother "by the hand, silent"; and his only major
speechless moment is that which Ophelia describes to Polonius,
when

> with a look so piteous in purport
> As if he had been loosed out of hell
> To speak of horrors—he comes before me.
>
> (II, i, 81–4)

The Ghost does indeed hint at unspeakable horrors—"I could a
tale unfold"—but he is very explicit about the effects its "lightest
word" would have, and the only reason he does not speak those

words is a purgatorial prohibition on telling "the secrets of my prison-house" to "ears of flesh and blood" (I, v, 13 ff.). Words govern the action of the play, from the ironical watchword— "Long live the King!"—which allays Francisco's fears at the opening, to Hamlet's "dying voice" which gives the throne of Denmark to Fortinbras at the end; and, beyond, to the speech which will be given by Horatio when it is all over, explaining "to th'yet unknowing world/How these things came about." Words control the fates and the development of the characters, and not only when they are spoken by the Ghost to Hamlet and turned by him into a principle of action ("Now to my word": I, v, 110). Words can open Gertrude's eyes, help to drive Ophelia mad, unpack Hamlet's heart (however much he regrets it); and if Claudius finds that "words without thoughts never to heaven go" (III, iii, 98), this merely validates those words which have thoughts. Sometimes the words deceive, sometimes they say what is felt and meant, sometimes they are inadequate—but the inadequacy reflects on the speaker rather than the language. In the study, where the play so readily presents itself spatially and thematically, it may be easy to speak of it as demonstrating the inadequacy of words. In the theatre, the words have to get us through the four-and-a-half hours traffic of the stage, and (when they have not been cut or played about with) they give us a play of relationships, of "comutual" (as the Player King would call them) interactions and dialogues—a world where it is natural to ask not only "What's Hecuba to him?" but also "or he to Hecuba?" *Hamlet*, for all its soliloquies, may well be the Shakespeare play which most confirms Ben Jonson's statement, in *Discoveries*, that language "is the instrument of society"; and in exploring the function of speech in the play we may do well to listen to Henry James's words to the graduating class at Bryn Mawr College in June 1905:

> All life therefore comes back to the question of our speech, the medium through which we communicate with each other; for all life comes back to the question of our relations with each other . . .
> . . . the way we say a thing, or fail to say it, fail to learn to say it, has an importance in life that is impossible to overstate—a far-reaching importance, as the very hinge of the relation of man to man.[10]

Looking at the world of "relations" in *Hamlet* from the outside,
we can have no doubt that its hinges are well oiled, by the sheer
size of its vocabulary. Long ago now, the patient industry of
Alfred Hart demonstrated that *Hamlet* has "the largest and most
expressive vocabulary" of all Shakespeare's plays, and that it
abounds in new words—new to Shakespeare and also, in many
cases, apparently new to English literature—a considerable
number of which do not recur in any later Shakespeare plays.[11]
And a new language for new and unique experiences is suggested
not only by the single words but by the new structures, images
and figures into which they are combined—as indeed by the new
uses of old syntactical patterns and rhetorical figures. (It is worth
remembering that, seen through the eyes of T. W. Baldwin and
Sister Miriam Joseph, Hamlet's forerunners are Holofernes and
Sir Nathaniel.)[12] Language is being stretched and re-shaped to
show the form and pressure of the *Hamlet* world. The extraordinary variety of language modes is important, too: we move,
between scenes or within a scene or even within a speech, from
moments of high elaboration and formality to moments of what
Yeats would have called "walking naked,"[13] where speech is what
the Sonnets call "true and plain" and we call "naturalistic."

If we view the world of *Hamlet* from the inside, we find that
what the still small voices in the play have in common with the
loud and eloquent ones is a general belief in the importance of
speaking. The play begins with three men repeatedly imploring a
ghost to speak and ends with Hamlet's concern for what Horatio
is going to "speak to th'yet unknowing world," and in between
characters are always urging each other to speak. It is as natural
for Laertes to part from Ophelia with a "let me hear from you"
(I, iii, 4) as it is for Polonius to react to Ophelia's "affrighted"
description of Hamlet's appearance with "What said he?"
(II, i, 86). In this particular instance there is no speech to report,
but the key-note of most of the character confrontations in the
play could, again, have been taken from the *Discoveries*: "Language
most shews a man: Speak, that I may see thee."[14] In *Hamlet*, unlike
King Lear, seeing is rarely enough. Ophelia's lament at the end of
the nunnery scene—

> O, woe is me
> T' have seen what I have seen, see what I see!—

follows upon an unusually (for her) eloquent analysis of both
what she has seen and what she is seeing ("O, what a noble mind
is here o'er-thrown!"); and Gertrude, we know, soon finds words
to translate into words her exclamation, "Ah, mine own lord,
what have I seen tonight!" Often seeing has to be achieved
through hearing. "You go not till I set you up a glass," Hamlet
tells his mother, but that "glass" is not so much "the counterfeit
presentment of two brothers" as Hamlet's speech on Gertrude's
lack of "eyes." Unlike Edgar, Horatio is left with the exact and
exacting task of speaking not what he feels, but what he ought to
say. One begins to feel that the ear is the main sense organ in
Hamlet, and concordances confirm that the word "ear" occurs in
this play more times than in any other of Shakespeare's.[15]
Through the ear—"attent," or "knowing"—comes the understanding which Claudius asks Gertrude for in IV, i; but through the
"too credent" or "foolish" ear come deception and corruption.
Claudius seems obsessed with a sense of Laertes's ear being
infected "with pestilent speeches" while he himself is being ar-
raigned "in ear and ear" (IV, v, 87–91). Well he might be, for in
the Ghost's speech all of Denmark had, as in a Bosch vision, been
contracted into a single ear:

> so the whole ear of Denmark
> Is by a forged process of my death
> Rankly abus'd;
>
>   (I, v, 36–8)

and the ironic source and sounding-board of all these images is of
course the literal poisoning by ear on which the plot of the play
rests.

   So the characters not only speak, they listen. Not only do we,
the audience, marvel at the variety of idioms heard, from Gravedigger to Player King, from Osric, who has "only got the tune of
the time and the outward habit of encounter" (V, ii, 185), to
Ophelia, whose real fluency comes only in madness. But the
characters themselves take a conscious and delighted interest in
the idiosyncrasies of individual and national idioms, in how people
speak, as Polonius says, "according to the phrase and the addition/
Of man and country" (II, i, 47–8). Hamlet's parodies of spoken
and written styles are outstanding, but Polonius—in instructing
Reynaldo—is just as good at imitating potential conversations.

Seen from our point of view or the characters', the play is alive
with interest in how people react to each other and to each other's
language.

Like Claudius, in the scene from which I began, the characters, when they urge each other to speak, expect to understand
the "matter," or meaning, of what is said. Hence they are particularly disturbed by the apparent meaninglessness of "antic"
speech—"I have nothing with this answer, Hamlet; these words
are not mine," is Claudius's sharpest and most direct rebuke to his
nephew/son (III, ii, 93-4)—and by the dim apprehension, again
expressed by Claudius, after overhearing the nunnery scene, that
the lack of "form" in such speech may conceal "something" (III, i,
162 ff.). Laertes does recognize that mad speech may reach
beyond rational discourse—"This nothing's more than matter"—
and be more effectively moving (IV, v, 171 and 165-6). But the
first we hear of Ophelia's madness is Gertrude's abrupt opening
line in IV, v: "I will not speak with her," followed by the Gentleman's long account of her language:

> Her speech is nothing,
> Yet the unshaped use of it doth move
> The hearers to collection; they yawn at it,
> And botch the words up fit to their own thoughts.
>
> (II. 7-10)

Yielding to Horatio's cautiously applied pressure—"'Twere good
she were spoken with"—Gertrude can attempt a dialogue only
through the usual request for *meaning*: "Alas, sweet lady, what
imports this song?"; and even Ophelia knows through her madness the kind of question that will be asked about her: "when they
ask you what it means, say you this: . . . ."

We have returned to the idea of translation, for in their
intercourse the characters seem unusually aware of their interlocutors' tendency to "botch the words up fit to their own
thoughts." One main aspect of this is the belief, demonstrated
throughout the play, in the importance of finding the right language for the right person. The opening scene is a model of this.
Horatio had been brought in as a translator ("Thou art a scholar;
speak to it, Horatio")[16] but, though the Ghost's first appearance
turns him from scepticism to "fear and wonder," he is unsure of
his language. His vocabulary is wrong: "What art thou that

usurp'st [a particularly unfortunate verb in the circumstances] this time of night . . . ?" and so is his tone: "By heaven I charge thee, speak!" On the Ghost's second appearance, Horatio's litany of appeals—"If . . . Speak to me"—more nearly approaches the ceremony which befits a king. The second "If," with its sense of "comutual" purpose, gets very warm—

> If there be any good thing to be done,
> That may to thee do ease and grace to me—

but Horatio then loses himself in the motivations of generalized ghost lore; and, in any case, Time in the form of a cock's crow interrupts any possible interchange. A "show of violence" signals the hopeless defeat of verbal communication. Horatio now knows that none but Hamlet can find the language needed, and so the scene ends with the decision to "impart what we have seen tonight/Unto young Hamlet," for:

> This spirit, dumb to us, will speak to him.

But the gap between speakers which—they are aware—must be bridged by translation is not always as wide as the grave. The king appeals to Rosencrantz and Guildenstern as being on the same side of the generation gap as Hamlet—

> being of so young days brought up with him,
> And sith so neighboured to his youth and haviour—
>   (II, ii, 11–12)

which should give them a language "to gather,/So much as from occasion you may glean"; and Hamlet conjures them to tell the truth "by the consonancy of our youth" (II, ii, 283). When the opening of the closet scene has demonstrated that Gertrude's language and her son's are in diametrical opposition—

> Hamlet, thou hast thy father much offended.
> Mother, you have my father much offended.—

and that he will not adopt the language of a son to a mother ("Have you forgot me?") but insists on a vocabulary and syntax which ram home the confusion in the state of Denmark—

> No, by the rood, not so:
> You are the Queen, your husband's brother's wife.
> And—would it were not so!—you are my mother—

then Gertrude can see no other way out of the deadlock but to call for translators:

> Nay then, I'll set those to you that can speak.

Hamlet's refusal to be thus translated is what leads to Polonius's death. Polonius spends much energy, in his last few days of life, on finding a language for a madman, trying—as in II, ii—at the same time to humour and to analyse Hamlet. But Rosencrantz and Guildenstern are perhaps even more supremely aware of the necessity of different languages for different persons. They take their colour, their style, tone and imagery, from their interlocutors, whether it is a question of speaking the snappy, quibbling dialogue of clever young students with Hamlet on first meeting him, or enlarging before Claudius on the idea of "the cease of majesty" so that it becomes an extended image of "a massy wheel,/Fixed on the summit of the highest mount" (III, iii, 10 ff.). They are in the end chameleons rather than caterpillars, and it is naturally to them that Hamlet speaks the words in which the play's interest in suiting language to persons is taken to the extreme of parody:

> Besides, to be demanded of a sponge—what replication should be made by the son of a king?
>
> (IV, ii, 12)

It is natural, too, that when the programming has gone wrong in their language laboratory they are helpless and can say nothing but

> What should we say, my lord?
>
> (II, ii, 275)

The characters of the play, then, are on the whole very self-conscious speakers, in a way which involves consciousness of others: they believe in the word and its powers, but they are also aware of the necessity so to translate intentions and experiences into words as to make them meaningful to the interlocutor. And not only vaguely meaningful: they know the effect they want to produce and take careful steps to achieve it. Perhaps the Reynaldo scene is the best model of this. Polonius, in a dialogue of superb naturalism, with its stops and starts, doublings back and forget-

tings what he was about to say, gives Reynaldo a lesson in
translation which is much closer to the heart of the play than any
mere plot function might suggest. Anyone who thinks Polonius
just a fool ought to look again at the almost Jamesian subtlety
with which Reynaldo is instructed to control the *tone* of his indirect enquiries into Laertes's Parisian life, to

> breathe his faults so quaintly
> That they may seem the taints of liberty,
>
> (II, i, 31-2)

and, in case he has not got the point, to lay "these slight sullies on
my son,/As 'twere a thing a little soil'd wi' th' working" (II. 39-40).
This is a situation less Machiavellian than the Revenge *genre* might
seem to demand, and more like the instruction of Strether where,
as here, facts tend to refract into opaque impressions rather than
moral certainties.

Perhaps I am now being seduced by the power of words—and
Polonius's of all people. Not that Shakespeare allows this to
happen for very long: the moment that Reynaldo exits, Ophelia
bursts in, and the contrast is blatant between the urbanity of the
preceding scene and the raw experience of her account—acted
out as much as spoken—of Hamlet's speechless visit to her.
Clearly, when the characters in *Hamlet* use their language, or
languages, for purposes of persuasion and diplomacy, they are
generally engaging in duplicity and deception. In the end, the evil
underneath is (as James also knew) made more, not less, pernicious by the bland surface of the dialogue. An outstanding example of this is the "witchcraft of his wits" (as the Ghost is to
describe the usurper's "power/So to seduce") practised by Claudius in the second scene of the play. His opening speech establishes him as a very clever chairman of the board. First he gets the
minutes of past proceedings accepted without query, by a carefully arranged structure of oxymorons:[17]

> Therefore our sometime sister, now our queen,
> Th'imperial jointress to this warlike state,
> Have we, as 'twere with a defeated joy,
> With an auspicious and a dropping eye,
> With mirth in funeral, and with dirge in marriage,

> In equal scale weighing delight and dole,
> Taken to wife.
>
> (I, ii, 8–14)

The oxymorons, in a relentless series of pairings, operate to cancel each other out, smoothing over the embarrassment (or worse) involved in "our sometime sister, now our queen," stilling criticism and enforcing acceptance of the apparent logic of the argument, so that by the time we finally get to the verb ("Taken to wife") the "Therefore" seems legitimate. Then he justifies chairman's action by suggesting that there have been consultations all along, spiking the guns of any potential rebel by thanking him in advance for his agreement:

> nor have we herein barr'd
> Your better wisdoms, which have freely gone
> With this affair along. For all, our thanks.
>
> (II. 14–16)

Having dealt with the minutes, he then proceeds to the agenda and polishes off, in turn, the foreign policy problems with Norway, the home and domestic issue of Laertes, and finally the awkward business with Hamlet which—who knows—might be both personal and national, psychological and political. He intends to deal with Hamlet, too, through the technique of dissolving contradictions—

> But now, my cousin Hamlet, and my son—
>
> (I. 64)

but his briskness here comes to grief, as Hamlet becomes the first to raise a voice, albeit in an aside, which punctures such use of language:

> A little more than kin, and less than kind.
>
> (I. 65)

Intrepidly, Claudius continues in an image suggesting the tone of decorous grief which ought to be adopted—"How is it that the clouds still hang on you?"—but this again founders on Hamlet's pun on sun/son. The pun, according to Sigurd Burckhardt in *Shakespearean Meanings*, "gives the lie direct to the social convention which is language. . . . It denies the meaningfulness of words."[18]

But in their dramatic context here, Hamlet's puns do no such thing: they deny the logic and sincerity and meaningfulness of Claudius's words but suggest that there is a language elsewhere.

The rest of the scene, until it closes on Hamlet's decision to "hold my tongue," is a series of contrasts and clashes between different languages. Hamlet's "common" is not the queen's and implies a far-reaching criticism of hers. Gertrude's reply suggests that she is not aware of the difference, Claudius's that he is trying to pretend that he is not, as he follows Hamlet's terrible outburst against seeming with an, in its way, equally terrible refusal to acknowledge any jar:

> 'Tis sweet and commendable in your nature, Hamlet,
> To give these mourning duties to your father.
>
> (II. 87–8)

Hamlet has no reply to Claudius's appeal to the "common theme" of death of fathers, nor to the request that he give up Wittenberg for "the cheer and comfort of our eye"; his reply, promising to "obey," is made to his mother. But it is Claudius who comments on it as "loving" and "fair," and it is he who sums up the conversation, translating the tense scene just past into an image of domestic and national harmony—

> This gentle and unforc'd account of Hamlet
> Sits smiling to my heart—
>
> (II. 123–4)

and an excuse for a "wassail." The incongruity is as if a satire and a masque by Jonson were being simultaneously performed on the same stage. The ultimate clash comes as, immediately upon Claudius's summing-up, Hamlet breaks into his first soliloquy, giving *his* version of himself and of "all the uses of this world," particularly those involving his mother and uncle.

The different languages spoken in a scene like this clearly add up to a kind of moral map. That is, the adding up is clear, the map itself not necessarily so. It is not just a matter of Hamlet's words being sincere and Claudius's not. In the dialogue Hamlet is striving for effect in his way just as much as Claudius in his. And Claudius is soon going to be sincere enough, when we learn from his own mouth, in an image that could well have been used by

Hamlet, that he is aware of the ugliness of his deed as against his "most painted word" (III, i, 50–4) and that his words are unable to rise in prayer (III, iii, 36 ff.). Morality and sensitivity to language are peculiarly tied up with each other in this play; and in trying to think how they are related I, at least, am driven back to James and "The Question of Our Speech": to the importance of "the way we say a thing, or fail to say it, fail to learn to say it."[19] In a play peopled by translators, it is in the end the range of languages available to each character—those they "fail to learn" as well as those they speak—which measures their moral stature. Both Claudius and Gertrude at various times have their consciences stung, but neither seems able to find a language for his or her own inner self. Even Polonius is able to learn and, up to a point, articulate what he has learnt. "I am sorry," he says about having misunderstood the nature of Hamlet's love for Ophelia, "that with better heed and judgment/I had not quoted him" (II, i, 111–12). Hamlet himself never has such a moment of recognition in regard to Ophelia. But typically Polonius at once takes the edge off any personal pain of remorse by translating it into a sententious generalization:

> It is as proper to our age
> To cast beyond ourselves in our opinions
> As it is common for the younger sort
> To lack discretion.
>
> (II, i, 114–17)

Claudius similarly lacks a really private language. Even when he is alone and trying to pray, his speech retains the basic characteristics of his public "translations." Images which in content might seem to anticipate Macbeth's,[20] are turned out in carefully balanced phrases—"heart, with strings of steel" against "sinews of the new-born babe"; his similes have the considered effect of earlier tragic verse:

> And, like a man to double business bound,
> I stand in pause where I shall first begin,
> And both neglect;
>
> (III, iii, 41–3)

and the most trenchant self-analysis is as cleverly antithetical as anything he has to say before the assembled court in I, ii: "My stronger guilt defends my strong intent." Unlike Macbeth, Claudius seems to be talking *about* himself, not from inside himself, and his own evil seems to contain no mystery to him, nothing unspeakable. Gertrude has known less evil, and her moral imagination has an even narrower range. Even after the closet scene, her appearances suggest that, like Claudius and unlike Lady Macbeth, she is able to cancel and pass on. The woman who describes Ophelia's death, and strews flowers on her grave, is harrowed within her limits but not marked and changed by her experience, in language and being. The fact that Hamlet and Ophelia are thus changed (however variously) sets them apart. Each of them receives shocks and undergoes sufferings which are taken into their language; and at the extremest point each speaks—whether in madness or not—a language foreign to the other characters.[21]

And yet Hamlet's own language is in many ways that of Elsinore. As others, notably R. A. Foakes, have pointed out, his speech modes and habits are largely those of the court: wordiness, formality, sententiousness, fondness of puns and other forms of word-play, etc.[22] He too uses language in all the ways practised by Claudius and his entourage: for persuasion, diplomacy, deception, and so on. His sheer range, which is as large almost as that of the play itself, has made it difficult for critics to define his own linguistic and stylistic attributes. As Professor Foakes succinctly puts it, "Hamlet seems master of all styles, but has no distinctive utterance of his own." Up to a point we can explain this, as Professor Foakes does, by seeing Hamlet as "the supreme actor who never reveals himself."[23] But beyond that point we still need a way of talking about Hamlet's language which includes his uncontrolled and (surely) revealing moments, such as the nunnery scene or the leaping into Ophelia's grave, as well as his moments of deliberately antic disposition; and the simple statements in the dialogues with Horatio as well as the tortuous questioning in the monologues. It might be helpful, then, to think of Hamlet as the most sensitive translator in the play: as the one who has the keenest sense both of the expressive and the persuasive powers of words, and also and more radically the keenest sense both of the limitations and the possibilities of words. No one could be more disillusioned with "words, words, words." Even before he appears on stage, his mother's rush "to incestuous sheets" has had an impact which he later describes as having (in contemporary parlance) deprived language of its very credibility:

> O, such a deed
> As . . . sweet religion makes
> A rhapsody of words;
>
> (III, iv, 45–8)

and, though a Wittenberg scholar could hardly have lived unaware of the general maxim that "one may smile, and smile, and be a villain," the encounter with the Ghost proves it on his own pulses and leaves him permanently aware that language may be a cloak or masque. Yet no one could use his disillusionment more subtly or positively to fit his words to the action, the interlocutor and his own mood—so far indeed that the disillusionment is swallowed up in excitement at the power of words.

No other Shakespearian hero, tragic or comic, has to face so many situations in which different speakers have different palpable designs on him, and where he so has to get hold of the verbal initiative. No other hero, not even Falstaff or Benedick, is so good at grasping the initiative, leading his interlocutor by the nose while—as with Polonius and Osric—playing with the very shape and temperature of reality. Many of the play's comic effects stem from this activity, and the strange tonal mixture of the graveyard scene has much to do with Hamlet, for once, almost playing the stooge to the indomitable wit of the First Gravedigger. No other Shakespearian hero is so good at running his antagonists right down to their basic premisses and striking them dumb, as with Rosencrantz and Guildenstern in the recorder scene. He won't be played upon, and so he listens in order, with lightning speed, to pick up a key-word and turn it into a pun or some other device for playing upon others.

But, unlike many other Shakespearian tragic heroes, Hamlet also listens in a more reflective way—listens and evaluates, as Othello does not (but Hamlet surely would have done) with Iago. In some situations we begin to feel that his linguistic flexibility is founded on a sympathetic imagination. In him, alone in the play, the ability to speak different languages to different people seems to stem from an awareness that, in George Eliot's words, another being may have "an equivalent centre of self, whence the lights and shadows must always fall with a certain difference."[24] Other characters meet to plot or to remonstrate, or they step aside for an odd twitch of conscience. To Hamlet, conversations may become extensions of moral sympathy. Even under the immediate impact of encountering the Ghost he can stop to realize and regret that he has offended Horatio with the "wild and whirling words" which came out of a hysterical absorption in his own experience (I, v, 133 ff.). In retrospect the scene at Ophelia's grave is illuminated by the same sympathy:

> I am very sorry, good Horatio,
> That to Laertes I forgot myself;
> For by the image of my cause I see
> The portraiture of his;
>
> (V, ii, 75-8)

and the courtly apology to Laertes (V, ii, 218 ff.), which some critics have taken to be mere falsehood,[25] is surely a genuine attempt at translating his own "cause" into the language of Laertes. In a case like this, his verbal virtuosity seems to aim at an interchange, a two-way traffic of language between selves. It is worth noting that Hamlet's most explicit tribute to Horatio is to call him "e'en as just a man/As e'er my conversation cop'd withal" (III, ii, 52-3). Two senses of "conversation" merge in that phrase— "the action of consorting or having dealings with others; . . . society; intimacy" (OED 2) and "interchange of thoughts and words" (OED 7)—and, one feels, in Hamlet's consciousness.

There is a kinship here between Hamlet and Cleopatra, another character who in her language combines intense self-preoccupation with strong awareness of others. In North's Plutarch Shakespeare would have found an emphasis on her verbal powers, even at the expense of her physical beauty which,

> as it is reported, was not so passing as unmatchable of other women, nor yet such as upon present view did enamour men with her; but so sweet was her company and conversation that a man could not possibly but be taken.

Not the least part of the power of Cleopatra's "conversation" was her ability to speak different languages:

> her tongue was an instrument of music to divers sports and
> pastimes, the which she easily turned to any language that
> pleased her. She spake unto few barbarous people by in-
> terpreter, but made them answer herself.[26]

It may not be wholly fanciful to imagine that North's comments
on Cleopatra's inter-lingual dexterity have in Shakespeare been
translated into an intralingual flexibility. Cleopatra is able to
speak different languages to Emperor and to Clown as well as to
forge her own variety of idioms according to situation and
mood—and finally to create, through language, her own reality
and Antony's ("Methinks I hear/Antony call. . . . Husband I
come"). In her case, as in Hamlet's, the vitality which comes from
superb handling of language affects us both aesthetically and
morally. To measure it we need only turn to Octavia who is "of a
holy, cold and still conversation."

Yet by the same measurement there is only a hair's breadth
between moral sympathy and callousness, and *Hamlet* shows this
too. Hamlet's awareness of others as autonomous beings with
"causes," and accordingly with languages, of their own also helps
to explain why he despises Rosencrantz and Guildenstern so, and
can so unflinchingly let them "go to't," recounting his dealings
with them as "not near my conscience" only a few lines before he
speaks to Horatio of his regret for what he did and said to Laertes.
To him they lack any "centre of self"; they are instruments used
to turn others into "unworthy" things (III, iii, 353); they are
sponges whose only function is to be "at each ear a hearer" (II, ii,
377). Hamlet's sympathetic imagination falls far short of Stoppard's, and of Christian charity. The killing of Polonius, whom he
sees only as an over-hearer and a mouthpiece, affects him no
more than a putting-down in verbal repartee:

> Take thy fortune;
> Thou find'st that to be busy is some danger.
>
> (III, iv, 32–3)

At this point, his whole sense of "conversation"—of dealings with
others—is narrowed onto speaking "daggers" to Gertrude:

> Leave wringing of your hands. Peace; sit you down,
> And let me wring your heart.
>
> (III, iv, 34–5)

Everyone knows that Hamlet speaks rather than acts, and therefore delays; but it is worth pointing out that his peculiar involvement with words can be at the expense of humanity as well as of deeds. It is worth remembering, when we speak of Hamlet as an actor (who can "act" but not act), that what he remembers from plays are great speeches; and that his own acting—as against his advice to the actors and his full admiration of their art—is almost entirely a matter of handling language: of the ability to control other people's reaction to his words. His self-reproach after the Hecuba speech is not that he can do nothing but that

> I . . . unpregnant of my cause
> . . . can say nothing.
>
> (II, ii, 562-3)

Yet, less than twenty lines later he is reproaching himself for saying too much,

> That I, the son of a dear father murder'd,
> Prompted to my revenge by heaven and hell,
> Must, like a whore, unpack my heart with words.
>
> (II, ii, 579-81)

There is no contradiction here for, while the words with which he unpacks his heart are merely therapeutic, even an anodyne, directed at no object and no audience, the "saying" which he admires in the First Player is the absorption of the self in a purposeful act of communication, "his whole function suiting/With forms to his conceit." The language needed for his own "conceit" is nonverbal, the act of revenge to which he is "prompted." Yet in the logic of this soliloquy, transferring his own "motive" and "cue for passion" to the Player and imagining the result, the act is translated into a theatrical declamation:

> He would drown the stage with tears,
> And cleave the general ear with horrid speech;
> Make mad the guilty, and appal the free,
> Confound the ignorant, and amaze indeed
> The very faculties of eyes and ears.
>
> (II, ii, 555-9)

It is natural for him to translate intention into language—into verbal rather than physical violence—hence the apparent relief as he finds gruesome reasons not to murder the praying Claudius, or as the "bitter business" of the "witching time" can, for the moment, be allowed to be resolved into a matter of words:

> I will speak daggers to her, but use none.

Hence, too, the play to be put on excites him beyond its detective purpose. It is going to speak for him, or he through it—and at least at the outset of II, ii his hopes of the effect of the play seem to hinge on the speech "of some dozen or sixteen lines" which he has composed himself—to Claudius, to form a translation fully and terribly meaningful only to Claudius. If, besides, it means different things to the rest of the court,[27] all the better a translation. Murder speaks metaphorically in much Elizabethan-Jacobean tragedy, but rarely is the speaking so completely *heard* by the imagination as in Hamlet's plan for the effect of "The Murder of Gonzago":

> For murder, though it have no tongue, will speak
> With most miraculous organ.
>
> (II, ii, 589–90)

Hamlet's excitement with speech as translation of deeds would help to explain, too, why in the graveyard scene it is Laertes's rhetoric which becomes the centre of Hamlet's grievance and object of his aggression. The leaping into the grave is a kind of act fitted to the word, a rhetorical flourish:

> Dost come here to whine?
> To outface me with leaping her grave?
> . . . Nay, an thou'lt mouth,
> I'll rant as well as thou.
>
> (V, i, 271–2, 277–8)

We return here to the notion of human sympathy, as well as positive action, being absorbed and lost in speech. For it is in his dealings with Ophelia—which is as much as to say his language to Ophelia—that Hamlet most shows the destructive powers of speech. His vision of the world as "an unweeded garden" ultimately drives Ophelia to her death, wearing the "coronet weeds" of her madness. I do not wish to turn the play into a *Hamlet and Ophelia*: the love story is played down in the structure as a whole, its pre-play course known only by the odd flashback and inference, and it disappears altogether after the graveyard scene. All the responsibility that Laertes can remember to remove from Hamlet with his dying breath is "mine and my father's death." But I still believe that the Hamlet-Ophelia relationship reveals something essential to Hamlet's and his creator's vision of the power of words; and also that it illuminates the way in which Hamlet contracts what Kenneth Muir has called "the occupational disease of avengers"[28]—how he is tainted by the world in which he is trying to take revenge.

The poisoning of that relationship within the play is full of searing ironies. Hamlet never says "I love you" except in the past tense and to unsay it at once. By the time he tells the world "I loved Ophelia," she is dead. The first time he refers to her it is antically, as the daughter of Polonius, the fishmonger. From Hamlet's love-letter—which we are surely meant to take more seriously than Polonius does—we learn that in his wooing he was both as exalted and as tongue-tied as any lover who hesitates to sully the uniqueness of his love by common speech. When he tries to write a love sonnet, the attempt to look in his heart and write turns into a touching version of the conventional idea that the beloved is inexpressible:

> O dear Ophelia, I am ill at these numbers. I have not art to reckon my groans; but that I love thee best, O most best, believe it.
>
> (II, ii, 119–21)

When, his world shattered, he came to her in the scene she recounts to Polonius, he was speechless and, though he frightened her, he also, as her mode of telling shows, drew out all her sympathy. But when he actually confronts her on stage, he has translated her into a whore, like Gertrude, and he is only too articulate, in a language which is meaningless and yet desperately hurtful to her—one to which she might well have responded in Desdemona's words:

> I understand a fury in your words,
> But not the words.[29]
>
> (*Othello*, IV, ii, 32–3)

Hamlet's vision of Ophelia has changed with his vision of the world. The language to be spoken to her is that current in a world where frailty is the name of woman, love equals appetite, vows are "as false as dicers' oaths" (III, iv, 45), and nothing is constant. It is a terrible coincidence, and a masterly dramatic stroke, that before Hamlet and Ophelia meet within this vision, Laertes and Polonius have been speaking the same language to her, articulating out of their worldly wisdom much the same view of their love as the one Hamlet has arrived at through his shock of revulsion from the world. In I, iii, while Hamlet off-stage goes to meet the Ghost, Ophelia meets with equally shattering (to her world) commands from her father, attacking her past, present and future relations with Hamlet.

Laertes is made to open the attack, all the more insidiously since it is by way of well-meaning brotherly advice, and since it is phrased in the idiom of the courtly "songs" to which he is reducing Hamlet's love:

> For Hamlet, and the trifling of his favour,
> Hold it a fashion and a toy in the blood,
> A violet in the youth of primy nature,
> Forward not permanent, sweet not lasting,
> The perfume and suppliance of a minute.

> (I, iii, 5–9)

On highly reasonable social grounds he argues that Hamlet's language must be translated:

> Then if he says he loves you,
> It fits your wisdom so far to believe it
> As he in his particular act and place
> May give his saying deed.

> (II. 24–7)

I need not point out how deeply rooted this is in the language assumptions of the play as a whole. Laertes's tone is not unkind in its knowingness; his final thrust has some of the ineluctable sadness of the Sonnets when contemplating examples of the precariousness of youth and beauty—

> Virtue itself scapes not calumnious strokes;
> The canker galls the infants of the spring

Too oft before their buttons be disclos'd;
And in the morn and liquid dew of youth
Contagious blastments are most imminent—

(II. 38–42)

and Ophelia, as her spirited reply suggests, is on the whole able to
cope with both the matter and the manner of his preaching. But
when Polonius picks up the attack, it is different. His technique is
far more devastating: an interrogation where each answer is
rapidly demolished. Ophelia does not have the speech-habits of
most of the other characters; she is brief, simple and direct—and
therefore particularly vulnerable. In a play where rhetorical units
of measurement may be "forty thousand brothers," there is a
moving literalness about her statement that Hamlet has "given
countenance to his speech . . . /With *almost* all the holy vows of
heaven." She does not have the worldy wisdom to produce translations which protect her feelings and hide her thoughts. So to
Polonius's opening question—"What is't, Ophelia, he hath said to
you?"—she simply, and vainly, tries to be non-specific:

So please you, something touching the Lord Hamlet.

(I. 89)

Some fifteen lines later her confidence is already undermined:

I do not know, my lord, what I should think.

Polonius's method is particularly undermining in that he lets
Ophelia provide the keywords which he then picks up and translates by devaluing them—painfully literally so when Ophelia's
"many tenders/Of his affection" provokes:

. . . think yourself a baby
That you have ta'en these tenders for true pay
Which are not sterling.

(II. 105–7)

His translation is partly a matter of devaluation by direct sneer
("think" and "fashion" are thus dealt with), partly a matter of
using the ambiguities of the English language to shift the meanings of words (thus "tender" is translated into the language of
finance and "entreatment" into that of diplomacy); and partly a

dizzifying matter of making one meaning slide into another by a
pun. In this last way Hamlet's vows are translated, first into
finance, then into religion—

> Do not believe his vows; for they are brokers,
> Not of that dye which their investments show,
> But mere implorators of unholy suits,
> Breathing like sanctified and pious bonds—
>
> (II. 127–30)

but always in proof of their falsehood: "The better to beguile."
What supplies the power of Polonius's words is also a logic which,
like Iago's, strikes at the root of the victim's hold on reality:

> You do not understand yourself so clearly
> As it behoves my daughter and your honour;
>
> (II. 96–7)

and which has a kind of general empirical truth—such as in the
comedies might have been spoken by a sensible and normative
heroine:

> I do know,
> When the blood burns, how prodigal the soul
> Lends the tongue vows.
>
> (II. 115–17)

By the end of the scene, Polonius's words have left Ophelia
with no hold on her love and with nothing to say but "I shall obey,
my lord."[30] When there is no one left even to obey, she will go to
pieces. But before then she has to be pushed to the limit by
Hamlet's verbal brutality which doubly frightens and hurts her
because it seems to prove both that Hamlet is mad and that
Polonius was right. A first and last intimation of the intimacy and
tenderness which might once have prevailed in their dialogues
rings out of her greeting to Hamlet in the nunnery scene—

> Good my lord,
> How does your honour for this many a day?—

but by the end of that scene there is not even a dialogue. The two
of them are speaking *about* each other, Hamlet's stream-of-con-
sciousness circling around nuns and painted harlots and Ophelia

appealing, twice, to an invisible and silent audience: "O, help him, you sweet heavens!" and "O heavenly powers, restore him!" She is left to speak her only soliloquy over the ruins of what used to be her reality, and to lament the most terrible translation of all: "the honey of his music vows" is now "like sweet bells jangled, out of time and harsh."

Hamlet and Ophelia no longer speak the same language. I dwelt at some length on the Polonius–Ophelia scene because it brings out, ironically and indirectly, an important aspect of the "tainting" of Hamlet. Though he does not know it, and would hate to be told so, his language has moved away from Ophelia's and towards Polonius's. It is a language based on the general idea of "woman" rather than a specific awareness of Ophelia (to whom he now listens only to score verbal points off her, usually bawdy ones, too). Even his technique is like Polonius's as he picks up words only to demolish them, and her. Thus, in perhaps the cruellest stretch of dialogue in the whole play, Ophelia is allowed, briefly, to think that she knows what Hamlet means, only to have this understanding taken from her:

> *Hamlet.* . . . I did love you once.
> *Ophelia.* Indeed, my lord, you made me believe so.
> *Hamlet.* You should not have believ'd me; for virtue cannot so inoculate our old stock but we shall relish of it. I loved you not.
> *Ophelia.* I was the more deceived.
> (III, i, 115–20)

Polonius turned her into an object, an instrument, by "loosing" her to Hamlet in the nunnery scene; Hamlet turns her into a thing—as "unworthy a thing" as he ever may accuse Rosencrantz and Guildenstern of attempting to make out of him—in the play scene where, in public and listening to a play which from her point of view must seem to be mainly about women's inconstancy and sexual promiscuity, she is all but sexually assaulted by Hamlet's language.[31] We have no evidence that Hamlet ever thinks of her again before he discovers that the grave he has watched being dug is that of "the fair Ophelia," and no redeeming recognition that the power of his own words has helped to drive her into that grave. In their story speech functions, in the end, as part of a vision of man's proneness to kill the thing he loves.

So we seem in the end to be left with a long row of contradictions: Hamlet's use of language is sensitive and brutal; he listens and he does not listen; his speech is built on sympathy and on total disregard of other selves; his relationship with words is his greatest strength and his greatest weakness. Only a Claudius could pretend that these are not contradictions and only he could translate them into a simple unity. Hamlet's soliloquies are not much help to this end. Even they speak different languages and add up, if anything, to a representation of a man searching for a language for the experiences which are forcing themselves upon him, finding it now in the free flow of I-centered exclamations of "O, that this too too solid flesh would melt," now in the formally structured and altogether generalized questions and statements of "To be, or not to be." It is tempting to hear in Hamlet's self-analytical speeches a progression towards clarity, reaching its goal in the fusion of the individual and the general, of simple form and complex thought, in the speech about defying augury—

> If it be now, 'tis not to come; if it be not to come, it will be
> now; if it be not now, yet it will come—the readiness is all—

and coming to rest on "Let be." It is tempting because many Jacobean tragic heroes and heroines were to go through such a progression, through tortured and verbally elaborate attempts at definition of their vision of life to simple statements of—as in Herbert's poem "Prayer"—"something understood." But to me this seems too smooth a curve, too cathartic a movement, more indicative of critics' need to experience the peace which Hamlet himself happily appears to gain at the end than of the true impact of the language of the play as a whole. That impact is surely much closer to the sense that for a complex personality in an impossible situation—and in "situation" I include a number of difficult human relationships—there is no single language. This does not mean that the play ultimately sees speech as meaningless, or that Shakespeare (or even Hamlet) is finally trapped in a disillusionist attitude to language. It means that we are given a very wide demonstration of the power of words to express and communicate—it is, after all, words which tell Horatio and us even that "the rest is silence"—but also, and at the same time, an intimation that there is something inexpressible and incommunicable at the heart of the play.

Shakespeare—whatever the true facts of the *Ur-Hamlet*—must have seen himself as producing a new "translation" of what the title page of the second Quarto describes as "The Tragicall History of Hamlet, Prince of Denmark." Like Gertrude's translation, in IV, i, it meant both changing and interpreting his raw material. Like Gertrude, he concentrated on the speech and deeds of the prince, and their ramifications, merging any personal pressure of experience in a concern for communicating with an audience. The analogy ends here, for Gertrude was, even like Hamlet himself, only part of his translation—a translation which T. S. Eliot criticized for trying to "express the inexpressibly horrible."[32] To me the final greatness of the play lies just there: in its power to express so much and yet also to call a halt on the edge of the inexpressible where, to misquote Claudius, we must learn to say "'Tis fit we do not understand." This, I think, is the hallmark of Shakespeare as a translator, into tragedy, of the human condition.

NOTES

1. Lawrence Danson, *Tragic Alphabet: Shakespeare's Drama of Language* (New Haven and London, 1974), p. 48; John Paterson, "The Word in *Hamlet*," *Shakespeare Quarterly*, 2 (1951), 47.
2. Though Gertrude herself does not use the verb "harrow," I use it advisedly, as it seems to be a *Hamlet* word. It occurs once in *Coriolanus*, in its literal sense, but Shakespeare's only two metaphorical uses of it are in *Hamlet*: by the Ghost (I, v, 16) and by Horatio describing the impact of the Ghost (I, i, 44).
3. *A Doll's House*, act III (*Et dukkehjem*, in *Henrik Ibsens Samlede Verker*, Oslo, 1960, II, 474).
4. Some other examples of "translated" versions of an episode we have already seen are: Rosencrantz and Guildenstern's slanted report, in III, i, 4 ff., of their meeting with Hamlet in II, ii; Polonius's to Claudius and Gertrude, in II, ii, 130 ff., of how he admonished Ophelia in I, iii; and Polonius's attempt to bolster up Claudius, in III, iii, 30 ff., by attributing to him his own plan hatched at III, i, 184–5. Signifi-

cantly, at the end of the nunnery scene Polonius and Claudius
specifically do not want a report from Ophelia: "We heard it all"
(III, i, 180).

5. That is, in the punctuation of modern editors (e.g. Alexander and
Dover Wilson). In Q 2 Hamlet says "a Rat," and Gertrude "a Rat,
a Rat,"; in F 1 the readings are, respectively, "a Rat?" and "a Rat,
a Rat."

6. As Dover Wilson points out in his note on "a weeps for what is
done," "the falsehood testifies to her fidelity" (New Cambridge
Shakespeare, Hamlet, 1934, p. 218).

7. See A Midsummer Night's Dream, III, i, 109; Hamlet, III, i, 113; The Merry
Wives, I, iii, 47; 2 Henry IV, IV, i, 46–8; Troilus and Cressida, IV, v, 112.

8. The OED, for example, uses both Claudius's line and the one from
The Merry Wives to illustrate the meaning "to interpret, explain"
("Translate" 11.3. fig.)

9. After Babel: Aspects of Language and Translation (1975), p. 47 (Dr. Steiner's
italics).

10. See Discoveries, 128, and Henry James, The Question of Our Speech (Boston and New York, 1905), p. 10 and p. 21.

11. Alfred Hart, "Vocabularies of Shakespeare's Plays," Review of English
Studies 19 (1943), 128–40, and "The Growth of Shakespeare's Vocabulary," ibid., 242–43. The subject was freshly illuminated in the paper
on "New Words between Henry IV and Hamlet" given by Professor
Marvin Spevack at the Seventeenth International Shakespeare Con-
ference in Stratford-upon-Avon, August 1976, and by the booklet of
word lists which he distributed in connection with his paper.

12. T. W. Baldwin, William Shakspere's Small Latine and Lesse Greeke, 2 vols.
(Urbana, Ill., 1944), passim; and Sister Miriam Joseph, Shakespeare's Use
of the Arts of Language (New York, 1947), esp. p. 12.

13. W. B. Yeats, "A Coat." (Collected Poems, 1933, p. 142.)

14. Discoveries 132 (Oratio imago animi).

15. "Ear" and "ears" occur, together, 24 (16 + 8) times. The second
largest figure is for Coriolanus: 17 (3 + 14) times. The different
lengths, in lines, make comparisons somewhat unreliable; though
Coriolanus is less than 500 lines shorter than Hamlet, and King Lear,
with 3,205 lines as against Hamlet's 3,762, has only 5 (4 + 1) occurrences of "ear" and "ears." (I take my figures for lengths in lines
from Hart, "Vocabularies of Shakespeare's Plays," and for word
frequencies from Marvin Spevack's Harvard Concordance to Shakespeare,
Cambridge, Mass., 1973).

16. As Professor A. C. Sprague has pointed out to me, G. L. Kittredge
exploded the idea (still adhered to by Dover Wilson; see his note on
I, i, 42) that this line refers to the fact that exorcisms of spirits were

usually performed in Latin. "Horatio, as a scholar, knows how to address the apparition in the right way, so as neither to offend it nor to subject himself to any evil influence." (G. L. Kittredge, ed., *Sixteen Plays of Shakespeare* (Boston, 1939), p. 1021.)

17. Danson, *Tragic Alphabet*, p. 26, has some excellent comments on Claudius's use of the oxymoron.

18. Sigurd Burckhardt, *Shakespearean Meanings* (Princeton, N.J., 1968), pp. 24-5, quoted also by Danson, p. 27, n. 2.

19. See note 10, above.

20. Claudius wonders whether there is not "rain enough in the sweet heavens" to wash his "cursed hand . . . white as snow," and he associates innocence with a "new-born babe."

21. Marvin Spevack has a very interesting discussion of how Hamlet's imagery shows him transforming all he sees, and how he is thus isolated by speaking, as it were, a foreign language; see "Hamlet and Imagery: The Mind's Eye," *Die Neueren Sprachen*, n.s. v (1966), 203-12.

22. R. A. Foakes, "*Hamlet* and the Court of Elsinore," *Shakespeare Survey*, 9 (Cambridge, 1956), pp. 35-43.

23. R. A. Foakes, "Character and Speech in *Hamlet*," in *Hamlet: Stratford-upon-Avon Studies 5* (1963), 161.

24. *Middlemarch*, end of chap. 21 (Penguin ed., p. 243).

25. For a conspectus of these, see Dover Wilson's note on V, ii, 230, and the Furness *Variorum* edition of *Hamlet*, I, 440. Dr. Johnson wished that Hamlet "had made some other defence; it is unsuitable to the character of a brave or good man to shelter himself in falsehood"; and Seymour believed that the passage was an interpolation: "The falsehood contained in it is too ignoble."

26. *Shakespeare's Plutarch*, ed. T. J. B. Spencer in the Penguin Shakespeare Library (Harmondsworth, 1964), p. 203. Cleopatra, it is pointed out, differs from "divers of her progenitors, the Kings of Egypt," who "could scarce learn the Egyptian tongue only."

27. A. C. Bradley, *Shakespearean Tragedy* (paperback ed., 1955, p. 109, note), finds it strange that while everyone at court "sees in the play-scene a gross and menacing insult to the King," no one "shows any sign in perceiving in it also an accusation of murder." Dover Wilson, in his note on III, ii, 243, points out that "Hamlet arranges *two* meanings to the Play, one for the King (and Horatio), the other for the rest of the spectators, who see a king being murdered by his nephew."

28. Kenneth Muir, *Shakespeare's Tragic Sequence* (1972), p. 57.

29. I have discussed some aspects of Ophelia's and Desdemona's language, especially the way in which the hero and the heroine in these tragedies become unable to speak the same language, in a short

paper to the Second International Shakespeare Congress, held in Washington, D.C., in April 1976.

30. To "obey" (which is of course also what Hamlet promises his mother in I, ii, 120) is a troublesome matter in Shakespearean tragedy. Cf. *Othello*, I, iii, 180 and *King Lear*, I, i, 97.

31. I have found Nigel Alexander's study of Hamlet, *Poison, Play and Duel* (1971), esp. chap. 5, "The Power of Beauty," the most illuminating analysis of Hamlet's relationship with Ophelia.

32. "Hamlet and His Problems," in *Selected Essays* (New York, 1932), p. 126.

PART 5:
The Theatre

Samuel Pepys

From *Diary and Correspondence,*
August 31, 1668

To the Duke of York's playhouse . . . and saw *Hamlet*, which we have not seen this year before, or more; and mightily pleased with it, but, above all, with Betterton, the best part, I believe, that ever man acted.

Mr. Mackenzie

From *The Mirror*, April 22, 1780

That gaiety and playfulness of deportment and of conversation which *Hamlet* sometimes not only assumes, but seems actually disposed to, is, I apprehend, no contradiction to the general tone of melancholy in his character. That sort of melancholy which is the most genuine as well as the most amiable of any, neither arising from natural sourness of temper, nor prompted by accidental chagrin, but the effect of delicate sensibility, impressed with a sense of sorrow, or a feeling of its own weakness, will, I believe, often be found indulging itself in a sportfulness of external behaviour, amidst the pressure of a fad, or even the anguish of a broken heart. Slighter emotions affect our ordinary discourse; but deep distress, sitting in the secret gloom of the soul, casts not its regard on the common occurrences of life, but suffers them to trick themselves out in the usual garb of indifference, or of gaiety, according to the fashion of the society around it, or the situation in which they chance to arise. The melancholy man feels in himself (if I may be allowed the expression) a sort of double person; one that, covered with the darkness of its imagination, looks not forth into the world, nor takes any concern in vulgar objects or frivolous pursuits; another, which he lends, as it were, to ordinary men, which can accommodate itself to their tempers and manners, and indulge, without feeling any degradation from the indulgence, a smile with the chearful, and a laugh with the giddy.

The conversation of *Hamlet* with the *Grave-digger* seems to me to be perfectly accounted for, under this supposition; and, instead of feeling it counteract the tragic effect of the story, I never see him in that scene, without receiving, from his transient jests with the clown before him, an idea of the deepest melancholy being rooted at his heart. The light point of view in which he places serious and important things, marks the power of that great impression, which swallows up every thing else in his mind, which makes *Caesar* and *Alexander* so indifferent to him, that he can trace their remains in the plaster of a cottage, or the stopper of a beer-barrel. It is from the same turn of mind, which, from the elevation of its sorrows, looks down on the bustle of ambition, and the pride of fame, that he breaks forth into the reflection in the 4th act, on the expedition of *Fortinbras*.

It is with regret, as well as deference, that I accuse the judgement of Mr. *Garrick*, or the taste of his audience; but I cannot help thinking, that the exclusion of the scene of the *Grave-digger*, in his alteration of the tragedy of *Hamlet*, was not only a needless, but an unnatural violence done to the work of his favourite poet.

Shakespeare's genius attended him in all his extravagancies. In the licence he took of departing from the regularity of the drama, or in his ignorance of those critical rules which might have restrained him within it, there is this advantage, that it gives him an opportunity of delineating the passions and affections of the human mind, as they exist in reality, with all the various colourings which they receive in the mixed scenes of life; not as they are accommodated, by the hands of more artificial poets, to one great undivided impression, or an uninterrupted chain of congenial events. It seems, therefore, preposterous, to endeavour to regularize his plays, at the expence of depriving them of this peculiar excellence, especially as the alteration can only produce a very partial and limited improvement, and can never bring his pieces to the standard of criticism, or the form of the *Aristotelian* drama. Within the bounds of a pleasure-garden, we may be allowed to smooth our terrasses and trim our hedge-rows; but it were equally absurd and impracticable to apply the minute labours of the *roller* and the *pruning-knife*, to the noble irregularity of trackless mountains and impenetrable forests.

Thomas Davies

From *Dramatic Miscellanies*

Hamlet's address to the ghost, in this act, is justly esteemed one of those situations in which the actor of merit may display, to the full, his greatest abilities.—Taylor was the original performer of Hamlet; and his excellences, in that character, were so remarkable, that, from the remembrance of them, Sir William Davenant taught Betterton a lesson which gained him universal and lasting reputation. His manner of address to the vision is recorded, by Cibber, in language so lively and terms so apposite, that the reader will not be displeased to see them quoted here:

"He opened the scene with a pause of mute amazement; then, rising slowly to a solemn, trembling, voice, he made the Ghost equally terrible to the spectator and himself; and, in the descriptive part of the natural emotions which the ghastly vision gave him, the boldness of his expostulation was still governed by decency; manly, but not braving; his voice never rising to that seeming outrage or wild defiance of what he naturally revered." And in this manner our late admirable Roscius addressed the vision.

Mr. Macklin, whose judgement merits the utmost deference, differs in his opinion, respecting the behaviour of Hamlet to the Ghost, from Betterton and Garrick. With pleasure I have heard him recite the speech of Hamlet to the Ghost, which he did with much force and energy. After the short ejaculation of "Angels and ministers of grace, defend us!" he endeavoured to conquer that fear and terror into which he was naturally thrown by the first sight of the vision, and uttered the remainder of the address calmly, but respectfully, and with a firm tone of voice, as from one who had subdued his timidity and apprehension. Mr. Henderson, a most judicious actor and accurate speaker, seems to have embraced a method not unlike that of Mr. Macklin.

How far tradition may be permitted to govern, in this question, I will not say: but Downs, the stage-historian, in his peculiar phrase, informs us, "That Mr. Betterton took every particle of Hamlet from Sir William Davenant, who had seen Mr. Taylor, who was taught by Mr. Shakspeare himself."

If we give credit to Downs, we must grant that the author was the best interpreter of his own meaning. Nor can I, indeed, conceive, that any sudden resolution, on the appearance of so questionable a shape as the vision of a dead father, can so far support a son as to be free from terror and affright. It is not in nature to assume such courage as will withstand a sight so awful and tremendous.

Towards the close of Hamlet's speech, the words themselves are strongly expressive of the uncommon impression still remaining on his mind:

> And we, fools of nature,
> So horridly to shake our disposition
> With thoughts beyond the reaches of our souls.

Colley Cibber, when in company with Mr. Addison at the tragedy of Hamlet, tells us, that they were both surprised at the vociferous manner in which Wilks spoke to the Ghost. This was greatly censured by them both, and with justice; for awe and terror will never excite a loud and intemperate exertion of the voice.

Wilks was so far mistaken, in this treatment of Hamlet's Ghost, that Booth, one day at rehearsal, reproached him for it. "I thought," said he, "Bob, that last night you wanted to play at fisty-cuffs with me: you bullied that which you ought to have revered. When I acted the Ghost with Betterton, instead of my awing him, he terrified me. But divinity hung round that man!" To this rebuke, Wilks, with his usual modesty, replied,—"Mr. Betterton and Mr. Booth could always act as they pleased: he, for his part, must do as well as he could."

The Ghost, though not meanly represented since the time of Booth, has never been equal to the action of that comedian. His slow, solemn, and under, tone of voice, his noiseless tread, as if he had been composed of air, and his whole deportment, inspired the audience with that feeling which is excited by awful astonishment! The impression of his appearance in this part was so powerful, upon a constant frequenter of the theatres for near sixty years, that he assured me, when, long after Booth's death, he was present at the tragedy of Hamlet, as soon as the name of the Ghost was announced on the stage, he felt a kind of awe and terror, "of which," said he, "I was soon cured by his appearance." Quin, who loved and admired Booth, some years before he left the stage, to oblige his old friend, Ryan, acted the Ghost with the approbation of the public, and as near to the manner of his old master as he possibly could.

****

In the delineation of Polonius's character, two great writers, Dr. Warburton and Dr. Johnson, differ widely. The first makes him a weak man and a pedantic statesman. The other places him in a much superior rank: with him, Polonius is a man who has been bred in courts, exercised in business, stored with observations, confident of his knowledge, proud of his eloquence, but declining into dotage; in short, it is by the advance of age alone that Dr. Johnson solves the seeming inconsistency in the conduct of Polonius. The whole argument is elaborately written; but I cannot submit to that decision, which pronounces that this statesman was ever strong in intellect or eloquent in discourse. There is but one passage in the play which favours the supposed dereliction of this man's faculties; and that is, in the instructions he gives his servant, in the 1st scene of the 2d act, relating to his observations of his son's conduct; but, in the recapitulation of precepts, or maxims, independent of each other, and where there is no concatenation of reasoning, a very young, as well as an old, man may easily suffer a lapse of memory. In all other situations of the character, he is ever ready and furnished with such materials as are suited to his incapacity and presumption. His logic and rhetoric, to prove that Hamlet is in love with his daughter, are sufficiently flowing, and, though weak and absurd, betray no declension of his faculties. Such powers of mind as Polonius ever had he seems to enjoy with vigour; and can boast, with Charon, the *cruda viridisque senectus,*—While the body remains unhurt, by disease or outward accident, the mind, by being kept in continual exercise, stretches its faculties, and improves more and more. I could produce instances in Tully and Bacon; and, with still more propriety, in Sophocles and Bishop Hoadley. But why need I go farther than Dr. Johnson himself? He is advanced some years above the age of seventy, without the least symptom of intellectual decay. Is not his last work, of the Critical and Biographical Prefaces, equal to any book he hath written?

****

The constant practice of the stage, from the revival of Hamlet, soon after the Restoration, to this day, may perhaps contribute to justify my opinion of this character. Polonius was always acted by what is termed a low comedian: By Lovell, Nokes, and Cross, in former times; who were succeeded by Griffin, Hippisley, Taswell, and Shuter; and these again by Wilson, Baddeley, and Edwin, in the present times.

Charles Shattuck

From *The Hamlet of Edwin Booth*

Hamlet opened on Wednesday, January 5, 1870. It played five nights and a Saturday matinee each week for a total of sixty-four performances, and closed on Saturday, March 19. From first to last it was immensely popular. Seats were booked two weeks in advance, and except on extremely wintry nights the sign "Only Standing Room Left" was regularly hung up at the box office. "Not to have seen *Hamlet* will be an unenviable distinction," observed a reporter to the *Telegram* (January 29);[1] during this 1870 run well in excess of 100,000 persons did see it.

The only serious competition that turned up seems to have done it no harm at the box office—the appearance of Charles Fechter, whose "modern" Hamlet had delighted London nine years earlier. His American visit had been heralded for months. The August issue of the *Atlantic Monthly* had carried a glowing introduction of him by Charles Dickens, as if his coming were a cultural event of extraordinary importance, and the New York critics anticipated hungrily the contest of "the actor who has taken the first rank in the Old World with the one who holds so securely the esteem of the new." Booth, who did not care for contests, had invited Fechter to play at Booth's Theatre—even to play Hamlet there on alternate nights in Booth's own settings; but Fechter, more cunning than wise, declined the invitation on the grounds that he was committed to perform at Niblo's.[2] There during his first four weeks he confined himself to modern plays—

Reprinted from *The Hamlet of Edwin Booth*, pp. 67–71, by Charles Shattuck (1969), by permission of University of Illinois Press.

459

Hugo's *Ruy Blas* from January 10 and Brougham's *The Duke's Motto* from January 26. Rumor persisted that he might yet go to Booth's for *Hamlet*, but nothing came of it, and beginning on February 14 he gave a single week of *Hamlet* to conclude his Niblo's engagement. His performance attracted ardent partisans, of course, but in limited numbers; the bulk of critical and popular support remained with Booth, whose reputation and profit were rather enhanced than diminished by the unsought-for competition.

Another sort of competition which sprang up was flattering and delightful. As *Hamlet*-fever swept the town, the clowns came forward with *Hamlet* burlesques. The best of these was George Fox's at the Olympic. Fox made up his face to resemble Booth's, and the more exactly and earnestly he imitated Booth's melancholy, the more hilarious was the effect. Booth's production had been much paragraphed for its "wintriness," especially as reflected in its heavy costumes, so that Fox garbed himself in a gigantic fur-collared overcoat, enormous mittens, and Arctic overshoes. His First Actor was a stage Irishman. His Actress was a fat blond woman six feet tall. The duel was fought with parasols. Booth himself always enjoyed Fox's burlesques, and his daughter Edwina recalls his particular delight in this spoof of *Hamlet*.[3] Other burlesques included Tony Pastor's at his theatre in the Bowery; Dan Bryant's minstrel-show version featuring the perennially favorite silly song "Shoo Fly, Don't Bother Me";[4] and a pair of theatrical pugilists, Jem Morse and John Heenan, who performed the duel as a boxing match.

That Booth withdrew *Hamlet* in mid-March was something of a puzzler to the town, for its popularity had not at all abated and it could obviously have outlasted the old record of a hundred nights, and probably have run to the end of the season. Booth gave out the excuse (obviously specious) that he was committed to producing certain other works. To William Winter he confided his real reason: "I do not wish to surfeit the *dear pub* with it—as it is my standby & must be done a little each season."[5] The nightly expenses were very high too, he noted, and if he could bring in full houses to less costly performances the profit would be greater. He was still under the illusion that he could one day pay for Booth's Theatre.

First Testimonials, Including Some Words from
William Shakespeare

The audience on the opening night was enormous, and no one present could have failed to be aware that the event was a historic one. Crowds swarmed through the aisles and lobbies before curtain time, and once the play began the *Evening Post* reporter counted standees seven rows deep. "Beauty and fashion mingled and glittered in the brilliant crowd," according to the *Tribune*, and a correspondent to the *Atlas* (January 8) reckoned from the vast number of high-polished bald heads that "intellect" was well represented too. Fechter and his leading lady Carlotta Leclercq, who had just arrived in town, were guests in Booth's own box; Fechter applauded generously and often, and the audience, who recognized him, were pleased that he was pleased. When Booth appeared at the opening of the second scene, he was greeted with the expectable ovation. "It was many moments before he could make his voice heard," said the *Home Journal* (January 12); "he stood, with pale face and glowing eyes, clad in the mourning garb of the Danish prince, inclining his head slightly with stately grace, but not for an instant separating himself from the part he had assumed." He was summoned for applause at the end of every act, and finally a speech was called for, but he gave none. The performance lasted past midnight.

To celebrate the event the reviewers spared no hyperboles. "In the production of Hamlet last night," said the *Post*, "the most admired actor and manager on the American stage achieved the greatest triumph he has yet known." To the *Herald* critic, it was "a genuine feast of reason, of beauty . . . of histrionic intelligence and splendor. . . . It was, in fact, just such a treat as 'professionals' and critical old playgoers would almost risk the shortening of their span of life to enjoy." The boldest writers favored an international gambit. "Outside the Grand Opera House of Paris," said the critic of the *Globe*, "we may well doubt if the world has seen the equal of that which thousands had the pleasure of seeing last night." The *Home Journal* declared it "a magnificent honor, not only to the American stage, but to the drama of the entire civilized world," and, overleaping time as well as oceans, found it "doubtful if any future attempt can greatly surpass it." Sentimentality and self-gratulation united to produce this pretty whimsy in the *Spirit of the Times* (January 8):[6] "For us there was but one drawback to the pleasure of the occasion—this was a regret that Shakespeare in his life could not have seen his play so produced; the resources of the stage in his day were bare indeed. Yet if his spirit did not hover delightedly over the battlements of the castle scene, and walk among the trees and tombs of the churchyard when the body of Ophelia was given to the earth, 'tis only because a sad tyranny is exercized in the other world."

But Shakespeare *was* there, wonderful to relate, and the *Leader* (January 8), achieving a first-rate scoop, published a long statement from him, dated "Dramatic Sphere, Spiritual World, Jan. 7th," and communicated by way of a medium identified as "O.K."[7] The statement was addressed to Booth, and its burden is Shakespeare's insistence that "from the rising of the curtain until the going down thereof, you are *my* Hamlet. . . . You are my young, quick-witted, ready-tongued, psychical, impassioned, emotion-swayed Prince. Of whom it may be said as an elegy—I quote from my brother Gray—'And Melancholy marked him for her own.'" Often before this, Shakespeare says, he has wanted to communicate with the living world, but he has waited for the proper time and the proper man. He wishes the modern public to understand that when as "a member of the most worshipful fraternity of player folks" he had worked over the play of *Hamlet*, it had *not* been one of his favorites. It was not an original work. He had not given it much thought, had not even looked into its documentary backgrounds—indeed, in those days he had never heard of Saxo or Belleforest. He was in fact only recarpentering an old play of Thomas Kyd's. But as the generations have passed until the present time, when one can find so many young Hamlets at the Cambridges of England and Massachusetts, he has come to appreciate how much of humanity is caught up in it, so that he thinks better of it now than he used to do.

Shakespeare has a very low regard for most of the closet critics of *Hamlet*, past and present: "Many of my so-called beauties have been only the complacencies of writers who wished to wrap themselves in the habiliments of my fame." The moguls of criticism, from Johnson to Guizot, he dismisses as pretentious obfuscators or deifiers of self. He mentions articles in nine or ten contemporary magazines which he thinks may have amused Booth, but are worth no more. He does approve of two writers, William Maginn and Richard Grant White, whose scholarship is sane and whose heartiness and affinity to the theatre match his own. But the Hamlet of the closet is not, for the most part, *his* Hamlet.

He allows that Hamlet on the stage has fared somewhat more successfully: Betterton and Kemble, at least, came close to the mark. But most stage Hamlets, too, have been all wrong: "I have seen men essay acting their own Hamlets; but they were monstrously bothered with my words. They were perpetually kicking with rhetorical gyves on!" The worst of them all was William Charles Macready, who was "freaky," a sort of elocutionary ropedancer. Whatever else may be said of Edwin Forrest, Shakespeare is indebted to him for having hissed Macready's Hamlet at Edinburgh. He thanks Booth, in passing, for the scenic production. The play has been "equally well propertied on the stage in England, but never better." And, of course, "in my day, all the machinery of scenic effect, this variety of property and the combinations of science which on the modern stage come to aid my illustrations of men and manners, were utterly undreamed of."

NOTES

1. The first reviews (daily newspapers) appeared on Thursday, January 6. Reviews in the weeklies appeared on January 8 and 9, and a vast number more appeared throughout the run. When quoting the reviews I have regularly given the date of issue except for the morning-after ones. When the date is not given, it may be assumed to be January 6.
2. A letter from Fechter excusing himself from the invitation is in Booth's souvenir letterbook at The Players.
3. Edwina Booth Grossman, *Edwin Booth* (New York, 1894), p. 15.
4. A folksong or minstrel-show song which had been popular from Civil War days. See Vance Randolph, *Ozark Folksongs* (New York, 1946–50), II, 352.
5. Booth to William Winter. The Folger Shakespeare Library, Y.c. 215 (212).

6. The *Spirit of the Times* carried two major reviews, both perhaps guest-written. This one of January 8 praises the production in nearly every point; the one of February 5, almost certainly written by Nym Crinkle, though beginning with an acknowledgment of the "beautiful and artistically exact presentment," is mainly hostile.

7. Apparently this letter from Shakespeare to Booth was updated from an earlier psychic transmission. William Stuart quoted a scrap from it in his advertisements for the Winter Garden *Hamlet*. See the *Times*, December 24, 1864.

Henry Irving

From "An Actor's Notes on Shakespeare"

The riddle of this scene [Act III, Scene 1] may be read in many ways, and in attempting to give any idea of its interpretation I do so with all reverence and modesty, believing that an honest confession of one's thoughts on such a subject may be received at any rate with some interest, if not with assent.

The first point, and one upon which differences of stage business have often turned, is whether Hamlet knew throughout the scene that he was watched by the King and Polonius. It is all enacted under espial. The interview between Hamlet and Ophelia is contrived. Is he conscious of this from the outset, or does he discover it in the course of the scene?

The text tells us that he knew he was being watched from the first, for in the quartos of 1603 and 1604 (the complete play) Hamlet enters before the *exeunt* words of Polonius to the King— "Let's withdraw, my lord"—catches sight of them as they retire "into the study" (an ante-room leading from the hall), and evidently guesses them to be intent on eaves-dropping. We know, besides, that the King had sent for him, and that he was quite shrewd enough to suspect some design. No doubt his mind is much preoccupied—preoccupied, too, with sublimer matters, and unlikely to be greatly fretted for the moment by any incident which he would regard as despicable. His thoughts on death reveal the bent, the tension, and the gravity of the mood in which he is when he observes the significant withdrawal of the King and Polonius, but when aware of the presence of Ophelia all else is banished from his consciousness. It is therefore not only conceivable but probable that the circumstances which indicated a set design to spy upon him fell at first on an only half-awakened sense, and that the fact, though clear, but faintly lingered in his mind beneath the surface of his nobler contemplations. It is when he perceives the spies that he remembers he is watched.

The second point of interest is whether Ophelia knew that her father and the King were eaves-droppers. Superficially this may be assumed, and allowance may be made for a girl under the influence of deep and anxious affection, whose first personal desire must have been to ascertain the present feelings of a man who had been her lover. But there is nothing in the text or stage directions that convicts Ophelia of actual complicity. Her feeling was probably somewhat vague and confused, especially as she would not be taken more into confidence than was necessary. Much that was said in the preceding interview between the Queen, the King, and Polonius might have been spoken apart from Ophelia, the room in the castle being probably a large one, in which a knot of talkers might not be overheard by a preoccupied person. When suggestions of this sort are condemned as over-refined, it is, I think, too often forgotten that it must be settled between stage managers and players in every case how the latter are to dispose themselves when on the stage; that Shakspeare himself must have very much affected the complexion of his plays by his personal directions; that the most suggestive, and therefore most valuable, of these have been lost; and that in reproducing old plays, in which there is much scope and even great necessity for subtle indications of this kind, nothing can be too refined which intelligibly conveys to an audience a rational idea of each individuality and a consistent theory of the whole.

That Ophelia burns with a desire to meet Hamlet, and that her thoughts are full of the meeting she expects, we can well believe. I would suggest as the natural and desirable course of things, in order to limit in the most probable manner Ophelia's share in the transaction, that after Polonius says to her "Walk you here," his words, "Gracious, so please you we will bestow ourselves," should be spoken to the King aside. If this be so accepted, there is no other evidence that Ophelia was fully possessed of the nature of the plot, though she knew that the interview with Hamlet was devised. The words addressed by the King to the Queen previously, in explanation of this plan—

> Her father and myself (lawful espials)
> Will so bestow ourselves, that, seeing, unseen,
> We may of their encounter frankly judge—

do not sound as if intended to be heard by Ophelia, and suggest that it was part of the project to observe both the lovers unawares. Note, also, how unlikely it is that Polonius, after directing his daughter to colour her loneliness by reading a book of devotion (perhaps hanging from her girdle), would utter in her hearing the cynical words which follow:—

> We are oft to blame in this—
> 'Tis too much proved—that with devotion's visage
> And pious action we do sugar o'er
> The devil himself.

When we consider the poignant "aside" of the King thereupon—

> O, 'tis too true.
> How smart a lash that speech doth give my conscience!—

nothing can be more natural than to suppose that Polonius has turned to him from Ophelia to utter his characteristic scrap of morality. Hamlet's first address to Ophelia, "Nymph, in thy orisons be all my sins remembered!" implies that he knows what she is reading, and it is a pretty idea (suggested, I believe, by Mr. F. A. Marshall in his beautiful *Study of Hamlet*) that she may probably be at a *prie-dieu* when he catches sight of her, having, in greater seriousness than had been expected, turned her mind to prayer—praying, not merely reading, and praying not as a mere colour for loneliness, but with that sincerity which, in a maiden placed as she was, would far exceed the cold instructions of her father which prompted to action her anxiety for Hamlet's restoration to his former self.

There is nothing venturesome in the supposition that remembrances of Ophelia have mingled with the more tragical matter of Hamlet's thoughts before he meets her. He has mentioned in his soliloquy "the pangs of despised love" among the things which make death almost preferable to life; and although it is possible to take these as mere general words, it is difficult to suppose that he could have uttered them without tender thoughts of the poor girl to whom he has been compelled to appear heartless, without the power to explain the cause. Hamlet knows how deeply she must have felt this, and his sense of her pain is now revived by the flood of memories which pours upon him when he finds himself in her presence. He cannot escape. He cannot again play the madman. He stands before her the forlorn and weary, the sad and loving prince. In mere courtesy he must address her, but it is not in mere courtesy that his words are conceived. In their very accent, as in their very spirit, there is a plaintive reminiscence of the tender past.

How eagerly must poor Ophelia drink in the sweet sounds, and for a moment dream that her bright sun will shine on her again! The "pangs of despised love" will give place to a feeling of "the pity of it, the pity of it," as she reads the pale face of her lost lover, gazes into his sleepless eyes, notes the deep-shaded hollows of his cheeks, and wonders at the mystery of pain which, in a few short months of unexplained and seemingly capricious separation, has ploughed furrows on his brow. Poor Ophelia? Nay, poor Prince! Thy "golden lamp of day" is dimmed indeed.

Her response to Hamlet's first words is full of tender solicitude, and yet is quite within the limits of maidenly reserve and inferior rank: "How does your honour for this many a day?" What must be the effect of this all but mute appeal upon Hamlet? The voice of Ophelia recalls the past. He shrinks from the revival of the influence its tender tones once had upon him. No doubt the words of his vow recur to his mind. He is pledged from his memory to wipe away "all trivial fond records." His "Well, well, well" is a nervous, hurried reply, with a quick glance around as if for exit or relief. But there is none. The hour he would most have avoided has come. His choking words uttered, we may suppose him hurrying from the scene, when Ophelia's next words arrest him and compel his attention. This time it is not in appeal for compassion that she speaks. It is with maidenly dignity in the simple act of returning presents which in times past were tokens of her lover's devotion—"remembrances" that she had "longed long to redeliver." In the imbecility of helplessness, rather than with any resort to his previously assumed manner, he replies, "No, not I; I never gave you aught." And then follows Ophelia's most beautiful and heart-rending answer:

My honoured lord, you know right well you did;
And with them words of so sweet breath composed,
As made the things more rich: their perfume lost,
Take these again; for to the noble mind,
Rich gifts wax poor when givers prove unkind.

Under any circumstances such words must have wrung the very heartstrings of such a nature as Hamlet's. "There, my lord"—she presses the casket into his hands. He cannot but take it, and he can speak no word of solace to her. She is no puppet of a wooden tragedy, remember—no faint gauzy figure in the background of a stilted classic play. She is the idol of this young man's heart—a living, loving, pleading woman—fair, pure, and fascinating, with all the most thrilling memories of her lover's life trembling at her lightest breath. But he knows she is lost to him for ever. He knows, too, that he must appear to her, from the very contradictions of his case, a mere heartless trifler. It is at this point that the scene takes its sudden and violent transition. The next words are "Ha! ha! are you honest?" May we not form a rational explanation of the swiftness with which this exclamation was conceived?

In all Hamlet's assumptions of mental wandering he is greatly aided by the excitability of his temperament. His emotions are always ready to carry him away, and his wild imaginings easily lend themselves to the maddest disguises of speech. A flash of volition may often be the exponent of a chain of thought, and perhaps the action of Hamlet's mind was somewhat after this manner: He feels the woe of Ophelia and his own. He writhes under the stigma of heartlessness which he cannot but incur. How remove it? How wipe away the stain? It is impossible. Cursed then be the cause. His whole nature surges up against it— the incestuousness of this King; the havoc of illicit passion, which has killed his noble father, wrecked his fairest hopes, stolen from him his mother's love—nay, robbed him even of the maternal ideal which remains to many a man in unblemished purity and even sweetness long after a breach has taken place between his mother and himself. His (Hamlet's) mother was once fair and honest, honest as Ophelia now. *Is* Ophelia honest? Impossible to think otherwise. But it were a mad quip to ask her, and let the after dialogue take its own course. Take what course it will, it must dwell on the one subject which will harden Hamlet's heart, and give rigour to his nature. Thus comes the paradox:—

> *Hamlet.* Ha, ha! are you honest?
> *Ophelia.* My lord!
> *Hamlet.* Are you fair?
> *Ophelia.* What means your lordship?
> *Hamlet.* That if you be honest and fair, your honesty should admit no discourse to your beauty.
> *Ophelia.* Could beauty, my lord, have better commerce than with honesty?
> *Hamlet.* Ay, truly; for the power of beauty will sooner transform honesty from what it is, than the force of honesty can translate beauty into his likeness; this was some time a paradox, but now the time gives it proof.

Did it occur to listening old Polonius, with the statesman's head, of which he was so proud, that this, and not "my daughter," was the idea on which Hamlet was harping? His knowledge was probably not sufficient, but the wily Claudius saw it—note his first speech after the interview—and the course of Hamlet's thought is clear enough to those who are in the King's secret. Hamlet's mother's beauty had been her snare, had tempted her adulterous lover. His mother's honesty had fallen a victim to her beauty. Let beauty and honesty therefore—here was the stroke of mad exaggeration—have no discourse.

> *Hamlet.* I did love you once.
> *Ophelia.* Indeed, my lord, you made me believe so.
> *Hamlet.* You should not have believed me; for virtue cannot so inoculate our old stock, but we shall relish of it.

The thought underlying this is one of almost peevish aggravation of the root-grievance cankering in the speaker's mind: "I am nothing but vicious. You should not have believed me. My old stock—that is, the vice I had from my mother—would so contaminate all that was honest in my nature, or all the good I might have got through my intercourse with you would be so polluted by the overpowering bad impulses in me, that you had better not have known me—infinitely better not have loved me." And then with a wild "bolt," as it were, he utters the words that may most sharply end all—"I loved you not." This is the surgeon's knife for such complaints, and many a man has used it coolly and callously. But such men were not Hamlets. He uses it more in frenzy than in judgment, in an agony of pain, amid a thousand fond remembrances, but dominated by the one conviction that he must break with Ophelia, cost what it may. His instincts were accurate, though his temperament was not calculating, and the impetus of necessity drove him, in that moment of miserable stress, to use words which could not have been more ruthlessly and effectually chosen by the most cold-blooded of deceivers.

There is nothing more pitiable, tender, or forlorn, in the whole range of the drama, than Ophelia's reply: "I was the more deceived." These are her last voluntary words, except her ejaculations of prayer that Heaven may help and restore her lover; but these do not come till further wild and whirling words have convinced her that it is with a madman she is talking. For the moment it is enough that she is abandoned, and the past repudiated. Her heart is wrecked. She incoherently answers the one question Hamlet puts to her—"Where's your father?"—and gazes and listens in frozen horror to the tirades which he has now worked himself up to deliver.

But his words are not devoid of sequence, nor is their harshness untouched with sympathy. "Get thee to a nunnery." Where else, but in such a sanctuary, should so pure a being be sheltered? Where else could Ophelia so well escape the contamination on which her lover's mind was still running? The next lines, violent, self-accusing, cynical, almost gross in their libel of humanity, are probably uttered in desperate and yet restrained anxiety to snatch at and throw to the heart-pierced maiden some strange, morbid consolation, but without giving her any faint shadow of the one solace which he so well knows would be all-sufficing. It is neither necessary nor possible to suppose that all this was deliberately thought out by Hamlet. At such moments as he was passing through, the high pressure of a forcible mind carries it over the difficulties in its course, and as truly so when the leaps and bounds seem without system as when the progress is more regular. But, for any purpose of comfort, how utterly is this without effect! Mute is Ophelia, and after his burst of self-condemning, man-condemning fury, her lover is mute also.

Let us now pause and imagine them thus together, when

suddenly Hamlet remembers—there is no need for him to have any reminder—the hidden presence of the King. He sharply asks Ophelia "Where's your father?" How shall we interpret her reply?

Her words are "At home, my lord." How comes she to say this? If she had known her father and the King were behind the arras, she might still have made the same reply, so wrapt in her thoughts that all recollection of the King's and Polonius's presence might have left her: in short, the words might have been spoken in mere vacancy. If she did not know the King and her father were watching, as I have argued she did not, of course the words were simple sincerity and truth; or, taken by surprise by the question, and feeling herself to be an unwilling instrument in something that was going on, while, though her own motive was pure, she was at a loss how to explain it, she may have given a reply which she knew to be false in the desire to clear herself of complicity in what Hamlet would certainly think mean and despicable. This or worse is probably Hamlet's opinion for the moment, but that he banishes the thought is curiously proved by the tender passage which follows; for, after sternly rebuking Polonius, Hamlet may be said to excuse himself by implication, and to ask pardon indirectly for the seeming reproach. "Be thou as chaste," he says, "as ice, as pure as snow, thou shalt not escape calumny."

And now Hamlet's excitement reaches its greatest height. Goaded within and without, nay, dragged even by his own feelings in two opposite directions, in each of which he suspects he may have gone too far under the eyes of malignant witnesses, he is maddened by the thought that they are still observing him, and as usual, half in wild exultation, half by design, begins to pour forth more and more extravagant reproaches on his kind. He must not commit himself to his love, nor unbosom his hate, nor has he a moment's pause in which to set in order a contrived display of random lunacy. As usual, passion and preconceived gloomy broodings abundantly supply him with declamation which may indicate a deep meaning or be mere madness according to the ears that hear it, while through all his bitter ravings there is visible the anguish of a lover forced to be cruel, and of a destined avenger almost beside himself with the horrors of his provocation and his task. The shafts fly wildly, and are tipped with cynic poison; the bow from which they are sped is a strong and constant though anxious nature, steadily, though with infinite excitement, bent upon the one great purpose fate has imposed upon it. The fitful excesses of his closing speech are the twangings of the bow from which the arrow of avenging destiny shall one day fly straight to the mark.

The exit of Hamlet after this outburst can only be described—as it has been—as "a flash of frenzy." What that flash reveals—the tenderness, the hate, the despair, the lurid glimpse of a horrid future—must be left to the individual actor. For these things Shakspeare gives no counsel but the teaching of his previous text. If I have read that teaching aright in the few pages I have written, there can be little doubt that the aim of one who acts Hamlet should be to express in this scene as fully as finite powers will permit the conflict of motive and variety of passion which it is as necessary to unite in a credible and vivid personality as to bring out boldly and distinctly in separate relief.

I will only add that Ophelia's understanding of her lover, as revealed in her succeeding speech, is exquisitely compassionate. Her feeling is that of the deepest pity. She is unwounded, though overwhelmed by loss and sorrow. She thinks only of the wreck that fate has made of her beloved. She cannot know or even suspect his grief or his obligations, and to her his state is mere calamity—a sad and unmitigated visitation from Heaven.

George Bernard Shaw

"Hamlet"

2 October, 1897.

The Forbes Robertson "Hamlet" at the Lyceum is, very unexpectedly at that address, really not at all unlike Shakespeare's play of the same name. I am quite certain I saw Reynaldo in it for a moment; and possibly I may have seen Voltimand and Cornelius; but just as the time for their scene arrived, my eye fell on the word "Fortinbras" in the programme, which so amazed me that I hardly know what I saw for the next ten minutes. Ophelia, instead of being a strenuously earnest and self-possessed young lady giving a concert and recitation for all she was worth, was mad—actually mad. The story of the play was perfectly intelligible, and quite took the attention of the audience off the principal actor at moments. What is the Lyceum coming to? Is it for this that Sir Henry Irving has invented a whole series of original romantic dramas, and given the credit of them without a murmur to the immortal bard whose profundity (as exemplified in the remark that good and evil are mingled in our natures) he has just been pointing out to the inhabitants of Cardiff, and whose works have been no more to him than the word-quarry from which he has hewn and blasted the lines and titles of masterpieces which are really all his own? And now, when he has created by these means a reputation for Shakespeare, he no sooner turns his back for a moment on London than Mr. Forbes Robertson competes with him on the boards of his own theatre by actually playing off against him the authentic Swan of Avon. Now if the result had been the utter exposure and collapse of that impostor, poetic justice must have proclaimed that it served Mr. Forbes Robertson right. But alas! the wily William, by literary tricks which our simple Sir Henry has never quite understood, has played into Mr. Forbes Robertson's hands so artfully that the scheme is a prodigious success. The effect of this success, coming after that of Mr. Alexander's experiment with a Shakespearean version of "As You Like It," makes it almost probable that we shall presently find managers vieing with each other in offering the public as much of the original Shakespearean stuff as possible, instead of, as heretofore, doing their utmost to reassure us that everything that the most modern resources can do to relieve the irreducible minimum of tedium inseparable from even the most heavily cut acting version will be lavished on their revivals. It is true that Mr. Beerbohm Tree still holds to the old scepticism, and calmly proposes to insult us by offering us Garrick's puerile and horribly caddish knockabout farce of "Katherine and Petruchio" for Shakespeare's "Taming of the Shrew"; but Mr. Tree, like all romantic actors, is incorrigible on the subject of Shakespeare.

Mr. Forbes Robertson is essentially a classical actor, the only one, with the exception of Mr. Alexander, now established in London management. What I mean by classical is that he can present a dramatic hero as a man whose passions are those which have produced the philosophy, the poetry, the art, and the statecraft of the world, and not merely those which have produced its weddings, coroner's inquests, and executions. And that is just the sort of actor that Hamlet requires. A Hamlet who only understands his love for Ophelia, his grief for his father, his vindictive hatred of his uncle, his fear of ghosts, his impulse to snub Rosencrantz and Guildenstern, and the sportsman's excitement with which he lays the "mousetrap" for Claudius, can, with sufficient force or virtuosity of execution, get a great reputation in the part, even though the very intensity of his obsession by these sentiments (which are common not only to all men but to many animals), shows that the characteristic side of Hamlet, the side that differentiates him from Fortinbras, is absolutely outside the actor's consciousness. Such a reputation is the actor's, not Hamlet's. Hamlet is not a man in whom "common humanity" is raised by great vital energy to a heroic pitch, like Coriolanus or Othello. On the contrary, he is a man in whom the common personal passions are so superseded by wider and rarer interests, and so discouraged by a degree of critical self-consciousness which makes the practical efficiency of the instinctive man on the lower plane impossible to him, that he finds the duties dictated by conventional revenge and ambition as disagreeable a burden as commerce is to a poet. Even his instinctive sexual impulses offend his intellect; so that when he meets the woman who excites them he invites her to join him in a bitter and scornful criticism of their joint absurdity, demanding "What should such fellows as I do crawling between heaven and earth?" "Why would'st thou be a breeder of sinners?" and so forth, all of which is so completely beyond the poor girl that she naturally thinks him mad. And, indeed, there is a sense in which Hamlet is insane; for he trips over the mistake which lies on the threshold of intellectual self-consciousness: that of bringing life to utilitarian or Hedonistic tests, thus treating it as a means instead of an end. Because Polonius is "a foolish prating knave," because Rosencrantz and Guildenstern are snobs, he kills them as remorselessly as he might kill a flea, showing that he has no real belief in the superstitious reason which he gives for not killing himself, and in fact anticipating exactly the whole course of the intellectual history of Western Europe until Schopenhauer found the clue that Shakespeare missed. But to call Hamlet mad because he did not anticipate Schopenhauer is like calling Marcellus mad because he did not refer the Ghost to the Psychical Society. It is in fact not possible for any actor to represent Hamlet as mad. He may (and generally does) combine some notion of his own of a man who is the creature of affectionate sentiment with the figure drawn by the lines of Shakespeare; but the result is not a madman, but simply one of those monsters produced by the imaginary combination of two normal species, such as sphinxes, mermaids, or centaurs. And this is the invariable resource of the instinctive, imaginative, romantic actor. You will see him weeping bucketsful of tears over Ophelia, and treating the players, the gravedigger, Horatio, Rosencrantz and Guildenstern as if they were mutes at his own funeral. But go and watch Mr. Forbes Robertson's Hamlet seizing delightedly on every opportunity for a bit of philosophic discussion or artistic recreation to escape from the "cursed spite" of revenge and love and other common troubles; see how he brightens up when the players come; how he tries to talk philosophy with Rosencrantz and Guildenstern the moment they come into the room; how he stops on his country walk with Horatio to lean over the churchyard wall and draw out the grave-digger whom he sees singing at his trade; how even his fits of excitement find expression in declaiming scraps of poetry; how the shock of Ophelia's death relieves itself in the fiercest intellectual contempt for Laertes's ranting, whilst an hour afterwards, when Laertes stabs him, he bears no malice for that at all, but embraces him gallantly and comradely; and how he dies as we forgive everything to Charles II. for dying, and makes "the rest is silence" a touchingly humorous apology for not being able to finish his business. See all that; and you have seen a true classical Hamlet. Nothing half so charming has been seen by this generation. It will bear seeing again and again.

And please observe that this is not a cold Hamlet. He is none of your logicians who reason their way through the world because they cannot feel their way through it; his intellect is the organ of his passion: his eternal self-criticism is as alive and thrilling as it can possibly be. The great soliloquy—no: I do NOT mean "To be or not to be": I mean the dramatic one, "O what a rogue and peasant slave am I!"—is as passionate in its scorn of brute passion as the most bullnecked affirmation or sentimental dilution of it could be. It comes out so without violence: Mr. Forbes Robertson takes the part quite easily and spontaneously. There is none of that strange Lyceum intensity which comes from the perpetual struggle between Sir Henry Irving and Shakespeare. The lines help Mr. Forbes Robertson instead of getting in his way at every turn, because he wants to play Hamlet, and not to slip into his inky cloak a changeling of quite another race. We may miss the craft, the skill double-distilled by constant peril, the subtlety, the dark rays of heat generated by intense friction, the relentless parental tenacity and cunning with which Sir Henry nurses his own pet creations on Shakespearean food like a fox rearing its litter in the den of a lioness; but we get light, freedom, naturalness, credibility, and Shakespeare. It is wonderful how easily everything comes right when you have the right man with the right mind for it—how the story tells itself, how the characters come to life, how even the failures in the cast cannot confuse you, though they may disappoint you. And Mr. Forbes

Robertson has certainly not escaped such failures, even in his own family. I strongly urge him to take a hint from Claudius and make a real ghost of Mr. Ian Robertson at once; for there is really no use in going through that scene night after night with a Ghost who is so solidly, comfortably and dogmatically alive as his brother. The voice is not a bad voice; but it is the voice of a man who does not believe in ghosts. Moreover, it is a hungry voice, not that of one who is past eating. There is an indescribable little complacent drop at the end of every line which no sooner calls up the image of purgatory by its words than by its smug elocution it convinces us that this particular penitent is cosily warming his shins and toasting his muffin at the flames instead of expiating his bad acting in the midst of them. His aspect and bearing are worse than his recitations. He beckons Hamlet away like a beadle summoning a timid candidate for the post of junior footman to the presence of the Lord Mayor. If I were Mr. Forbes Robertson I would not stand that from any brother: I would cleave the general ear with horrid speech at him first. It is a pity; for the Ghost's part is one of the wonders of the play. And yet, until Mr. Courtenay Thorpe divined it the other day, nobody seems to have had a glimpse of the reason why Shakespeare would not trust any one else with it, and played it himself. The weird music of that long speech which should be the spectral wail of a soul's bitter wrong crying from one world to another in the extremity of its torment, is invariably handed over to the most squaretoed member of the company, who makes it sound, not like Rossetti's "Sister Helen," or even, to suggest a possible heavy treatment, like Mozart's statue-ghost, but like Chambers's Information for the People.

Still, I can understand Mr. Ian Robertson, by sheer force of a certain quality of sententiousness in him, overbearing the management into casting him for the Ghost. What I cannot understand is why Miss Granville was cast for the Queen. It is like setting a fashionable modern mandolinist to play Haydn's sonatas. She does her best under the circumstances; but she would have been more fortunate had she been in a position to refuse the part.

On the other hand, several of the impersonations are conspicuously successful. Mrs. Patrick Campbell's Ophelia is a surprise. The part is one which has hitherto seemed incapable of progress.

From generation to generation actresses have, in the mad scene, exhausted their musical skill, their ingenuity in devising fantasias in the language of flowers, and their intensest powers of portraying anxiously earnest sanity. Mrs. Patrick Campbell, with that complacent audacity of hers which is so exasperating when she is doing the wrong thing, this time does the right thing by making Ophelia really mad. The resentment of the audience at this outrage is hardly to be described. They long for the strenuous mental grasp and attentive coherence of Miss Lily Hanbury's conception of maiden lunacy; and this wandering, silly, vague Ophelia, who no sooner catches an emotional impulse than it drifts away from her again, emptying her voice of its tone in a way that makes one shiver, makes them horribly uncomfortable. But the effect on the play is conclusive. The shrinking discomfort of the King and Queen, the rankling grief of Laertes, are created by it at once; and the scene, instead of being a pretty interlude coming in just when a little relief from the inky cloak is welcome, touches us with a chill of the blood that gives it is [sic—its] right tragic power and dramatic significance. Playgoers naturally murmur when something that has always been pretty becomes painful; but the pain is good for them, good for the theatre, and good for the play. I doubt whether Mrs. Patrick Campbell fully appreciates the dramatic value of her quite simple and original sketch—it is only a sketch—of the part; but in spite of the occasional triviality of its execution and the petulance with which it has been received, it seems to me to finally settle in her favor the question of her right to the very important place which Mr. Forbes Robertson has assigned to her in his enterprises.

I did not see Mr. Bernard Gould play Laertes: he was indisposed when I returned to town and hastened to the Lyceum; but he was replaced very creditably by Mr. Frank Dyall. Mr. Martin Harvey is the best Osric I have seen: he plays Osric from Osric's own point of view, which is, that Osric is a gallant and distinguished courtier, and not, as usual, from Hamlet's, which is that Osric is "a waterfly." Mr. Harrison Hunter hits off the modest, honest Horatio capitally; and Mr. Willes is so good a Gravedigger that I venture to suggest to him that he should carry his work a little further, and not virtually cease to concern himself with the play when he has spoken his last line and handed Hamlet the

skull. Mr. Cooper Cliffe is not exactly a subtle Claudius; but he
looks as if he had stepped out of a picture by Madox Brown, and
plays straightforwardly on his very successful appearance.
Mr. Barnes makes Polonius robust and elderly instead of aged
and garrulous. He is good in the scenes where Polonius appears as
a man of character and experience; but the senile exhibitions of
courtierly tact do not match these, and so seem forced and farci-
cal.

Mr. Forbes Robertson's own performance has a continuous
charm, interest and variety which are the result not only of his
well-known familiar grace and accomplishment as an actor, but of
a genuine delight—the rarest thing on our stage—in Shakespeare's art, and a natural familiarity with the plane of his imagination. He does not superstitiously worship William: he enjoys
him and understands his methods of expression. Instead of cutting every line that can possibly be spared, he retains every gem,
in his own part or anyone else's, that he can make time for in a
spiritedly brisk performance lasting three hours and a half with
very short intervals. He does not utter half a line; then stop to act;
then go on with another half line; and then stop to act again, with
the clock running away with Shakespeare's chances all the time.
He plays as Shakespeare should be played, on the line and to the
line, with the utterance and acting simultaneous, inseparable and
in fact identical. Not for a moment is he solemnly conscious of
Shakespeare's reputation, or of Hamlet's momentousness in literary history: on the contrary, he delivers us from all these bore-
doms instead of heaping them on us. We forgive him the plati-
tudes, so engagingly are they delivered. His novel and
astonishingly effective and touching treatment of the final scene
is an inspiration, from the fencing match onward. If only Fortinbras could also be inspired with sufficient force and brilliancy to
rise to the warlike splendor of his helmet, and make straight for
that throne like a man who intended to keep it against all comers,
he would leave nothing to be desired. How many generations of
Hamlets, all thirsting to outshine their competitors in effect and
originality, have regarded Fortinbras, and the clue he gives to this
kingly death for Hamlet, as a wildly unpresentable blunder of the
poor foolish old Swan, than whom they all knew so much better!
How sweetly they have died in that faith to slow music, like Little

Nell in "The Old Curiosity Shop"! And now how completely Mr. Forbes Robertson has bowled them all out by being clever enough to be simple.

By the way, talking of slow music, the sooner Mr. Hamilton Clarke's romantic Irving music is stopped, the better. Its effect in this Shakespearean version of the play is absurd. The four Offenbachian young women in tights should also be abolished, and the part of the player-queen given to a man. The courtiers should be taught how flatteringly courtiers listen when a king shows off his wisdom in wise speeches to his nephew. And that nice wooden beach on which the ghost walks would be the better for a sea-weedy-looking cloth on it, with a handful of shrimps and a pennorth of silver sand.

Muriel St. C. Byrne

From "Fifty Years of Shakespearean Production"

This decline and revival of the prestige of Shakespearian acting cannot be overlooked in any account of post-1918 Shakespearian production. Historically, however, the next important
landmark was the London production in 1925 of Barry Jackson's
modern-dress *Hamlet* at the Kingsway. In spite of the "Hamlet in
plus fours" headlines, it was in general taken seriously by the
Press and intelligently received. For its audiences—average man
and Shakespearian scholar alike—it was a profoundly exciting
experience, and the best critics of the day were unanimous in
praise. One of the things which surprised people most was to
discover what an extraordinarily good play it was, and that all the
characters were as real and vital as Hamlet himself—they saw it,
in fact, as a play for the first time. It had always been one of the
most unsatisfactorily costumed plays, and the mere getting rid of
the theatrical fancy dress which did duty for most productions
would have helped to bring the play to life; but on to the scrap
heap, with the incredible clothes and the wigs and the beards,
went the whole accumulation of conventional characterization
which had been stifling everybody except the star performer who
had used it as his vehicle. Everything had been as freshly considered and was as freshly interpreted as if the play were being put
on the stage for the first time. And far from its "Elizabethanism"

Reprinted from *Shakespeare Survey*, vol. 2 (1949), pp. 12–13, by permission of Cambridge University Press. Copyright © 1949 by Cambridge
University Press.

suffering under this treatment, never—as William Poel pointed out in the *Manchester Guardian*—had the revenge motif been so well-handled or made more explicit. The incongruity of blank verse and modern dress was felt by some, but the verse was quickly and naturally delivered, and most of the audience, already accustomed to the speedy modern tempo of the Old Vic productions under Robert Atkins, took it in their stride.

Despite the success of the 1925 *Hamlet* the whole question of "Shakespeare in modern dress" remains fraught with difficulties. The idea does not yet meet with general, critical or theatrical acceptance, though it has received informed and discriminating support. Disregarding the usual contention that it is a mere stunt, an exercise in ingenuity, it is worth while to assume that most producers and actors who care for Shakespearian work and who try this experiment are at heart simpler and more simply sincere than their critics believe, and are attempting it in good faith. It is never an easy solution of the producer's problem, but the terms of reference it offers are wide—including the Ruritanian magnificence of Tyrone Guthrie's 1938 *Hamlet*—and provided the emotional associations are sensitively and truly keyed and that the acting is first class, then, as *The Times* critic said of the original experiment, there is "a clear gain in freshness and life and vigour." Whatever its future, it has earned the right to be regarded not as a stunt but as a serious excursion in search of authenticity, and one for which there is every theatrical and scholarly justification. After the work of Granville-Barker, therefore, Barry Jackson's *Hamlet* may be regarded as the most important single contribution to the history of modern Shakespearian production, which it has influenced in a similar and equally vital fashion. It stressed again, at a moment when such inspiration was much needed, the necessity for the fresh and original approach to the problem of production—the flight from Shakespearian acting in the twenties was at least partly due to the lack of any really outstanding Shakespearian producer. If the intellectual basis of Barker's approach to the text had to some extent been masked by the picturesque and pictorial qualities of the stage spectacle, now, in the Barry Jackson production, the intellectual approach and the realization were unmistakably identified. Translation into the idiom of modern life forces you to make your meaning clear to yourself: your understanding may be right or wrong, but you must make up your own mind and express yourself accordingly. By the "Shakespearian ritualists" your manner of proceeding is viewed from the start with the gravest suspicions: if you throw away tradition you must have the author: your scrupulous interpretation of his text in the entirety of its statement and implications is your only strength. For an engineer of a modern-dress production of *Hamlet* it must be "back to the text" with a vengeance, or he will be hoist with his own petard: he has forced his audience back to the text and the pursuit of the authentic Shakespeare. He has shocked them into thinking.

Richard L. Sterne

From *John Gielgud Directs Richard Burton in Hamlet*

The cast took a break, and then Gielgud resumed.

Gielgud: I know this is a difficult place to begin the act after an intermission, but it's really a question of how the vitality of the play holds up. Still, it's very hard for poor Ophelia to have to open the third act, but there isn't any other place to break it. The Fortinbras scene makes a marvelous curtain for the second act. I have an idea about Ophelia's mad scene. I thought we could get the idea that she was shut up in the castle. And you, Gertrude, come down the grand stairway saying "I won't speak with her, I won't speak with her." But then they let Ophelia in—and her one idea is to get out into the open air. And so she keeps on going to the center doors trying to find a way to open them. Gertrude knows it's dangerous and that Ophelia mustn't be let out. Finally she does find the door and she rushes out, which alarms the Queen.

Then the riot begins with Laertes, and Ophelia, coming back, hears all the noise. She has been down by the river already and her dress is stained with weeds and muck. And she thinks of the flowers. She's come back, she thinks, for the funeral—to offer the flowers for her father; she can't find the body because the King has done "but greenly in hugger-mugger to inter him." And I don't think she ever saw him after he was dead. So that when

she's come back the second time and Laertes is there, she's
looking for poor Polonius' body, and for Hamlet, too, who
went away, and she can't find either of them. She's distracted and looks about, under the rostrum and everywhere. Then finally, when she sees it's no good and she's
given away the flowers and doesn't know where she is
because there is no funeral, she kisses the Queen suddenly, and then very slyly, seeing the door is open, makes
a dash for it and goes rushing out. The Queen rushes out
after her, so we are prepared to hear the description of
Ophelia's death at the end of the scene.

I'm rather sick of the wild indecency that has been put
into the scene in recent productions, with Ophelia tearing
off her clothes and clutching all the gentlemen. I don't
think Shakespeare meant it. It must be a touching scene.
You see, I think in Shakespeare's time people always
laughed at lunatics. They visited madhouses right up to
the eighteenth century in England as we visit the zoo
today. And Shakespeare knew that the only way to make
madness pitiful, as is obvious with Lady Macbeth and
Ophelia, was to give them a poignant, agonized, though
not sentimental, scene. If that was not intended by Shakespeare, Laertes would never say "Thought and affliction,
passion, hell itself she turns to favor and to prettiness."
And to suddenly make Ophelia openly lewd on-stage is
against the intention of the writing. In this other way you
can be just as strong. I don't want to make it sentimental
and Victorian.

I think we must all play not as though we were going
to put this poor creature in prison or to lock her up, but as
though we were going to restrain her in the castle. After
all, "Denmark's a prison," as Hamlet says and as our set
conveys. Even Hamlet himself is trying to break away to
get to the outer world. All the people in the play are shut
up in this castle. You play that, really, all through the play.
There is this curious feeling, except on the battlements
and in the churchyard, that they are all really locked in the
castle, in a miasma of corruption and sensuality. It isn't
until Fortinbras comes at the end that the whole thing
opens and all are free. I had an idea to use a lute for
Ophelia as we once did in another production of mine. It
was beautiful to have her play it. But it's such a big prop to
manage and it's such an Elizabethan prop. It would really

only work well if the actress could play it properly herself.
I originally thought a lady-in-waiting might play it sitting
in a chair, but that was no good.

Herlie [Gertrude].[1] Do you want the Queen's speech about
Ophelia's death to be "read" or "acted"?

Gielgud: It must be frantic. But also, it has to be spoken very
beautifully. It's like the description of an automobile
crash, "Oh, there they were, all covered with blood and it
was horrible." Only the Queen describes the romantic
aspect of it with her own rather limited romantic attitude
even toward disaster.

During the reading of Act Three there were a few
discussions about cuttings and the possibilities of alternate line readings. Sir John had a comment on the Ham-
let-Horatio conversation at the beginning of the last
scene.

Gielgud: This scene is so difficult, following the big drama at
the end of the grave scene. It's such an anticlimax. I never
know how to make it interesting up to the entrance of
Osric. This is where they get restless and start to cough.
Let's cut all the lines about the letters—who cares about
that? You just told Horatio *offstage* that Rosencrantz and
Guildenstern are dead. We don't care particularly how
you did it. Anything belabored at this point, when both
the actor playing Hamlet and the audience are tired, is
very dangerous.

After finishing the reading Gielgud again called for the
timing. The third act took forty-two minutes to read.

Gielgud: That makes a total of three hours and a quarter. I
think we'd better have an eight-o'clock curtain so we get
them out on time.

Following an hour and a half lunch break, the company returned to the rehearsal hall to spend the four hours of the
afternoon session blocking[2] the first three scenes of the play.
Gielgud staged the production entirely from his head. He did not
use a prompt-script except for an occasional referral to his sparse
notes on a few entrance and exit positions. He invented most of
the blocking as he went along, and *never* stopped improving on
movements.

Gielgud knew every line in the play. He was his own prompter
and would correct an actor for the slightest change in the text. He

picked up even the misquotes made by the actors in the bit parts. He seemed to be everywhere at once—out front watching from every angle, always on his toes, and always moving about. At the same time that he was watching the play, he was also acting all the parts with the actors, mouthing the lines, reflecting the emotions in his facial expressions, and kinesthetically making all the gestures.

Sometimes he found it most expedient in dictating the moves to dash up on the set and guide the actor bodily where he wanted him to be placed. "Move over there. Cross back. No, no, go right," he would call. Yet one could not tell whether he meant stage right or audience right.[3] It didn't matter, because before the actor had time to question this, Gielgud was taking him by the shoulders and moving him bodily to where he wanted him. Gielgud did not hesitate to demonstrate while directing, so as not to waste time in needless theorizing. He had the actor stand in front of the set while he himself demonstrated lines in the passage on which he was working. Yet he would let people try any gesture or reading they felt strongly about. But once Sir John decided that something was not right, it was out.

Often, while he directed, he would be holding a glass of milk in his hand, or be popping Life Savers into his mouth. He would frequently squint during his close scrutiny of scenes. He demanded everything from his actors at that first blocking. For most, it was impossible to keep up with all his suggestions and criticisms, no matter how furiously the actor would write notations in his script or how accurately he could memorize the direction. Sir John pushed on rapidly with a minimum of discussion or review, expecting the actor to retain much. He would speak constant encouragement to his actors. "Much better!" "Beautiful!" "I like what you're doing with that speech."

Richard Burton walked through the first blocking rehearsals with the complete Cambridge text in his hand. He made no notes at rehearsals. Obviously, he had noted Gielgud's cuts in his script. As soon as a scene was run a second time, Burton discarded the book at once. Yet he did not duplicate the moves exactly as before; rather he felt his way through the scenes, making changes each time. He engrossed himself completely in some speeches and gave a plain, straightforward reading in others. He turned to Gielgud for help at some points and almost became annoyed with his suggestions at others. Burton would not try to imitate Gielgud's demonstrations and would sometimes go out of his way to be different. The Hamlet he played was his own, and Sir John only made suggestions to Burton and did not demand strict adherence to them. When not on set, Burton buried himself in the text and whispered his lines to himself.

Hume Cronyn [Polonius] constantly amused the company with his characterizations. His work had polish and distinction. He was careful and precise in all that he did. His pencil was poised constantly and he would write furiously immediately after leaving the set, to jot down all that he did or was given to do. Often he would remain an hour or two after rehearsals were over, continuing his notations while walking through the movements.

Before starting the actual blocking of the first scene, in which the Ghost appears to Horatio and the soldiers, Sir John had Horatio, Marcellus, Bernardo, and Francisco put on their overcoats to help them to feel the atmosphere of a cold night. He gave Bernardo and Francisco their entrance positions and then let them start their lines. They got as far as the fourth line when Sir John interrupted to demonstrate the exact tempo and vocal contrasts he wanted.

> *Gielgud:* The words of these opening lines must have height to give the sense of the open air. As it must be dark, the words must be pitched very clearly or they will not be heard. (Gielgud repeats the opening lines four times.) Don't set your readings. You've got to listen and refresh your ear each time. Keep the feeling of the cold. You've got to walk about to keep your circulation going. They all know there is something in the woodshed, yet they won't speak of it openly. There is so much they *don't* say in this scene. That's what's interesting—what is understood. People still go about their business, doing what they have to do, but with a terrible shadow hanging over them—like in the war. One does it with a heavy heart and this must be conveyed.
>
> Then Horatio comes in. He's the young philosopher-student without fear, and the old men have gone to him for help. I think that's very moving.

At the entrance of the Ghost Gielgud first had an actor walk across the platform to give the actors in the scene the proper timing for following the moving shaft of light that would be used instead of a "live" Ghost. When the actor walking for the Spirit could not get the right timing for the cross, Gielgud walked it himself. He would occasionally break his ghostly mien to turn to an actor and paraphrase a line or give a description of the surrounding mist.

Gielgud hammered away, building tension in Bernardo's speech preceding the Ghost's first entrance. Three times he demonstrated the lines.

> *Gielgud:* Each phrase must top the preceding one, as in a musical crescendo. "Last night of all,/When yond same star that's westward from the pole/Had made his course t'illume that part of heaven/Where now it burns, Marcellus and myself,/The bell then beating one—" Each phrase is a little louder and a little more excited and tense. Then at that point we hear the bell. *Dong!* And when you hear that bell you're terrified that the Ghost may come again— and it does. . . .
>
> When the Ghost disappears after his second appearance, the lights begin to change so that Marcellus' speech about "the season wherein our Savior's birth is celebrated" has a kind of benediction. And on Horatio's line, "But look the morn, in russet mantle clad/Walks o'er the dew of yon high eastern hill," everything must drop away to beauty and relief.
>
> Be careful not to move on that line, Bob Milli [Horatio]. Let's take it again, and Courtiers and Polonius be ready for the next scene because we go right on so that there is no break whatsoever between the scenes.

Seven times Gielgud ran the entrance of the court, each time taking the final lines of the preceding first platform scene so that the entrances of the court nearly overlapped with the exit of Horatio and the soldiers. Gielgud directed the seven Courtiers and the principals to their entrance positions. Prior to the entrance of the King and Queen, he inserted business[4] of Courtiers greeting each other along with Polonius and Laertes. While the Courtiers were coming on, Gielgud ran about, pushing them into their positions and groupings, demonstrating bows, changing them and readjusting them each time the entrance was repeated.

> *Gielgud:* I want you all to talk when you're coming on, but I don't want to understand what you say. I want it to be a lively and a decadent court. . . . More voices. It's much too soft. I can't hear a word. Sweep on, look at one another. Talk much louder so that we can have a hush when the King comes. I want this instead of the usual trumpet fanfare. More talking! Louder. Take some lines from any speech in the play. Then if the audience hears any of the words distinctly they will be Shakespearean lines, not modern ones. Polonius must be a busybody in this scene, and then he hushes everyone for the King's entrance, and then you all bow. . . . The King's first speech must be affable for the court. This is the first Privy Council meeting. You don't want anyone to think you're not sorry about the old King's death. Then Hamlet, after the King says "for all, our thanks," you come in. And everyone be aware of Hamlet's late entrance. Hamlet, you come down the stairway any way you like and sit at the end of the council table. So we're all waiting and the King doesn't know what to do, of course. He can't go on with the Prince behaving like that—Polonius tries to speak to Hamlet as he passes him on the way in, but Hamlet ignores him. Then Eileen [Queen], you go to him and touch him when you say "Good Hamlet, cast thy nightly color off," but he doesn't like it and so he gets up and moves away. Then Richard, when you say "Seems, madam? Nay it is. I know not seems," all through that speech there should be regret at having moved away from her, as if to say "I really love you but I can't do anything." But show some kind of tenderness. I would keep moving away from the King, too. You don't like the King but you don't think he is a murderer. He's only a bastard who cheated you out of the kingdom, and he sleeps with your mother, which you hate. But it isn't the same hate you've got to keep up your sleeve until after the Ghost tells you he's murdered your father. So we don't want too much reaction toward the King as yet.

Sir John had been working for an hour and a half on this court scene. He decided to take a five-minute break before tackling the exit of the court. After the break he started the scene over from the beginning. This time Ben Edwards, the scene designer, pointed out to him that actors would not be visible at the top of the stairway, which was out of sightlines; and so some further rearrangement was necessary. At the end of the scene Gielgud pondered over the exit of the court.

> *Gielgud:* This is where Tony Guthrie is so good at getting everyone off in one second.
>
> *Burton:* John, do you suppose I could start the "too, too solid flesh" before the court leaves?
>
> *Gielgud:* No, no. This is the most realistic of the soliloquies and it would seem odd that the Courtiers would fail to hear it if they were there.
>
> *Burton:* I would like to be close to the audience for this. (Burton moves downstage and says the soliloquy with great energy and passion.)
>
> *Gielgud:* That's fine, but I think it's too active. Keep it sad and simple. Soft. He's down—a very sad boy, but not morose.

Before going on to the last part of the scene between Hamlet, Horatio, and the soldiers, Gielgud dismissed the rest of the company. Most of them stayed on, however, to watch the proceedings.

Gielgud worked through the last section of the scene. He told Horatio, Marcellus, and Bernardo not to wear their coats now. "They've left them in the hall," he said. He concentrated on line interpretations as well as movements. When Burton spoke sharply the line "I prithee do not mock me, fellow student," Gielgud said it should be read warmly. When Burton shouted out "The King, my Father!" Gielgud felt the line should be said with quiet amazement. At the points in the scene where the text indicated that the soldiers speak in unison, Gielgud divided the lines between them to avoid a humorous "Tweedledee and Tweedledum" effect. Burton took his closing soliloquy, "My Father's spirit in arms, all is not well," very softly. Gielgud asked for it to be done louder to show a change of mood now that Hamlet had heard of the Ghost. The scene was repeated a second time without interruptions, except for a few minor changes and adjustments in the blocking.

The Laertes farewell scene, in which Polonius gives the famous parting advice to his son, was rehearsed in the same manner: worked through for movements and interpretation slowly, and then repeated with few interruptions. Gielgud gave the following directions during the first working:

> *Gielgud:* Ophelia [Linda Marsh], be more jaunty and playful in this opening scene. Laertes [John Cullum], be careful of sounding too colloquial. You mustn't ignore the verse. I like the ease, but sustain the poetry. First Laertes gives Ophelia a lecture, and then she lectures him on "Do not, as some ungracious pastors do." And then Pop comes in and gives another one. They're a most terrible family for lecturing one another. Then when Polonius comes in, Laertes should have a little more humorous attitude toward his father. He said goodbye in the hall but here he comes again.
>
> Polonius [Hume Cronyn], can you give us more fluster and busy-ness on your entrance? You're very anxious to get him off.
>
> *Cronyn:* John, I'm having trouble establishing that Polonius is in a high position as chief of state. I want to retain the dignity and not start being cute too soon.
>
> *Gielgud:* Oh yes, I agree. But he is a shrewd man. And shrewd men can sometimes be awfully tricky. And I think he's fond of both children in a very selfish way. But I think the scene is comic in that you are annoyed that Laertes is late and yet you give him a long lecture.

NOTES

1. Eileen Herlie
2. Process of setting the actors' movement patterns.
3. In the English theatre stage right means the right side as one looks at the stage from the auditorium. In America, the opposite is the case; a curious example of the differences in stage jargon in the two countries.
4. Any detailed pantomimic action other than movement about the stage.

PART 6:
Hamlet in Fiction

Henry Fielding

From *Tom Jones*

As soon as the Play, which was *Hamlet* Prince of *Denmark*, began, *Partridge* was all Attention, nor did he break Silence till the Entrance of the Ghost; upon which he asked *Jones*, "What Man that was in the strange Dress; something," said he, "like what I have seen in a Picture. Sure it is not Armour, is it?" *Jones* answered, "That is the Ghost." To which *Partridge* replied with a Smile, "Persuade me to that, Sir, if you can. Though I can't say I ever actually saw a Ghost in my Life, yet I am certain I should know one, if I saw him, better than that comes to. No, no, Sir, Ghosts don't appear in such Dresses as that, neither." In this Mistake, which caused much Laughter in the Neighbourhood of *Partridge*, he was suffered to continue, 'till the Scene between the Ghost and *Hamlet*, when *Partridge* gave that Credit to Mr. *Garrick*, which he had denied to *Jones*, and fell into so violent a Trembling, that his Knees knocked against each other. *Jones* asked him what was the Matter, and whether he was afraid of the Warrior upon the Stage? "O la! Sir," said he, "I perceive now it is what you told me. I am not afraid of any Thing; for I know it is but a Play. And if it was really a Ghost, it could do one no Harm at such a Distance, and in so much Company; and yet if I was frightened, I am not the only Person." "Why, who," cries *Jones*, "dost thou take to be such a Coward here besides thyself!" "Nay, you may call me Coward if you will; but if that little Man there upon the Stage is not frightned, I never saw any Man frightned in my Life. Ay, ay; *go along with you!* Ay, to be sure! Who's Fool then? Will you? Lud have Mercy upon such Fool-hardiness!—Whatever happens it is good enough for you.—*Follow you?* I'd follow the devil as soon. Nay, perhaps, it is the Devil—for they say he can put on what Likeness he pleases.—Oh! here he is again.—*No farther!* No, you have gone far enough already; farther than I'd have gone for all the King's Dominions." *Jones* offered to speak, but *Partridge* cried, "Hush, hush, dear Sir, don't you hear him!" And during the whole Speech of the Ghost, he sat with his Eyes fixed partly on the Ghost, and partly on *Hamlet*, and with his Mouth open; the same Passions which succeeded each other in *Hamlet*, succeeding likewise in him.

When the Scene was over, *Jones* said, "Why, *Partridge*, you exceed my Expectations. You enjoy the Play more than I conceived possible." "Nay, Sir," answered *Partridge*, "if you are not afraid of the Devil, I can't help it; but to be sure it is natural to be surprized at such Things, though I know there is nothing in them: Not that it was the Ghost that surprized me neither; for I should have known that to have been only a Man in a strange Dress: But when I saw the little Man so frightned himself, it was that which took hold of me." "And dost thou imagine then, *Partridge*," cries *Jones*, "that he was really frightened?" "Nay, Sir," said *Partridge*, "did not you yourself observe afterwards, when he found it was his own Father's Spirit, and how he was murdered in the Garden, how his Fear forsook him by Degrees, and he was struck dumb with Sorrow, as it were, just as I should have been, had it been my own Case.—But hush! O la! What Noise is that? There he is again.—Well, to be certain, though I know there is nothing at all in it, I am glad I am not down yonder, where those Men are." Then turning his Eyes again upon *Hamlet*, "Ay, you may draw your Sword; what signifies a Sword against the Power of the Devil?"

During the second Act, *Partridge* made very few Remarks. He greatly admired the Fineness of the Dresses; nor could he help observing upon the King's Countenance. "Well," said he, "how People may be deceived by Faces? *Nulla fides fronti* is, I find, a true Saying. Who would think, by looking in the King's Face, that he had ever committed a Murder?" He then enquired after the Ghost; but *Jones*, who intended he should be surprized, gave him no other Satisfaction, than "that he might possibly see him again soon, and in a Flash of Fire."

Partridge sat in fearful Expectation of this; and now, when the Ghost made his next Appearance, *Partridge* cried out, "There, Sir, now; what say you now? Is he frightened now or no? As much frightened as you think me, and, to be sure, no Body can help

some Fears, I would not be in so bad a Condition as what's his
Name, Squire *Hamlet*, is there, for all the World. Bless me! What's
become of the Spirit? As I am a living Soul, I thought I saw him
sink into the Earth." "Indeed, you saw right," answered *Jones*.
"Well, well," cries *Partridge*, "I know it is only a Play; and besides, if
there was any Thing in all this, Madam *Miller* would not laugh so:
For as to you, Sir, you would not be afraid, I believe, if the Devil
was here in person.—There, there—Ay, no Wonder you are in
such a Passion; shake the vile wicked Wretch to Pieces. If she was
my own Mother I should serve her so. To be sure, all Duty to a
Mother is forfeited by such wicked Doings.—Ay, go about your
Business; I hate the Sight of you."

The Grave-digging Scene next engaged the Attention of *Partridge*, who expressed much Surprize at the Number of Skulls
thrown upon the Stage. To which *Jones* answered, "That it was
one of the most famous Burial-places about Town." "No wonder
then," cries *Partridge*, "that the Place is haunted. But I never saw in
my Life a worse Grave-digger. I had a Sexton when I was Clerk,
that should have dug three Graves while he is digging one. The
Fellow handles a Spade as if it was the first Time he had ever had
one in his Hand. Ay, ay, you may sing. You had rather sing than
work, I believe."—Upon *Hamlet*'s taking up the Skull, he cried out,
"Well it is strange to see how fearless some Men are: I never could
bring myself to touch any Thing belonging to a dead Man on any
Account.—He seemed frightened enough too at the Ghost I
thought. *Nemo omnibus horis sapit.*"

Little more worth remembering occurred during the Play; at
the End of which *Jones* asked him, which of the Players he had
liked best? To this he answered, with some Appearance of Indig-

Our Critic was now pretty silent till the Play, which *Hamlet*
introduces before the King. This he did not at first understand,
'till *Jones* explained it to him; but he no sooner entered into the
Spirit of it, then he began to bless himself that he had never
committed Murder. Then turning to Mrs. *Miller*, he asked her, "If
she did not imagine the King looked as if he was touched; though
he is," said he, "a good Actor, and doth all he can to hide it. Well, I
would not have so much to answer for, as that wicked Man there
hath, to sit upon a much higher Chair than he sits upon.—No
wonder he run away; for your Sake I'll never trust an innocent
Face again."

nation at the Question, "The King without Doubt." "Indeed, Mr. *Partridge*," says Mrs. *Miller*, "you are not of the same Opinion with the Town; for they are all agreed, that *Hamlet* is acted by the best Player who ever was on the Stage." "He the best Player!" cries *Partridge*, with a contemptuous Sneer, "Why I could act as well as he myself. I am sure if I had seen a Ghost, I should have looked in the very same Manner, and done just as he did. And then, to be sure, in that Scene, as you called it, between him and his Mother, where you told me he acted so fine, why, Lord help me, any Man, that is, any good Man, that had such a Mother, would have done exactly the same. I know you are only joking with me; but, indeed, Madam, though I was never at a Play in *London*, yet I have seen acting before in the Country; and the King for my Money; he speaks all his Words distinctly, half as loud again as the other.—Any Body may see he is an Actor."

Goethe

From *Wilhelm Meister*

Wilhelm, when he saw the company so favourably disposed, now hoped that he might be able to converse with them about the poetic merit of the pieces which they played. "It is not enough," said he the next day when they had come together again, "for the actor just to glance superficially, to judge of it by his first impressions and to declare his satisfaction or dissatisfaction with it without investigation. This is indeed permissible for the spectator, who may be moved and entertained but is not expected to criticize. On the other hand, the actor ought to be able to give an account of the piece and of the reasons for his praise and censure; and how will he do this if he does not understand how to penetrate into the sense of his author and his intentions? I have seen the mistake of judging a play from one part and looking at a part by itself not in connection with the play as a whole. I have noticed this in myself in these days so clearly that I will give you an example of it if you will give me a well-disposed hearing. You know Shakespeare's incomparable Hamlet from a public reading which gave you the greatest pleasure at the Castle. We proposed to act the play, and I, without knowing what I was doing, undertook the part of the prince. I thought that I was studying it while I began to learn by heart the strangest passages, the soliloquies and those scenes in which force of soul, elevation and vehemence of feeling have their freest scope, when the agitated heart can display itself with expressive feeling. I also imagined that I penetrated right into the spirit of the part, while I took upon myself the load of deep melancholy and endeavoured to follow my prototype through the strange labyrinth of so many moods and peculiarities. So I learned by heart and practised and imagined by degrees I should become one person with my hero.

"But the farther I advanced the more difficult did the representation of the whole become for me and at last it seemed to me impossible to arrive at a general view of the whole. Now I went through the piece in an uninterrupted sequence and here, unfortunately, much would not suit me. Now the characters, now the manner of expression, seemed in contradiction, and I almost despaired of finding a general tone in which I could present my whole part with all its shadings and deviations. In these errors I toiled for a long time in vain, until at length I hoped to arrive at my aim in a quite special way. I sought out every trace of the character of Hamlet which showed itself before the death of his father; I noticed what this young man had been, independently of this tragic event and of the horrible events which followed upon it, and what without them he perhaps would have become. Gentle, and sprung from a noble stem, this royal flower had grown up amid the immediate influences of majesty; the conception of what is right with that of princely elevation, of what is good and dignified with the consciousness of high birth developed themselves in him simultaneously. He was a prince, by birth a prince, and he wished to reign only that good men should be good without hindrance. Pleasing in form, well mannered by nature, amiable in his feelings, he was to be the pattern of youth and the joy of the world. Without any prominent passion, his love for Ophelia was a silent presentiment of sweet requirements. His zeal for knightly exercises was not quite original, much rather was this desire to be quickened and elevated by the praise which is bestowed on others. Pure in feeling he knew the honourable minded and could value the repose which a sincere spirit enjoys on the bosom of a friend. Up to a certain degree he had learnt to recognize and appreciate the good and the beautiful in the arts and sciences; everything in bad taste was offensive to him, and if hatred could take root in his gentle soul it was only so far as was necessary to make him despise the changeful butterflies of the Court and to play with them in a scornful fashion. He was composed in his temper, simple in his behaviour, neither pleased with idleness nor too eager for employment. An academic leisureliness he seemed to continue at Court. He possessed rather mirth of humour than of heart; he was a good mixer, pliant, modest, careful and able to forgive and forget an injury, yet he could never unite himself with one who overstept the boundaries of the right, the good and the becoming. When we read the piece together again, you can judge whether I am on the right path. At least I hope to support my opinion completely with some passages."

* * * * * * *

"Much and everything," replied Wilhelm. "Picture to yourselves a prince, such as I have described him, whose father dies unexpectedly. Ambition and desire to rule are not the passions which animate him; he would have been satisfied to be a king's son, but now he is compelled to be more attentive to the difference which separates the king from his subjects. The right to the throne was not hereditary, yet a longer life of his father would have strengthened the claims of his only son and secured his hopes of the throne. On the other hand, he now sees himself excluded by his uncle in spite of specious promises, perhaps for ever. He is now poor in favour, in goods and a stranger in that which from his youth he could regard as his property. Here his temper assumes its first mournful direction. He feels that he is not more, indeed not so much, as any nobleman; he offers himself as the servant of everyone; he is not polite, not condescending; no, he is degraded and needy. He looks upon his former condition only as a vanished dream. It is in vain that his uncle wishes to cheer him and show him his position from another point of view; the sensation of his nothingness will not leave him.

"The second blow that struck him wounded him deeper, bowed him down still more. It is the marriage of his mother. For him, the faithful and tender son, when his father died there still remained a mother; he hoped in the society of his surviving noble-minded mother to honour the heroic form of the mighty departed one, but his mother too he loses, and it is worse than if death had robbed him of her. The truthworthy picture which a well-advised child is so glad to make of its parents vanishes away. With the dead there is no help, with the living no hold. She, too, is a woman and her name is Frailty, like that of all her sex.

"Now for the first time he feels himself bowed down and orphaned, and no good fortune in the world can replace what he has lost. Neither melancholy nor reflective by nature, melancholy and reflection have become for him a heavy burden. This is how he enters on the scene. I don't think that I have added anything to the piece or exaggerated any feature of it."

Serlo looked at his sister and said: "Have I given you a false picture of our friend? He begins well and he has still much to tell us and much to persuade us of."

Wilhelm asserted solemnly that he did not want to persuade, but to convince, and only begged for another moment's patience.

"Imagine this, you," he cried, "this son of a prince, represent to yourselves right vividly his condition and then observe him, when he learns that the spirit of his father is visible; stand by him in that terrible night when the venerable spirit itself appears before him; an unspeakable horror takes hold of him; he addresses the miraculous form, sees it beckon, follows it and listens. The fearful accusation against his uncle rings in his ears, the challenge to revenge, and the pressing, oft-repeated prayers: 'Remember me!' and when the ghost has vanished, whom do we see standing before us? A young hero, panting for revenge? A prince by birth, who feels himself fortunate in being called out against the usurper of his crown? No! Astonishment and trouble overwhelm the young man in his solitude, he is bitter against smiling villains, swears that he will not forget the departed spirit and closes with the significant sigh:

> The time is out of joint: O cursed spite,
> That ever I was born to set it right!

In these words, it seems to me, lies the key to the whole behaviour of Hamlet, and it is clear to me that Shakespeare wished to describe the effects of a great action laid upon a soul which was unequal to it. In this sense I find the play to have been thoroughly worked out. Here is an oak tree planted in a costly vase which should only have borne pleasing flowers in its bosom, but the roots expand and the vase is shattered.

"A beautiful, pure, noble, highly moral nature without the sensuous strength which makes the hero, sinks beneath a burden which it can neither bear nor cast away; all duties are sacred to him, this one too hard. The impossible is demanded of him, not what is impossible in itself but what is impossible for him. How he winds and turns and torments himself, advances and goes back, is ever putting himself in mind, at last almost loses his aim from his thoughts, without however ever recovering his peace of mind."

Charles Dickens

From *Great Expectations*

[*Pip Sees Mr. Wopsle As Hamlet*]

On our arrival in Denmark, we found the king and queen of that country elevated in two armchairs on a kitchen-table, holding a Court. The whole of the Danish nobility were in attendance; consisting of a noble boy in the wash-leather boots of a gigantic ancestor, a venerable Peer with a dirty face, who seemed to have risen from the people late in life, and the Danish chivalry with a comb in its hair and a pair of white silk legs, and presenting on the whole a feminine appearance. My gifted townsman stood gloomily apart, with folded arms and I could have wished that his curls and forehead had been more probable.

Several curious little circumstances transpired as the action proceeded. The late king of the country not only appeared to have been troubled with a cough at the time of his decease but to have taken it with him to the tomb, and to have brought it back. The royal phantom also carried a ghostly manuscript round its truncheon, to which it had the appearance of occasionally referring, and that, too, with an air of anxiety and a tendency to lose the place of reference which were suggestive of a state of mortality. It was this, I conceive, which led to the Shade's being advised by the gallery to "turn over!"—a recommendation which it took extremely ill. It was likewise to be noted of this majestic spirit that whereas it always appeared with an air of having been out a long time and walked an immense distance, it perceptibly came from a closely-contiguous wall. This occasioned its terrors to be received derisively. The Queen of Denmark, a very buxom lady, though no doubt historically brazen, was considered by the public to have too much brass about her; her chin being attached to her diadem

by a broad band of that metal (as if she had a gorgeous tooth-
ache), her waist being encircled by another, and each of her arms
by another, so that she was openly mentioned as "the kettle-
drum." The noble boy in the ancestral boots was inconsistent,
representing himself, as it were in one breath, as an able seaman,
a strolling actor, a grave-digger, a clergyman, and a person of the
utmost importance at a Court fencing-match, on the authority of
whose practised eye and nice discrimination the finest strokes
were judged. This gradually led to a want of toleration for him,
and even—on his being detected in holy orders, and declining to
perform the funeral service—to the general indignation taking
the form of nuts. Lastly, Ophelia was a prey to such slow musical
madness, that when, in course of time, she had taken off her
white muslin scarf, folded it up, and buried it, a sulky man who
had been long cooling his impatient nose against an iron bar in the
front row of the gallery, growled, "Now the baby's put to bed,
let's have supper!" Which, to say the least of it, was out of
keeping.

Upon my unfortunate townsman all these incidents accumu-
lated with playful effect. Whenever that undecided Prince had to
ask a question or state a doubt, the public helped him out with it.
As for example; on the question whether 'twas nobler in the mind
to suffer, some roared yes, and some no, and some inclining to
both opinions said "toss up for it"; and quite a Debating Society
arose. When he asked what should such fellows as he do crawling
between earth and heaven, he was encouraged with loud cries of
"Hear, hear!" When he appeared with his stocking disordered (its
disorder expressed, according to usage, by one very neat fold in
the top, which I suppose to be always got up with a flat iron), a
conversation took place in the gallery respecting the paleness of
his leg, and whether it was occasioned by the turn the ghost had
given him. On his taking the recorders—very like a little black
flute that had just been played in the orchestra and handed out at
the door—he was called upon unanimously for Rule Britannia.
When he recommended the player not to saw the air thus, the
sulky man said, "And don't *you* do it, neither; you're a deal worse
than *him!*" And I grieve to add that peals of laughter greeted
Mr. Wopsle on every one of these occasions.

But his greatest trials were in the churchyard: which had the
appearance of a primeval forest, with a kind of small ecclesiastical

wash-house on one side, and a turnpike gate on the other.
Mr. Wopsle, in a comprehensive black cloak, being descried entering at the turnpike, the grave-digger was admonished in a
friendly way, "Look out! Here's the undertaker a-coming, to see
how you're getting on with your work!" I believe it is well known
in a constitutional country that Mr. Wopsle could not possibly
have returned the skull, after moralizing over it, without dusting
his fingers on a white napkin taken from his breast; but even that
innocent and indispensable action did not pass without the comment "Wai-ter!" The arrival of the body for interment (in an
empty black box with the lid tumbling open) was the signal for a
general joy which was much enhanced by the discovery, among
the bearers, of an individual obnoxious to identification. The joy
attended Mr. Wopsle through his struggle with Laertes on the
brink of the orchestra and the grave, and slackened no more until
he had tumbled the king off the kitchentable, and had died by
inches from the ankles upwards.

We had made some pale efforts in the beginning to applaud
Mr. Wopsle; but they were too hopeless to be persisted in. Therefore we had sat, feeling keenly for him, but laughing, nevertheless, from ear to ear. I laughed in spite of myself all the time, the
whole thing was so droll; and yet I had a latent impression that
there was something decidedly fine in Mr. Wopsle's elocution—
not for old associations' sake, I am afraid, but because it was very
slow, very dreary, very up-hill and down-hill, and very unlike any
way in which any man in any natural circumstances of life or
death ever expressed himself about anything. When the tragedy
was over, and he had been called for and hooted, I said to Herbert,
"Let us go at once, or perhaps we shall meet him."

James Joyce

From *Ulysses*

From these words Mr. Best turned an unoffending face to Stephen.

—Mallarmé, don't you know, he said, has written those wonderful prose poems Stephen MacKenna used to read to me in Paris. The one about *Hamlet*. He says: *il se promène, lisant au livre de lui-même*, don't you know, *reading the book of himself*. He describes *Hamlet* given in a French town, don't you know, a provincial town. They advertised it.

His free hand graciously wrote tiny signs in air.

HAMLET
ou
LE DISTRAIT
Pièce de Shakespeare

He repeated to John Eglinton's newgathered frown:

—*Pièce de Shakespeare*, don't you know. It's so French, the French point of view. *Hamlet ou . . .*

—The absentminded beggar, Stephen ended.

John Eglinton laughed.

—Yes, I suppose it would be, he said. Excellent people, no doubt, but distressingly shortsighted in some matters.

Sumptuous and stagnant exaggeration of murder.

—A deathsman of the soul Robert Greene called him, Stephen said. Not for nothing was he a butcher's son wielding the sledded poleaxe and spitting in his palm. Nine lives are taken off for his father's one, Our Father who art in purgatory. Khaki Hamlets don't hesitate to shoot. The bloodboltered shambles in act five is a forecast of the concentration camp sung by Mr. Swinburne.

511

Cranly, I his mute orderly, following battles from afar.

> Whelps and dams of murderous foes whom none
> But we had spared . . .

Between the Saxon smile and yankee yawp. The devil and the deep sea.

—He will have it that *Hamlet* is a ghoststory, John Eglinton said for Mr. Best's behoof. Like the fat boy in Pickwick he wants to make our flesh creep.

> List! List! O List!

My flesh hears him: creeping, hears.

> If thou dist ever . . .

—What is a ghost? Stephen said with tingling energy. One who has faded into impalpability through death, through absence, through change of manners. Elizabethan London lay as far from Stratford as corrupt Paris lies from virgin Dublin. Who is the ghost from *limbo patrum*, returning to the world that has forgotten him? Who is king Hamlet?

John Eglinton shifted his spare body, leaning back to judge. Lifted.

—It is this hour of a day in mid June, Stephen said, begging with a swift glance their hearing. The flag is up on the playhouse by the bankside. The bear Sackerson growls in the pit near it, Paris garden. Canvasclimbers who sailed with Drake chew their sausages among the groundlings.

Local colour. Work in all you know. Make them accomplices.

—Shakespeare has left the huguenot's house in Silver street and walks by the swanmews along the riverbank. But he does not stay to feed the pen chivying her game of cygnets towards the rushes. The swan of Avon has other thoughts.

Composition of place. Ignatius Loyola, make haste to help me!

—The play begins. A player comes on under the shadow, made up in the castoff mail of a court buck, a wellset man with a bass voice. It is the ghost, the king, a king and no king, and the player is Shakespeare who has studied *Hamlet* all the years of his life which were not vanity in order to play the part of the spectre. He speaks the words to Burbage, the young player who stands before him beyond the rack of cerecloth, calling him by a name:

> Hamlet, I am thy father's spirit

bidding him list. To a son he speaks, the son of his soul, the prince, young Hamlet and to the son of his body, Hamnet Shakespeare, who has died in Stratford that his namesake may live for ever.

—Is it possible that that player Shakespeare, a ghost by absence, and in the vesture of buried Denmark, a ghost by death, speaking his own words to his own son's name (had Hamnet Shakespeare lived he would have been prince Hamlet's twin) is it possible, I want to know, or probable that he did not draw or foresee the logical conclusion of those premises: you are the dispossessed son: I am the murdered father: your mother is the guilty queen. Ann Shakespeare, born Hathaway?

—But this prying into the family life of a great man, Russell began impatiently.

Art thou there, truepenny?

—Interesting only to the parish clerk. I mean, we have the plays. I mean when we read the poetry of *King Lear* what is it to us how the poet lived? As for living, our servants can do that for us, Villiers de l'Isle has said. Peeping and prying into greenroom gossip of the day, the poet's drinking, the poet's debts. We have *King Lear*: and it is immortal.

Mr. Best's face appealed to, agreed.

Bibliography

Alexander, Nigel. *Poison, Play, and Duel: A Study in Hamlet*. London: Routledge & Kegan Paul, Ltd., 1971, pp. 119-52.

Bradley, A. C. *Shakespearean Tragedy*. London: Macmillan & Co.., 1904, pp. 120-29, 143-48.

Bucknill, John Charles. *The Mad Folk of Shakespeare: Psychological Essays*. London: Macmillan, 1867, pp. 102-12.

Byrne, Muriel St. C. "Fifty Years of Shakespearian Production." *Shakespeare Survey*, 2 (1949), 12-13.

Davies, Thomas. *Dramatic Miscellanies*, Vol. 3. London: Thomas Davies, 1784, pp. 28-33, 37-42.

Dickens, Charles. *Great Expectations. The Works of Charles Dickens*, Vol. 13. London: Chapman & Hall, 1901, pp. 200-02.

Doran, Madeleine. *Shakespeare's Dramatic Language*. Madison: University of Wisconsin Press, 1976, pp. 33-62.

Ewbank, Inga-Stina. "*Hamlet* and the Power of Words." *Shakespeare Survey*, 30 (1977), 85-102.

Fergusson, Francis. *The Idea of a Theatre*. Princeton: Princeton University Press, 1949, pp. 112-27.

Fielding, Henry. *Tom Jones. The Works of Henry Fielding*, Vol. 6. New York: International Publishing Co., 1903, pp. 153-58.

Foakes, R. A. (ed.). *Coleridge on Shakespeare: The Text of the Lectures of 1811-12*. Charlottesville: The University Press of Virginia for the Folger Shakespeare Library, 1971, pp. 124-28.

[Gentleman, Francis]. *Hamlet, Prince of Denmark: A Tragedy, by Shakespeare As Performed at the Theatre-Royal, Covent Garden*. London: John Bell, 1777, pp. 39-40.

Goethe, Johann Wolfgang Von. *Wilhelm Meister: Apprenticeship and Travels*, Vol. 1. Trans. by R. O. Moon. London: G. T. Foulis & Co. Ltd., 1947, pp. 186-87, 210-12.

Gottschalk, Paul. *The Meanings of Hamlet*. Albuquerque: University of New Mexico Press, 1972, pp. 87-97.

Granville-Barker, Harley. *Prefaces to Shakespeare*, Vol. 1. Princeton: Princeton University Press, 1946, pp. 86-93.

Hazlitt, William. *Characters of Shakespeare's Plays*. London: C. H. Reynell, 1817, pp. 103-11.

Irving, Henry. "An Actor's Notes on Shakspeare." *The Nineteenth Century: A Monthly Review*, 1 (May, 1877), 524-30.

516   *Bibliography*

James, D. G. *The Dream of Learning.* Oxford: Clarendon Press, 1951, pp. 33–62.
Jenkins, Harold (ed.). *The Arden Shakespeare: Hamlet.* London: Methuen & Co., 1982, pp. 136–42, 149–53.
Johnson, Samuel. *The Plays of William Shakespare,* Vol. 10. [Ed. by Isaac Reed] London: C. Bathurst, 1785, pp. 332, 370–71, 524–25.
Jones, Ernest. *Hamlet and Oedipus.* Garden City, N.Y.: Doubleday, 1954, pp. 59–79.
Joyce, James. *Ulysses,* Vol. 1. Hamburg: The Odyssey Press, 1932, pp. 192–94.
Kitto, H. D. F. *Form and Meaning in Drama.* London: Methuen & Co., 1959, pp. 329–34.
Kittredge, G. L. (ed.). *Hamlet.* Boston: Ginn & Co., 1939, pp. xvii–xx.
Kittredge, G. L. *Shakspere: An Address, 1916, Apr. 23.* Cambridge, Mass.: Harvard University Press, 1930, pp. 12–14, 36–40.
Levin, Harry. *The Question of Hamlet.* New York: Oxford University Press, 1959, pp. 47–75.
Mack, Maynard. "The World of *Hamlet.*" *The Yale Review,* 41 (1952), 502–23.
[Mackenzie, Mr.]. *The Mirror,* No. 100 (April 22, 1780), pp. 399–400.
Mincoff, Marco. "The Structural Pattern of Shakespeare's Tragedies." *Shakespeare Survey,* 3 (1950), 58–62.
Pepys, Samuel. *The Diary of Samuel Pepys,* Vol. 8. Edited by Henry B. Wheatley. London: Macmillan & Co., 1918, p. 90.
Schlegel, Augustus. *Course of Lectures on Dramatic Art and Literature.* Trans. by John Black. London: George Bell and Son, 1904, pp. 404–06.
Schücking, Levin L. *Character Problems in Shakespeare's Plays.* London: George G. Harrop & Co., Ltd., 1922, pp. 153–67.
Shattuck, Charles. *The Hamlet of Edwin Booth.* Urbana: University of Illinois Press, 1969, pp. 67–71.
Shaw, George Bernard. *Dramatic Opinions and Essays,* Vol. 2. New York: Brentano's, 1909, pp. 313–22.
Snyder, Susan. *The Comic Matrix of Shakespeare's Tragedies.* Princeton: Princeton University Press, 1979, pp. 91–136.
Sterne, Richard L. *John Gielgud Directs Richard Burton in Hamlet.* New York: Random House, 1967, pp. 19–28.
Stoll, Elmer Edgard. *Hamlet: An Historical and Comparative Study.* Research Publications of the University of Minnesota. Vol. 8, No. 5. Minneapolis: University of Minnesota Press, 1919, pp. 22–25, 47–54, 57–60, 63–69.
Waldock, A. J. A. *Hamlet: A Study in Critical Method.* Cambridge: Cambridge University Press, 1931, pp. 50–60.
Wilson, John Dover. *What Happens in Hamlet.* Cambridge: Cambridge University Press, 1935, pp. 174–97.
Zitner, Sheldon P. "Hamlet, Duelist." *University of Toronto Quarterly,* 39, No. 1 (October, 1969), 1–18.